D1402692

Extraordinary Leadership

Join Us at
Josseybass.com
▼

JOSSEY-BASS™
An Imprint of
WILEY

Register at **www.josseybass.com/email**
for more information on our publications,
authors, and to receive special offers.

Extraordinary Leadership

ADDRESSING THE GAPS
IN SENIOR EXECUTIVE
DEVELOPMENT

Kerry A. Bunker
Douglas T. Hall
Kathy E. Kram

Editors

Center for
Creative
Leadership
NORTH AMERICA EUROPE ASIA
www.ccl.org

JOSSEY-BASS
A Wiley Imprint
www.josseybass.com

Copyright © 2010 by John Wiley & Sons, Inc. All rights reserved.

Published by Jossey-Bass
A Wiley Imprint
989 Market Street, San Francisco, CA 94103-1741—www.josseybass.com

No part of this publication may be reproduced, stored in a retrieval system, or transmitted in any form or by any means, electronic, mechanical, photocopying, recording, scanning, or otherwise, except as permitted under Section 107 or 108 of the 1976 United States Copyright Act, without either the prior written permission of the publisher, or authorization through payment of the appropriate per-copy fee to the Copyright Clearance Center, Inc., 222 Rosewood Drive, Danvers, MA 01923, 978-750-8400, fax 978-646-8600, or on the Web at www.copyright.com. Requests to the publisher for permission should be addressed to the Permissions Department, John Wiley & Sons, Inc., 111 River Street, Hoboken, NJ 07030, 201-748-6011, fax 201-748-6008, or online at www.wiley.com/go/permissions.

Readers should be aware that Internet Web sites offered as citations and/or sources for further information may have changed or disappeared between the time this was written and when it is read.

Limit of Liability/Disclaimer of Warranty: While the publisher and author have used their best efforts in preparing this book, they make no representations or warranties with respect to the accuracy or completeness of the contents of this book and specifically disclaim any implied warranties of merchantability or fitness for a particular purpose. No warranty may be created or extended by sales representatives or written sales materials. The advice and strategies contained herein may not be suitable for your situation. You should consult with a professional where appropriate. Neither the publisher nor author shall be liable for any loss of profit or any other commercial damages, including but not limited to special, incidental, consequential, or other damages.

Jossey-Bass books and products are available through most bookstores. To contact Jossey-Bass directly call our Customer Care Department within the U.S. at 800-956-7739, outside the U.S. at 317-572-3986, or fax 317-572-4002.

Jossey-Bass also publishes its books in a variety of electronic formats. Some content that appears in print may not be available in electronic books.

Library of Congress Cataloging-in-Publication Data

Extraordinary leadership : addressing the gaps in senior executive development / Kerry A. Bunker, Douglas T. Hall, Kathy E. Kram, editors.
    p. cm.
  "A joint publication of the Jossey-Bass business & management series and the Center for Creative Leadership."
  Includes bibliographical references and index.
  ISBN 978-0-470-47990-2 (cloth)
  1. Leadership. 2. Executive ability. I. Bunker, Kerry A. II. Hall, Douglas T. III. Kram, Kathy E.
  HD57.7.E94 2010
  658.4′092—dc22
                                    2009051937

Printed in the United States of America
FIRST EDITION
HB Printing   10 9 8 7 6 5 4 3 2 1

A Joint Publication of
The Jossey-Bass
Business & Management Series
and
The Center for Creative Leadership

CONTENTS

This book is the product of a collaborative effort among the three editors and twenty esteemed scholars and practitioners of leadership development.

FROM THE EDITORS

The journey began when Kerry Bunker, Tim Hall, and Kathy Kram discovered a common interest in understanding the critical ingredients that differentiate talented managers from extraordinary senior leaders and a shared passion for understanding and facilitating the learning and development process that enables the transformation. Each editor brings unique life and career experiences to bear on the issue, and in working together and with our contributors, we have discovered many common threads in terms of our core beliefs and values and our approaches to leadership development.

Tim Hall

I have always been interested in understanding how things work so I could fix them or make them work better. I loved learning the theory of electrical networks, and I studied electrical engineering in college. I took a course in organizational behavior in my senior year at Yale with Chris Argyris, who kept asking not just "how" questions but "why" questions. They helped me see how the complexities of organizational systems could be analyzed with concepts and models similar to those of electronic networks. The next semester I took another course with Chris, and I was hooked.

In graduate school at MIT in the 1960s, I came into contact with the foundational work of the Sloan School faculty: Ed Schein, Warren Bennis, Dave Berlew, Doug McGregor, Dick Beckhard, Bob Greenleaf, and Bob Kahn (as a visiting professor from Michigan). I started my research experience by working on the AT&T Management Progress Study, a pioneering study of assessment center methods led by Doug Bray and Richard Campbell. (I later learned that Kerry Bunker began his research career there too.) Along with my experience at Yale, my studies at the Sloan School supported an understanding and a set of values related to the goodness of people, their capacity and need to grow, and the impact that organizations can have on human growth, for good or ill.

In the second half of my career, I have been blessed to work with colleagues like Kathy Kram, who arrived at Boston University at the same time I did. I soon realized we were kindred spirits who had grown up in the same ground for our academic training (just as Kerry and I had for our early research experience). The only difference was that her training in the field was the reverse of mine: Kathy started at MIT and then moved to Yale for graduate school. We have been collaborators and peer coaches to each other since 1980. Human development and the theory-practice link are core parts of our identities.

My research has focused on career and leadership development. Through my work with the Executive Development Roundtable (where I first met Kerry), I have seen the gap in much of the work on leadership development that fails to see that leaders are complex human beings who have personal lives, families, and communities that they care about. I find it very exciting to see this book's rich collection of work by the best scholar-practitioners in our field that helps us see the whole leader and how that person grows.

Kathy Kram

I began my career with a strong interest in adult development, stemming from a desire to better understand my own experiences as I entered the world of full-time professional work. In particular, I was interested in the role of mentoring in early adulthood and how relationships with mentors shaped the challenging transition from student to individual contributor and then to manager of others. I was equally curious about how gender and racial identity seemed to influence the nature of these key life experiences.

Early in my career, I was very fortunate to have had mentors who encouraged me to pursue my passion and who modeled an approach to research that valued self-inquiry as an important source of data, as well as a rigorous approach to clinical methods. I am grateful to Clay Alderfer, Richard Hackman, David Berg, and Dan Levinson, who guided me through the most important years of my development as a scholar-practitioner. In my earliest research, I quickly saw that mentors benefited from these growth-enhancing relationships in unique ways that supported their development at midcareer and midlife. A decade into my research program, I was quite certain that relationships of a certain quality were essential vehicles for learning at every stage of career and life. This insight led me to examine relationships with peers, subordinates, family members, coaches, and others whom individuals (knowingly and unknowingly) enlisted as part of their developmental networks.

One of my early associations with the Center for Creative Leadership (CCL) involved working with Kerry Bunker and Sharon Ting on understanding the nature of effective executive coaching and how peer coaching might play an important role in coaches' development of critical emotional competencies. At the same time, my mentor and colleague, Tim Hall, helped me to broaden my research agenda to the point where we identified relational learning as a core element in executive growth and development. Our writing, research, and consulting collaborations led us to clarify a relational approach to careers. Other colleagues who share my passion for this work, including Ilene Wasserman, Polly Parker, and Scott Taylor, as well as the work in Positive Organizational Scholarship as represented by the work of Jane Dutton, Emily Heaphy, and Karen Golden-Biddle, have enabled me to move forward with this line of inquiry.

Kerry came to Boston University several times to speak with our Executive Development Roundtable about his work on learning agility, authenticity, and coaching. It was at one of these meetings that the three of us confirmed our shared interest in the role of relationships in leadership development. We also knew of many thought leaders who could greatly enrich our conversation, and we began to reach out to them for the purpose of creating a forum where we could elaborate on several new ideas about how to enable aspiring leaders to develop the emotional competencies, cognitive complexity, and systemic understanding of organizations necessary in today's turbulent context and to help great leaders become extraordinary at a time when nothing less suffices.

Kerry Bunker

Like Tim, I began my college career as a student in electrical engineering. But I quickly determined that higher mathematics was neither a strength nor a passion and turned to psychology at the University of Montana. I became enamored with understanding the total person as a necessary approach to understanding human behavior. My graduate education in industrial and organizational psychology, first at Western Michigan University and later at the University of South Florida, guided my research and practice in the direction of helping leaders learn to operate effectively in their roles. I had the privilege of learning applied organizational psychology from Herbert Meyer, who joined the faculty after twenty-five years as director of personnel research at GE.

My professional career began at AT&T, where I joined a four-person basic human resource research team directed by Douglas Bray, father of the Assessment Center Method and architect of the seminal Management Progress Study (Manuel London and Ann Howard were the other two). The MPS experience shaped us all to appreciate longitudinal, total-life experience and to integrate multimethod and multiperspective data into our research and interventions. My studies of stress and coping during the breakup of the Bell System helped shape my subsequent work with organizations and leaders confronting change and transition.

I joined CCL as a researcher in 1987. My early work focused on understanding how aspiring leaders learn how to learn from experience. For more than a decade, I have primarily divided my attention between two interests: one, designing and leading large-scale leader-development projects for organizations facing difficult challenges such as layoffs and positioning those interventions toward enhancing authentic leadership capacity for leading the human side of learning and change; and two, managing and delivering senior executive coaching and development in CCL's Awareness Program for Executive Excellence.

My personal interest in producing this book grows out of repeated observations of developmental gaps among senior executives striving to lead in the face of the complexity and ambiguity of contemporary organizational life. Like Tim and Kathy, I have a thirst for understanding the nature and pattern of these missing ingredients and a passion for broadening the knowledge and practice of how to fill them.

THE COLLABORATIVE PROCESS

Attempting to identify and remedy the gaps in senior executive learning presents a daunting challenge that demands a wider lens and broader focus than any one, or three, development professionals or scholars could generate alone. We quickly determined that we wanted to draw on the wisdom of thought leaders and practitioners with unique viewpoints and recognized credibility in the development field. In addition, we applied relational criteria in our selection process, seeking out experts with a demonstrated interest and capacity for collaborating with others whose opinions might differ significantly. Indeed, one potential author declined our invitation, saying that he has repeatedly demonstrated low ability to "play well with others."

The authors and editors came together for two days early in the process to identify the nature and pattern of the gaps in senior executive development, structure the format for the book, and identify and shape the content for individual chapters. We all returned to CCL after completing first drafts to identify and strengthen the collective themes in our work, fine-tune the structure, and give and receive input on individual chapters. The integrative involvement and commitment of the chapter authors played an important role in teasing out the subtle and often invisible dynamics that either cement or undermine the development of extraordinary leadership.

SPECIAL THANKS

We are deeply indebted to the premier group of leadership scholars and practitioners who invested their time, experience, and energy to both the design of this book and the writing it required. The depth of their wisdom and passion is truly a gift, one we are glad now to share with readers. We also were blessed with financial and professional support from the Alfred J. Marrow New Directions in Leadership Series Fund at CCL. The generous gift from this endowment allowed the authors to come together and participate in the integrative learning that led to this book's publication.

We also owe a huge dept of gratitude to Peter Scisco, whose tireless guidance and wisdom in developing and editing the book formed the cornerstone of the project. We are grateful to CCL not only for providing Pete to the project, but for hosting the collaborative sessions and supporting the book's development.

We have been extremely fortunate to be working with such a high-quality book publisher as Jossey-Bass. We extend our deep gratitude to our editor, Kathe Sweeney, and her colleagues, Kathleen Davies, Dani Scoville, and Mary Garrett, for all of the help, support, and creative ideas (and patience!) they gave to us during the writing and production process. A special thanks goes to Alan Venable for his developmental editing.

We also acknowledge the assistance of a number of other individuals who made enormous contributions to making this project possible: Dave Altman, Laurie Dennis, Beth Dixson, Marianne Ganley, Kelly Lombardino, Marianne Moorhead, Kat Pappa, Jeni Powell, John Ryan, and so many others. In addition to providing specific help at key times, they all contributed to an atmosphere of quality and collaboration at CCL, which contributes to generating products such as the one you have in your hands right now. Our thanks to all of you.

Greensboro, North Carolina   Kerry A. Bunker
January 2010   Douglas T. Hall
    Kathy E. Kram

ABOUT THE AUTHORS

Stacy Blake-Beard

Stacy is an associate professor at the Simmons School of Management and a research affiliate with the Center for Gender in Organizations at Simmons. Her research examines the challenges and opportunities offered by mentoring relationships, with a focus on how these relationships may be changing as a result of increasing workforce diversity. She is particularly interested in the issues women face as they develop mentoring relationships. She also studies the dynamics of formal mentoring programs in corporate and educational settings. Stacy has published research on gender, diversity, and mentoring in several publications, including *Journal of Career Development, Academy of Management Learning and Education,* and *Psychology of Women Quarterly.* She sits on the advisory board of a number of organizations, including MentorNet, Teen Voices, and the Harvard Medical School Center for the Study of Diversity in Science. Stacy holds a B.S. in psychology from the University of Maryland at College Park and an M.A. and Ph.D. in organizational psychology from the University of Michigan.

Peter C. Browning

Peter has a wide range of experience in business. Beginning as a sales trainee, he spent twenty-four years with the Continental Can Company, last serving as executive vice president–operating officer. He joined National Gypsum Company in 1989 and was elected chairman, president, and chief executive officer in 1990, seeing the company through and out of bankruptcy. He joined Sonoco Products Company in 1993, last serving as president and chief executive officer before retiring in 2000. Later that year, he was elected to the position of nonexecutive chairman of Nucor Corporation and became lead director in 2006. He was appointed dean of the McColl Graduate School of Business at Queens University of Charlotte in 2002 and served until 2005. Since 1989, Peter has served on the board of directors of eleven publicly traded companies, two as CEO. In that time, he has also been nonexecutive chair, lead director, and chair of governance/nominating and compensation committees. He currently serves on the board of the Daniel Stowe Botanical Gardens and of the Palisades Episcopal School, and the board of trustees of Presbyterian Hospital Foundation. Peter holds an A.B. in history from Colgate University and an M.B.A. from the University of Chicago.

Kerry A. Bunker

Kerry is founder and president of Mangrove Leadership Solutions, an executive development firm specializing in improving organizational leadership and performance through senior executive learning and coaching. Prior to forming his current organization, Kerry was senior fellow and manager of the Awareness Program for Executive Excellence at the Center for Creative Leadership. Kerry is an industrial/organizational psychologist with a B.A. from the University of Montana, an M.A. from Western Michigan University, and a Ph.D. from the University of South Florida. He has authored, coauthored, or edited more than forty books, chapters, and articles on various aspects of leadership, including the book *Leading with Authenticity in Times of Transition,* a *Harvard Business Review* article entitled "The Young and the Clueless," and a chapter in *The CCL Handbook of Coaching: A Guide for the Leader Coach* entitled "Coaching Leaders Through Change and Transition."

Peter C. Cairo

Peter is a senior partner and consultant at Oliver Wyman Leadership Development. He specializes in the areas of leadership development, executive coaching, and executive team effectiveness. He spent twenty years as a full-time faculty member at Columbia University, where he served as chairman of the Department of Organizational and Counseling Psychology. He is a member of the American Psychological Association and a licensed psychologist in the state of New York. He has been a primary consultant and coach to numerous senior executives and leadership teams at Time Warner, Citi, Avon Products, Colgate-Palmolive, Boehringer-Ingelheim, KPMG, Bank of America, Johnson & Johnson, Cox Communications, and the Carlyle Group. Peter earned a B.A. at Harvard University and a Ph.D. at Columbia University. He coauthored *Leading in Times of Crisis: Navigating Through Complexity, Diversity, and Uncertainty to Save Your Business*; *Head, Heart and Guts: How the World's Best Companies Develop Complete Leaders*; and *Why CEOs Fail: The 11 Behaviors That Can Derail Your Climb to the Top—and How to Manage Them.* He has also published numerous articles, book chapters, and reports on topics such as counseling in business and industry, career adjustment in the workplace, and assessment of high-potential managers.

Cary Cherniss

Cary is a professor of applied psychology and director of the organizational psychology program at Rutgers University. He specializes in the areas of emotional intelligence, work stress, leadership development, and planned organizational change. In addition to his research and writing, Cary has consulted with many organizations in both the public and private sectors, including American Express, Johnson & Johnson, the U.S. Coast Guard, AT&T, Telcordia, Colgate-Palmolive, the U.S. Office of Personnel Management, the Defense Finance and Accounting Service, and PSEG Power. He currently is the director and cochair (with Daniel Goleman) of the Consortium for Research on Emotional Intelligence in Organizations. He is a fellow of the American Psychological Association and past president of its Division 27 (Society for Community Research and Action), and he is a member of the Academy of Management. He received his Ph.D. in psychology from Yale University and has published more than sixty scholarly articles, book chapters, and books, including *The Emotionally Intelligent Workplace* with Daniel Goleman, *Promoting Emotional Intelligence in the Workplace: Guidelines for Practitioners* with Mitchel Adler, and *The Human Side of Corporate Competitiveness* with Daniel Fishman.

Jay A. Conger

Jay holds the Henry Kravis Research Chair Professorship of Leadership at Claremont McKenna College. Author of more than one hundred articles and book chapters and fourteen books, he researches leadership, organizational change, boards of directors, and the development of leaders and managers. His most recent books include *Boardroom Realities, The Practice of Leadership, Growing Your Company's Leaders, Shared Leadership, Corporate Boards: New Strategies for Adding Value at the Top, The Leader's Change Handbook,* and *Building Leaders.* He was chosen by *Business Week* as the best business school professor to teach leadership to executives and as one of the world's top ten management educators.

David L. Dotlich

David is a senior partner with Pivot Leadership, a consortium of senior business advisers that focuses on global executive learning programs around issues of growth, sustainability, and wellness. He is a former executive vice president of Honeywell International, founder and former president of Oliver Wyman—Delta Executive Learning Center, and former president of Mercer Delta Consulting. He consults to executive committees, CEOs, and senior leaders in the areas of leadership, business strategy, and executive coaching. His clients include Johnson & Johnson, Nike, PG&E, Kraft, Bank of America, Fidelity, Sara Lee, Target, Sun, Shell, Novartis, Medtronic, and Toshiba. David earned his M.A. and Ph.D. at the University of Minnesota. He is the coauthor of nine books, including *Head, Heart, and Guts: How the World's Best Companies Develop Complete Leaders* and *Leadership Passages: The Personal and Professional Transitions That Make or Break a Leader.* His newest book is *Leading in Times of Crisis: How to Navigate Complexity, Diversity, and Uncertainty to Save Your Company.* He is the coeditor of *The Pfeiffer Annual: Leadership Development,* which each year compiles the research and practice of leading thinkers and practitioners in the field of leadership development throughout the world.

Joyce K. Fletcher

Joyce is a distinguished research scholar at the Center for Gender in Organizations, Simmons School of Management, and a senior research scholar at the Jean Baker Miller Training Institute, Wellesley College. She uses relational theory to study a wide range of workplace issues, including leadership, organizational learning, and gender dynamics. She is a frequent speaker at national and international conferences on the topic of women, power, and leadership. Joyce holds a bachelor's degree in education from Eastern Michigan University, a master's degree in industrial psychology from Northeastern University, and a doctoral degree in business from Boston University. She is the coauthor of a widely read *Harvard Business Review* article, "A Modest Manifesto for Shattering the Glass Ceiling." She is the author of *Disappearing Acts: Gender, Power, and Relational Practice at Work,* a book that explores the subtle dynamics that often cause women's leadership behavior to disappear at work, and the coauthor of *Beyond*

Work-Family Balance: Advancing Gender Equity and Workplace Performance, about how to lead organizational change efforts to achieve the dual outcomes of equity and effectiveness.

Douglas T. (Tim) Hall

Tim is the Morton H. and Charlotte Friedman Professor of Management in the School of Management at Boston University and director of the Executive Development Roundtable and faculty director of the M.B.A. program. He is a core faculty member of the Human Resources Policy Institute. He has held faculty positions at Yale, York, Michigan State, and Northwestern universities. In 2007 he was the H. Smith Richardson Jr. Visiting Fellow at the Center for Creative Leadership, where he has also been a member of the board of governors. His research and consulting activities have dealt with career development, women's careers, career plateauing, work/family balance, and executive succession. He received his graduate degrees from the Sloan School of Management at MIT and his undergraduate degree from the School of Engineering at Yale University. He is the author of *Careers in and out of Organizations* and, with Brad Harrington, coauthor of *Career Management and Work/Life Integration: A Guide to Meaningful Work and a Meaningful Life.* He is also the author of *The Career Is Dead—Long Live the Career: A Relational Approach to Careers.*

Deborah Helsing

Deborah is a senior coach at Minds at Work and a senior program associate at the Change Leadership Group (CLG). As a coach, she works with clients in the fields of education, business, finance, and the nonprofit sector to diagnose and overcome their immunities to change. She works with her colleagues at CLG to better understand school transformation and to design high-quality professional development programs for educational leaders. Her background in teaching includes a lectureship at the Harvard Graduate School of Education, primary school TESOL instruction and teacher training in the Kingdom of Tonga, and secondary English literature and writing instruction at an alternative high school in Kansas City. Deborah holds an M.A.C. from the University of Michigan and an Ed.D. from the Harvard Graduate School of Education. She is a coauthor of *Change Leadership: A Practical Guide to Transforming Our Schools,* "Putting the 'Development' in Professional Development: Understanding and Overturning Educational Leaders' Immunities to Change" in the

Harvard Educational Review, and "Learning to Walk, Walking to Learn" in *Phi Delta Kappan.*

Frances Hesselbein

Frances is the chairman of the board of governors of the Leader to Leader Institute (formerly the Peter F. Drucker Foundation for Nonprofit Management) and its founding president. She was awarded the Presidential Medal of Freedom, the highest civilian honor in the United States, in 1998. This award recognized her leadership as CEO of the Girl Scouts of the USA from 1976 to 1990, her role as the founding president of the Drucker Foundation, and her service as a "pioneer for women, diversity, and inclusion." She is the recipient of numerous other awards and has received twenty honorary doctoral degrees. She is editor-in-chief of the quarterly journal *Leader to Leader* and a coeditor of the book of the same name. She also is a coeditor of the Drucker Foundation's three-volume Future Series and the first two books in the foundation's Wisdom to Action Series: *Leading Beyond the Walls* and *Leading for Innovation, Organizing for Results.* She is coeditor with Marshall Goldsmith of *The Leader of the Future 2: Visions, Strategies, and Practices for the New Era* and is the author of *Hesselbein on Leadership.*

George P. Hollenbeck

George is an industrial/organizational psychologist specializing in leadership development; he consults in the areas of individual executive coaching, assessment, and development with senior executives. His career includes positions at Merrill Lynch in New York City (vice president and division director—human resources), Fidelity Investments (vice president, organization planning), and the Harvard Business School (senior director, executive education). George teaches, writes, and speaks about leadership; he is an adjunct professor at Boston University's Graduate School of Management. In 2003, he was the recipient of the Distinguished Professional Contributions Award of the Society of Industrial/Organizational Psychology. He is a fellow of that society, a licensed psychologist in New York and Massachusetts, and a diplomate of the American Board of Professional Psychology. George received his Ph.D. in psychology from the University of Wisconsin. He was a James McKeen Cattell Fund Fellow at the University of California, Berkeley, and, as a Merrill Lynch executive, he attended Harvard Business School's Advanced Management Program. He is the author of "Executive Selection—What's Right ... and What's Wrong" in

Industrial and Organizational Psychology. He coauthored *Developing Global Executives: The Lessons of International Experience* and "Getting Leader Development Right: Competence Not Competencies" in *The Practice of Leadership,* edited by Jay A. Conger, and Ronald E. Riggio.

Kathy E. Kram

Kathy is professor of organizational behavior at the Boston University School of Management and Everett Lord Distinguished Faculty Scholar. She teaches courses in global management, leadership, team dynamics, and organizational change. Her primary interests are adult development, mentoring, diversity issues in executive development, leadership, and organizational change processes. She is currently exploring the nature of peer coaching and mentoring circles as part of her ongoing program of research on relational learning, adult development, and leadership development. She consults with private and public sector organizations on a variety of human resource management concerns. She is a founding member of the Center for Research on Emotional Intelligence in Organizations. During 2000–2001, she served as a visiting scholar at the Center for Creative Leadership and is now serving a second three-year term as a member of the center's board of governors. Kathy received her B.S. and M.S. degrees from MIT Sloan School of Management and her Ph.D. from Yale University. She is the author of *Mentoring at Work* and the coeditor of *The Handbook of Mentoring at Work: Theory, Research, and Practice.* She has also published in a wide range of journals.

Lisa Lahey

Lisa is associate director of the Change Leadership Group at the Graduate School of Education at Harvard University and cofounder and codirector of Minds at Work. An expert in adult development and an experienced practicing psychologist and educator, she works with leaders and leadership teams in for-profit and nononprofit organizations. She combines her expertise of individual development with a deep knowledge of organizational psychology and teamwork. Lisa is credited with a breakthrough discovery of a hidden dynamic that impedes personal and organizational transformation. This work on what she and Robert Kegan call "the immunity to change" has found its way into the practice of leaders and senior teams in business, governmental, and educational organizations in the United States, Europe, and Asia. She and Robert Kegan received from Boston University the Gislason Award for exceptional contributions to organizational leadership, joining past recipients Warren Bennis, Peter Senge, and Edgar Schein. Lisa holds a doctorate in developmental psychology from Harvard University. She is the coauthor of *Immunity to Change: How to Overcome It and Unlock the Potential in Yourself and Your Organization, How the Way We Talk Can Change the Way We Work,* and *Change Leadership: A Practical Guide to Transforming Our Schools.*

Mireia las Heras

Mireia is a professor at IESE Business School in Barcelona, Spain. In the past two years she has lectured about career development and work-family balance at conferences in Brazil, Colombia, Uruguay, Mexico, Greece, Norway, the United States, and Spain. She is involved in an international project on career management and is also working on other projects that focus on career management and the dynamism of career success and its interplay with work and family integration. She has been a consultant in the area of work-family balance in Mexico. Mireia studied industrial engineering, specializing in industrial organization, at the Polytechnic School of Catalonia in Barcelona, Spain, and holds an M.B.A. from IESE Business School and a doctorate in business administration from Boston University. She has written and published in such areas as work and family, career development, and leadership.

Jina Mao

Jina is a doctoral candidate in the department of organizational behavior at Boston University. Prior to joining the program, she worked as an engineer at IBM. Her research interests include work, occupations, and culture. She teaches international management at the undergraduate level at Boston University.

Naomi S. Marrow

Naomi is an organizational consultant in private practice. She is a human resource executive with extensive experience leading global training, talent identification, leadership development, succession planning, change management, and organizational consulting functions. She has worked in major global corporations in the banking, publishing, and reinsurance sectors. She was past vice chair of the board of governors of the Center for Creative Leadership and chair of Boston University's Executive Development Round Table. She continues to hold board leadership positions in nonprofit organizations. Naomi earned an M.A. in psychology at the New School for Social Research.

Morgan W. McCall Jr.

Morgan is a professor of management and organization in the Marshall School of Business at the University of Southern California (USC). He is also affiliated with the Center for Effective Organizations. He spent his most recent sabbatical as director of HR Labs, HR Strategy and Planning at Sun Microsystems. Before joining USC he was director of research and a senior behavioral scientist at the Center for Creative Leadership. Executive leadership is the primary focus of his research and writing—more specifically, the early identification, assessment, development, and derailment of executives. An active speaker, teacher, and consultant, Morgan has worked with a variety of organizations. The Executive Development Roundtable at Boston University honored him with the Marion Gislason award for Leadership in Executive Development in 1997. He received the 2008 Distinguished Professional Contributions Award from the Society for Industrial and Organizational Psychology. After receiving a B.S. with honors from Yale University, Morgan earned his Ph.D. from Cornell's School of Industrial and Labor Relations. He coauthored *Developing Global Executives: The Lessons of International Experience* and coedited *Advances in Global Leadership, Volume 2.* He is the author of *High Flyers: Developing the Next Generation of Leaders* and the coauthor of *The Lessons of Experience.*

Barry Oshry

Barry is president of Power + Systems, Inc. For over forty years, his focus has been on helping people see, understand, and master the systemic contexts in which they and others live. He is the developer of the Power Lab, a five-day total immersion experience focusing on issues of class and power. He is also the developer of the Organization Workshop on Creating Partnership and When Cultures Meet. His network of associates delivers these programs to organizations and institutions around the globe. Barry has a Ph.D. in psychology from Boston University. He was selected to participate in the National Training Laboratories' first Applied Behavioral Science Intern Program. He is the author of numerous articles and books, including *Seeing Systems, Leading Systems,* and *In the Middle.* His current writing projects include *Waiting for Homo Systemicus* and *The Adventures of the*

Count of Context. His organizational plays, *What a Way to Make a Living* and *Hierarchy*, have had multiple stagings.

Laura Curnutt Santana

Laura is a faculty member at the Center for Creative Leadership in Greensboro, North Carolina. She facilitates CCL's public leader and leadership development in Spanish and English within Latin America, Europe, the Middle East, and the United States. As a lead faculty and executive coach, she also works closely with clients to design and deliver customized leadership initiatives. Instrumental in implementing CCL's online follow-through system for increased application and transfer of learning, her doctoral research focuses on postclassroom program impact. An author, researcher, and speaker, Laura has presented her research internationally and is published in the areas of integral leadership development, the cultural dimension of leadership, and mind-body wellness. She holds a doctorate in leadership and change from Antioch University, having earned a B.A. in psychology from the University of California and an M.S. in management and organizational development from the United States International University campus in Mexico.

Trina L. Soske

Trina is a partner and head of the Americas at Oliver Wyman Leadership Development. She has more than twenty-five years of strategy consulting and leadership development experience with companies ranging from start-ups to Fortune 50. Her industry background includes health care, medical instruments, technology, financial services, entertainment, consumer products, education, and nonprofits. Her particular areas of domain expertise are corporate and business unit strategy; market research, strategy, and positioning; organizational change; and leadership development. Before going to Oliver Wyman, Trina was a partner and global practice lead for Monitor Executive Development, president of Linkage Professional Services, and president and CEO of Interaction Associates, which she led through a successful turnaround. She was also a founder of two strategy boutique consulting firms. She has been active in education reform efforts over the past ten years, involving policy, assessment, curriculum design, teacher professional development, and high-performance management of school districts. Trina earned an undergraduate degree in political science from Whitman

College and an M.B.A. from Harvard Business School. She is the coauthor of the *Sloan Management Review* article "Consulting: Has the Solution Become Part of the Problem?"

Peter B. Vaill

Peter is emeritus professor of management and a senior scholar in the Ph.D. program in leadership and change at Antioch University. Prior to joining the Antioch faculty, he held the Distinguished Endowed Chair in Management Education at the University of St. Thomas, and before that he was for many years professor of human systems at George Washington University, where he also served as dean. He is a leader in the movement to explore the role of spirituality in the lives of leaders and organizations. Peter has M.B.A. and D.B.A. degrees from Harvard University. His publications deal principally with the extremely turbulent and unstable environments within which all organizations are functioning—what he calls permanent white water—and with the implications of these conditions for managerial leaders. His most recent books are *Managing as a Performing Art, Learning as a Way of Being,* and *Spirited Leading and Learning.*

Ilene C. Wasserman

Ilene is the founder and principal of the ICW Consulting Group, a small consulting firm specializing in fostering organizational excellence by leveraging diversity and enhancing communication and collaboration. She is an adjunct faculty member at Teachers College, Columbia University, and at St. Joseph's University Haub School of Business. She teaches courses on diversity, leadership, and managing change. She has worked with Fortune 100 companies, universities, and nonprofit health care institutions. She regularly presents at conferences, such as the Academy of Management, the Transformative Learning Conference, and the National Communication Association. Ilene received her Ph.D. in human and organizational development from Fielding Graduate University and holds master's degrees in counseling psychology and social work from Washington University and a bachelor's degree from Cornell University. Her specialties are gender and diversity in organizations, transformative learning, leadership development, team building, and communication. She has recently published "Engaging Diversity: Disorienting Dilemmas That Transform Relationships," in *Innovations in Transformative Learning: Space, Culture, and the*

Arts, edited by Beth Fisher-Yoshida, Kathy Dee Geller, and Steven A. Schapiro; "Dancing with Resistance: Leadership Challenges in Fostering a Culture of Inclusion," in *Diversity Resistance in Organizations,* edited by Kecia Thomas; and "Enacting the Scholar-Practitioner Role: An Exploration of Narratives," in the *Journal of Applied Behavioral Science.* She has also been a visiting editor for *AI Practitioner.*

Extraordinary Leadership

Introduction

Kerry A. Bunker
Douglas T. (Tim) Hall
Kathy E. Kram

Perhaps no greater challenge faces contemporary organizations than the identification and development of senior executives who have the potential not only to master the complex and ambiguous business demands of our turbulent global existence, but also to engage the human and relational challenges associated with inspiring and supporting leadership in such an environment. Organizations and the people who lead them no longer operate in a world of predictable, incremental change and transition. More than ever before, successful leadership hinges on learning agility and the experience necessary to navigate and lead others through complex situations. It's not about the perfect pedigree or knowing all the answers anymore. It's about resiliency and openness. Sheer intellect, savvy business sense, bottom-line focus, and solid management skills are necessary, but they are clearly not sufficient for meeting the demands of leadership in the twenty-first century.

Despite this clear call for better, different, more agile leadership, many top executives arrive in their high-impact roles without being fully prepared to meet contemporary challenges. There is ample evidence of reduced tenure and dramatic derailment among prominent CEOs (Weisman, 2008; Spencer, 2007; Booz Allen Hamilton, 2007). Similarly, multiple reports point to a high failure rate for the significant organizational change efforts that CEOs and other top leaders have undertaken over the past several decades (Grint, 1994; Henry and Jespersen, 2002; Marks and Mirvis, 1998). Almost two-thirds of such initiatives fail to attain hoped-for goals and outcomes, under even the best of circumstances.

The combination of these trends—turmoil at the top and unsuccessful change efforts—suggests that the demands and complexity of contemporary leadership have exposed significant gaps in the process of executive development. Much has been written about the nature and importance of effective leadership, but far less attention is directed at understanding what it takes to produce leaders capable of applying the latest knowledge in effective ways.

PURPOSE OF THIS BOOK

This book examines the substance and pattern of leadership gaps evidenced among contemporary executives, and it offers multiple lenses for examining that pattern and multiple strategies for enhancing the learning journey from proven manager to extraordinary senior leader. The chapter authors offer fresh insights that anticipate and fill subtle yet powerful learning gaps in executive development that can derail otherwise talented and successful managers.

We began with the hypothesis that the more potent developmental gaps in leader and leadership development have their roots in skills, attributes, and behaviors that are largely learned and shaped through powerful experience. Those experiences create a compelling, paradoxical combination of pressure and opportunity and a context that provokes deep, reflective learning. Connection with others is the site for such development, and relational learning is among the key outcomes produced there. Under such conditions, leaders are challenged to remove their masks of invulnerability and release, or at least reshape, the mental models of leadership they carry from prior learning.

The chapters in this book address the subtle yet powerful forces that combine to differentiate outstanding leaders from the also-rans. The authors share their collective wisdom on the elusive factors of leadership effectiveness that often fall through the cracks of traditional development programs and institutionalized succession management systems. The end product is a process guide for leader development, a valuable resource for executive coaches, human resource professionals, mentors, corporate officers, and aspiring senior leaders themselves. The chapters provide guidance relative to such issues as enhanced career pathing, developmental job assignments, inside-out learning experience, coaching, mentoring, peer learning, and more.

ADDRESSING GAPS IN EXISTING MODELS OF LEADERSHIP DEVELOPMENT

One of the key triggers for this book lies in our own experience coaching C-level executives. We typically encounter managers who are highly valued by their organizations and yet are perceived to be missing one or two of the leadership attributes they need to realize their full potential in a senior executive role. We believe there is pattern and meaning to the missing ingredients evidenced by these high-level, highly accomplished managers—that there are subtle reasons for such gaps. Top-level leaders almost never show up in a coaching engagement because they lack intelligence, or strategic or financial acumen, or because they display a pattern of poor business performance. Instead, top-level leaders who engage coaching or other developmental initiatives are for the most part exceedingly gifted and talented individuals with a history of succeeding at whatever they have set out to do. It is more typical for their developmental gaps to involve such matters as interpersonal relationship challenges, difficulty adapting to rapid change and spiraling complexity, problems partnering and sharing responsibility and accountability, or a leadership style that not only fails to inspire and motivate the masses but may actually foster a culture of fear and risk aversion.

A subtle and persistent stubbornness clings to the patterns of learning that facilitate success (up to a point) while simultaneously planting the seeds for problems or even failure when confronted with the demands of higher-level leadership. Uncovering the positive and negative consequences of these underlying dynamics and charting a course for new learning often requires an individualized and tailored approach to assessment, feedback, and development. Traditional training and development approaches don't lend themselves well to the reflective experiential learning required. Guidance and support are generally required and may take the form of a professional coach, a savvy HR advocate, a mentor in senior management, or some combination of these roles.

It is the rare executive who voluntarily reaches out for in-depth learning and development of this nature. Efforts to redirect or fine-tune the attributes and behaviors of leaders at this stage of their careers can be difficult and challenging. Successful executives can point to a track record of success brought about by behaviors that are shaped by core personality, driven by needs and preferences, and reinforced through successful implementation in a variety of work and nonwork settings. Choosing to enter the next level of learning inevitably requires leaders to go against the grain and let go of some of their most cherished and highly rewarded behaviors. To succeed at the next level, managers must embrace demanding and novel learning agendas, and they must tackle these new initiatives with learning strategies and tactics that lie outside their comfort zones. Accepting such deep learning challenges brings with it the emotional risks of vulnerability, a fall-off in performance, or even outright failure (those who are learning something new are, by definition, not competent at it). It is particularly difficult for highly skilled managers—especially those who have built a career on being recognized as star performers—to undertake such learning amid crises, stress, or organizational turbulence (Bunker and Webb, 1993).

A FRESH VIEW OF LEADERSHIP DEVELOPMENT

Clearly the leadership bar has been raised. People expect their leaders to be simultaneously "larger than life" and "just like me." The requisite core characterics now include authenticity, emotional competence, integrity, and the ability to inspire leadership with and through others. While followers will always look to leaders for strength, courage, direction, wisdom, and knowledge, it has become increasingly clear that they will also expect to find openness, emotional intelligence, empathy, vulnerability, and a sense of humility and humanity.

The evolving complexity of the world economy and the ever-shifting competitive marketplace call out for the effective building and use of teams. Those situations also call for a sharing of leadership, responsibility, and accountability across the organization. The time of the high-profile and egocentric CEO who prefers to manage by exerting control and influence while maintaining emotional distance from others (Lucier and Wheeler, 2007; "Super-Star CEOs Are Out," 2007) has passed. Ironically, this elevated focus on elements of interpersonal and relational competence has emerged at a time when multiple factors may be operating to create gaps in the learning and mastery of such skills—for example:

- Accelerated career advancement for high-potential managers means that the average age of senior executives in our own executive coaching practice dropped seven to ten years during the period 1999 to 2009. Talented young managers are moving upward at a pace that makes it difficult for them to learn the experiential lessons of powerful assignments.

- The rapid pace of technology and globalization has decreased the face-to-face connections required to nurture the development and maturation of both self-awareness and relational learning.

- Reward systems are rarely tied to development and the expression of emotional and interpersonal maturity. Young managers are sometimes given a pass on problems with these softer skills if they maintain bottom-line performance.

- Corporate cultures can sometimes stunt growth by overlooking negative patterns of behavior or failing to mandate development to mitigate the consequences.

- The trend toward careers that include rapid and frequent movement across organizations sometimes allows high-potential managers to escape account-ability for learning to lead with emotional intelligence (Bunker, Kram, and Ting, 2002).

Some organizations have attempted to fill the learning gap by investing energy and resources in the creation of talent management and leadership pipeline programs, but the fact remains that individual managers continue to bear the brunt of responsibility for directing and shaping their own learning and career pathing. This is especially true when it comes to honing the intrapersonal and interpersonal skills needed to lead others in today's emotionally charged workplace.

Thus, we began developing this book with concerns about the gap between how much we know about leading effectively and how little we have learned relative to making effective leadership happen. For example, there were many powerful lessons to be learned from underestimating the emotional fallout associated with the widespread downsizings in the early 1980s and mid-1990s (Bunker and Wakefield, 2005; Cascio, 2003). Yet many of these same leadership blunders were repeated in the face of the economic crises beginning in 2008. While much has been written about the core elements of high-impact change leadership, far less attention has been focused on how to develop and nurture these requisite skills and attributes. Learning to lead in our complex contemporary world tends to be a subtle, invisible, experience-based process that is not sufficiently addressed through traditional approaches to leadership development.

MAKING THE INVISIBLE VISIBLE

This book is the product of a collaborative effort of twenty esteemed leadership scholars and practitioners who partnered with the editors (and with each other) to shed light on the subtle and hidden ingredients of extraordinary leadership and, more important, on how to develop them. Each of these experts came to the table with a wealth of experience, a unique lens on leadership, and a focused approach for facilitating learning and development. They shared their research and practical experience and collaborated in an effort to tease out the convergent themes and patterns that underlie their various models. We asked them to identify the subtle gaps in learning and experience that operate to undermine the development and expression of effective leadership and to offer strategies, tools, and tactics for filling those gaps. It is important to emphasize that our goal was not to achieve consensus in developmental models or approaches, but rather to leverage the breadth and depth of expert insight and gain multiple perspectives of the problem. The richness of our collaborative effort emerges across the chapters, opening up to divergent lenses and approaches, teasing out common threads, and seeking ways to integrate interventions.

WHOM THIS BOOK IS FOR

This book offers tools, techniques, approaches, and tips for those who play important roles in the development process, such as executive coaches, internal HR managers, and sponsoring members of the senior leadership community. The language and format of the book were crafted to be practical and relevant for both HR professionals and practicing managers. Each chapter is enriched with examples and cases drawn from real-world leadership learning situations. Our aim was to enlighten, inspire, and guide leaders in implementing the developmental lessons that emerge from this collaborative initiative.

This book also provides aspiring senior executives with a comprehensive and multiperspective look at the subtle elements of intrapersonal, relational, organizational, and contextual development that differentiate good managers from outstanding leaders. The focus throughout is on assisting various reader constituencies to craft and customize personal agendas for strengthening the learning process for individuals who hold or are asked to serve in executive-level leadership positions.

HOW THIS BOOK IS ORGANIZED

We began this book by asking the authors to reflect on the nature of the gaps they encounter. What is missing? Why is it important? What is required to fill the gaps? What stands in the way? Collaborative sessions between the editors and authors identified four lenses for examining the existing gaps in leader and leadership development:

1. The gap within: Intrapersonal learning and development issues within an individual

2. The gap between: Interpersonal and relational issues that operate between individuals

3. The gap in the system: Organizational issues that operate among systems, organizations, groups, and individuals

4. The gap at the institutional level: External and contextual issues such as cultural differences, dramatic change, paradigm shifts, and economic fluctuations

Each of these lenses carries its theme in a separate part of the book. For each part, the editors have compiled a short introduction about the nature of the gaps addressed in that part and briefly describing the work explored in each chapter.

The Gap Within

Intrapersonal development addresses the learning and maturation required for a leader to gain access to and an understanding of his or her feelings, dreams, aspirations, expectations, preferences, fears, and so on. Understanding the self is an important component of executive development because expressions of these inner dynamics are closely linked to behaviors that others experience as strengths, weaknesses, and gaps in leadership ability. Personal knowledge turned inward to the self leads to a heightened awareness that enhances one's ability to do an accurate self-assessment of one's intentions, behaviors, and impact on others. Gaps in learning at this level tend to block subsequent stages of leadership development.

The Gap Between

Interpersonal and relational development addresses the ability of leaders to build collaborative and mutually growth-enhancing relationships with others. Empathy, listening, conflict management skills, team building, coaching skills, and other competencies come into play when senior-level leaders must engage organizational members (peers, subordinates), as well as strategic partners and customers, to create organizational growth and sustainability.

Recent research in psychology and neuroscience suggests that these skills can be developed, provided that the intrapersonal learning process has produced the self-awareness and humility required to support deeper levels of interpersonal engagement and learning. Some of the keys to success are regular practice, candid self-reflection, and a willingness to invite and embrace the feedback that will enable personal change and improvement in this area. Business pressures have a way of driving out attention to relational shortcomings. The challenge for coaches and developmental partners lies in capturing a senior executive's attention and keeping him or her engaged in the hard work of changing embedded behaviors and mental models that might otherwise undermine the development and maintenance of authentic relationships.

The Gap in the System

The organizational level of learning addresses the strategic, cultural, and systemic perspectives that leaders require in order to effectively adapt or transform their organizations in response to changes in the environment. This domain includes appreciation for the importance of establishing meaningful linkages among vision, strategy, culture, and practices. It also demands a deep understanding of how technology, workforce diversity, and the pace of change affect individual and organizational performance. Extraordinary leaders take into account the subtle yet powerful forces created by hierarchy, subcultures, and environmental jolts. Perhaps more so than at the intrapersonal and interpersonal levels, cognitive complexity and emotional maturity are essential to understanding and working with these dimensions of leader capability.

The Gap at the Institutional Level

This part focuses on the skills an executive needs in order to respond to the complex and unpredictable demands of the external environment. We characterize developmental gaps in this arena as institutional in nature because they tend to be exposed when leaders are responding to powerful institutional forces such as the expanding global economy, generational and cultural dynamics, governmental intervention, labor unions, or social and religious movements.

To achieve extraordinary leadership, senior managers must learn how to engage and capitalize on the diversity of perspectives that arises when cultural viewpoints are expressed. Those managers should also consider how individual and personal development can be reframed as collective or organizational development. In this realm, an emphasis on educational credentials, intellect, and business acumen provides the requisite technical competence. Senior managers aspiring to extraordinary performance must match that ability with an ethical stance that supports the character and the capacity required to lead in the context of uncertainty and ambiguity. That can be a tall order for executives who are not experiencing guided development in their personal growth and learning.

HOW TO USE THIS BOOK

We have organized this book to facilitate its use as a reference guide for both aspiring senior executives and those charged with contributing to their growth and development. Each of the four parts addresses a focal point for development that may be of particular interest to the reader. The introductory essays at the beginning of each part offer a preview of the chapters that follow and a quick understanding of the developmental gaps addressed. Our suggestion is that you start by focusing on chapters that address the developmental gaps evidenced either by you or by the leaders you are supporting. But do not limit your attention solely to those chapters. Part of the power of this collaborative initiative resides in its examination of developmental issues from multiple learning perspectives. Organizational interventions can often be enhanced by weaving in individual leader development tactics, for example, or by weaving in the opposite direction.

In summary, this book contains a rich collection of wisdom, experience, and insight for addressing the gaps in learning and development that the traditional models for training, talent development, and succession planning fail to address. As you address your own executive development needs or those of others, we hope you'll create your own recipe for pulling everything together. A rich stock of openness, vulnerability, and learning readiness forms the base for developing leadership capacity and can carry all of the ingredients that high-performing managers need to set the table for extraordinary leadership.

PART ONE   The Gap Within

Our quest to identify and understand the missing ingredients in extraordinary leadership begins with an examination of the gap within: intrapersonal learning and development. Intrapersonal intelligence (self-insight or self-awareness) is the bedrock of learning and development for aspiring leaders because it is difficult to change what you do not acknowledge or understand. In many ways, leader development consists of the lifelong journey to understand, accept, and take responsibility for who you are and how you came to be that way. The ongoing objective is to reexamine and fine-tune yourself to maximize the positive impact of your leadership. Gaps in learning at the intrapersonal level tend to block the pathway to growth and success at subsequent stages of leadership development (Hogan and Warrenfeltz, 2003). For example, the genuineness, authenticity, humility, and empathy requisite to relational and social learning have their roots in the heightened self-awareness that is dependent on openness to feedback and self-acceptance.

Naomi Marrow opens Part One with a chapter grounded in the reflective observations of six savvy and seasoned C-suite executives. Marrow interviewed all of these executives with the goal of tapping into their career and personal histories in order to identify the attributes, skills, and experiences that contributed most to their personal leadership success. She also asked each executive to characterize the nature and pattern of attributes and skills that will be required to lead successfully in the years to come and to share any concerns about preparing the up-and-coming pool of leaders to meet these challenges.

In looking back across their own developmental histories, these senior executives offer insights into the critical lessons and attributes that contributed most to their own growth and maturation as leaders and, perhaps more important, where and how they learned these lessons. Connectedness and relational learning emerge as common themes, along with shared concern about the challenge of learning to lead with authenticity, integrity, and inspiration. The so-called harder skills of finance, strategy, and globalization were also acknowledged but were referenced more as givens than as differentiators of extraordinary leadership. All of the executives spoke to the subtle yet provocative nature of experiential learning, and each voiced a concern that the emerging cadre of new leaders will likely arrive with gaps in this arena. Marrow offers insight into the nature and origin of these gaps, as well as developmental strategies for filling them.

Chapter Two is an interview with Peter Vaill, a noted organizational and leadership thought leader, who widens the lens for examining the gap within by proposing what he calls the *learning premise.* Vaill draws on a long career at the forefront of both the study and practice of leadership and puts forth the learning premise that leading and managing *are* learning. It is not that they express learning, apply learning, or result in learning, but rather that leading and learning are opposite sides of the same coin. Furthermore, he joins managing and leading in a concept he calls *managerial leading,* that is, leading with managerial issues in mind. In his view, when you observe managerial leadership, you are in fact looking at a learning process.

Having established managerial leadership as a continuous learning challenge, Vaill proposes a model outlining five interactive categories of the leadership-learning challenge: purposing of mission/vision, drive or implementation, permanent white water, managing the mess, and people. Vaill, who admits to a lifelong preoccupation with what he calls *leaderly learning,* contends that gaps in developing effective managerial leaders can often be linked back to learning failures in one or more of the five domains of his model.

In Chapter Three, Deborah Helsing and Lisa Lahey apply a constructive developmental lens to the issue of leadership. Using several case examples, they illustrate a powerful reflective process designed to help leaders unearth competing assumptions and gaps in stage development that can derail intentional learning. They also illustrate how the successful acquisition and expression of many of the attributes of extraordinary leadership described in other chapters in this book (for example, emotional intelligence, self-awareness, and learning agility) may actually be dependent on the ability to access unlearned or untapped developmental capacities.

Views from the C-Suite

Naomi S. Marrow

Three enduring touchstones of leadership success are authenticity, persistently working to connect with a wide range of key players inside and outside one's organization, and communicating honestly and persuasively. Effective future executives must possess (and many in the talent pool do not) the abilities to translate complexity into understandable terms and to inspire confidence among key players and constituents. To ensure sustainable success, developing leadership capability must be an ongoing and core priority of top management and must be embedded in the organization's culture.

This chapter describes the leadership development experiences and insights of six highly successful C-suite executives. It shows them and their perspectives, immersed in the thick of day-in, day-out leadership challenges, and it draws some conclusions about developing leaders for the future.

The chapter also includes some of my own observations based on a career in human resources (HR) in three large for-profit businesses in vastly different industries and on my experience as a board member of several nonprofit organizations. Over the years, I have come to appreciate the inherent complexities of developing leaders and the frustrating gap between the needs and intent of organizations committed to developing talent and the reality experienced by individuals who have been identified as having high potential for leading. This chapter offers recommendations for minimizing the continuing gap between the intended end goal of development and current practices.

I interviewed the six executives just prior to the start of the global financial meltdown in 2008. As I wrote up the results, that event was still unfolding. The six executives described and endorsed fundamental, sound practices that remain important, regardless of the business model an organization subscribes to or the context in which it operates. The evidence in this chapter is anecdotal, and the conclusions are drawn mainly from the experiences of just six leaders, but I believe what these outstanding leaders have to say will prepare readers to gain more from the chapters that follow than they are likely to gain without the on-the-ground perspective of these leaders. To protect confidentiality, the names of the six and their organizations have been changed. When we spoke, the executives were asked to comment on the following topics:

- The experiences that had shaped their readiness to lead
- The skills most critical to their achievements
- What they expect leaders of the future will face
- Their observations about the needs of talented up-and-comers
- What they recommend to prepare future leaders to tackle major responsibilities
- Additional observations about ways to maximize development processes

LEADERSHIP, NOW MORE THAN EVER BEFORE

Leadership capability has long been recognized as a factor (perhaps the key one) in simultaneously guiding organizations through challenges and driving them toward higher performance. With so many pressures testing organizations of all kinds worldwide, the value and impact of exceptional leadership are greater than they have ever been before. At the same time, senior executives voice profound concern about whether the necessary talent will be available and ready to lead when the time comes for the next generation to take the reins. That concern is shared by nonprofits, educational, governmental, military, and other organizations.

The financial crisis that began in mid-2008 brings those concerns into bold relief. The world economy was pushed to near collapse by extreme and poorly understood complexity and exacerbated by diverse vulnerabilities. Together these conditions nearly shredded whatever limited safety nets were in place and left strong indications that new thinking and new business models will be necessary going forward. Among top executives, managers, and highly trained technical specialists, a paucity of good judgment, an excessive comfort with ends justifying means, a shortage of courage, and simple greed brought about a severe financial meltdown. Hindsight revealed shared responsibility and accountability (to varying degrees) by those making decisions in major financial institutions and other organizations and by those passively benefiting from a seemingly ever-expanding economy. Mounting signs of impending crises were largely ignored, and judgment was suspended.

The depth and scope of this financial crisis and other serious vulnerabilities looming on the horizon (for example, epidemics and pandemics, access to health care, adequacy of global food and water resources, climate change, economic and political security), demonstrate how quickly and stunningly threats arise to face leaders and to challenge the survival of their enterprises. Leaders can anticipate some threats, but others will arrive with unexpected fury. These challenges bring new urgency to developing flexibility and agility among candidates for senior leadership positions (Johansen, 2007).

In light of recent changing circumstances, in addition to looking at current business models, it is relevant to ask whether the models of leadership and the developmental methods used to improve it are satisfactory. Indeed, we've seen numerous real-life models spotlighted in scholarly work and in the media as examples of extraordinary effectiveness. All too often, though, initial excitement about these near icons fades to silence. Meanwhile leaders and their organizations appear to glide along, racking up one purported triumph after another, until, for some previously unexpected reason, they hit a significant speed bump and sometimes crash. After-the-fact analysis often uncovers long-simmering problems not recognized earlier.

One such crash took down Ramalinga Raju, founder and chairman of Satyam Computer, a leading Indian technology and outsourcing firm. In 2008 Raju was lauded by Thomas Friedman for superior entrepreneurial ability, prescient strategic foresight, and philanthropic generosity, yet in January 2009, a mere six months after publication of Friedman's *Hot, Flat, and Crowded*, Raju was arrested and resigned from Satyam in disgrace. He publicly admitted to having overseen a massive, multiyear financial fraud, similar in scope to the Enron fraud in the United States just a few years earlier. The falsifying of Satyam's accounting records and inflating of profits represent the largest example of financial mismanagement in Indian corporate history (Dolnick, 2009). As of early 2009, Satyam Computer was acquired by Mahindra Group and renamed Mahindra Satyam, and multiple investigations continued to determine the fate of funds illegally transferred from the company before the fraud was uncovered.

THE SIX INTERVIEWEES

The executives interviewed for this chapter are CEOs of highly successful corporate groups, major divisions of corporations, or educational institutions. They are diverse in terms of sector, location, ages, and gender. They work in shipping, financial services, pharmaceuticals, and higher education; their ages range from their early forties to seventies; four are men and two are women; and two are non-Americans who are based abroad.

Those in businesses run multibillion-dollar organizations; our educational CEO leads a preeminent graduate school with a main campus in the United States and programs conducted abroad. Each boasts a long and sustained record of success. All of them and their organizations have experienced significant crises during their careers. Just as one would expect, these executives are seasoned, sophisticated, curious, and optimistic, and they have a broad worldview.

Early in their careers, each of the executives interviewed anticipated and looked forward to the challenges ahead. In our discussions, they projected character, appear guided by their values, and routinely reflect on their experiences. Maybe most appealing, each recognizes that he or she remains a work in progress. Their experiences range from the extraordinarily dramatic to being pushed well beyond their comfort zone.

Leading in Traumatic Times

Hostin Maritime is a major global maritime group headquartered in Europe, and Marti Amberg has a sterling record in the transportation industry, first as a senior executive of a leading national airline and subsequently leading a global maritime business. He lived abroad prior to taking the top spot at Hostin and traveled the world extensively, meeting employee teams and customers around the world. The story of Amberg's ascension to the CEO position at Hostin in 1990 and what he has accomplished there since are at the heart of why he is regarded as an exceptional leader.

When Hostin recruited Amberg to lead the business, it had just experienced an unprecedented trauma that endangered its very survival: its entire executive team had recently perished in an air crash en route to a company meeting. In one fell swoop, the business lost its leadership team, and many in the company lost valued friends and colleagues with whom they had worked for decades. The shock was profound and palpable on all levels and created deep personal pain.

Any wise executive being recruited under these circumstances would think through what might be faced before jumping on board. Amberg did just that. He considered what he might encounter professionally and personally if he accepted the job, and he discussed with valued advisors whether this position would be a match for him.

Amberg's prior positions had taught him that bringing about change is at the core of effective leadership, and to accomplish this requires creating common ground with others based on personal authenticity. He learned this lesson from previously running a business unit that was losing ground rapidly in its market because of lax management. He quickly concluded that reorganization and significant reductions in force were required to stabilize, energize, and develop the unit. To build a platform conducive to implementing these changes, Amberg put his values into practice. He communicated honestly, directly, and frequently to his staff across the company and endeavored to be open and available to employees and customers alike. He appreciated that people are acutely adept at judging integrity and operated accordingly.

As a first step in this earlier assignment, he presented in explicit terms his assessment of the state of the business and what had to be done. Simultaneously he stressed to his management team that they should work diligently to avoid casualties—meaning that they had to financially buffer those being asked to leave as much as possible and treat everyone with respect and dignity. The shared goal was to minimize fallout while allowing change to proceed. Amberg's mix of bluntness and sensitivity helped the process play out well.

An additional experience stood him in good stead when joining Hostin. During an assignment in the United States years before, Amberg had proved himself particularly effective at building bridges with the U.S.-based staff and upgrading the company's bottom line. He received numerous accolades for his accomplishments. When he returned to his home country, he faced a serious union problem but fully expected his adversaries to appreciate his impressive skills. As Amberg describes it now, he had developed a "major helium head" while in the United States. Once back home, he quickly discovered that his overinflated self-assessment jeopardized his effectiveness. He came to understand how easy it is to become disconnected from reality. This experience became formative and highly valuable to him.

When Amberg joined Hostin, he used his accumulated experiences to deal with a situation that turned out to be as serious as he anticipated, if not more so. The company was nearly paralyzed by profound shock and needed time to find its way to a new "normal." In Amberg's view, one of his immediate priorities was to rebuild confidence in the company among staff, suppliers, and customers. It was imperative that he convincingly assure everyone that the company was on a firm footing in spite of the trauma it had experienced. As he worked on this, he frequently used Hostin's long and successful history as a touch point and announced that he would delay making any significant change for a full year.

He expected that this year-long hiatus would offer three advantages: (1) he would respect (and be seen as respecting) the company's need to restabilize, (2) he would have an opportunity to get a firsthand understanding of the true state of the business and what was necessary to move it forward, and (3) he would have the opportunity to build relationships and trust with staff, suppliers, and customers. In Amberg's estimation, thrusting new challenges onto the Hostin staff too quickly would endanger a fragile organization. As he put it, "The company needed time to grieve."

For his first twelve months as Hostin's CEO, Amberg ran the company as promised: in a business-as-usual mode without significant change. At the one-year mark, he felt the interlude had accomplished what he had intended. He had become highly knowledgeable about the company, had learned whom he could rely on, and had developed a plan for next steps with the active help of key players. In turn, the staff had had a chance to get to know him, had developed a sense of renewed confidence in themselves, and had come to trust and respect their new leader. Together Amberg and Hostin were ready to move forward.

Amberg's experiences illustrate the importance of leadership presence—the willingness and the capacity to be visible in the most difficult times, to be open to others during times of crisis, and through it all to remain, in the midst of change, focused on what needs to be done to ensure the organization's success.

Relationships Work, Clarity Leads

Greentown National is a large investment organization in the United States. Meredith Rangster's progression throughout her career has been based on the strength of her technical skill, relationship-building skills, and highly competitive nature. She has always relied on her gut and sheer persuasiveness, finely tuned over twenty-four years as a salesperson in financial services. The combined power of these skills had worked so well for her that she came to expect she would win every argument and overcome any obstacle in her path.

Reality struck a few years ago when the president of Greentown National gave Rangster the assignment to "reduce the white space between the bank's silos and leverage the capabilities of each to augment overall effectiveness." To this point in her career, Rangster says she had been operating as "a typical salesperson, thinking facts were less important than relationships." But after months of trying to accomplish her new mandate and coming up against one frustration after another, she realized she was directly interfering with what the employees in those silos felt was working quite well for them. Rangster was challenging a comfortable status quo and facing abundant resistance. Her inability to move the situation forward to a successful conclusion came as an unfamiliar surprise. She readily admits she came to hate the job.

For several months, Rangster pressed ahead with minimal progress. She began to realize that she had to not only rely on her gut and influence skills, but highlight convincing facts to support her positions and deliver the information in a compelling manner. As she put it, her arguments had to "let the story tell itself." After all, the decision makers in her target audience were experienced and skeptical executives who were trained to look at facts and numbers. She would have to impress them intellectually and convince them that she had a firm grasp of their world. Credible solutions would have to be developed with her internal clients, not for them.

Encouraging the involvement of those closest to the work required Rangster to look critically at the style she was most comfortable with and draw out the perspectives and ideas of her internal clients. She also had to recognize and resolve disagreements in a patient, inclusive, and respectful manner in order to build relationships with those most inclined to resist her involvement. The power of her position would not buffer her from conflict or carry the day. So with rigor and persistence, Rangster marshaled data to support her arguments and used information, persuasiveness, and process skills to help others think with her, project ahead, and avoid the constraint of initial assumptions and objections. She also found that as a by-product of inclusiveness, she had an opportunity to understand the shortcomings others saw in her arguments. Their comments provided early alerts to possible risks and unintended consequences she might not have anticipated on her own. As a result, she was also able to garner solid support for the major structural and behavioral changes needed to accomplish her mission. She turned things around, accomplished the goals of the project, and was rewarded with a major new line assignment.

As Rangster's career progressed, two additional lessons stand out in her mind—one involving personal style and the other a work-life balance issue. The first represented what might be thought of as the underbelly of being an extraordinarily effective multitasker. While Rangster routinely juggled multiple priorities, she did not always realize that her attention and clarity were at times deflected from strategic issues and onto small fixes. She received feedback about this and empowered her team to send up a warning flag when they saw her lunging toward small fixes rather than attending to the bigger picture. These alerts, which she needed, strengthened bonds with her team.

Another and very different kind of experience, which has had a lasting impact on Rangster, came when she learned she was pregnant with her second child at a time when she was leading an extremely demanding business unit. With some apprehension about her manager's possible response, she proposed working four days a week for several months after her baby was born. She had carefully worked through the dynamics of managing her toddler and newborn along with her job and was confident her multitasking skills would make it work. Although she understood that her strength as a multitasker sometimes endangered business goals, she knew that adroitly leveraging this skill would be her salvation in balancing this work-life issue. To her surprise and delight, her manager unhesitatingly approved her request despite the potential risks to the business.

His positive response and the confidence he exhibited in her left a lasting impression. She terms it "soft kindness," and she in turn intentionally extends soft kindness to others. She believes the arrangement cost Greentown National nothing, minimized disruption in the office and at home, and transmitted to her that her manager and the company appreciated the importance of trusting a talented employee to professionally work through a difficult personal issue. As she sees it, her manager's decision turned into a benefit that keeps on giving and one that she passes along to others.

Leading others is not about having all the answers all of the time. In Rangster's story, we see a leader who learns to access others, expands the range of choices available when decisions must be made, and understands that the balancing point between competing priorities is often the fulcrum of an effective personal leadership style.

Transformation and Change

At various times prior to leading Lester Steel, Davion Marcon was chair and CEO of American Corrugated, CEO of Lamour Products, and a dean of the Wayland Graduate School of Business. He has had a stellar career across industries at the CEO and board levels, facing unexpected and trying situations several times, including the following:

- Early in his career, having to reduce a sales staff from 120 to 10 while maintaining prior sales levels
- Taking a company through bankruptcy and returning it to good health
- Having his company acquired by a business in a different industry and needing to bridge the gap in perspectives with new owners so he could return his company to a growth position

Marcon's career at Lamour Products exposed him to a variety of leadership challenges. Early in his career, he was tasked with turning around a poorly performing, rapidly deteriorating unit. It was widely understood that drastic improvement was urgently needed; inaction was not an option. The division faced imminent bankruptcy, and Marcon executed a massive and rapid restructuring.

First, he quickly gathered his direct reports and empowered them to develop a plan to stabilize the business. He told them that because they were the technical experts in the division with the greatest day-to-day depth in its operations, they alone could map out the necessary actions. Although he would make the final decisions, they would chart the course for his review. This strengthened the team's collaborativeness, ensured a viable plan, and gave key players a vested interest in a successful outcome.

Second, he took the full staff off-site to explain what was happening, the potentially disastrous outcomes they were facing, and the steps being planned. The all-staff session allowed him to initiate more open communications than had previously existed in the company, express his confidence in their shared ability to turn things around, and directly and frankly respond to their questions. He shared his beliefs that while nothing endures but change, there was no going back to the familiar. It was essential to hold on to what was important (values, pride in self and company, and a belief in what they could accomplish together) and necessary to get on board with the new direction. He reiterated his core themes repeatedly, and his confidence that success lay ahead never flagged. The deeper meaning embedded in Marcon's message was that alignment and collaboration significantly improve the likelihood of success in the face of extraordinary and complex challenges. Going it alone makes progress difficult to achieve.

Marcon's approach created a workable platform of shared understanding and trust among the division's management and employees. Results were highly positive, and his star continued to rise within Lamour.

His next assignment, by contrast, presented a situation in which supreme diplomacy and finesse had to be meshed with clear, swift action. Marcon was positioned as second in command of a division that top corporate management considered its crown jewel, but one that was operating under growing competitive challenge. His orders from the corporate CEO were to bring about fundamental change "without breaking the china."

This new assignment was made all the more difficult because division management and employees sensed no emergency. As far as they could see, the profits they generated were the highest in the corporation. To them, nothing was wrong that wouldn't right itself with time, and they rejected headquarters' concerns. In addition, their culture was one of benign complacency. Employees, including senior managers, were content with the status quo and felt their market position was secure for the indefinite future. Division management operated in a maintenance mode, with a business-as-usual attitude. Even if profits were not up to expectations, the division still provided an essential revenue cushion to the parent company.

In light of these circumstances, Marcon decided to honor the positive aspects of the culture: respect for the division's heritage and loyalty to and pride in the company. He would work hand-in-glove with the division's existing leadership and avoid at all cost any appearance of a breach within division management or with corporate headquarters. He accomplished this latter goal by pledging to keep his division boss informed on an ongoing basis and promised no surprises. To his direct reports, he outlined his stretch expectations, privately shared his concerns about individual performance capabilities with them, and committed to working closely and supportively with each of them to improve results. This was time-consuming, but vital to establishing trust and producing positive outcomes.

Simultaneously one of Macron's top priorities was to dramatically upgrade the quality of communications within the division's senior ranks. Staff meetings were transformed from one-on-one serial updates to the boss in a group setting to goal-oriented, problem-solving discussions. No longer would bad news be buried or ignored. Rather, it would be shared and addressed promptly. Interactions with staff became more casual, and the gap between management and employees was progressively narrowed to expand openness and increase interaction and substantive exchanges.

Beyond this, new life was breathed into the division's orientation toward customers. They would no longer be taken for granted. Presentations were orchestrated to explain the value of the division's products and services directly to the client, and they were positioned as a total system. The pace, focus, and energy exhibited in the division toward customers quickly changed with Marcon showing the way. Customers would no longer be kept at arm's length.

These actions reflect Marcon's belief that the best way to protect the profitability of the division and improve its market share was to keep morale high and renew and refresh relationships with its customers. The outcome was successful. The guiding principle that carried Marcon through the challenges he faced was a demonstrated commitment to being direct, honest, and empathic to others. To his mind, constructively engaging staff, especially during difficult times, increases trust and heightens the likelihood of success.

The mantle of leadership carries the responsibility of making difficult decisions. As Marcon's experience indicates, *how* a leader makes such decisions spells the difference. Transmitting trust and respect and engaging in robust communication figure into any leader's transformational efforts.

Creating a Sustainable Organization

Paul Richland has spent his career in a family business, Vita Health Pharma, watching his father and uncle build the largest pharmaceutical processing and distribution business in North America. Finding his own voice and differentiating himself and his leadership style from what had been successful for family elders became a key personal and professional challenge.

Vita Health had been growing nicely for years under the direction of his father and uncle, but in Richland's view, what had worked in the past would no longer suffice. The expectations of employees and demands of the marketplace were changing rapidly. A hierarchical structure, an autocratic though benevolent leadership style, and decision making largely restricted to the senior suite could no longer keep the company competitive and agile. If anything, these characteristics were becoming increasingly counterproductive.

Staff and customer loyalty were fading in spite of his father and uncle's sincere generosity (as described by Richland, "their big hearts and numerous beneficent deeds") over the years. Employees were now looking for a different kind of relationship with their employer, and loyalty was no longer a viable tool to ensure retention and increase productivity. In addition, the business had become far too complex to allow a few individuals in top positions to run everything.

Vita Health's success from the beginning had been attributable to the entrepreneurial foresight, business acumen, and sheer drive of Richland's father and uncle. But as the younger Richland took on assignment after assignment and tried to establish himself on his own merits within the company, he witnessed increasing friction between the founders. Family businesses are far from apolitical, and Paul Richland was coming to realize that he was being drawn into the center of a family power struggle, which added a personal level of pressure to already demanding assignments.

Richland's circumstances were exacerbated by his own style and way of expressing himself. He was demanding and critical of others and failed at efforts to win the trust and admiration of his colleagues. His way of operating was also of serious concern to the senior team running Vita Health and making succession decisions at the time. With hindsight, Richland now readily describes his early style as brash, blunt, judgmental, and impatient. He was quick to display frustration with others and did so frequently. He knew he was exceptionally smart, and he now realizes he operated under the assumption that he was smarter than everyone else.

As would be expected, these attributes were off-putting and worked against him. When the time came to select a new CEO, Richland was not the obvious choice. Fortunately for him, a senior member of the selection team recognized that as much as Richland's day-to-day style dismayed and upset many, he was also deeply talented and insightful about the business. Instead of rejecting his candidacy out of hand, the selection team opted to have Richland participate in an in-depth coaching initiative tailored to expanding his leadership repertoire and moderating his style. Fortunately for Richland, he dove into the development experience, and the results have been highly positive. He has become adept at controlling his impatience, fosters collaboration and teamwork, crafts consensus, and works diligently to establish trust with others.

In effect, he has learned to leverage his strengths and address his weaknesses. Richland's brush with nearly losing the job he felt he had been raised for stunned him into addressing the aspects of his style that had alienated even his fans. Not only did he participate in the intense coaching experience, but when he returned to the office, he charged his colleagues with raising a flag whenever they saw a relapse in his behavior. In addition, he later returned for a follow-up coaching session when he felt a refresher was needed. One immediate indication of the value and impact of Richland's development is that his staff (some of whom had formerly been more senior to him and in some cases in line for his position) now herald him as an impressive and respected leader who has led the company to a dramatic increase in its size and stature.

A second outcome is more serious: it concerns Richland's handling of a contamination problem that surfaced after a Vita Health product was shipped to drugstores. This serious challenge highlighted Richland's values, professionalism, and leadership savvy during a harrowing crisis. Dozens of customers were sickened, and several died as a direct result of the contamination, and an investigation determined that the source of the contamination was an overseas supplier that had provided one of Vita Health's key additives. When he learned that the additive had slipped through Vita Health's safety regimen, Richland immediately issued public statements taking personal and organizational responsibility, expressing profound regret, committing to strengthening safety practices, and promising to quickly work with the victims or their families to address damages. His rapid response and subsequent follow-up have been widely recognized as extraordinarily open, sensitive, and ethically responsible.

In the parlance of the investment industry, "past performance does not indicate future success." Every organization is at some measure of risk from competition, internal stagnation, and external and uncontrollable forces. Those risks don't disappear, and new ones inevitably arise. A leader who stands on core values without wavering and learns to temper strength and not wield it irresponsibly earns the trust that's necessary for guiding organizations over the long term.

Leaders Are Learners

Remy Toulous has a long and stellar career in higher education and in leading positions in professional associations. The roles she has held demand that she connect with highly independent and naturally skeptical intellectuals who often resist, to their core, being managed or led.

Her sense of how to succeed with faculty and administrators is to engage them on an intellectual level about the challenges confronting their part of the university and its academic goals and administrative challenges. She draws synergies across ideas and brings people together on an intellectual level where their ideas intersect. She works hard to create a spirit of collaboration. By doing so, she believes she's communicating a deep appreciation for their opinions, concerns, and needs, and she gradually wins their trust. The respect of colleagues and staff for her academic credentials was a given, but willingness to accept her leadership was something to be gained and regained on an ongoing basis. Her ability to listen, interpolate, and connect ideas has been powerful. She has been able to clarify and frame issues in a way that engages critical others.

One way Toulous demonstrates respect for her staff and retains her balance is to request their feedback. Is she keeping her priorities in balance—or stumbling over herself to ensure her next success? She knows she has a tendency to wonder after each success whether she'll be able to achieve additional successes going forward. Her openness about this has helped build a sense of team with her staff.

The role models who influenced her early in her career are renowned academic leaders. While training under them, Toulous experienced both their hard-headedness and their soft touch. She contrasted this with the relationship she had as a child with her mother. Toulous's mother was a full-time businesswoman who had little time to spend with her daughter or listen to the details of her life. While Toulous readily credits her as having been a good mother, she missed sharing the little everyday things that are part of life and grew up appreciating how important these moments are.

Lessons from all of her teachers have had an impact on Toulous as a leader and as a mother in her own right. She believes her style is businesslike and firm, but with a warmth that helps her connect with others and establish a shared comfort level. One example is her socializing with her school's board members as a way of relaxing and getting to know one another informally. She holds that this nurturing and collegial style has significantly contributed to her effectiveness professionally and with her family. Being clear, available, and warm with her sons and grandchildren has also provided enormous personal satisfaction.

Collaboration is in high demand, but leaders face the risk of appearing weak if they seek too many voices and make no stand of their own. One approach, as Toulous demonstrates, is to synthesize varied perspectives into a singular vision to which everyone in the organization can aspire. Leaders should not confuse collaboration with cacophony or consensus. Everyone can have a voice, and respectful listening creates common goals and actions.

Building the Adaptive Leadership Network

Paxar is a leading global reinsurer. Earlier in his career, Jerry Holland was president and chief operating officer of Foremost Specialty Insurance Group (a primary insurer and a Paxar subsidiary). He has moved rapidly into ever more responsible positions within the insurance and reinsurance arena throughout his career. These moves have been based on his deep technical expertise and acuity, a nonstop work ethic, and an intuitive ability to relate authentically to others.

Holland learned his values in childhood, watching family members work in their neighborhood bakery. Hard work, reliability, and turning out quality goods were their guiding principles. Later, while attending university, he held internships in several small to medium-sized businesses. These positions gave him opportunities to observe the presidents of modest-sized companies invest their spirit, hard work, and heart in their enterprises. He also learned the importance of rolling up his sleeves and working with the team.

Shortly after graduation, Holland signed on to work in his home state's insurance commissioner's department and was quickly promoted to head an auditing unit. Approximately forty seasoned auditors found themselves reporting to a twenty-four-year-old newly hired boss. At the time, Holland recalls being completely confident that his technical skills would stand him in good stead, but he also understood that as the *kid* in the department, he needed to learn the leadership side of his role, gain the respect of his team, and learn from those more experienced. He quickly decided that his job was "to observe, learn, and be adaptive" as he went about shaping an environment in which "everyone rowed in the same direction and understood they'd be rewarded for doing so."

A few years later, Holland was recruited by Foremost Specialty as CEO. Within his first six months, he became acutely aware that the company was in deep economic distress and on the verge of collapse. He followed his instinct and drew on the senior staff to develop a comprehensive turnaround plan for survival. His earlier experience working with others rather than solving problems on his own worked well.

One element of the turnaround strategy strained the entire senior team professionally and personally. For the economics of the plan to work, half the company's employees would have to be laid off. The company's environment was unaccustomed to layoffs. Turnover had historically been low at the company, and many of the employees had worked together for decades. Their families often socialized with one another and did volunteer work together. Holland recognized that in such a climate, he had to address the layoffs on an emotional level for the plan to succeed, not just present the business case. As he put it during our discussion, the employees had always taken great pride in the company and had devoted themselves to it for many years. It would come as an ugly shock to discover that the business model, which had guided their efforts over time, had neither allowed the company to be successful nor created a financial structure to protect their jobs. Holland's challenge was to downsize while recognizing the work of all the employees, maintaining the dignity of those leaving, retaining the trust and commitment of the survivors, and sensitively transmitting optimism that the changes would prove effective. Again, like Amberg and Marcon in their respective organizations, Holland believed that the way a leader treats those asked to leave sets a tone for how well that leader can work with those workers who remain.

The sensitivity Holland and his team displayed throughout the process allowed Foremost Specialty to successfully implement its turnaround plan and return to a firm footing. Its success and strength were soon noticed by Paxar Reinsurance, a top global reinsurer, which subsequently acquired Foremost. Paxar understood the value of a strong, disciplined, and highly dedicated professional team. Holland continues as CEO at Foremost and has become a highly regarded senior executive within Paxar's global operation as well.

In each new role or position, leaders face the task of creating the right network of resources that will bring positive results. In some instances it's a case of proving leadership mettle every day. Holland created a base of support not by stacking a team using the authority granted to his position, but by weaving the interests of team members into a cohesive web. A web's strength comes from its flexibility and its links between strands. Faced with uncertain times, those are two leadership elements that infuse sustainability.

LEARNINGS FROM THE SIX

The stories of these six executives reveal clear, pronounced, recurring patterns of leadership in spite of their varied backgrounds and profiles. Of course, many competencies and factors influence leadership effectiveness, but the core themes expressed in the interviews with these leaders communicated some key messages. Let's look at seven skills and propensities:

- Authenticity
- Relational skills
- Building networks
- Joining the give-and-take
- Translating complexity
- Collaborating and deferring
- Showing confidence

Authenticity

All six executives felt strongly that being authentic is essential to connecting meaningfully with others and gaining their trust. Translated to practice, *authenticity* includes the following:

- Knowing yourself and who you are
- Remembering where you came from
- Remaining grounded
- Staying true to the values you hold most dear
- Knowing your strengths and creatively enlisting resources to address or compensate for shortfalls
- Reflecting on the stresses and circumstances that affect you and how you're responding

Each leader enacts authenticity in his or her own way, but the power of being true to oneself and working hard to relate genuinely to others is centrally important in their efforts to build, mine, and sustain vibrant relationships. They would agree with Warren Bennis's statement that becoming a leader means becoming yourself—that simple and that hard (2003).

Relational Skills

An allied set of communication and connecting, or relational, skills surfaced in each interview as a platform on which to persuade, mobilize, and motivate others. In the view of our executives, robust and persistent communications were must-have and must-use skills. These executives described effective communication and relational skills as persuasive and empathic. Although all six are hard-headed, no-nonsense professionals, all emphasized without hesitation the importance of demonstrating an understanding of the issues at hand and of being empathetic about the concerns of key constituencies. Showing sensitivity and speaking compellingly while offering credible, timely information to back up their positions were part of the mix. I'd add that crafting and following a communication plan can provide rigor, clarifying key messages and increasing the likelihood they'll get through.

Building Networks

Building, nourishing, and sustaining vibrant and diverse networks were also considered instrumental to gathering useful information and fine-tuning intuitions. While data are absolutely necessary for sound decision making, they are not sufficient. A clear sense of the situation is required for context and texture.

Joining the Give-and-Take

Complementary to networking is a willingness to dive into an ongoing give-and-take with others. Being extroverted and displaying an always cheery, upbeat persona are not required; rather, being seen as truly interested in and respectful of the perspectives and contributions of others is what is needed. Being articulate is the baseline requirement, but listening to the many nuanced messages that fly in and around organizations is an absolute necessity. Amberg and Marcon observed that they needed to be and be seen as present, avoiding at all cost appearing detached or unreachable.

Translating Complexity

On the substantive side of communication, translating complexity into understandable and compelling messages gave these executives an extra edge. It demonstrated that they could be relied on to be straight with others. It allowed them to cut through the noise, capture attention, and mobilize the resources that otherwise might have remained resistant or on the sidelines.

Marti Amberg, Davion Marcon, and Jerry Holland all noted that as they led through crisis, they knew they were being judged on how well they presented issues in clear, credible terms. Holland added that the success of the turnaround he led depended on both exquisite clarity and how well he demonstrated an emotional understanding of the situation and its impact on others (again, the empathy factor).

An intuitive and empathic sense of the situation helped guide these executives and those around them through the morass of turmoil. It also helped others become more comfortable with and more open to how these leaders interpreted the situation and the plan of what had to be done (Goleman, 2000). A CEO I worked with some years ago often said the hairs on the back of his neck stood up when he knew something was wrong but could not quite put his finger on the problem. He had become adept at sensing emerging issues and reading cues. His network provided the signals, and his hair-spiking moments focused his attention on finding out what was going on.

Collaborating and Deferring

Given the range of diverse responsibilities senior executives carry routinely and the insistent expectations by boards, shareholders, and others that senior leaders be on top of *everything* at *all times,* our executives also mentioned that collaborating with others and deferring (for content rather than ultimate decision making) to those with greater expertise in particular arenas were underappreciated but especially important skills.

Showing Confidence

Finally we heard several times during these interviews that leaders need to display realistic confidence that a satisfactory outcome will result from the actions they plan. Exuding a sense of confidence helps to stabilize uncertain situations.

SOFT SKILLS VERSUS HARD

A mix of so-called soft skills allowed the executives we interviewed to stand prepared and deal with current circumstances while minimizing the risk of becoming isolated or missing relevant information. These soft skills have been highlighted for decades as key competencies, and their value is increasing as the world becomes even more interconnected and uncertain and technology becomes more pervasive. Technology makes data more readily available, but it does not simplify and clarify issues, and it can never build openness, trust, or collaboration.

In contrast with the soft skills they displayed and discussed, it was surprising to hear our executives raise no concern at all about deficits in technical skill as possible future threats to executive readiness. Our executives assume that high performers and high potentials have the required technical depth to be able to fill knowledge gaps quickly.

That position meshes with what I have heard in numerous discussions about talent and succession planning. Hard skills are, almost offhandedly, considered comparatively easy to develop, while relationship and communication shortfalls are believed to be much more difficult to master and sustain under pressure. In fact, gaps in soft skill proficiency far more often put a candidate's next logical promotion at risk, while shortfalls in hard skills (like financial acumen, or strategic thinking) fell into a grouping of manageable developmental steps (Bunker, Kram, and Ting, 2002).

When asked how they had developed key soft skills, several of our interviewees volunteered that they had learned their best and most lasting lessons about authenticity, relationships, and communication during childhood. A few felt these skills came naturally to them or they learned them by observing others. Others in our group realized as working professionals that they needed greater proficiency in, comfort with, and reliance on solid interpersonal skills. In this regard, they all mentioned the value of working with coaches or mentors, or both, to build the requisite skills. With time, they learned that they had to be disciplined about practicing their newly acquired skills, especially when under stress.

For all the valuable lessons learned, the senior executives we spoke with appreciate that along with their strengths, they grapple with shortfalls that could potentially jeopardize their effectiveness. Several shared that they easily become impatient and highly critical of themselves and others because of the extremely high expectations they set. Two others mentioned that they at times allow themselves to be deflected onto small matters and procrastinate about dealing with big challenges.

To prevent these tendencies from derailing them, they have routinely turned to trusted colleagues, coaches, or mentors for reliable feedback. This support, in addition to self-imposed discipline, helps them remain focused. In spite of their best efforts, though, they know they are not always successful and that defaulting to autopilot is a risk they dare not take.

VIEWS ON PREPARING YOUNG EXECUTIVES

Readying young professionals (whether we label them Generation X or Y, millennials, or some other name) for future leadership is an ongoing challenge and very much on the minds of the six executives. Their observations on the problems and opportunities of developing future talent were consistent.

Entitlement

Although they recognize that recruits over the past five to ten years have remained impressive for their intelligence, spark, curiosity, and exposure to international settings at a younger and younger age (as a result of overseas schooling and travel), entitlement has surfaced prominently as an obstacle. (The comments that follow are not intended to describe an entire generation; rather, they highlight an increasingly significant characteristic that should be considered when planning development strategies.)

This entitlement phenomenon has been described extensively in the past dozen years by many observers. Specifically, many young high potentials no longer accept the standards of the past (such as paying dues, gaining knowledge and practical experience over time, patiently working for promotions, and making personal sacrifices along the way). Loyalty to companies is dead (or close to it), and frustration that formerly prompted an employee to dig deeper into himself or herself and the assignment at hand now often leads to complaints or a leap to another organization.

Young professionals often show palpable impatience with traditional development processes. New recruits and high potentials operate on a different time line than many managers are accustomed to. Often they expect rapid growth, attention, recognition, visibility, and assignments that provide fulfillment, substantive growth, and accelerated career progression. As Jerry Holland notes, "They're not willing to wait until we're ready to develop them." To give just one extreme example, I recall hearing a new recruit in an elite financial services training program say, without humor, humility, or apparent self-doubt, that his goal was to become CEO within five years. And, by the way, he believed it was the company's obligation to prepare him. In sum, the expectations and behavior of young recruits is notably different from those of their predecessors and sometimes results in a conflict of perspectives between generations (Bennis and Thomas, 2002). Time will tell if the financial crisis of 2008 will have any impact on such views.

Working in a context of aggressive competition for top-flight young recruits and in market conditions that stretch and stress organizations, current managers frustrated by the entitlement factor often find they have to press ahead developing new recruits quickly—even when those managers remain somewhat skeptical about reliable outcomes. Not only does not moving forward on development risk a lack of organizational competitiveness in the marketplace, but it tempts high potentials to jump to any competitor who promises more.

Several of our executives commented that they had been alarmed in managing development for some high potentials who persistently pushed hard for plum assignments even when they were aware that the work was likely well beyond their capabilities. Meredith Rangster, in particular, warned that these developing stars risked moving up well ahead of their readiness and could find themselves unprepared for large-scale challenges when they erupt. She was also concerned that organizations might mistakenly assume that they had capabilities on hand that they did not actually possess.

In a similar vein, Davion Marcon strongly expressed the vital importance of keeping rising stars in a position long enough to experience the impact of what they have put in motion. He worries that moving them from one position to another ahead of outcomes could mask gaps in capabilities and diminish learning. As he said, "There's no substitute for [the] experience of going through good and bad times. Give people time to get bruised, recover, and gain insight about themselves." Real learning comes from doing, feedback, and reflecting on the outcomes.

Filling Key Positions

Another theme relates to the selection of outsiders for leadership roles. When companies conclude they do not have internal candidates to fill key positions, they often turn to the outside for rising stars—in some cases, the very people who may have moved ahead of real, substantive growth in their former organizations. Hiring teams frequently see top external candidates through rose-colored glasses, anointing them with a halo effect and anticipating that once on board, they will be ready to roll right away. Too often impressive résumés and interview skills can overplay what can and will actually be delivered. The costs of these exaggerated expectations can be very high.

The input from our executives about how they personally developed and what they recommend going forward harkens back to breakthrough research conducted at the Center for Creative Leadership and later work by Morgan McCall (McCall,

Lombardo, and Morrison, 1988; McCall, 1998). There's agreement that leadership readiness is significantly bolstered in these ways:

- Accumulating diverse experiences in one's repertoire (but not too rapidly)
- Allowing time to develop and practice the necessary skills
- Openness to feedback and input
- Taking time to reflect on one's experiences and responses to them
- Readiness to adjust one's style and behaviors as needed

Ongoing Tensions About Young Talent

The pressures of organizational realities today often amplify tensions between executives' expectations and assumptions as they evaluate and develop young talent and young talent's avid quest for growth. The combination can raise leadership development hurdles. Our executives posed a number of questions about whether highly talented young managers will have the emotional depth and durability to lead effectively in ambiguous and threatening conditions. For example, will young recruits rising to senior positions:

- Have a realistic grasp of what they do and do not know, or will they expect their limited and possibly superficial repertoire to be adequate? In effect, will intelligence and ambition be enough?
- Be interested and patient about trying to understand the perspectives and cultural sensitivities of others?
- Build diverse, vibrant, and sustained relationships across a range of stakeholders within and outside their organizations?
- Direct their primary attention to bettering the organization and meeting its goals versus tending to their own careers?
- Reach deep within themselves or reach out to others for assistance if the challenges outstrip their readiness or expertise?
- Create an environment in which colleagues, staff, or other relevant constituencies can be quickly and effectively mobilized to tackle issues?

From my own practice arises a related question: In increasingly dispersed workforces that afford managers limited face-to-face time with their reports, will they have adequate opportunity to directly observe up-and-comers in action and so be able to accurately judge their abilities?

As the crisis events of 2008 show, the world can lurch in unexpected directions. We should expect that traditional evaluation and assessment methodologies will have to be rethought and adjusted for the conditions of the future. We can only wonder at this time whether executives who developed and progressed up the hierarchy in a different world will readily adjust their lenses, consider the circumstances in which younger talent is operating, and relate successfully to the perspectives and values they bring to the workplace.

MORE IMPLICATIONS FOR THE FUTURE

Good current common sense has not outlived its day, but leadership development will need to change in several respects.

Tried and True

Time and again our executives reiterated the commonsense wisdom of connecting well and often with others. I'm reminded of the truism that common sense is often not common practice. The good news is that the tried-and-true methods available to human resource professionals and their clients already highlight relational and communication skills and are generally well regarded. For example, the executives we interviewed were uniformly enthusiastic about the feedback they had received through the years, with several saying they wished they had had greater access to feedback earlier.

Based on this, I'd expect a number of current standard development resources to remain in wide use, albeit in need of periodic rejiggering to keep their content timely. Among them are coaching and mentoring opportunities, appraisal input, survey instruments, the growing range of assessment tools, and development experiences blended with action-learning assignments on priority business issues. Selection interview processes for internal candidates can also be strengthened by requiring feedback to those offered a position about the strengths they presented in the interview and capabilities they might further develop to maximize success in the new role and what those not given an offer can do to prepare for increased responsibilities. Too often these messages are left unspoken, with development opportunities missed.

More Aggressive, More Tailored

The key message from our executives about how development needs to change in the future is that the processes will have to be far more aggressive and far more tailored than in the past. While today's systems and processes present a reasonable base, more attention needs to be paid to meeting individualized needs. One size fits all and quick, facile judgments about the competencies of candidates will waste opportunities and resources. Those assessing candidates need to be able to observe their behavior numerous times before drawing conclusions about performance and potential. Numbers and measures are essential, but knowledge of how employees achieve results will differentiate those organizations that simply meet their immediate objectives from those that also build organizational strength in the process.

In dispersed organizations, executives managing staffs located around the world may be reluctant to offer critical judgments about performance or development needs for fear of weakening individuals' motivation and potentially risking both bottom-line results and the possible loss of key people. To address this, such organizations should establish a strong development culture that carries the expectation of performance feedback, development planning, and input. Organizations need well-stated and widely shared statements about the organization's development philosophy, and managers need to demonstrate their own active commitment to those views. These are essential pieces of the development puzzle. Technology certainly enables, but it can never substitute for direct one-to-one interaction and endorsement. Otherwise, for the listener, too many assumptions about intent, politics, and cultural overlays will interfere.

Top Leaders Must Own Development

Development efforts are more successful when the top of the organization not only owns but demonstrates interest and ongoing involvement in talent identification, succession planning, and development. This is the case in several notable organizations with solid reputations for developing talent, but it is not yet the norm. Time and again, managers and HR take on the lion's share of responsibility for getting the right talent ready for the right positions, and this diminishes the viability of results. High potentials and high performers interpret senior involvement (or lack thereof) in development and succession issues carefully—not just for the obvious personal reasons but also as a signal about the importance and value of the process to the organization. The most critical responsibility of senior leadership is to ensure that the top positions in their organizations are filled by those ready to lead effectively (Sorcher, 1985; Welch and Welch, 2007).

Paul Richland's practice at Vita Health exemplifies these standards. He is exquisitely and emphatically clear about what it takes to make effective development processes work well and about how critical he feels they are to building a strong, resilient and competitive organization. He expects all managers at Vita Health to consider development a business imperative and to spend the time necessary to develop capabilities and leadership capacity. To him, development is a core business process, not a sideline. He has positioned HR professionals to guide and support the process. In his words, "If you have time to do a budget, you have time to develop your staff." He accepts no excuses.

The essence of his message rang through other interviews as well. At Hostin and at Greentown National, for example, development is a core responsibility of line executives. It is ongoing and facilitated by a senior HR professional. There is organizational recognition that the stakes are high regarding talent, and significant time is invested observing, evaluating, and developing staff. Feedback is an everyday occurrence, not a once-a-year appraisal.

In recent years, HR professionals have increasingly acted as partners with their clients, transmitting that they too have a stake in the process and are not operating solely as third-party counselors. Our most admirable and effective development colleagues work smartly to help design development plans that are highly relevant to the needs of the organization. In addition, they are seen as honest brokers who offer sensitive but direct feedback to those being developed and to their managers. They do not merely monitor from the sidelines but mesh their professional expertise and business knowledge with influence skills to advance development.

Criteria for Judging Future Leadership Development Work

Beyond the knowledge already in place about what defines a robust development process, experience teaches that evaluating the processes on the following criteria will prove useful and boost their impact:

- *Simplicity.* Complexity frustrates busy people and usually adds nothing to the results.
- *Intuitiveness.* Development processes should make sense to both line executives and those being evaluated. The key messages about what the organization is looking for and how it measures effectiveness should be explicit and ring out loudly.
- *Objectivity.* The process is as objective as possible.

- *Clarity.* The objectives, process steps, and ground rules are understood by all involved.

- *Communication.* Messages about development and succession planning are separated. Mixing the two confounds the process and creates unrealistic and possibly unmanageable expectations.

- *Necessity.* Individual development experiences are tailored to address the business needs of the organization (action learning to generate real and needed business results) and the individual's professional growth.

- *Oversight.* An HR professional stays connected with the individuals being developed and with their managers, adjusting plans as necessary.

- *Credibility.* All development plans include credible measures (bottom-line results and qualitative judgments about behaviors) to assess progress and organizational impact.

The magic of leader development depends less on the processes or details within them (assuming they are generally well conceived) than on how well the details are communicated, managed, and linked to the priorities of the organization's strategy and long-term needs. Classroom learning does not have the same impact as working on substantive business issues important to the life and success of the organization. And the inclusion of structured opportunities to reflect, interpret, and recalibrate while working on complex issues in ambiguous environments augments learning and growth. That is how to set in motion good habits for the future—habits, as Rangster notes, that keep on giving.

CONCLUSION

The common sense resonating from these six highly talented executives has helped them lead through turmoil. Although there were certainly some magical moments in their careers, they found no silver bullets or quick fixes to facilitate or guarantee their ultimate success. Based on their comments, they do not expect their successors to find a silver bullet either. Leading, as well as developing leaders, is complex, hard, and often subtle. Discipline and persistence are needed, especially during stressful times, and the guidance and support of development professionals as partners smooth the way.

The Learning Premise

A Conversation with Peter B. Vaill

Peter B. Vaill
Kerry A. Bunker
Laura Curnutt Santana

Seasoned executives are intensive learners. And learning is a skill, a mentality, that we barely understand. Leaders must be nearly relentlessly able to move things along in a complex system. In their vast arena of continual learning, it is useful to look for five basic qualities, realities, and concerns: purpose, drive, people, permanent white water, and messiness. A managerial leader constantly learns and relearns how to balance and integrate these factors, sometimes simultaneously, always recurrently, usually unexpectedly. These are just a few of the many ideas for which Peter Vaill, University Professor of Management in the Ph.D. in Leadership and Change program at Antioch University, is known. Kerry Bunker and Laura Santana spoke with him in March 2009.

Peter Vaill: Based on the lineup of authors for this book and the concept of filling gaps in executive learning and so forth, I think this book is going to be very important in providing CCL and other organizations with an agenda for new kinds of development.

I'm particularly glad that you have some practitioners in the group. Because it's the practitioners like Frances Hesselbein and Peter Browning, both transformational leaders in my opinion, who in one way or another will say something like, "Speaking of missing ingredients and leadership, could we please cut the crap?"

The crap is the vast overintellectualization and "academicization" of leadership and leader behavior and the maze of concepts and distinctions academics have created. I like to say that professors seek distinction by making distinctions. In some ways, the concept of "gaps" or "missing ingredients" itself is sort of an academic notion. I can just hear a professor starting the last class of a term by saying, "Well, ladies and gentlemen, we've been together for a whole semester discussing leadership. What are we missing here? Where are the developmental gaps?" and getting spirited discussion going. But no practitioners I know go through their day wondering, "What are the missing ingredients in leadership?" They might be asking at a personal level how they can be more effective, but they tend not to ask the abstract question. Our field of leadership is overburdened with carefully crafted abstract questions.

Kerry Bunker and Laura Santana: That's a good, frank start!

Vaill: The point is that in the moment, so to speak, in the instant of acting, of leading, all these distinctions are so much deadweight. You can't possibly stop to think of all those things and still retain your energy and your focus for what it is you're trying to get done. And so one of the things that I am going to emphasize is this very point: that leaders are immersed in getting things done. Before anything else, they're immersed in getting things done.

THE MANAGERIAL LEADER

Bunker: Let's talk about the kind of leader you have in mind.

Vaill: All right. You hear me using the expression "managerial leader." Leadership for me is concerned with change, with doing things differently on both a small and a large scale. Management is concerned with doing well what we have already decided we are intending to do. My managerial leader has both types of mentality. A managerial leader leads in some context where he, she, or someone else is going to need to be doing some serious managing, that is, providing for the basic operations of the system and coordinating it toward some objectives. Some leadership is detached from managerial realities, but by and large, I have not focused my interests on it. I am interested in leadership in organizations and other types of structured systems. My managerial leader is also quintessentially a practitioner concerned with getting things done.

Also I am talking about managerial leadership at all levels of organizations. Leadership jobs differ up and down the hierarchy, of course, and among various kinds of organizations. But I think the comments I make in this conversation will apply broadly to managerial leadership virtually everywhere it is found.

Bunker: So, quintessentially oriented to act?

Vaill: Yes. A good example of what I'm talking about can be found in the Ph.D. program I am part of at Antioch University. Some of the students are seasoned executives with major responsibilities. For example, one of our Ph.D. candidates, Lynn Olsen, is a senior executive in a major supermarket chain and a member of the adjunct faculty in the Opus College of Business, University of St. Thomas. He's doing major conceptual work on leadership that is imbued with his understanding of what it actually takes to move things along in a complex system. Many of our other students are much younger practitioners or consultants or academics who need a Ph.D. Like any other Ph.D. program, the curriculum is filled with juicy concepts about leadership, change, ethics, personal development, and so on.

A major difference between the seasoned executives and all of the others, including many of the faculty, is dramatic. The seasoned executives continually ask, "What difference does it make?" and "Can you give me an example?" and "How would this actually work?" Most of the other students do not ask such questions but instead focus on understanding ideas for their own sake. The seasoned executives don't ask their questions in a skeptical or challenging way (not usually!); they're just revealing their particular response to a new idea: How will it work in practice?

A second major difference is that the seasoned executives tend to bring to their studies a mentality of goal setting and planning. I never have to prod any one of them to stay on track, work faster, be more conscious of deadlines, and so forth. This again is in dramatic contrast to the other students, who tend to be much more leisurely in the way they approach their course of study. The seasoned executives are intensive learners; they aren't casual learners, and they are very aware of whether they are learning.

DETERMINATION AND DRIVE TO LEARN

Vaill: When executives feel they are not learning, for whatever reason, they tell you so, and they intensify their efforts. Their learning occurs within a mental context of their particular responsibilities and particular roles at work. They are, you might say, highly determined learners. This has its advantages and its disadvantages for the learners (and for the faculty). On balance, because much of what happens in an academic setting is so ethereal, I think it is an advantage to be a highly determined learner.

Santana: We see both kinds of learners in CCL programs also. "Highly determined learners" nicely describes the more senior participants.

Vaill: I am not saying one mentality, determined learner or leisurely learner, is better than the other. Rather, I am suggesting that our study of leadership emphasizes the slower-paced, more reflective side of leadership, whereas what distinguishes the successful leaders I have known is their can-do side, so to speak.

Bunker: We know how to talk to the more leisurely, reflective side of participants' thinking. In fact, we often try to slow the determined learners down.

Vaill: A lot of training, development, and educational approaches do the same. M.B.A. programs as I know them certainly do. I am more of the leisurely, reflective kind of learner myself. But in my role as a leadership researcher, my data and my reflections tell me we don't know enough about the can-do side. So what capacity does someone who can move things along in a complex system possess?

Bunker: That's a good way to put it. You're not talking about beating on the system necessarily, but about stroking it and coaxing it along—leading it.

Vaill: That itself is a mentality and a skill that in my opinion we just barely understand—the ability to just move things along in a complex system. It calls for near relentlessness. It calls for a whole style of being oneself that is not typical of academics and of training and development experts. The leadership field, as an academic discipline, practically disqualifies itself from understanding these very men and women who supposedly are its focus. This is true even though the best educational institutions, including consulting firms and training and development organizations, can look back along a line of men and women who are superb practitioners of moving things along in a complex system.

The quality I'm talking about used to be called drive. You don't hear *drive* used as a descriptor very often anymore except in the expression "hard-driving executive," and there it's a negative. You don't want to be seen, especially if you are a woman, as a hard-driving executive. [See Chapter Five for an exploration of leadership and gender.] I'm talking about a more neutral quality.

Avid, Hands-On Learners

Vaill: Let me give you an example that makes this and a second important point about missing ingredients in leadership. Some years ago I had the pleasure of attending one of Tom Peters's "skunk camps," where he brought together leaders of excellent companies he had discovered, a few academics interested in "excellent organizations," and other organizational leaders who were "in search of excellence" for their own organizations. This last group was intended to be the learners, but in fact we were all learners in those days [Vaill, 1998].

One evening I sat at dinner with the late Frank Perdue, CEO of the famous company of the same name that he had built into the third largest player in the national retail poultry market. But Perdue didn't want to be at dinner that evening, didn't particularly want to be on display as a leader of an excellent company. In fact, he didn't even want to be at the seminar at all. Where he wanted to be was back in Salisbury, Maryland, where the company was taking delivery on a new state-of-the-art machine called a poultry eviscerator.

Santana: A rather graphic set of actions comes to mind.

Vaill: Yes, it means "rip the guts out of." If you're a chicken man like Perdue, you are very interested in doing this as efficiently as possible. I had heard Tom Peters say that Perdue's margin per chicken was one hundred times the industry average: most companies made a penny per chicken; Perdue's made a dollar per chicken. As Perdue talked about his new machine that evening, I could see why his relentless commitment to efficiency and quality could produce such extraordinary margins. However, we were at dinner, and many of us at the table were not particularly interested in exactly how this machine worked. But Perdue was undeterred. For much of the meal, that was all he talked about.

Two things in particular were very clear. One was Perdue's complete immersion in the details of his business and his commitment to making it as successful as possible. He obviously possessed the singular drive I was talking about a minute ago. But the other thing was that he wanted to have the direct, hands-on learning experience of bringing this machine on line. There was nothing passive about his interest; he wanted to know how the machine worked and how it could be fitted smoothly into ongoing operations. He obviously was not an executive who would sit in an office and read a report of the machine's delivery and early performance.

Perdue wanted to have that concrete learning experience because of its central importance to the company's basic purpose. He was clear about that. Leadership learning—"leaderly learning," as I call it—has been a preoccupation of mine for practically my whole career. How do leaders develop this mentality of drive and of commitment and ability to get things done? That is our big blind spot. The consensus seems to be that it's somehow learned in the school of hard knocks; it's not learned from books.

Dialing Down the Reflection, Dialing Up Work

Vaill: A personal mentor of mine named David Brown, a professor of public administration, once said to me that an executive has to want something. His phrasing captures the active, concrete nature of this mentality and the conscious agenda effective leaders have. This is what makes them determined learners.

Bunker: These qualities have always been on CCL's agenda for research and training.

Vaill: Another anecdote involves one of my colleagues in the Executive M.B.A. program at the University of St. Thomas. I said to him, "You know, there's one thing that every successful executive is good at that we don't mention in this program and is completely absent from our curriculum, and yet every good executive possesses it." My colleague said, "What do you have in mind?" I said, "Drive, single-mindedness, ability to get things done." And he looked at me and he said, "What do you mean?" And I said, "That's my point."

Santana: If he didn't recognize it, he didn't have it?

Vaill: Right. At some point, you have to dial down the reflection, dial down the double-loop learning, dial down the reflexivity and the phenomenological reductions, set aside the speculations about the nature of the leader's consciousness—just lower the volume on all these things that we're telling executives they need to be able to do. We need to dial that down and dial up the energy required to move people to action and enlist people in projects, which is the content of leadership.

One of the challenges of leadership, especially with what I call managerial leadership, is that the leader may confuse people with too much thinking, too much reflection. People walk away sort of saying, "What'd she say?" "What does this memo mean?" "Are we gonna do it or are we not gonna do it?" The lack of clarity, the very qualities of reflection and so forth that we value, could have the effect of confusing people—the very people whose energy we're trying to mobilize.

Santana: But leadership is not choosing between action and reflection, is it?

Vaill: No, it certainly is not either-or. It is balance and integration, but I wonder if those of us with a passion for developing leaders sufficiently emphasize the need for a balance between an action mentality and a reflective mentality [Vaill, 1998]. The best practitioners have a sense of the balance, I think. My sense, though, is that executive development programs don't talk very much about this kind of balance.

When I was doing research on high-performing systems twenty-five or thirty years ago, in every successful high-performing systems leader I found this clarity. People knew where these leaders stood, and they knew what the managerial leader's priorities were. The leader had a predictability; system members knew how the leader was going to react to things. You know, if you're playing football for Bill Parcells, you know how he's going react to things, and it's no mystery. If he blows his cork, it's not a mystery. If he has a good laugh, it's not a mystery. So the possibility that too much reflection, too much complexity, too much consciousness of the interconnections of things, and the contingencies and all that could have an effect of confusing people.

Learning and Communication Versus Confusion or Technicality

Vaill: Before we move on from what I mean by *managerial leader,* I'd like to introduce one more stylistic element, which I described in my stories about Frank Perdue's intense desire to learn and Antioch executive students being determined learners.

I was dean of the School of Business and Public Management for five years at George Washington University, and then I resigned because I decided I wanted to return to being a classroom professor. Teaching was more fun than being a dean, and I had become fascinated with theory and research and teaching about this managerial leader. In the succeeding twenty years that I was on the faculty, three people followed me: two men and a woman. All three of them were far more seasoned executives than I had been when I took the dean's job. They'd had careers in the military, careers in government, careers in industry that reached the top levels of all three of those spheres. They were well thought of, and they understood the academic culture pretty well.

But I knew the job intimately because I'd done it myself. Academic environments are a pretty open world, so there aren't too many secrets, and I could observe these three deans doing whatever deans do. After several years I realized that what I was watching was a continual learning experience on the part of all three. They were having these learning experiences even though they were well-seasoned executives. They were constantly having to engage in the learning process, and if they couldn't engage in a learning process or if they procrastinated that engagement or if they didn't have the capability to engage with it, then that lack showed up right away in the ineffectiveness of their leadership.

I didn't have the need for continual learning in my mind when I had served as dean. Instead I had framed my qualifications in starker terms: Was I qualified or not to be a dean? I concluded that I was, and I think I was right. But I didn't ask the learning question: Am I a good enough learner to handle the learning challenges this job is continually going to throw at me?

It took me three years to really understand my budget, for example, even though I was not confused or intimidated by it, and I brought an M.B.A. degree and lots of academic experience to the task of understanding it. But it just took me much longer than I expected; I didn't understand the budget as a tool for instituting major change in the system. Slowly and clumsily I learned, but I've often wondered if I had explicitly defined my budget as a strategic learning challenge, and not just tried to learn about it on the fly, so to speak, whether I might have been more effective as a dean than I felt I was.

Bunker: Do you think such strategic learning challenges can be identified more clearly?

Vaill: Exactly. As another example, I remember when one of my successors was trying to explain degree accreditation criteria for the M.B.A. degree to the faculty. He created just an enormous swirl of confusion in the room; one faculty member after another stood up and asked ill-informed questions, and the dean gave awkward and misleading answers. I had been preoccupied with accreditation myself as a dean and understood the standards very well.

This scene taught me the learning lesson, though: communicating the criteria required much more than just understanding the technicalities. The dean himself didn't understand the criteria well enough or understand the challenges they posed. So not understanding the technicalities well enough himself, he was not communicating them effectively. And he was unable to perceive in real time, in the nature of the questions they were asking, the learning that faculty members had yet to do in order to grasp the meaning of accreditation.

I could see that in such situations members of the system won't understand what the issues are and why the action the managerial leader is taking or proposing makes sense. Or if the proposed action is founded on inadequate learning, the members of the system may not understand enough to know that it doesn't make sense. [See Chapter Eight for a discussion on building systems insight.]

Santana: It seems that what you're saying applies to everything, not just to the rules and regulations the system must live by.

THE LEARNING PREMISE

Vaill: Definitely. There are issues arising all the time, some involving a lot of technical complexity, some involving a lot of psychological tension and stress, some involving legal issues where one misstep could cost the organization millions of dollars, some involving all three, or something else entirely like Hurricane Katrina or like an economic meltdown.

Just think of the amount of learning that necessarily occurred in 2008–2009 for all executives, particularly in the nonprofit world, where funding may rest heavily on an endowment and when its value, and the cash it generates, suddenly drops by a third or by half. Or consider an organization that lives off contributions and grants that suddenly shrink dramatically. The for-profit world has endured sales declines of 20 or 30 percent or more, creating enormous consequences for cash flow.

The learning experience, the learning challenge in such an environment, is enormous. Nobody ever told any of those executives when they took on their jobs that they needed to understand the sensitivity of financial dynamics to generate a revenue shortfall of 30 or 40 percent. They did not know they would need to understand such a scenario intimately and that they'd have to make a whole set of really tough strategic decisions. For one thing, any warning like that suddenly makes the job much less attractive. Why would anyone want a job in which they had to deal with such a calamity? I am sure a lot of managerial leaders have asked themselves that question since the fall of 2008. What CEO wants to preside over a bankruptcy? What college president wants to preside over a campus closing?

When the problems are at a sufficiently strategic level, a managerial leader can't just rely on a staff specialist to make the decisions. The fact that continual learning is needed, and continually is going on, I call the *learning premise*. The learning premise says, "When you are looking at a managerial leader moving things along in a complex system, you are looking at a learning process."

If you can understand that, then you can ask the really key questions: What are the learning needs or challenges? How is the person, or the team, confronting them? Are there learning needs that are not getting addressed? How are the results of learning showing up in decisions, operations, and results? Are these results shuttled back into the organization as continual learning? It is a whole learning system I am talking about, all triggered by the learning premise: when observing managerial leadership, you are looking at a learning process.

THE CONTENT OF LEARNING IN MANAGERIAL LEADERSHIP

Bunker: You've said quite a bit about the style of your managerial leader, but what is the content? What does that person focus on? What are the main kinds of learning we are looking at when we're observing managerial leadership?

Vaill: Since I'm suggesting that everything the managerial leader does is potentially an arena of learning, there is a vast range of answers to that question. But I would like to bring it down to five main categories. I believe these represent major gaps in leadership studies, because they are not getting the kind of emphasis they deserve. This diagram [see Figure 2.1] illustrates the five qualities. The learning premise applies to everything on this diagram.

Santana: What is the significance of the five all being connected by two-way arrows?

Vaill: That they are all related and influence each other. I'll get to that in minute. First, let me talk about the five.

Purpose

Vaill: Let me first talk about purpose and "purposing the mission/vision." I have put this in the center because of its importance. Mission and vision ground everything else. *Purposing* is the behavior of continually emphasizing these things to oneself and to others [Vaill, 1998].

Bunker: Are you treating mission and vision as pretty much the same thing?

Vaill: Definitely not, something I'll explain in a minute. I keep them together at the center, though, because both are essential in providing the fundamental meaning of the organization (or group or team) for everyone. Mission and vision are the content—the organization's reason to be. They express the managerial leader's overall understanding of what it is the people in the organization are up to, the big picture. Purposing is the process.

I think of the managerial leader as the voice of the mission and the painter of the vision. If leaders do nothing else—if leaders don't do another darn thing for

Figure 2.1
Five Interrelated Qualities as Missing Ingredients

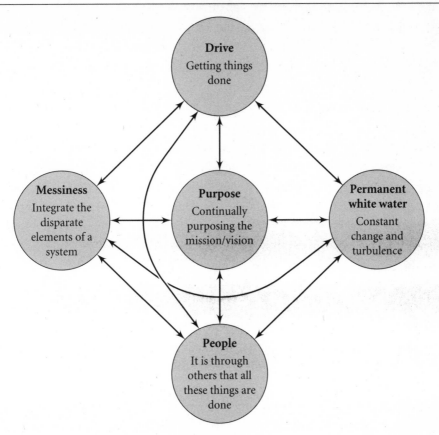

Source: ©Peter B. Vaill, 2009. Used with permission.

their organizations—they are the voice of the mission and purpose. That's why they're paid the big salary—to make the mission meaningful to everybody else. If they don't do that—if they themselves are confused or forget what is important, if they get immersed in details and micromanaging, if they abdicate or are just never around, always on the road or something, if people in the organization are not sure where they stand, not sure what their take is on one issue or another facing the organization—then they're not earning their keep.

Santana: How is what you're saying different from all of the other statements from leadership textbooks that emphasize the importance of mission?

Vaill: Three things. One, since mission and vision ground everything, the managerial leader in the system needs to talk about it continually. It is not something to hang on the wall or put on a wallet-sized plastic card and forget about. Second, its meaning is a matter of continual learning and reflection. All organizations are dynamic environments, and the meaning of all mission statements is problematic. Someone has to take the lead on articulating what the mission means under dynamic circumstances and take the lead from time to time in revising the mission if necessary. Third, this ongoing articulation is a special kind of behavior itself, which I call *purposing*.

For example, when and after Frank Perdue was on site for the start-up of his chicken eviscerator, I am pretty sure he talked to others about what that piece of equipment meant for the company and possibly for other stakeholders. Purposing is special behavior; it's not speech making. Furthermore, purposing occurs all along the line. Even the drive I was talking about earlier is expressed in terms of the meaning of the work that is being done and what it will mean in terms of the mission.

To answer your earlier question about mission versus vision, one of the biggest confusions in the leadership field is the relation between the two. I've seen so many organizations first write a mission statement and then write a vision statement, and the two are practically indistinguishable. Both are very high-flown rhetoric. Somebody at the table might mumble, "Don't they say the same thing?" or, "Why do we need both?" The statements might even conflict with each other.

But to me, the vision statement is completely different from the mission statement. Leaders, at whatever level in the organization, need to be aware of the roles that the vision and the mission play. In fact, the vision "statement" may not be primarily a statement at all. It's a picture—that's why we call it a "vision." The vision is a picture of what things will look like when the organization is fulfilling its mission or purpose. There can be many vision statements because there are many things happening in an organization as it fulfills its mission. Visions can be very specific, like a physical therapist helping a disabled child to walk, or they can be sweeping, thrillingly grandiose, like the Statue of Liberty welcoming newcomers into the United States.

The vision can be people talking to each other, or it could be people driving somewhere in a car, or it could be people sitting at desks, or it could be people talking to customers; it could be all kinds of visualizations. Leaders all up and down the line of an organization, from the highest to the lowest in the hierarchy, so to speak, can participate in visualizing and helping the people they supervise and lead to visualize, "What will the organization look like when we're doing what the mission calls us to do?" The response might be, "Our piece of the organization will look like this" or "We in the mailroom . . ." or "We in the customer service department . . ." The great power and role of vision is how it allows people to see what they will look like when they act consistently with the organization's mission.

The vision is not necessarily a high-level, abstract, flowery statement, but it can express the highest of ideals. One of the most famous corporate visions of the twentieth century is Theodore N. Vail's vision for the AT&T of the 1920s: "We will build a telephone system so that anyone anywhere in the world can talk with anyone else quickly, cheaply, and satisfactorily." Fifty years later, AT&T had largely fulfilled Vail's vision. You could have a master vision, like a slogan, a song, a costume. CCL's symbol, for example, that wonderful winged figure, is a master vision of what CCL tries to be. It's a wonderful visualization of the optimism, hope, promise, innovation, creativity, and, hopefully, the lightness and the playfulness that characterize your organization. Advertisements are primarily vision statements designed to portray the organization fulfilling its mission.

If I were a consultant to a group trying to write a vision statement, I would not encourage them to craft an ambitious high-level statement of what the organization is trying to do. Instead, I would encourage them to identify some generic settings in which the organization's fulfillment of its mission is particularly dramatic or significant, and work on how to communicate those visions.

I actually like the word *purpose* better than *mission*. *Mission* is a little too military for me.

Santana: *Purpose* also plays directly into the behavior you call "purposing."

Vaill: Yes, and let me add one additional thought about purposing. My three descriptors of purposing are behaviors that, on the part of the managerial leader, have the effect of inducing the clarity, consensus, and commitment:

- Clarity means people know what the mission or purpose is.
- Consensus is knowing that we all know it together, not just me personally, but everybody more or less knows what the purpose is and understands it similarly—not in a lockstep, mind-numbing conformity, but as a general agreement of what the mission and purpose say and why.

- Commitment is the emotional side of it: "Dammit, this is right! I want to be part of this. I want to contribute to this. This is worth doing," and so forth.

If you don't have all three, you're not going to have a very effective mission or purpose. I derived these three Cs from studying what I called high-performing systems [Vaill, 1998, 1978].

Drive—Getting Things Done

Bunker: What about the item at the top of the diagram?

Vaill: *Implementation* is often the word people use for this. It is a cumbersome and neutral word. There is wide agreement that it is important but not very wide understanding of what it entails. Not much happens if the managerial leader does not possess this ability and is unable to stimulate it in others. In fact, if it does not arise in others, if the managerial leader is the only one concerned with "getting it done," the work ultimately proves exhausting.

Purpose/vision, and the drive to follow up and translate mission into policies and programs that result in action, "purposing," are the sine qua non of effective leadership. I am willing to forgive a lot of defects if a man or woman has this proven ability and can sustain it over time.

As to the other three circles in the diagram—permanent white water, messiness, and people—I think of them as constant contexts for the managerial leader who is voicing mission, painting the vision, and purposing what the mission calls for. These contexts keep coming up over and over; you can't do mission/vision and implementation without encountering them. "Permanent white water" means that all of your action occurs in a context of constant change. "Messiness" means that the managerial leader continually encounters a heterogeneous collection of elements that he or she must somehow harmonize and integrate into coherent, directed, action. And "people" simply reminds us that none of what we are talking about can be done without doing it through others.

Bunker: Would you say a bit more about each of the three?

Permanent White Water

Vaill: As I said, managerial leaders are continually learning. They have to be continual learners because they live in environments of continual change–change they have initiated themselves, perhaps, but more often change that others have initiated and that affects them and the groups they lead [Vaill, 1996]. It's a cliché to say things are constantly changing. But it's not a cliché to experience that fact in relation to one's responsibilities in some system.

Managerial leaders are in vigorous, continual dialogue with the world around them, the people around them, and the missions around them. They're continually learning, continually modifying their own behavior in relation to what they're encountering and experiencing. That's a learning process.

By "permanent white water," I mean events with five characteristics. First, they arrive as surprises. Second, they frequently have novel components and character. Third, they don't fit neatly into any capability the organization already possesses. Fourth, although they are frequently so weird and bizarre as to be amusing, they cannot be brushed aside but must be dealt with. And fifth, while conceivably any one of these events can be anticipated, what cannot be planned for is the continual occurrence of further surprising, novel, ill-structured, and obtrusive events. This fifth characteristic makes *permanent white water* a descriptor of the overall system over which a managerial leader is in charge or facilitates. As that famous philosopher of the human condition, Roseanne Roseannadanna, used to say on *Saturday Night Live,* "It's always something."

We hear about these events all the time: a hospital operating room staff discovers it has put the wrong heart in a patient's body after sending him to recovery; a credit card company accidentally releases fifty thousand phone numbers to a telemarketing firm; "Naval" was spelled "Navel" on the 1990 diplomas of the U.S. Naval Academy; a new plumbing system in a large government building dumps all the human waste from the building into the basement of the building next door; the gun sight on a tank prototype is reliable only if soldiers squint with their right eye; a school principal is visited by a delegation of angry parents who want a particular teacher fired because the individual is allegedly using voodoo to control the children; and so on and on.

One surprising, novel, ill-structured, obtrusive event after another. We hear about these kinds of things, and we often laugh out loud or our jaw drops. What we often forget is that for every such event, one or more managerial leaders now have to absorb the event and keep it from entirely ruining an organization's pursuit of its purpose. Of course, many executives have several of these on their desks at one time, particularly in the fast-paced high-tech industry or just about anywhere in the health care business. White water increases in frequency and intensity in times of great stress and confusion. War, especially with hit-and-run guerrilla or terrorist fighters, is the archetypal context of permanent white water.

It is not often observed that what a terrorist does is to create as much permanent white water for his enemy as he can.

Bunker: That's what makes such actions terrifying.

Vaill: Yes, exactly. A year ago, if someone had said a rogue financial institution was controlled by terrorists and was attempting to destabilize the world financial system, most people would have laughed it off. Now we know just how fragile some of our big systems are. It's ironic to me that all of what organizations have been doing since the fall of 2008 fits my definitions and my descriptions of white water so well. Yet for thousands of organizations, that economic meltdown has been white water on top of white water because their work environments were extremely unstable even before the meltdown occurred.

But I'm not just talking about the economic turmoil; I'm talking about a whole range of different issues that can hit the organization and about which executives have to make strategic decisions that they never dreamed they would have to have the knowledge or the competence to engage.

So they're in white water par excellence, and, of course, what many of these managerial leaders are asking is, "When will we get out of this?" In my opinion, because of the size of these federal deficits and the instabilities that have been introduced in the economic system as a result of these federal deficits, and the changing global power realities due to changes in economic relationships as well as other factors, plus the worldwide march of ever more powerful and exotic technologies, the answer is that we're not going to get out of it. The game has fundamentally transformed, regardless of your profession or your type of organization. That's what all of the commentators seem to be starting to say. I have been saying for years that permanent white water is transforming the leadership environment, and I think it is coming to pass. We have reached a tipping point. They say Wall Street is not going to be what it used to be; it's a different industry entirely, and that's going to have reverberations throughout the entire economy. We call a business a "firm." All I can say is, the firm is not so firm anymore.

Bunker: What is managerial leadership in such a world?

Vaill: Answers are emerging. They are pretty much what you would expect, but there are some surprises [see, for example, Bennis and Slater, 1998]. One big surprise from my research reveals how important it is for leaders to have the ability to stay clear on purpose, both for themselves and for the group they lead. Another finding points to being very conscious of the impact on the system and people's feelings. White-water events can isolate people as well as exhaust them. An isolated, exhausted person is not having a very good experience. Team development is important, but it's more important than ever in permanent white water. Many of the managers I talk to use the term *inclusiveness* to refer to a managerial leader's ability to keep people conscious of each other's needs and to make sure people don't get lost in the swirl of ad hoc events. One manager said to me once, "You're saying we need to enlarge the raft!" I thought that was a great expansion of the metaphor: leaders need not shoot the rapids all alone.

Two more abilities that are important are to keep one's sense of humor and to stay grounded in core values and wisdom—to retain and develop one's spirituality, if that is not too grandiose a phrase.

Bunker: Why is developing one's spirituality especially important in the context of permanent white water?

Vaill: Because, fundamentally, permanent white water is an assault on meaning, an assault on the values one holds dear. We need a spirituality that is robust enough to handle such assaults and not evaporate on us at the first sign of trouble. Viktor Frankl's study of survival in the Nazi death camps showed that survivors tended to have some kind of spirituality that helped them through the horror [2006; see also Pattakos, 2004].

So these white-water events are novel, they're surprising, they don't fit into neat categories, they force themselves on your attention, and they will always arrive in some form or another. They take up enormous amounts of your time. Leaders may spend the whole day fighting fires and then feel like they haven't accomplished a darn thing.

Messiness

Vaill: On the left side of the diagram, "messiness" appears in a related but somewhat different sense. I'm aware of only two scholars who have made this fundamental observation about the world of the managerial leader. One was Russell Ackoff, the father of strategic planning, operations research, and many other seminal concepts in the strategy and leadership field. In *Redesigning the Future* [1974], he writes:

> We have also come to realize that no problem ever exists in complete isolation. Every problem interacts with every other problem and is therefore part of a set of interrelated problems, a *system of problems*. Furthermore, solutions to most problems produce other

problems; for example, buying a car may solve a transportation problem but it may also create a need for a garage, a financial problem, a maintenance problem, and conflict among family members for its use.

English does not contain a suitable word for "system of problems." Therefore, I have had to coin one. I choose to call such a system a *mess*. This concept is as central in this book as is that of a "system." This book is about messes. This chapter is about "mess management" [p. 21].

The left side of Figure 2.1 represents Ackoff's idea of a mess. Every managerial leader has a heterogeneous set of functions and units to coordinate. They don't automatically go together, even if the organization is very carefully designed. Even if you're in charge of just the mailroom, you have multiple different pieces and they don't automatically go together. You have the configuration of the mailroom, and you have the kind of mail that comes through. And you have sanitary issues. You have human resource issues. You have deadlines and expectations of your customers and other stakeholders around the building. There's no mathematical formula that integrates all these things. The integration is a soft process, and it's done by what Chester Barnard called the leader's own "feeling, judgment, sense proportion, balance and appropriateness," not by science [1938, p. 235]. Ackoff calls it "mess management."

My other source for thinking about messes is Eric Trist, the father of the sociotechnical systems approach to organizational change. I don't know if he ever published this idea, but on several occasions, most notably at the University of Pennsylvania's Wharton School in 1972, I heard him say that a human organization is composed of a heterogeneous range of pieces, and among them are people, equipment, information, physical plant, laws and other rules it must conform to, and the values and norms bearing on the organization and a wider physical, social, political, and economic environment. Each of these elements has its own dynamics and patterns; most of these elements have been the object of rigorous analysis on their own terms.

However—and here is Trist's point, which I consider brilliant—none of these elements necessarily have anything to do with each other. Equipment follows one set of laws; human beings follow another. The physical environment has its nature, the economic environment has its nature, and so forth. The job of the managerial leader—of anyone in the organization—is to blend and harmonize these disparate elements so that they contribute to the organization's purposes without grossly violating the laws that govern them. Trist didn't call this collection of disparate elements "a mess," as Ackoff did, but Trist was always crystal clear that the elements have to be blended and integrated by leaders in the first instance; the elements don't go together naturally.

Following Trist's lead, as a dean I had a huge range of different kinds of things going together that didn't go together. I had faculty, students, physical plant, curriculum, alumni, higher-level executives in the university; I had financial opportunities and constraints. I had myself—my own energy and ideas. This much heterogeneity dramatically underlines the learning process that is managerial leadership as one tries to harmonize and integrate these elements for the educational purposes of the system.

I heard Warren Bennis say one time that as president of the University of Cincinnati he found that he didn't so much solve problems as he managed predicaments—ongoing tensions among various parts of the system. These are the elements I am talking about that never finally get into fixed stable relationships with each other. These tensions are such things as long term versus short term, quantity versus quality, financial objectives versus educational objectives, the faculty as employees of the institution versus the faculty as independent professionals, students as learners versus students as participants in the institution's affairs, and so on.

Bunker: "Predicaments" captures the idea that these things are never solved once and for all.

Vaill: Yes, that's the point. You're managing an Ackovian-Tristian-Bennisist mess! Rocket science it isn't. It's harder than rocket science! The predicaments just keep coming up over and over and over again, and just because you managed it fairly well a year ago doesn't mean it's going to go automatically more easily this year. I always thought that was very profound insight on Bennis's part—that the notion of managing and leading is not problem solving; it's a predicament—confronting and working through predicaments.

People

Vaill: Finally, there's "people" at the bottom of the diagram. I don't want to beat this one to death—we know it's all people. But we keep forgetting it; we keep stating requirements for the system and what ought to be done in it that don't take account of the human complexities we are talking about. I say casually, for example, that the managerial leader is the "voice of the organization's purpose." Most I think would agree with me. Well, then, why do so many leaders fail to continually voice purpose as I have advocated? It should be fairly simple.

The reasons many leaders don't voice purpose are many and various. They may not know exactly what the purpose is. They may think others are supposed to know. They may not be articulate enough. They may not agree with the purposes and be intending to change them. They may be waiting to see what ideas about purpose bubble up from the system. A leader may know she should be the voice of purpose, but that's abstract; her reading of this system and these people may tell her it is not appropriate at the present time. And these speculations are just on the one idea of being the voice of purpose. The same kind of speculative analysis could be made on everything we think a managerial leader should do.

The effectiveness of everything a managerial leader does depends on the meaning that other people attach to it. You can't lead money; you can't lead physical resources; you can't lead plant and equipment; the only thing you can lead is people. It's all about the meaning others attach to one's actions.

So you're in the world of human beings, and that means you better darn well understand how human beings form meanings, change meanings, what role meanings play in their overall psychological well-being and functioning. If you just take for granted that everybody knows what things mean around here and everybody knows what the mission means and everybody knows what the job means and all that, if you just take that for granted, you are in peril. Human beings' meanings are extraordinarily important psychologically and spiritually, and they are also resistant to change. They form and re-form out of sight of other people. They go deep back into the person's own head, to their history, into their childhood, as we know.

So the meanings that people attach to the things that the managerial leader does are extraordinarily important but extraordinarily elusive and resistant. If there ever was a lifelong learning challenge, it's to get better and better, more and more comfortable with working with the meanings that other people possess about the organization, about the work to be done, about you the leader, about themselves, and so forth. You never can get enough of that in my opinion.

As I say, these points are not so debatable, but we keep forgetting them or downplaying them. We keep assuming that the members of the system can be brought along, so to speak, with whatever it is the managerial leaders of the system want to do.

Bunker: You may be preaching to the choir on this one, Peter.

Vaill: However, it's the choir that needs to consider this point. I consider it—this is a strong word but apt, I think—nothing less than a scandal that we, the choir, have allowed "working effectively with people" to become just one more subject in the field of leadership and management. There's marketing and there's operations and there's strategy and there's stakeholders and there's regulations of laws, there's ethics, there's international, and then there's the people problem. "Oh, yeah, right, the people problem," people roll their eyes.

For those of us who understand how important the human issues are in organizations, the scandal is ours. The scandal is mine, as I've watched subjects like organizational behavior, leadership, and organization development become electives. In practically every M.B.A. program in the country, there is one required course on human behavior in organizations and then a handful of electives, most of them on very specialized and very academic subjects. Most behavioral professors don't even know what goes on in the rest of the curriculum and have not taken most of those other courses themselves. I think what I am saying is true of other professional schools too—in education, health services administration, engineering, and public administration. I have some exposure to those schools, but not as much as to business schools.

Bunker: One implication of what you're saying is that training and development organizations also may be guilty of ignoring organizational operations in favor of a detailed discussion of behavioral dynamics.

Vaill: I think that's right. If a software company, for example, hires psychologists for its human resource development function, it should not be surprised if these professionals remain vague about what the company actually does, what its business realities are, and where the touch points are, so to speak, where human relationships are especially problematic.

Bunker: Should it *not* hire such psychologists?

Vaill: The company should give top priority to making sure that what the psychologists are teaching addresses the actual operating problems of the organization. I'm not saying this is not happening at all; rather, that I don't think it is happening systematically with top priority.

Bunker: Do you think other priorities may crowd out that approach?

Vaill: I'm not sure the issue is even understood in these terms—namely, that the behavioral content will become marginalized in favor of other pressing issues if the decision is not made to keep the people factor at the center of people's thinking.

Bunker: What does stop that point of view from taking hold?

Vaill: I think it is our own lack of courage, our own lack of drive and single-mindedness, that has allowed that to happen, plus not appreciating how important it is to keep the behavioral material connected to all the other things students and trainees are being exposed to. In my own opinion, working effectively with people ought to be the queen subject of every leadership development program, every M.B.A. program in the world, and it's not. Furthermore, when somebody in a leadership position demonstrates an inability to work with people effectively, this person should be penalized, if not outright removed. I mean, if you had a surgeon who didn't give a damn about infection in every surgery he or she performed, who just casually sneezed into the wound or used dirty instruments or didn't hold others around the operating table to standards of hygiene and antiseptic, if the doctor was indifferent to hygiene, how long would that doctor last in that job? Not very long. And yet in the organizational world, the human organizational world, we often tolerate toxic managers long past the point where they are perceived as toxic [see, for example, Charan and Colvin, 1999].

Bunker: Such managers are not only tolerated but sometimes celebrated.

Vaill: It's as if there is a massive group norm: "Oh, well, he's not very good with people. He's got a good mind, just not too good with people. We just gotta be kinda careful around him. He's kinda rigid, kinda stiff, or outright abusive." And why we tolerate that year after year after year, decade after decade, is a mystery to me. I really don't know the answer to that question, or why I tolerate it in my own career, or why I have not confronted my colleagues in other fields like finance or accounting. It should not be a mystery to me, because such toleration is a phenomenon of organizational behavior. But still, it always astonishes me when I see a toxic managerial leader being tolerated or, as you say, even celebrated.

As I read all the articles about the crash on Wall Street, it seemed clear that it was not a failure of finance; it was a failure of human relationships. The vocabulary was finance, but the failure was in people's unwillingness to trust each other, to be open with each other, to speak the truth to each other. They knew the system was vulnerable to collapse; they just were whistling past the graveyard: "I won't bring up the fact that you don't understand your balance sheet if you don't bring up the fact that I don't understand mine." That's collusion! You see it every day in a thousand different forms in organizations: letting obvious examples of weakness, incompetence, and ineffectiveness with people go by. We're paying the price of massive collusion.

Bunker: The human side of enterprise is ever new.

Vaill: I shouldn't complain; it means there'll always be a market for what we do! But it just struck me that "the human side of enterprise" is the title of Douglas McGregor's book [1960], still probably the largest-selling management book of all time, and definitely one of the major foundations of the leadership development field. But I'm saying that there is no other "side" to enterprise than the human side. Sure there are other subjects that are important to organizations and managerial leaders, but all of those subjects are mediated through human relationships, or failures of human relationships.

THE BROAD AGENDA

Bunker: You are establishing a pretty large agenda, one that many members of the leadership development field have probably never thought of before in quite this way.

Vaill: I want to make it even a little harder with two final comments. First, all five of those elements operate simultaneously [see Figure 2.1]. They're a sandwich, not a list. They're all operating at the same time, some perhaps more intensely on a given issue than others, but they're all in play all the time. It might be tempting to talk about one while ignoring the others, and we do it all the time, but it is a mistake. We have to learn to talk about the whole complex of projects and their contexts that a leader is experiencing at a given time.

The field, as you know, is obsessed with lists of factors, key things that leaders do. It's a growth industry to come up with yet one more list. Have you noticed, by the way, how few of the writers refer to each other's lists as they are presenting their own?

Purpose, getting it done, white water, messiness, and people are integrative ideas: they are all operating all the time, not one after another. The next time you look at someone's list of the key things managerial leaders do, ask yourself what it would look like to have the leader performing all these key factors at the same time: listening and inspiring *and* reflecting and mediating; or planning and organizing *and* staffing and directing *and* controlling, to use Koontz and

O'Donnell's famous list of five key functions [1968]. Of course I would agree that not all members of a list are equally present all the time, but it is never the case that they are present one at a time, yet that is the way that they are presented.

Vaill: To add one final piece of complexity to this whole scenario, consider that it's easy enough for me to say these elements make a sandwich, easy enough for me to say that the items on a list of functions or abilities are all operating at the same time. What is much, much harder is to show what this looks like in some concrete form.

Bunker: You mean as a research report, a set of findings?

Vaill: Yes, or as a teaching or training design. How do we show a managerial leader keeping all these balls in the air at once?

Bunker: We suspect you have ideas.

Vaill: I have four thoughts about this, no one of which is original. Each has already been done. First, cases. The best way to portray the complexity that a managerial leader deals with is to describe it as a story. Cases have a distinguished tradition in leadership development, but they are continually on the defensive against claims that we should be teaching theory and technique.

Second, leader biographies. At present, these tend to be laudatory more than critical, but there's no reason that we have to put a halo around a particular managerial leader. Biographies tend to be about renowned men and women, but there's no reason that a researcher, who comes across an "ordinary" leader doing extraordinary things, can't pause to write up that person's biography to show how they have learned to do what they are doing.

Third, consider the "up-and-out" of systems thinking rather than the "down-and-in" of analytical, reductionist thinking. The latter is overwhelmingly the dominant mode at present, and it results in the familiar lists of skills, abilities, and behaviors a managerial leader engages in. "Up-and-out" means taking the system as it is, with its leader doing what he or she is currently doing, and asking, "What in this system's environment is leading it to be what it is and act how it is acting?" This gives a learner a big picture of a leader's awareness rather than the small picture of what the leader is good at. The up-and-out approach has been advocated by Russell Ackoff for many years.

Finally, phenomenological studies by managerial leaders themselves or by researchers on their behalf. A phenomenological approach asks, "How is this situation presenting itself to the managerial leader? What is in the individual's awareness? What is he or she not aware of?" This leads to a very complex picture but if well done conveys what is actually going on as the managerial leader is exercising his or her influence on the surrounding system.

To find ways of writing about organizations and their leaders more holistically is my final missing ingredient. I hope you can see the continuity of this last idea with what I said earlier. I realize I am creating a very, very tough problem. If, for example, you're going to talk about Frances Hesselbein as a whole person, then how can you do that other than to tell her story? You might argue that that is biography, not science, but maybe biography is what we need to be better than we are. You might suggest that there are two or three things that Frances Hesselbein does really well, but if you write down these two or three things, then you put them in a textbook, and then five years from now somebody says, "It was found that the great Frances Hesselbein did this and this and this," suddenly those things take on a life of their own, and they get detached from each other. They become foundational elements that aren't located in the context that they were in when Frances Hesselbein first practiced them. There, in a nutshell, is what happened with "excellent organizations": we were so busy writing down their characteristics that we lost sight of how the system as a whole contributed to their extraordinary character and achievement.

CONCLUSION

Bunker and Santana: Thank you, Peter, for sharing these perspectives. It seems you have been saying there is not just one missing ingredient, there is a missing system of ingredients, organized generally around effective action as continual learning in very complex and dynamic contexts, staying as close as possible to the actual practice of managerial leadership.

Vaill: Yes, that sums it up nicely.

Unlocking Leadership Potential

Overcoming Immunities to Change

Deborah Helsing
Lisa Lahey

Some senior leaders find it difficult to make progress on their personal change goals, leaving a potential gap between the developmental demands of a leadership role and their current developmental capacities. The immunity-to-change process proposed by developmental psychologists Robert Kegan and Lisa Lahey offers the possibility of increasing success in accomplishing personal change goals those leaders have previously found frustrating and hard to achieve. Kegan described stages of development in terms of how a person knows things, not just what things a person knows. For leaders, developing requires gaining additional mental functions that may be crucial to their success in their roles. For example, leaders can increase their capacities to analyze their own and others' values and commitments, give and receive criticism more productively, tolerate and even welcome disagreement and diversity, work in a more self-directed and self-regulated manner, and take responsibility for the conditions and products of their work.

Stefanie was recently promoted to a senior executive position in a large insurance company after she spent several years successfully managing the company's law department. With this promotion, her work centers less on her knowledge and skill in analyzing legal issues and more on her ability to communicate effectively with staff, colleagues, and senior executives. Stefanie has always felt confident of her ability to offer wise legal analysis and advice, but she is less confident about how to communicate her ideas and opinions. When she received her promotion, Stefanie was told that other senior executives had only one reservation about her leadership abilities: some felt that Stefanie can be difficult to interact with because she doesn't always listen carefully to what others are saying. In meetings, she often asks questions or makes comments that reveal her lack of awareness of previously expressed information or ideas. Stefanie found this feedback both familiar and embarrassing and vows to turn this around. She now leaves meetings worrying about how she has communicated and how others have perceived her. Stefanie has always been ambitious and hard working, and she is eager to work on her communication in order to succeed in her new position.

Edward is the director of global competitiveness in a large nonprofit research and public policy institute. Long frustrated by what he sees as the bureaucratic nature of his organization, he has always prided himself on being something of a maverick, willing to bend rules or butt heads whenever he disagrees with the organization's official stance on a matter or with his colleagues' opinions. For the past year, Edward has been working with other directors and senior fellows on developing a cross-departmental project focused on a complex environmental issue. Edward feels extremely frustrated by their meetings, which he sees as unnecessarily long and unproductive. Before a meeting begins, he often vows that he won't get so angry when others make comments that seem blatantly ill informed or unnecessary. Yet he is rarely able to uphold this vow and finds himself berating his colleagues for their poor judgment, fundamental misunderstanding of the global economy, and inefficiency. Although he realizes that his outbursts tend to make the meetings even longer and less productive, Edward has not been able to change the ways he participates.

Both of these leaders have decided it's time to change how they lead. Their self-initiated efforts haven't led to the gains they hoped for (in good part, as both would readily admit, because they haven't been able to sustain their attention or gain any momentum on their change goals given all their other demands). Now, however, it is clear to both that the costs of not changing are too great. In her heart, Stefanie knows that listening well is a key to earning the trust of people in her department, let alone being successful in motivating and influencing them. She recognizes that if she doesn't improve her listening skills, she will not succeed in her new position. Edward knows that the environmental project will fail if the participants cannot work together productively.

The stakes are high for Stefanie and Edward. They know what is on the line: their sense of efficacy, their reputations, the effectiveness of their organizations, and perhaps even their jobs. But Stefanie and Edward are also realists: their own efforts to change have not succeeded, despite their sincerity, hard work, and eagerness to change, and so the odds are slim that willing themselves to change will succeed this time just because the stakes are higher. Both feel stuck, caught in a familiar tangle of their own habits and tendencies.

We begin this chapter with these descriptions of their struggles because we suspect that there are many Stefanies and Edwards out there. While the particular details of a leader's problem—how exactly he or she gets stuck—vary, we have met countless leaders who experience their own kind of "stuckness" and see other forms of "stuckness" in their colleagues, their employees, and their bosses. All of them seem to experience or exhibit an immunity to change that hinders their capacity to lead or, worse, threatens to block further development altogether.

DEALING WITH STUCKNESS

If we can understand why leaders like Stefanie and Edward are stuck, we are better positioned to help them get unstuck. A powerful lens for these purposes is adult development psychologist Robert Kegan's constructive-developmental theory (1982, 1994), which shows how adults make meaning of their lives, how meaning systems grow and change, and how, where, and why adults might get stuck. Central to this view is that every individual is inherently a meaning maker, actively making sense of what is going on around and inside him or her. People are not, by contrast, like cameras, faithfully recording images. Perhaps you have had the experience of leaving a movie that you loved, only to hear your companion's endless criticisms of it. It may even seem as though you had attended different movies. That is meaning making at work, the constructive aspect of the theory.

Also central to this view is that meaning systems are coherent and can develop over time. Imagine you have eyeglasses on. Early on in our development, that eyeglass is a monocle. You can see, but your vision is more limited than if you were wearing a pair of eyeglasses and could see depth and perspective. An even more powerful set of eyeglasses might include polarized sunglasses that enable you to see what before you saw only as glare. In each case, you see or understand the world using a consistent lens, and that lens gives way over time to another one that enables you to see more. In like manner, each stage of meaning making incorporates the capacities of the prior stage within a larger, more complex meaning system. In this way, our mental complexity, or psychological capacity, increases—the developmental aspect of the theory (see Basseches, 1984; Belenky, Clinchy, Goldberger, and Tarule, 1986; Daloz, 1986; Kegan, 1982; Kohlberg, 1984; Mezirow, 1991; Piaget, 1952; Weathersby, 1976).

In addition to this focus on the individual, specifically his or her psychological capacities and meaning making, the theory also attends to the person's larger context—his or her roles, relationships, the organizational culture—and its tacit expectations. Being effective in adulthood turns out to demand certain developmental capabilities, and being an effective leader is no exception. From our view, a leader's problem is not located in the individual or the context, but is about the relationship between the two.

Specifically, problems are generated whenever a gap exists between a leader's current capacities, or mental complexity, and the psychological demands of his or her role and work context (Kegan, 1994). It is as if the prescription in a leader's glasses is not strong enough so that he or she cannot adequately see what is occurring. In these cases, leaders such as Stefanie and Edward are in over their heads; consequently, they experience the personal angst and stress of not meeting expectations, and they fail to create conditions within their organizations that enable it to thrive. In a nutshell, these leaders are missing the critical psychological capabilities demanded by their roles. The good news, however, is that a motivated leader can develop his or her meaning-making system given proper supports and challenges at any age or phase in life.

In this chapter, we provide a brief overview of Robert Kegan's (1982, 1994) constructive-developmental theory, showing how this theory explains Stefanie's and Edward's current developmental capacities, the ways in which they are in over their heads and make sense of the challenges they consequently face, and what their next evolutionary steps might be. We also describe a process for supporting the development of leaders, which helps them overturn their immunities to change (Kegan and Lahey, 2001, 2009).

KEGAN'S THEORY AND ITS RELEVANCE TO LEADERSHIP DEVELOPMENT

A leader's way of knowing fundamentally shapes how that individual conceives of work, leadership, and the kinds of competencies he or she can demonstrate in this role. Looking more deeply into the ways that Stefanie and Edward make sense of their situations helps to clarify how their problems arise from the fundamental ways they make meaning of themselves and their work. We can quickly gain access to how people make sense of a problem by asking what they would fear if they were to change their behaviors. When Stefanie and Edward consider that possibility, each is able to identify particular fears. For example, when Stefanie thinks about what it would be like to listen more openly to her colleagues, she fears that she might lose track of her own thinking. "If I listen more openly," she tells us, "I won't be able to hold on to my own perspective. My view will be influenced by the other person's. The way a person adds value to any project is by offering insights and ideas. If I lose mine, get persuaded by other ideas, I won't add value."

Edward does not like to think of himself as someone who has fears that influence his behaviors, and at first, his list of fears about what would happen if he were to be friendlier to colleagues sounds more like an evaluation of others than self-reflection. "These people really push my buttons. I've worked with them in some manner or another for a few years, although not as closely as we do now. But I've seen how they work, and I've heard stories. I really wonder about their motivations for the decisions they make. They've done things that seem patently ignorant, narrow-minded, and shortsighted to me. I've also seen how hypercompetitive and aggressive they can be when it comes to promoting their own ideas. They need to demonstrate that they understand and value my perspective." As he reflects further, he identifies this fear: "Because I don't like or trust them, I see everything they do as suspect, as evidence that they'll try to override my opinions or discount my perspective."

Using a constructive-developmental lens, we see some fundamental similarities in the ways these two leaders make sense of themselves, others around them, and their work. The constructive-developmental perspective helps us understand how Stefanie and Edward make meaning of their experiences, how the meaning they make grows and changes, and how they might meet obstacles when their meaning making proves inadequate to furthering their development as leaders. In various ways, Stefanie and Edward are experiencing problems at work because each is encountering the limits of a system of meaning making governed by others' opinions and assessments of them. In putting a premium on others' opinions, they allow others to be the ultimate authorities for measuring their worth, which also means that they don't take responsibility for the ways that they contribute to their problem and so can't take responsibility for their part in solving it. In other words, they share some basic ideas about the nature and location of authority and responsibility, and these similarities reveal that they are at the same developmental stage or order of consciousness.

Stefanie and Edward from Kegan's Developmental Perspective

In Kegan's developmental framework, each stage is characterized not by the contents of what one knows or is able to do but with *how* one knows, referring to the structures that organize and regulate our meaning making. That is how Stefanie and Edward, who have quite different personalities, skills, and knowledge, can both be described as sharing a developmental stage. These two leaders make meaning at Kegan's third order of consciousness, the *Socializing* perspective (Table 3.1 provides a synopsis of Kegan's theory). Socializing individuals are able to exercise many capacities that are necessary for successful leadership, including the ability to reason abstractly, reflect on their own inner states, and understand their relationships in a reciprocal manner (subordinating their individual interests on behalf of shared feelings, agreements, and expectations). But their orientation to the opinions of experts and important others means that their own theories, values, and expectations about personal and professional relationships and responsibilities are essentially made up by the theories, values, and expectations of these others.

Kegan (1994) describes these internalized authorities as being similar to a board of directors that has been welcomed into Socializing individuals' meaning making and therefore is a part of their decision making. These various perspectives may usefully guide individuals' decision making and behavior, but if there is conflict

Table 3.1
Robert Kegan's Five Stages of Development: Childhood Through Adulthood

Stage of Development	Capacities and Limits

Impulsive Perspective: First Order of Consciousness (mostly young children)	Can . . .
	    Exercise control over their own movement
	    Perceive basic sensation, others' moods
	Cannot . . .
	    Reliably distinguish between fantasy and reality, between how something appears and how it actually is
	    Consistently follow rules and meet expectations without supervision
	    Control one's own impulses

Instrumental Perspective: Second Order of Consciousness (older children, adolescents, and some adults)	Can . . .
	    Understand the difference between how something or someone appears and how it actually is
	    Control their impulses
	    Identify their own needs and preferences
	    Understand that others have separate feelings and desires, views relationships in terms of what is tangibly shared and exchanged
	Cannot . . .
	    Reflect on concrete information to reason abstractly
	    Understand another person's perspective, point of view, or emotional state except for what is explicitly stated

Socializing Perspective: Third Order of Consciousness (older adolescents and a majority of adults)	Can . . .
	    Reflect on the concrete to reason abstractly and think hypothetically
	    Internalize the feelings of others
	    Orient to values and ideas that are important to them and identify with values or belong to a group to which they are loyal

(continued)

Table 3.1
(*continued*)

Stage of Development	Capacities and Limits
	Draw their source of authority, self-assessment from external sources
	Cannot . . .
	Reflect on or critique assessments, values, or group positions with which they are identified
	Mediate conflict between external authorities
	Take responsibility for their internal reactions to others
Self-Authoring Perspective: Fourth Order of Consciousness (some adults)	Can . . .
	Generate their own (and develop critiques of others') values, commitments, and assessments
	Set limits or boundaries on relationships where necessary
	Tolerate or welcome disagreement with important others
	Take responsibility for their inner lives
	Cannot . . .
	Reflect on or critique their own ideologies or governing theories of self and leadership
Self-Transforming Perspective: Fifth Order of Consciousness (a very few adults, not before mid-life)	Can . . .
	Reflect on own and others' belief systems or ideologies to identify larger patterns
	Orient to the dialectical or paradoxical, welcoming contradiction and oppositeness
	Understand own selves and leadership identities as always revisable, evolving

between any of the board members, then these individuals feel torn. They cannot find a way to make a decision since they have no internal authority to rely on for mediating such conflicts.

Stefanie's tendency to "lose" her own perspective when she listens carefully to others indicates that she is not yet able to demonstrate the Self-Authoring capacity to hold and mediate between conflicting ideas. And although Edward's tendencies toward hostility and feelings of superiority might seem initially uncharacteristic of the Socializing perspective, his elaborations on his fears actually reveal that he also locates responsibility externally. He conceives of his relationships with colleagues as determined completely by *their* past actions and tendencies and takes no responsibility for defining and contributing to these relationships.

Moving from a Socializing to a Self-Authoring Stage or Perspective

The development of a Self-Authoring perspective is a move to a more integrative structure that permits individuals to exercise qualitatively new capacities. Self-Authoring adults are able to reflect on and reconsider the abstractions, values, and social prescriptions with which the Socializing individual is identified. Therefore, when they experience conflicts between their own emotional states or values, they are able to mediate these conflicts for themselves. They understand themselves as authorities who are responsible for determining their own beliefs and emotions, and so an individual who makes meaning at the Self-Authoring stage of development has metaphorically become the chair of the board of directors. These individuals may value the differing opinions of the board members yet ultimately decide what is best themselves. With the Socializing perspective, these differences may be upsetting to individuals and threaten their feelings of closeness or connection in a relationship. With a Self-Authoring perspective, however, "closeness" does not require an absolute correspondence of beliefs, and one can be more comfortable with and welcoming of such differences.

The gradual movement individuals make from one way of knowing to another is a transformational change, a qualitative shift in how they understand themselves and their worlds. In Kegan's (1994) language, they "can reflect on, handle, look at" (p. 32) the reactions and beliefs they previously held as truths. In making this movement, individuals develop increasingly complex capacities for conceptualizing responsibility, authority, conflict within the self, and conflict with others. They are therefore better able to manage the demands of their daily lives and their roles as leaders. Furthermore, because transformative change happens at the most basic levels of our meaning making, these types of change can enable people to take a broader perspective not only on a particular area that has been targeted for improvement but on all aspects of their work and personal lives (Cranton, 1994; Kegan, 1982, 1994, 2000; Kegan & Lahey, 2001, 2009; Mezirow, 1991).

It is not surprising that Stefanie and Edward are at this point in their development as adults. Research with large samples, using a variety of robust measures, suggests that roughly one-half to two-thirds of the adult population in the United States has not yet fully developed Self-Authoring capacities (Kegan, 1994, 2001). In this way, the Socializing and Self-Authoring perspectives, and the evolution from one to the other, are particularly relevant to issues of leadership development.

DEVELOPMENT AND LEADERSHIP EFFECTIVENESS

It's not surprising that these Socializing leaders are feeling challenged by the demands of their work. Research indicates that leaders who can exercise Self-Authorship are better able to handle the demands of leadership and more likely to be effective in their roles (for a review of this research, see McCauley, Drath, Palus, O'Connor, and Baker, 2006). In general, higher levels of development are associated with increased leadership competence. For example, in his study of twenty-one CEOs of large and successful organizations, Keith Eigel (1998) found that leaders' developmental capacities correlated with their abilities to challenge existing processes, inspire a shared vision, manage conflict, solve problems, delegate, empower, and build relationships. These associations exist because typically, the skills, behaviors, and knowledge of effective leadership necessitate an increased complexity of consciousness and an ability to construct one's own internal belief system, standard, or personal filter that enables one to make meaning of oneself and one's work in new ways.

For his book, *In over Our Heads* (1994), Kegan surveyed the literature describing the competencies needed for effective leadership (as well as those competencies commonly expected of parents, intimate partners, citizens of an increasingly diverse world, and adult learners). His book illustrates how many of these expectations are aligned with and attainable only in conjunction with Self-Authorship. His list of workplace competencies includes that we

- Be the inventor or owner of our work (rather than see it as owned and created by the employer) and distinguish our work from our job
- Be self-initiating, self-correcting, self-evaluating (rather than remaining dependent on others to frame the problems, initiate adjustments, or determine whether things are going acceptably well)

- Be guided by our own visions at work (rather than be without a vision or captive of the authority's agenda)

- Take responsibility for what happens to us at work externally and internally (rather than see our present internal circumstances and future external possibilities as caused by someone else)

- Be accomplished masters of our particular work roles, jobs, or careers (rather than see our present circumstances and future external possibilities as caused by someone else)

- Conceive of the organization from the "outside in," as a whole; see our relation to the whole; see the relation of the parts to the whole (rather than see the rest of the organization and its parts only from the perspective of our own part, from the "inside out") [Kegan, 2001, p. 198]

Taken together, these competencies require development beyond the Socializing perspective. For example, if leaders are to be guided by their own visions at work, they must not only be well Socialized into the visions of other leaders in the organization but also be able to gain some psychological distance from those visions in order to be able to reflect on and evaluate them. Similarly, if leaders are to take responsibility for the circumstances and possibilities for their work, they must be able not only to reflect on their inner lives of feelings and thoughts but also to see themselves as the authors of and responsible for their inner lives. Finally, if leaders are to be self-initiating, self-correcting, and self-evaluating, they must have their own ideology or organized set of beliefs and values that allows them to prioritize and resolve conflicts among specific beliefs and values. In sum, Kegan writes that "the very idea of managing . . . suggesting as it does the activities of handling, arranging, configuring, deciding, executing, finessing, operating, and presiding would seem to require or to imply the authoring capacities of the fourth order of consciousness" (1994, p. 168). Drath (1990) makes a similar assertion, suggesting most modern organizations are structured in ways that reward a Self-Authoring manager's strengths and minimize weaknesses.

In a nutshell, some capacity for Self-Authorship is necessary in order to exercise a host of abilities and skills that are valuable for success across many aspects of an adult's life and work and can clearly bear on one's capacity to lead. The Self-Authoring adult can think critically and thereby examine and evaluate the opinions and expectations of others—for example, by analyzing the appropriateness and potential risks and benefits of adopting a new marketing strategy; asking hard, pertinent questions during meetings; or giving and receiving criticism about the quality of one's work. Self-Authorship fosters the development of respectful but detached relationships and empathizing with but not becoming captive of the emotions of others. Adults who can exercise this capacity are able to make tough decisions that can involve disappointing others on behalf of a larger vision or purpose. Self-Authoring adults can achieve some distance from their own tendency to privilege that which is familiar and comfortable, and so to be open to disagreement and diversity that can lead to improved strategies and approaches for achieving the organizational mission. In doing so, they can seek out and promote the sharing and consideration of novel ideas and perspectives for solving problems, promoting organizational growth, and cultivating new learning. Self-Authoring individuals also can work in a more self-directed and self-regulated manner, establishing a clear focus and sense of accountability and taking responsibility for results, actions, and decisions.

If leaders provide support and challenge that differ according to their followers' capacities, then the followers themselves are more likely to experience that leadership as growth enhancing. Cultivating these appropriately varying types of relationships with their followers means that the leaders themselves will likely need to have more complex developmental capacities than those of their followers. Accordingly, research suggests that a leader's stage of development predicts followers' satisfaction with that leader (Harris, 2005; Strang, 2006, as cited in McCauley et al., 2006). Leaders may therefore need to possess and exercise these particular developmental capacities in order to be successful.

The application of constructive-developmental theory to issues of leadership competency illustrates why and how leaders may face a gap between the demands of effective leadership of most modern organizations and their own developmental capacities. In other words, these demands of the role are more complex than individuals' abilities to meet them. We are not suggesting that individuals who have not yet developed Self-Authoring capacities are lacking in other capacities such as intelligence, work ethic, or motivation to succeed. Individuals can possess (or lack) such qualities at any developmental stage. What we do suggest is that if leaders like Stefanie and Edward are to make maximal progress and increase their effectiveness in meeting the demands of their work, they will benefit from access to development programs designed to nurture this transformation.

FOSTERING LEADERS' DEVELOPMENT

Adult development psychologists Robert Kegan and Lisa Lahey (2001, 2009) have formulated a process for supporting transformational learning and increasing participants' effectiveness in their roles. In this process, a first step is diagnostic: individuals make explicit the contradictions between their intended goals and the behaviors that they enact, and they uncover their hidden assumptions, beliefs, or mental models that give rise to those contradictions. In doing so, a person sees his or her immunity to change. Next, the process of overcoming one's immunity to change provides opportunities for participants to envision and then experiment with new, more effective behaviors and to mindfully form new relationships to the commitments and assumptions that underlie them (for a fuller illustration of the immunities-to-change diagnostic and change process, see Kegan and Lahey, 2001, 2009). In this section, we provide snapshots of the journey our two leaders took to diagnose and overturn their immunities. In doing so, we seek to illustrate something of the nature of these processes; show how individuals progress through the work in different ways, according to their needs; and highlight the types of learning and change they achieve.

Immunity Maps

To diagnose their own immunities to change, participants complete an exercise that helps them to make explicit the contradictions in their thinking and behaviors, recording their responses in a four-column template, or "immunity map." (Often the work of diagnosing and overturning immunities to change takes place under the direction of a trained coach. However, many groups and individuals also successfully undertake this work guided by published descriptions of the process. See Kegan and Lahey, 2001, and Wagner et al., 2006.)

Stefanie begins her map with a commitment to improve her ability to communicate effectively with her colleagues. Looking at the behaviors she engages in that undermine this commitment, Stefanie lists: "I don't listen well enough. I resist considering others' ideas seriously. I advocate too strongly for my own opinions. I am not always very clear in my explanations." Stefanie fears that if she were to listen more openly to her colleagues, she might lose track of her own thinking, and that she wouldn't be adding value unless she was offering her own ideas. These fears show Stefanie that she is also committed to "feeling like my ideas are the best ideas and having others see my ideas as the best ideas." In fact, Stefanie admits that she is committed to "having others agree with me and see me as valuable" and "not allowing myself to change my mind . . . , not feeling like I don't know what to think." These commitments counterbalance her starting commitment to communicating more effectively, thereby creating an immunity to change (see Table 3.2).

Underlying Stefanie's immunity are several assumptions about what it means to be seen as valuable and what it means to have an opinion. Stefanie assumes if she doesn't have distinct ideas to contribute, or if her ideas are not accepted by the team, then she is not a valuable part of the team. She also realizes that she has been assuming that listening to others is not viewed as making a valuable contribution. And she has been assuming that if she listens carefully, she will necessarily be persuaded by what others are saying. She lists these in her map as the big assumptions that underlie her immune system and keep it running. As long as she views these assumptions as true, she continues to be immune to change. However, if she can begin to alter those assumptions, she has the potential to disturb the counterbalance of her commitments and make progress on her goals.

Edward's first-column commitment (see Table 3.3) is to having more productive relationships with his colleagues. In his second column, he lists behaviors that undermine his commitment: "My comments are often rigid and dogmatic. I use my own knowledge of economics to bully others into submission. I give speeches and tirades that show my anger. I take up too much airtime in meetings." As we have described, Edward saw that his history with and knowledge of his colleagues were influencing the ways he related to them and that his fears were based on this information. "Because I don't like or trust my colleagues," Edward concluded, "I see everything they do as suspect, as evidence that they'll try to override my perspective or discount my opinions." These fears showed Edward the hidden commitments he held that were in tension with his first-column commitment: "I am committed to not being manipulated by them, not finding out I can be manipulated by them. I am committed to being the one with integrity, as setting the standard for professional conduct." As he wrote these words, Edward laughed, realizing that his own conduct in the team meetings was less than professional. He also discovered a possibility that surprised him some—a commitment "to not having to find out that I like anything about them, that they actually might have anything of value to contribute."

As he looked at his map (see Table 3.3), Edward recognized several assumptions that were holding his immunity in place. He assumed that his colleagues had

Table 3.2

Stefanie's Four-Column Immunity Map

1. Commitment	2. Doing/Not Doing and Therefore Keeping Commitment from Being More Fully Realized	3. Hidden Competing Commitment	4. Big Assumption
I am committed to improving my abilities to communicate effectively with my collegues, especially in team meetings.	I don't listen well enough. I resist considering others' ideas seriously. I advocate too strongly for my own opinions. I am not always very clear in my explanations.	I fear that I will lose track of my own thinking. I fear that if I am not offering and advocating for my own ideas, I won't be adding value. I am committed to feeling like my ideas are the best ideas and having others see my ideas as the best ideas. I am committed to having others agree with me and see me as valuable. I am committed to not allowing myself to change my mind, to not feeling like I don't know what to think.	I assume that if I do not have distinct ideas to contribute to a discussion, and if others don't accept those ideas, then I'm not a valuable part of the team. I assume that just listening to others is not seen as a valuable contribution. I assume that if I listen carefully to others' ideas, I'll get persuaded to agree with them and adopt their ideas.

Table 3.3

Edward's Four-Column Immunity Map

1. Commitment	2. Doing/Not Doing and Therefore Keeping Commitment from Being More Fully Realized	3. Hidden Competing Commitment	4. Big Assumption
I am committed to having more productive relationships with my colleagues.	My comments are often rigid and dogmatic. I use my own knowledge of economics to bully others into submission. I give speeches and tirades that show my anger. I take up too much airtime in meetings.	Because I don't like or trust my colleagues, I see everything they do as suspect, as evidence that they'll try to override my perspective or discount my opinions. I am committed to not being manipulated by them, not finding out I can be manipulated by them. I am committed to being the one with integrity, as setting the standard for professional conduct. I am committed to not having to find out that I like anything about them, that they actually might have anything of value to contribute.	I assume that if given the chance, my colleagues could manipulate me, although I can't actually say how they'd do this or in what ways I'd be manipulated! I assume that if I don't voice my disagreement with and disapproval of them, they will see me as a approving of them, and I will lose power. I assume that I must not ever agree with my colleagues or find their comments or perspectives valuable without compromising my own stance as a critic of their positions and their characters.

power to manipulate him, although he could not name what this manipulation might potentially involve or how it would happen. He assumed that if he did not regularly voice his disagreement and disapproval, his colleagues would mistakenly assume that he approved of them and he would lack power. Finally, he could see that he had been assuming that he must never agree with his colleagues or find their perspectives valuable without compromising his stance as a critic of their positions and their characters. In naming these assumptions, Edward recognized immediately that they seemed a bit irrational and overstated. Nevertheless, he could clearly see how powerfully (if unknowingly) his thoughts and actions had been guided by these beliefs.

Overcoming Immunities to Change

In completing their maps, these leaders come to understand how and why the assumptions they hold generate immunities to the types of change they need to make in order to meet their desired goals.

To overcome their immunities to change, participants envision and enact behaviors that run counter to their own assumptions, look to see what happens when they do so, and on the basis of such data consider whether those assumptions need modification. It is not easy to call into question and potentially alter the assumptions we have taken as truths. Often we have held particularly big assumptions for years and years, with their roots lodged deep in our pasts. In practicing new behaviors that explicitly test these assumptions, participants can begin to form new understandings of and relationships to their previous commitments and the assumptions that underlie them. In this way, the process powerfully engages people's behaviors and beliefs, which are linked in a reciprocal, reinforcing relationship. Changes to behavior, when reflected on, can lead to changes in belief. Similarly, when changes in belief occur, they have necessary implications for changes in practice. Ultimately this process leads in many cases to significant advances in the stated goal (Kegan and Lahey, 2009). In addition, the immunities-to-change technology offers the potential for a type of change that is of even greater magnitude: leaders may undertake transformation—a fundamental change or qualitative shift in their entire meaning-making system (thereby enabling them to accomplish a great deal more than just their original goal).

In describing how these individuals began to overturn their immunities, we provide snapshots of their work on two of the steps in the process (see Table 3.4;

Table 3.4
Two Steps in the Process of Overturning Immunities

Step	Key Actions and Guiding Questions
Observing the big assumption in action	Participants do not yet attempt to change their behavior or their big assumptions.
	PART ONE: For approximately two weeks, participants look for information that illustrates the influence of their big assumptions on their lives and seek to answer the following question: "What do you notice does or does not happen as a result of holding your big assumption as TRUE?" Participants record what happened and how it is an instance of their big assumptions at work.
	PART TWO: Participants search for data and experiences—whether in their professional lives or personal lives—that counter or cast doubt on the absolute quality of their big assumptions.
Designing and running a test of the big assumption	Participants design a simple experiment that leads them to do something different from what they ordinarily would do when routinely holding their big assumptions as true. An ideal test (1) is both safe and modest, (2) allows them to collect data related to their big assumptions (including data that would qualify it or call it into doubt), and (3) is actionable in the near term (within a week or so).

for a fuller account of all the steps in this process, see Kegan and Lahey, 2009). These snapshots allow us to illustrate something of the nature of the process most individuals follow, while also showing how participants' learning can potentially occur across the span of our learning objectives: increasing their effectiveness in their roles by gaining new skills and behaviors, altering their meaning making and the underlying assumptions they have brought to their work, and making transformative change toward a more Self-Authoring perspective.

Observing the Big Assumption in Action and Staying Alert to Natural Counters

As part of the process of overturning their immunities, we ask participants to be alert to what happens, and fails to happen, as a result of holding their big assumptions as true. They spend at least a week keeping track of situations where they see (or have recently seen) their big assumptions at work, influencing how they look at things, feel about things, take action (or not), make choices, and direct their energies. We also ask them to watch for any experiences that might lead them to question the truthfulness or widespread applicability of their big assumptions. Our big assumptions typically lead us to attend to certain data and avoid or ignore other data, but if we can deliberately look at data we might otherwise ignore, we may begin to cast doubt on these assumptions.

Stefanie decides to pay more attention to how she participates in senior executive meetings. She notices that she is preoccupied with her own thinking, her own ideas. As a result, "I listen to others only for the purposes of devising a response to them. Often I have a response in mind after the other person has uttered only a sentence. Then I stop listening and am simply waiting for my turn to speak next." She also uncovers new assumptions: "I assume I know what the person is going to say next, how they'll complete their thought. I also assume that I don't have to take time to entertain their idea seriously. I have already decided to discount it."

She looks for natural counters to her assumption and discovers times when she actually is a good listener and communicator. For example, she has a good relationship with a young lawyer she used to manage. Stefanie considers herself a mentor to that lawyer and enjoys the times when they have conversations about specific aspects of the law. She says, "Often I'm being more of a sounding board for him as he works out an issue on his own. Other times I may engage in some Socratic questioning, like in law school." The young lawyer has thanked Stefanie for being willing to help him, telling her how much he has learned from their conversations and how much he appreciates the opportunity to talk. Stefanie realizes that these interactions counter several of her assumptions. She says,

> I listen to this lawyer because I assume his own thinking is valuable; he has something good to say. I also listen and don't feel I need to tell him my ideas because I'm not trying to impress him. But, interestingly enough, I *do* impress him. So my value to him comes through the listening, the questioning. Also, because it's not so important for me to give him *my* opinions, I don't worry about whether I can hold onto them. I can listen to him openly, think about what he's saying,

consider what I think of that and not focus on whether or not I'll lose my own thoughts.

In completing this step, Stefanie's learning extends across the three types of changes we seek to promote: behavioral change, changes in meaning making, and transformational change. For example, although this step does not ask her to change her behaviors yet, Stefanie is realizing that she in fact does know how to listen well, as evidenced by her interactions with her protégé. In discovering this fact, Stefanie's goal shifts from wanting to learn how to listen more effectively to learning how and when she should be exercising this skill. Furthermore, she is coming to new insights about the value of listening. She now sees that listening can and does add value, perhaps enough so that she decides she'd like to listen more even if that sometimes causes her to lose track of her own ideas.

Finally, Stefanie comes to an insight with transformational potential when she discovers that whether she listens well depends on whether she thinks she needs to impress people. "I have been thinking a lot about that issue," she muses.

> It has really been nagging at me because I feel like maybe I've been selfish and shortsighted, although that hasn't been my intention. But I see now that impressing others and getting to the best result are two different things. I've been focused mostly on impressing people with my dazzling ideas, but if I focus *only* on impressing them, we might not get to the best result. Of course, I know that my own ideas might not always be the best ones. I can count on that. So I need to start focusing less on *whose* idea is getting taken and more on how together we can come up with the *best* idea. I want to do some more observing, to try to be more aware of the times when trying to impress is my goal, and think how and why that might be unrelated to getting the best results. And then I want to change it!

Reconsidering her goals in this way, Stefanie is also beginning to question her reliance on others' opinions of her as the source of her own self-evaluation. The fact that she can consider the possibility that her contributions might be less impressive to others, but more useful in moving a team toward a better result, suggests that she is beginning to develop a qualitatively different understanding of authority. Although she is still a long way from internally authoring a new standard, she has begun to take noticeable steps.

Deliberately Testing Big Assumptions

One of the most powerful steps in the overturning process asks participants to create a safe, modest test of their big assumptions. In effect, they run a small experiment in which they do something different from what they ordinarily would do when routinely holding their big assumptions as true. The experiments should be safe, modest, and actionable, allowing participants to consider what happens when they make even small changes in their usual behaviors. The purpose of the test is not to see whether they can successfully enact the new behaviors, or even to see if the new behaviors are more effective, although often participants do learn about these things. The main purpose is for them to collect data that will help shed light on whether, and under what circumstances, their big assumptions are not true. It is very important, therefore, that participants try to maintain their focus on how what they are doing, thinking, and learning has an impact on their big assumptions. As powerful as it is to experience oneself behaving in new ways or getting results one never thought possible, these changes are likely to become permanent, fully realized ways of leading only when the fundamental ideas and beliefs (the big assumptions) that generated old ways of being are directly challenged, tested, and amended.

When Edward designed his first test of his big assumptions, he purposefully decided not to think about behaving differently in the project development meetings. Having tried and failed to change that behavior in the past, he begins with a modest test: he chooses to change his behavior by talking to a colleague, Terry, whom he respects and who also works well with the coworkers Edward dislikes. In planning the conversation, Edward is deliberately seeking data that will disrupt his assumptions about feeling constant dislike for and disapproval of his coworkers. To do so, he asks Terry what contributions he thinks the others make to the organization and to Terry's work, as well as what Terry does to make his working relationships with these coworkers successful. Terry responds by telling Edward that getting along with these coworkers makes good political sense, that it is better to have them as allies than as enemies.

"I wasn't really persuaded by that argument," Edward explains, "because I've never been motivated by those types of political considerations. I understand the line of thinking, but that doesn't mean I agree with it." Then Terry went on to provide additional explanation that Edward did find compelling:

> First, he told me that he thought I was lumping all these coworkers together when actually, they can be quite different from each other. While some of them might at times be intellectually sloppy and prone to self-promotion, it could be I am exaggerating the problem a bit and applying those labels to some individuals who might actually show a lot more promise. I think it is possible that I've done that.
>
> Then Terry said something else that I've really been thinking quite a lot about. He pointed out that these coworkers are actually all at a more junior rank in the organization than either he is or I am. So Terry thinks that their tendency toward self-promotion is a by-product of their current position and their desire for advancement. That's not new information to me, but I guess I haven't really thought about this issue much from that kind of political perspective. Again, it's not how I like to operate. But Terry understands it because he remembers behaving in that kind of way himself.

Reflecting on his conversation with Terry, Edward realizes that the way he looks at these coworkers has shifted a bit, although it takes him a while to identify how and why. Eventually he concludes that while he still doesn't really value the way these coworkers conduct themselves, he no longer feels threatened by them. Instead, he notes, "I feel kind of old and a little silly that I get so provoked by them. I guess I worry that they represent the future of our organization, and I don't want to see things change too much around here." In coming to this conclusion, Edward feels as if he still harbors some dislike of and distaste for these coworkers, but he also recognizes that the intensity of these feelings has lessened considerably. "I think," he reflects, "I had been assuming that if I wasn't expressing my dislike and disapproval, I had somehow lost my own passion for this work and was giving it up to them."

The transformational potential in these insights becomes clearer as Edward considers how he'd like his relationship with his coworkers to change:

> I can see now that I was reacting to them, or to my interpretations of them, I suppose. In that way, I was allowing their behavior and their personalities to define the way I responded; I was letting them

determine how I'd relate to them. In my conversation with Terry, he suggested that I could actually be a kind of teacher to them, and that completely changed the way I think of relating to them. I'm not sure I want to be their teacher, and I doubt that's what they would want either. [laughs] But it did help me see that I can decide what I want my relationship to them to be like. I can determine who I'd like to be in these meetings. I'm not sure what that looks like yet, but I'll figure it out.

Edward's colleague has helped him begin to accept responsibility for the terms of his relationship with his colleagues. He now sees that by reacting blindly, he was captive of their approach to their work and their conception of how to communicate. Instead he can now entertain the possibility that they are not responsible for the way he reacts to them; he is ultimately responsible for that. With this realization, he is reconceiving a fundamental assumption in his meaning making system, demonstrating an increasing capacity for Self-Authorship.

In both examples, Stefanie and Edward illustrate the potential that the immunity-to-change process has for bringing about change in individuals' behaviors, in their meaning making, and for fostering transformation. We can also see that this process does not occur overnight; continued experimentation, reflection, and reconsideration of their former ways of making sense of their work will be necessary for the process to yield the results each leader hopes to see.

APPLYING THE PROCESS TO INDIVIDUALS AND ORGANIZATIONS

The immunity-to-change process is a personal learning program. It is not a quick fix; time and focused reflection are necessary if deep-seated (and typically long-held) assumptions are to be examined and reworked. But it is professional education, not treatment or psychotherapy, and the learning process can be structured in varying ways depending on the needs of the participants and the organization. In a common delivery model, individual leaders request the services of an immunities coach (who can be internal or external to the organization). In such cases, a participant typically works one-on-one with the coach who has been trained in the immunities process. The experimentation and reflection process typically takes four to six months, through a series of weekly e-mails and phone calls. Participants commit to spending approximately one hour each week on a structured assignment or phone meeting (or both) with their coach. Once participants complete all of the steps in the process, they can continue with the process on their own, replicating the methodologies without the assistance of the coach, thereby sustaining the long-term impact of the process.

In other cases, organizations use immunities coaching more expansively. For example, each member of an executive committee may create individual immunity maps and begin the process of overturning their immunities, supported by a coach. Along the way, the members of the committee share the results with each other and help to hold each other accountable for making changes. In this way, not only can individuals make progress on their stated commitments, but the committee can make powerful changes in the way it works. New kinds of conversations and learning become possible. Another possibility is for a coach to lead a collective (such as a work team, a leadership group, or even an entire organization) in the process of diagnosing and overturning their groupwide immunities to change. In such cases, the focus is not on each individual group member's immunity but on the ways that they collectively prevent themselves from making the kinds of progress that the team or group desires. The group then can engage in a process of experimentation and reflection leading to new insights that can unleash the power of the group to function more effectively.

CONCLUSION

When fully implemented, the immunities-to-change process leads to changes in mind as well as behavior, and it can increase participants' effectiveness in understanding and enacting their complex roles. It engages and links various growth and change processes and has the potential to yield lasting results. Perhaps its most powerful result is providing a vehicle for participants to make transformative change: a qualitative shift in how they understand themselves and their world and the relationship between the two. In that way, it can provide valuable opportunities for leaders to develop the Self-Authoring capacities demanded of them by their roles. This process is rooted in constructive-developmental theory, which provides a comprehensive framework for understanding and analyzing a leader's meaning making and psychological capacity, bringing those into relationship with the demands of the leader's role, and offering a picture of what the leader's developmental progress could look like.

In this chapter, we have argued that Stefanie's and Edward's developmental capacities and limits contribute to their struggles in performing their leadership functions. We know that linking transformational change and professional competence can lead to misunderstandings, so we want to be clear that we are not suggesting that to operate out of a higher-order meaning making translates into being a better person or having a more meaningful life and the like. "Higher is better" only in the sense that a person can perform the mental functions of the prior levels as well as additional functions. Nor are we suggesting that the specific challenges these leaders face are endemic to the Socializing perspective. A leader could be a bad listener or an intellectual bully at any stage along the developmental continuum. It is also possible for a leader to evolve to a higher stage of development without effectively solving a specific leadership challenge.

What we are suggesting is that the ways that Stefanie and Edward make meaning of their challenges render them immune to the changes they would like to make and are indicative of the Socializing perspective. In undertaking transformative change toward developing the Self-Authoring perspective, these leaders have greater potential to renegotiate their relationship to the specific challenges they face. They not only acquire an increased capacity to reflect on and reevaluate their relationship to these challenges but to all other aspects of their leadership. In doing so, they are better able to meet the mental demands of leadership in most organizations.

As we have shown earlier in this chapter, in many organizations and for many followers, leaders who can exercise Self-Authorship will be well equipped to succeed in their roles and across these relationships. However, some contexts and some followers will be best served by leaders who can exercise capacities that go beyond Self-Authoring. Followers who have already developed Self-Authoring capacities, for example, may be nurtured most by leaders who can make meaning in a manner more complex than they can. In addition, the needs of some organizations may begin to outstrip the Self-Authoring leader's capacities. In recent years, it has become increasingly important for organizations to become learning organizations (Senge, 1990), which can adapt quickly and fluidly to constant change in order to maintain their competitiveness. The organization itself can no longer be committed primarily to preserving itself by upholding predetermined purposes, tasks, and standards. Instead organizations may need to be committed most to their own evolution and development, operating with the assumption that the current organizational configuration is always incomplete and under construction. Where the pace and nature of change are more manageable, leaders who are Self-Authoring or slightly beyond may be well enough equipped to reflect on and reconsider their organization's existing ideology and current identity. But in situations where change is constant, requiring perpetual organizational transformation, leaders need to be committed most not to any particular ideology or identity but instead to a process of constant reinvention.

Leaders who have begun to win some distance from their own Self-Authorship are evolving toward Kegan's fifth developmental stage, the Self-Transforming perspective. As the term suggests, these leaders are committed to holding and mediating among multiple ideologies, individual identities, and organizational possibilities. They may therefore be uniquely suited to running dynamic, constantly transforming organizations. Few studies that measure leadership capacities have included individuals who operate fully with the Self-Transforming perspective. However, these studies often include individuals who make meaning somewhere between Self-Authorship and Self-Transformation, illustrating that such development is possible and suggesting ways that such individuals are uniquely qualified (Torbert, 2004; Joiner and Josephs, 2007). It may be the case then that our organizations currently face an unprecedented need for leadership development programs that can assist leaders in making transformational changes, nurturing Self-Transforming capacities.

PART TWO

The Gap Between

In this part of the book, three authors highlight several subtle yet powerful dynamics within individual leaders that, if not clearly understood, can undermine relations with colleagues at work and ultimately impede critical work outcomes. Sharing the basic premise that leadership is a relational process, each chapter examines how hidden dynamics can create unintended consequences for the relationships that leaders depend on to move their visions forward. From different perspectives, the authors offer specific strategies for transforming these invisible dynamics into positive influences.

In Chapter Four, Cary Cherniss calls attention to what happens when leaders lack emotional intelligence. Drawing on recent studies of the impact of emotional intelligence on work performance, he demonstrates how information flow and decision making are compromised when leaders are unable to manage their own emotional reactions effectively and to respond to the emotions of others with empathy, social skill, and adaptability. He offers examples of how the absence of self-awareness, resilience, self-regulation, and other competencies in this domain strains work relationships and undermines employee engagement. Many of these social and emotional skills are regularly overlooked in traditional executive development programs, and they remain insufficiently developed in leaders who face complex challenges in a global, fast-paced, and technology-driven economy. Cherniss provides a new, highly cost-effective, group-based approach to developing emotional intelligence in leaders at all levels. A systematic evaluation of this approach demonstrates its success in increasing social and emotional skills that are targeted for development.

In Chapter Five, Joyce Fletcher extends the scope of emotional intelligence to include the ability to create conditions in which organization members can operate effectively in their relational interactions. She suggests that relational leadership is difficult to enact because of two hidden challenges: (1) gender and power dynamics that undermine both men and women as they attempt to practice relational leadership and (2) relational skills employed in the service of instrumental ends (accomplishing work, for example) that can be experienced as counterintuitive. Several vivid workplace examples illustrate how effective relational practice is often marginalized by misunderstanding and mislabeling the leader's motives, the limits of language to explain how supportive and yielding behavior could be acts of leadership, and the tendency to equate relational practice with femininity rather than leadership. The chapter ends with a rubric that defines relational practice, nonrelational practice, and relational malpractice. Leaders can use this framework to develop greater self-awareness and ultimately to practice relational leadership that will result in better work outcomes.

In the interview with Frances Hesselbein in Chapter Six, readers have an opportunity to learn what it means to lead with authenticity and how critical this capacity is for catalyzing groups and organizations to work toward a meaningful mission that hinges on service to others. Through her many years of leading, writing, and teaching about leadership, Hesselbein has clearly demonstrated that knowing oneself—one's core values, talents, and passions—and acting consistently with that knowledge lie at the core of transformational leadership. As CEO of the Girl Scouts of America from 1976 to 1990 and as founding president of the Peter Drucker Foundation (now called the Leader to Leader Institute), she draws on her own experiences and those of other well-regarded leaders in private industry, government, and education to illustrate the criticality of transparency and integrity in leading authentically and in transforming organizations. She strongly believes that young adults today are demonstrating a desire to serve and living consistently with a set of core values that promise good work in the world. She calls for all leaders to be models of authentic leadership for this next generation of leaders.

Helping Leaders to Become Emotionally Intelligent

Cary Cherniss

A leader's inability to manage his or her emotional reactions adversely affects relationships with others in ways that compromise information flow and communication. In addition, a leader's emotional intelligence (or lack thereof) strongly influences employee engagement. This chapter highlights the social and emotional skills that often are overlooked in executive development programs. It provides a new, highly cost-effective, group-based approach for developing emotional intelligence in leaders at all levels.

A large aerospace firm fired a division president for the first time in its long history. Although many reasons were given, an employee of the company who knew the situation well said that the real problem was his lack of emotional intelligence. More specifically, it was the way in which he managed—or failed to manage—his emotions. He was one of those leaders who would explode in anger whenever he received bad news from a subordinate—the kind of leader who shoots the messenger. As a result, his subordinates were reluctant to come to him with bad news. It all finally caught up with him when he negotiated a large deal with a major airline. Because he was not aware of problems with the division's manufacturing capacity, he negotiated a contract to deliver twenty more planes than the company could deliver. When Wall Street learned of this lapse, the company's stock plummeted. This executive, who had been with the company for over thirty years, was fired.

This senior executive lacked a critical ingredient for effective leadership, but what was it? And how can we help leaders fill this gap earlier in their careers before they make the kind of mistake that cost this executive his job?

For decades, the conventional wisdom has been that traditional intelligence is the most important ingredient for leadership effectiveness. Those who become leaders, it was thought, stand out from the rest because they are smarter. And among leaders, it is the smartest ones who rise to the top. However, neither personal experience nor research has supported this view. For instance, very few leaders have derailed because they were not smart enough to do the job. In their classic studies of executive derailment, researchers at the Center for Creative Leadership found that leaders who derail are more likely to have problems with interpersonal relationships than to suffer from an intellectual deficiency (Lombardo, Ruderman, and McCauley, 1988). They are more likely to fail to build effective teams than to master the technical requirements of the job. And they are more likely to find it difficult to adapt to change than to break a complex problem down into its component parts.

A study at Cambridge University found that a high level of mental ability by itself actually can be a liability, at least in some situations. Researchers put together 120 simulated management teams and gave them mock businesses to run. Some of the teams were made up exclusively of people with high IQs. To the researchers' surprise, these teams performed worse than the other teams. When they examined more closely what went on in these groups, they found that the high-IQ teams got bogged down because the members often engaged in endless debates in which they would try to show each other up (Belbin, 1996).

These results do not appear to be isolated findings. A meta-analysis of dozens of studies conducted in many different settings found that IQ and other measures of mental ability account for only about 8 percent of the variation in leadership performance (Judge, Colbert, and Ilies, 2004). Apparently there is something else that is important—a missing ingredient that is crucial for effective leadership.

THE ROLE OF EMOTIONAL INTELLIGENCE IN FACING CRITICAL CHALLENGES

In the case that opened this chapter, a gap in effective leadership seemed to open along the lines of managing one's emotions. The division president did not have the information he needed to make a critical decision because he became so angry when a subordinate brought him bad news. The ability to manage one's emotions is a core element of emotional intelligence (EI). Other components are the abilities to perceive accurately and express effectively one's emotions, use emotions to make decisions, understand emotions, and perceive and manage other people's emotions (Mayer, 2006). In addition, some writers believe that EI also includes a larger set of social and emotional competencies that are important for effective leadership, such as adaptability and resilience, achievement drive and initiative, empathy, and the ability to influence and inspire others (Bar-On, Handley, and Fund, 2005; Goleman, Boyatzis, and McKee, 2002).

Consider another situation in which an EI deficit adversely affected a leader. Sarah was a midlevel manager who directed a group of technical employees. One member of the group, Chuck, was bright and motivated, but he also seemed to be disgruntled. Most of the time, his attitude did not affect his performance, but in staff meetings, he often became angry and belligerent. Sarah felt she needed to intervene, but she was not sure what to do. She met with an executive coach, and he suggested that she sit down with Chuck and talk about his behavior. Sarah went pale and said she could not do that. It was clear that she, like the other team members, was afraid of Chuck and worried about antagonizing him further if she tried to discuss the problem with him.

In this situation, an otherwise highly successful leader was unable to manage the emotions of one of her subordinates. In discussing the problem with her and exploring ways of handling it, the coach realized that this inability was linked to another one: she could not effectively manage her own emotions—in this case, the anxiety that increased whenever she thought about confronting Chuck about his behavior. Again, a deficit in certain aspects of EI contributed to less-than-optimal leadership.

This example illustrates another important point about EI: the core abilities are often related. Sarah's difficulty in managing Chuck's emotions (and thus those of the rest of the group) was connected to her difficulty in managing her own emotions. Simply advising her on how to deal most effectively with Chuck was not enough. The coach also needed to help Sarah address the more basic EI problem, which had to do with emotional self-management.

Sarah is not alone. Many leaders find it difficult to deliver tough messages. Those who do so effectively use several EI competencies. First, they are aware of their own feelings, which might involve frustration, irritation, and uncertainty, as well as anxiety about the impact of the message on the other person. They also understand why they feel this way and the impact that those feelings could have on the discussion. Second, effective leaders use their self-awareness to modulate those feelings so that they are adaptive rather than dysfunctional. For instance, the anxiety about how the other person might respond to the tough message helps the leader take the time to think through carefully the best way to convey the tough message. Third, the effective leader is able to identify accurately how the other person is feeling, and why he or she is feeling that way. The leader uses this information to develop the most effective message and context for the discussion. The leader also is able to anticipate how the other person will respond to the message.

All of this preparation, which is as much emotional as it is cognitive, helps set the stage for a conversation in which the leader is able to deliver the message in a way that minimizes defensiveness on the part of the other person and helps the other person to see how he or she can improve. If the leader is able to perceive, understand, and manage her own emotions and those of the other person effectively, the conversation will be productive. The other person will view the leader more positively. There will be increased respect and appreciation for the leader, which will make the other person more willing to hear what the leader is saying and less likely to respond with anger or defensiveness. A tough message that is delivered in an emotionally intelligent way will help improve the relationship between the leader and the other person. And it will probably result in a mutually agreeable solution to the problem at hand, and thus better performance.

Generating support for change and innovation is a particularly important challenge for leaders, and it is another situation in which EI is a critical ingredient. A vivid example of how a group of leaders successfully gained support for an innovative and risky course of action was the Colombian hostage rescue (Lehrer, 2008). A revolutionary guerrilla organization known as FARC had captured over seven hundred hostages, including several Americans, and had held many of them in the jungle for over five years. The Colombian government seemed incapable of doing anything about the problem, in spite of one of the best-equipped and best-trained armies in Latin America and strong support from the U.S. government. Then a few junior military officers came up with a daring plan: a group of military intelligence operatives, disguised as aid workers, would arrange to meet with the rebels and their captives in the jungle. During the meeting, the military operatives would separate the hostages from their captors, get them into their helicopter, and whisk them away.

Securing support from their superiors for this risky endeavor proved to be almost as challenging as the rescue itself. The Colombian defense minister admitted that when the junior officers first brought the plan to one of their superiors, he considered it "crazy" and rejected the idea. But the junior officers persevered. They considered the senior officer's objections, revised the plan, and brought it back to him. According to the defense minister, they said, "This can work. Let us try." Eventually their superior approved the plan and sent it up the chain of command. Ultimately the president of Colombia gave his approval, and the plan was put into operation. It worked perfectly. Fifteen hostages were freed, including the daughter of a former Colombian presidential candidate and three Americans. Eleven Colombian soldiers also were rescued, and the local guerrilla commander, along with one other rebel, was captured. Not a single shot was fired. Following this dramatic rescue, 282 FARC guerrillas surrendered on their own.

The junior officers who initially proposed the daring plan faced considerable resistance, as is often the case when leaders attempt to gain support for innovative ideas. In order to overcome that resistance, they needed to employ a number of EI competencies that Goleman (1998) and others have identified. (See Table 4.1.) For instance, they needed *initiative*, which is the ability to see opportunities for change and to act on them. They also needed *self-confidence* so that when people told them that their plan was a bad idea, they would persist rather than give up. *Influence* also was important. Influence is more than just mustering facts and rational arguments; it also requires knowing how to use different approaches to persuade different people on an emotional level as well as intellectually. *Organizational awareness* also played a role by enabling the officers to be aware of how different groups would be affected by the idea and where the levers of power and influence were in the organization. And the officers needed *optimism*—the belief that change is really possible. Otherwise they would give up at the first sign of resistance.

Table 4.1
Emotional and Social Competencies Associated
with Superior Leadership

Self-awareness	Knowing one's internal states, preferences, resources, and intuitions
	Emotional self-awareness: Recognizing one's emotions and their effects
	Accurate self-assessment: Knowing one's strengths and limits
	Self-confidence: A strong sense of one's self-worth and capabilities
Self-management	Managing one's internal states, impulses, and resources to facilitate reaching goals
	Self-control: Keeping disruptive emotions and impulses in check
	Transparency: Living one's values and openly admitting mistakes or faults
	Adaptability: Flexibility in handling change
	Initiative: Readiness to act on opportunities; being comfortable with novel ideas, approaches, and new information
	Achievement: Striving to improve or meet a standard of excellence; persistence in pursuing goals despite obstacles and setbacks
	Optimism: Rolling with the punches and seeing the glass as half full
Social awareness	Awareness of others' feelings, needs, and concerns
	Empathy: Sensing others' feelings and perspective, and taking an active interest in their concerns
	Service: Anticipating, recognizing, and meeting customers' needs
	Organizational awareness: Reading a group's emotional currents and power relationships

(continued)

Table 4.1
(*continued*)

Relationship management	Adeptness at inducing desirable responses in others
	Inspiration: Inspiring and guiding individuals and groups; aligning with the goals of the group or organization
	Influence: Wielding effective tactics for persuasion
	Developing others: Sensing others' developmental needs and bolstering their abilities
	Change catalyst: Initiating or managing change
	Conflict management: Negotiating and resolving disagreements
	Teamwork and collaboration: Working with others toward shared goals; nurturing instrumental relationships.

Source: Adapted from Goleman et al. (2002).

RESEARCH INTO LEADERSHIP AND EMOTIONAL INTELLIGENCE

Recent research has suggested that these social and emotional competencies may be developmental gaps in many leaders who fail at some point in their careers. For instance, one study examined the relationship between emotional and social competencies and organizational success in a group of top-level executives working in a large financial services organization (Hopkins and Bilmoria, 2008). Using the Emotional Competence Inventory (ECI), a 360-degree measure, the executives' bosses, peers, clients, and subordinates rated the executives in terms of how much they displayed these competencies on the job. Organizational success was based on annual performance and potential ratings over a three-year period. Results indicated that the most successful executives, compared to the others, scored significantly higher on several of the competencies, including Self-Confidence, Achievement Motivation, Organizational Awareness, Inspirational Leadership, and Change Catalyst.

Another study, which also used the ECI, looked at a group of 358 managers and executives at Johnson & Johnson, a large, multinational manufacturer of pharmaceuticals and other health care products (Cavallo and Brienza, 2002).

Those who were rated as superior by their bosses scored higher on all four dimensions of EI: Self-Awareness, Self-Management, Awareness of Others, and Relationship Management. Even more noteworthy was a follow-up study, which found that leaders who scored higher in EI posted higher salary increases during the next five years.

Research using other measures of EI also has found a positive link between EI and leadership performance. One such study involved supervisors in a large manufacturing organization (Kerr, Garvin, and Heaton, 2006). In this study, EI was assessed with the Mayer-Salovey-Caruso Emotional Intelligence Test (MSCEIT), an ability test that asks the participants to complete a number of tasks designed to measure different aspects of EI. Managerial effectiveness was assessed through subordinate ratings. The results indicated a strong relationship between EI scores and effectiveness ratings: the most effective supervisors scored much higher on EI.

Yet another study using the MSCEIT examined EI's relation to the effectiveness of a large group of public service managers (Rosete, 2007). The researcher found that EI correlated with both business performance (for example, "focuses strategically") and interpersonal effectiveness (for example, "guides, mentors, and develops people," "communicates clearly").

Emotional intelligence also was linked to leadership effectiveness in a study of military personnel. Bar-On and his colleagues (2005) found that soldiers who were nominated most often by peers as having officer potential scored significantly higher on the EQ-I, another popular measure of emotional intelligence, than those nominated least often. They also compared those accepted for officer training with a random sample of recruits and found that those accepted for training scored 108 compared to 100 on the EQ-I.

One other study looked at division presidents in a large, multinational beverage firm (McClelland, 1998). In this case, 50 percent of the division presidents had left during the previous two-year period, mostly because of performance problems. The company then began to select presidents based on an assessment of the competencies that seemed to be most strongly linked to performance—most of these social and emotional competencies. During the next two years, only 6 percent of the division presidents left. In addition, 87 percent of the new group were in the top third based on salary bonuses and outperformed their targets by 15 to 20 percent.

HELPING LEADERS TO BECOME MORE EMOTIONALLY INTELLIGENT

A fairly large body of research suggests that we can help leaders develop many of the emotional and social competencies associated with superior performance (Cherniss and Adler, 2000). This research points to several model programs that have been used successfully in many different settings with hundreds or even thousands of leaders.

A particularly popular approach uses some kind of assessment followed by feedback and coaching. For instance, the M.B.A. programs at Case Western Reserve's Weatherhead School of Management begin with a semester-long course involving extensive personal assessment, feedback, and coaching provided by specially trained faculty (Boyatzis and Saatcioglu, 2008). The coaches help the students use the feedback from the assessments to develop a personal learning plan for the rest of their time in the program. There also is an ongoing support group facilitated by trained doctoral students. The assessment emphasizes the emotional and social competencies associated with superior leadership. In a series of studies extending over twenty years, researchers have found that students who have gone through the program demonstrated more improvement in several key competencies than did a comparison group.

Not all model programs use assessment, feedback, and coaching. For instance, the Emotional Competence (EmoComp) training program, developed at American Express Financial Advisors in the early 1990s, brings participants together to engage in a variety of activities, including lectures, discussions, videos, role plays, and visualization. The participants use these activities to learn about the role of emotion in the workplace, norms for expressing emotion, and how their own self-talk influences their emotional reactions. Participants also learn to become more aware of their own emotional reactions and how to better describe and label what they are feeling at any given moment. The program teaches participants how to help others better manage their emotions through careful listening.

The EmoComp training program has been offered to both financial advisors and their managers. One evaluation study compared the performance of advisors working under managers who had received the EmoComp training with those working for managers who had not yet received training. The sales performance of the advisors from both groups was compared for one year prior to and following training. The findings indicated that advisors working in regions with trained leadership saw their businesses grow at a rate of 18.1 percent over a period of fifteen months compared to a 16.2 percent growth rate for the controls (Cherniss and Adler, 2000).

These model programs demonstrate that leaders can increase their social and emotional competence, and they point to specific strategies that work. However, they also share some inherent limitations. One is cost. Any leadership development program that includes an adequate degree of assessment, carefully delivered feedback, and supportive coaching is expensive. Even an approach that omits the assessment, feedback, and coaching, such as the EmoComp program, is costly if it is intensive enough to make a difference (Cherniss and Adler, 2000). Large, successful corporations have been willing to spend that kind of money for leadership development efforts in the past, when times were good. Unfortunately, when the economy begins to shrink, such efforts are often the first to be cut. Also, in an organization that is not large or successful, spending large sums of money on well-designed and carefully implemented leadership development programs typically brings forth little enthusiasm.

Another limitation with such programs is that they depend heavily on the personal qualities of the trainer or coach (Boyatzis, 2006). Although there are many competent coaches and trainers helping executives to become more emotionally intelligent, there are no professionally enforced standards for training programs or practitioners. Physicians, attorneys, certified public accountants, teachers, nurses, psychologists, and many other professionals must graduate from accredited programs and be licensed in order to practice. Such is not the case for executive coaches or those who deliver management training programs. And even if there were licensing, we know all too well that it cannot guarantee every practitioner will be equally proficient.

PROCESS-DESIGNED TRAINING: A NEW GROUP APPROACH

These limitations have led to the development of a new approach for helping executives become more emotionally intelligent leaders. This approach, called process-designed training (PDT), uses a group of peers who meet monthly and follow a carefully prescribed set of rules and processes. In addition to the monthly meetings, which last about three hours and are followed by dinner together, a weekend retreat is held at the end of each year. Unlike more typical approaches, there is no formal assessment, feedback, coaching, or training of any kind.

Each group of nine participants has a moderator, but the moderator's role is limited to ensuring that the group follows the rules and procedures. Participants develop greater self-awareness, self-control, and empathy primarily through the process-directed interactions that take place in the group.

Developed by Jim Liautaud, a retired businessman and a clinical professor at the University of Illinois College of Business, the PDT approach was inspired by the use of ISO (International Standards Organization) principles in industry. The aim was to create a process that would follow a specific sequence, be identical in every group, and never change. ISO principles typically are used in manufacturing contexts. What is unique about this program is that these principles were used to design a low-cost, highly reliable process for helping leaders to become more socially and emotionally intelligent. In addition to ISO principles, the PDT approach includes concepts drawn from Liautaud's study of positive psychology (Seligman, 1993, 2002) and existentialist group psychotherapy (Yalom, 2005), as well as the work of EI theorist Daniel Goleman (1998) and educator Parker Palmer (2004).

The process each group follows is defined by a set of rules and procedures, referred to as the protocol. The protocol, spelled out in an eighteen-page manual (Liautaud, 2006), is designed to create a safe, supportive, and caring environment. Every participant reads the manual prior to beginning of the program and must pass a test on it.

The protocol sets out five basic ground rules, summarized in Table 4.2. These rules spell out how to listen, how to speak, how to ask questions, and how to think about problems. For instance, the listening section of the protocol includes the following:

> *WHEN OTHERS SPEAK:*
> I will listen with my eyes and body, and understand that side conversation, paper rustling, note taking, interrupting, or in any way diverting from their attention, is extremely disrespectful....
> *Effective listening focuses the listening energy on the feelings or emotions being projected. Positive body language, like nodding and smiling, are important comfort signals. Short, affirmative phrases like "I hear you," "I can see that," "I'd feel the same had that happened to me," etc., indicate to the speaker that he is connecting with you.*

Table 4.2
Summary of Protocol Rules for Process-Designed Training Groups

Protocol Rule	Brief Summary of Rule
When others speak	Listen attentively.
When I speak	Be specific; don't repeat or give advice; share own experiences, perspectives, and feelings; use "I" statements.
When I ask questions	Acknowledge what has been said; state own opinions or prejudices first.
How I will think	Put group members' best interests first; do not attack or demean others; keep everything confidential.
Attendance rules	Commit to making all meetings and dinners on time, barring medical or family emergencies.

Source: Adapted from Liautaud (2006, pp. 2–3).

The protocol also spells out expectations for attendance. For instance, members cannot miss more than one meeting during the year, and attendance at the year-end retreat is mandatory.

Each meeting of the group focuses on a different member. The meetings begin with the target member, called the "host," talking about his or her personal history and the history and highlights of his or her company. This is followed by "clarifying questions" from the group members. Then the host presents his or her "biggest concern or problem at this time." The members are not allowed to interrupt during this presentation. When it is clear that the host is finished, the members ask clarifying questions to make sure they understand the issues. No advice is allowed. Once the question phase is completed, the members share with the host personal experiences of their own that posed similar issues and concerns. The discussion then ends unless the host wishes to ask the other group members for advice. At that point, group members are limited to one minute to offer what they would do if they were in the host's situation.

Each meeting ends with a brief update from each member, and then the moderator presents one "EI habit" that all of the participants are expected to practice during the next month. An example of an EI habit is, "Make a daily effort to compliment someone sincerely." Another habit is "practicing good listening." During the updates segment of the meeting, the members describe their experiences in trying to use the EI habit assigned to the group during the previous month.

The first year-end retreat is based on an exercise called the "Life Line." Each group member graphs his or her life on a chart. The vertical scale corresponds to happiness, scored 1 to 10, and the horizontal scale corresponds to the person's age. The resulting plots show how the person's happiness has varied across the years, based on what was happening in his or her life. Each member takes thirty-five to forty-five minutes to present his or her chart. The retreat is intended to increase self-awareness and cohesiveness within the group. The second year-end retreat is based on an exercise called the "Soul Trail," in which each member recalls all the events in his or her life, both positive and negative, that shaped his or her values and beliefs.

Each group is facilitated by a moderator. The moderators are individuals who have had comprehensive management experience and strong leadership qualities and have participated as members in similar groups in the past. They also are selected based on their ability to be vulnerable and self-disclosing. The moderators meet with the program chair each month to discuss how the meetings are going and to address any problems. They also send a monthly meeting summary to the program chair, who reviews the reports and discusses with the moderators any apparent deviations from the protocol.

Within the group, moderators are expected to be caring, warm, and genuine. They also are to make sure that the group is safe by ensuring that the members adhere to the protocol. Moderators are supposed to avoid dominating the discussions and to speak as little as possible. But they also are expected to intervene when necessary to keep the discussion from getting bogged down, and they are encouraged to summarize what group members said once they are sure that the member has finished.

For the second year, each PDT group selects one of its members to serve as the moderator. The new moderators attend a two-day training session prior to the start of the second year and a one-day training session during the fall of the second year. In all of the training sessions, a strong emphasis is placed on following the written protocol.

A recently completed evaluation by an independent researcher found that managers who participated in a PDT group became more emotionally and socially competent leaders, based on ratings by those who worked most closely with them; a control group showed no such improvement. Groups included entry, midlevel, and senior-level managers from nine companies. There were nine groups with nine managers in each group. Outcome measures included the ECI. Outcome data were collected before the program started, one year later, and two years later. Results indicated that participant reactions to the groups were highly positive. And after two years, the intervention group had improved more than did the controls on all ECI variables. The PDT participants also did better than the controls in terms of salary increases and promotions, but these differences were not as statistically significant.

In addition to PDT leadership groups for business managers and executives, groups have been developed for human resource professionals and public school principals. A program also is under way with surgeons, with the goal of helping them learn EI skills that can lower malpractice lawsuits.

The PDT Group Experience

I interviewed thirteen individuals who had gone through the group experience. Many of them were intrigued by the idea when they were invited to participate, but some were ambivalent. For instance, one manager, who joined mainly because his CEO encouraged him to do so, was more than a little skeptical. As he put it, "I'm a regulator with a background in accounting. My motto was, 'Just show me the numbers.' Everything was black or white." The first couple of sessions were a challenge, but over time he came to appreciate the program as he learned new ways of interacting with people and discovered how effective these approaches were on the job and in his personal life. "The group helped me to go from a yeller and screamer to a listener. If you really focus on the other person and hear what they are saying, you discover there is a lot of hidden meaning. You start noticing how people are expressing emotion in their tone of voice or the way they sit. Then if you realize that what they are talking about is a difficult subject for them, you respond differently."

This manager's skepticism dissipated when he discovered how useful it could be just to compliment a coworker. For instance, after he praised one of the people with whom he works, the person was so appreciative that "he now comes and asks if there is anything he can do to help. He had never done that before." Asking clarifying questions has proven to be another useful skill, and not just at work. He mentioned that he had been trying to get his teenage son to take out the garbage for weeks without any success. Yelling and scolding did not seem to be working. So one day he tried using what he learned in his PDT group: he started a conversation by asking clarifying questions. And it worked. His son said, "Okay, Dad, I get it." He has continued to do the chore ever since without being asked.

A participant in a PDT group for high school principals summed up how he benefited: "I feel that my [PDT group] experience has enhanced my leadership ability at work because it has made me a better listener. On a daily basis I am approached by parents, colleagues, and others with problems they need assistance to solve. As a result of my [PDT group] experience I have learned to ask clarifying questions that give me more information and understanding of the problems they are presenting, and I am better able to resolve the issue with them. Also, I have learned to be more complimentary to others. In the past I would think good things about someone, but I would not verbalize it so that the person could benefit. Now I am more deliberate in verbalizing those thoughts, and I enjoy seeing the expressions on people's faces when they receive my unexpected compliments. This has also made others around me more cooperative and more willing to work together."

Participants brought up a wide range of topics in the groups. As one person put it, "They ran the gamut of everything that goes on in life." Business-related issues included career-related concerns such as how to move up in their company, transitioning from one job to another, negotiating for a new job, and work-life balance. Participants also talked about problem employees and how to deal with them, how to address an underperforming subordinate, and how to work with a difficult boss. Senior-level executives addressed succession planning, responding to board members, marketing a new product, dealing with rapid growth, and concerns about their leadership style. In the principal groups, participants discussed how to deal with parents and teachers. In all the groups, participants also brought up personal issues, especially as trust developed. These issues included a close friend or family member who was dying, trouble with family members, marriage issues, and personal money issues such as concerns about retirement.

The PDT groups helped participants develop a number of useful social and emotional skills, but the one mentioned most often in the interviews was listening. The participants stressed that through the group experience, they learned how to "really listen" to others, to focus just on them and their needs, and to be attentive to what they were saying. And the participants discovered that devoting their full attention to another person often had powerful results. As one participant put it, "Any person who feels they have been listened to will talk more, which gives you more information. Also, when you listen really well to someone else, they remember better what you say. I now have some of my people telling me that they remember me saying something that I don't remember saying myself! So listening better to my staff has made them listen better to me."

The PDT group experience also expanded the participants' self-awareness. For instance, as they began to use their new listening skills, the participants became more conscious of how they usually listened to others—or failed to do so. As one participant said, "After following the [PDT] protocol for a few months, I realized that I had been talking too much at work. I interrupted people all the time. And it was getting in the way of my being more effective." Another participant said, "You know, I never noticed before how people will keep looking at their computer when I go into their office to talk with them. But after a few months in the [PDT] program, I began to notice it. And it bothered me. I didn't want to be that way. So I began to put everything aside whenever someone came into my office to talk."

Greater self-awareness led to other kinds of changes at work. One participant observed that after he had been participating in a PDT group for a few months, he began to get frustrated at work with how other people often would talk and not listen. So he started running his meetings differently: "I started calling people on it when they didn't listen. I tried to re-create the [PDT] group's rules for listening in our business meetings." Much to his delight, the meetings became more productive.

Being in a PDT group also helped some of the participants develop greater self-confidence. One midlevel manager said that he felt a "little intimidated" when he was promoted to a director position because he had never gone to college and now was working with people who had. But his PDT group helped him to see that everyone is the same in many ways: "We all have stuff in our lives that we have to deal with." Another participant said that she often came away from the meetings feeling that if others could cope successfully with situations similar to those she was facing, then she could as well. "If they could deal with this, then so can I."

The PDT groups also helped many of the participants develop greater self-control. For instance, they began to curb the impulse to interrupt others and "jump in to solve someone else's problems." Instead, they spent more time sitting back and reflecting. This new way of dealing with their role actually made it less stressful. As their stress levels went down, they were able to make better decisions. "I now am calmer and think more before I make decisions," said one participant.

Many participants also curbed the tendency to engage in overly simplistic, all-or-none thinking. The group experience helped them realize that there were more ways of thinking about the world than they previously had thought. As one participant, a senior vice president for finance, put it, "Being in the group helped me understand that there are more options, more ways of dealing with issues." Another participant said that one of the most valuable lessons for him was seeing how he could start a discussion holding a certain point of view, and then after hearing the clarifying questions that others posed, his opinion would change. "It was interesting to see how you could have a belief about something at the beginning of the process and then your opinion changed during the questioning." He believed that this discovery helped him to be a more thoughtful and effective decision maker on the job. One other participant said, "I believe I have an even greater realization about the complexity of people. We make far too many assumptions about people's values, motives, and interests. We need to spend more effort in getting to know people by asking questions and allowing them to share who they are."

A strong emphasis in the groups was on participants' keeping their commitments, and this aspect of the protocol carried over into the work setting. The human resource head at one of the participating companies observed that his participants "got better at keeping their commitments and holding their colleagues to be more accountable—for example, coming on time for meetings and following through on commitments." A participant said, "In my family when I was growing up, we were late in everything. It was just a way of life, a cultural thing. I didn't think much of it other than being stressed. Then I had a light bulb go off after being in the program. I realized that being late is rude."

Although most of the participants focused on the social and emotional skills they developed in their PDT group, some also commented on the social support that the experience provided. For one participant, the greatest benefit of the program was getting to know everyone in the group and seeing how supportive they were of each other. "We were all very different on the surface. We ranged in age from twenty-eight to sixty-two. We were married, single, and divorced; kids and no kids. We never would have developed a relationship with each other if we were in a bar together. But it took only one meeting to realize that we all are human beings going through similar experiences and problems." A participant in a PDT group for public school principals said, "The first year of the [PDT group] was also my first year as a school principal, and I have often thought if

I was not a participant in this process, I would not have made it through that first year with my sanity. The monthly meetings provided a safe place for me to speak about what was troubling me in that first year, and having the opportunity to hear others speak about their similar circumstances gave me validation of my actions."

These personal accounts suggest that the PDT group provides a vehicle for what Parker, Hall, and Kram (2008) refer to as peer coaching, which organizations increasingly are using as an alternative to professional coaching, mentoring relationships, and classroom learning. PDT groups possess all the critical qualities associated with peer coaching, including equal status of partners, focus on personal and professional development, integration of reflection on practice, emphasis on process as well as content, and acceleration of career learning. And like all other good coaching, the PDT group experience provides a combination of thought-provoking questions, shared experiences, and direct advice in a context of safety, respect, support, and confidentiality.

What Makes a PDT Group Effective

When I asked participants what made the PDT group most helpful in bringing about positive growth and development, virtually everyone agreed that the protocol was key. One participant, the vice president for sales and marketing in his firm, said, "I have worked in several companies over the past twenty-three years, and I have been involved in many different types of meetings and groups. Having specific rules for communicating, and having them stated as absolute necessities was very different. Having someone there who could explain the rules and make sure they were followed had a dramatic effect on the process. It was really refreshing to engage in a format that truly allowed everyone to listen and ask what they were wondering and then say what they felt in an orderly way."

One participant conceded that he and some other members of his group initially were put off by having to follow what he referred to as "rigid rules." And another participant said that at first the approach "seemed a little religious or cultish" because of the "guidelines and rules." However, both agreed that after two or three meetings, "everyone got used to it, and it seemed fine." Eventually they came to appreciate the value of following the prescribed procedures so closely. One of the participants called the protocol "the key to learning the skills. It really drills them into you." And another said, "The protocol really helps because it forces you to get there on time, not miss meetings, and to really listen with care and concern when you are there. This helps everyone to feel more special."

The confidentiality rule, restated at the beginning of every group session, was an especially important part of the protocol. When I asked one participant what made the PDT group effective as a development experience, he said, "The confidentiality and trust that develop over time were important parts of it. They enable you to open up, and the more you open up, the more you get out of the program."

Another participant pointed out that "being able to share personal experiences with each other really makes people open to change." He went on to say that when he does training in his company, he gets the most attention from the trainees when he shares his personal experiences with them. "Their eyes light up!" He thought that the same process occurred in the PDT groups: the emphasis on sharing personal experiences enhanced the impact on participants' learning.

Repetition and practice also are important elements of the program. The participants use the skills each month for two years in the groups. They practice the skills with each other, using real issues, not role plays or simulations. And then the EI habits assignments provide more practice. As the participants practiced using the skills, they saw how effective they were, which was reinforcing. These positive experiences also helped overcome some of the initial skepticism and increased commitment to the process. As a result, the skills became habitual in many different settings.

Many participants also believed that the amount of time required by the program, though sometimes a burden, was another important ingredient. Several participants commented that the real payoffs did not come until the second year. As one manager put it, "You don't see the value the first year because you're developing new habits, and that takes time. It is an evolution." He then said, "The fact that we did this month after month for two years really helps you develop the habit. Everyone got it at the end. Some people developed it faster than others, but everyone got it at the end." Another participant remarked that the monthly meetings were more "in-depth" during the second year. "We were very close to each other by then. It wouldn't have happened with the first year of meetings and the retreat. They helped create such a trusting atmosphere. People could challenge each other more through the questions they asked. People also could ask more penetrating questions because they could build on the Life Line exercise and other discussions during the previous year."

The extended time commitment required by the PDT approach distinguishes it from many other types of management training. Many management training programs use a workshop lasting no more than a day. Another popular format is the residential experience that occurs over a few consecutive days and ends without any follow-up. Sometimes a training program offers a few sessions spread out over a few weeks. The PDT approach, in contrast, uses three-hour meetings followed by a dinner every month for a period of two years, plus the year-end retreats. This extensive time commitment not only allows much practice and reinforcement but also helps the group members form close bonds.

The PDT group approach is more experiential than many other leadership training models, and this seemed to be another positive aspect. Several participants commented that the program was less academic than typical management training because there were no lectures or structured exercises. One participant believed that sharing personal experiences at each meeting, rather than lectures or structured exercises, opened more participants to change. The opportunity to talk about an issue for a long period of time without any interruptions or time pressure, followed by clarifying questions and shared experiences from others in the group, helped every participant "feel special" and contributed to increased self-awareness.

Some participants mentioned the year-end retreats and the dinners that they shared after each group meeting during the year. The year-end retreats were especially helpful in increasing the participants' self-awareness and self-confidence. One participant remarked that the Life Line exercise forced him to reflect on his life more than he would normally. It also made him more aware of his strengths. As a result, he has become more reflective generally than he used to be. The retreats also helped build "camaraderie and trust," as did the monthly dinners.

Potential PDT Group Pitfalls, Unresolved Issues, and Concerns

The PDT group offers a promising new approach to the development of social and emotional competence in senior leaders. However, some potential pitfalls need to be kept in mind. Also, the model is evolving, and some issues and concerns need to be addressed.

The most important potential problem in any PDT group is failure to follow the protocol consistently. For instance, if participants do not listen attentively with a genuine interest in understanding what other people are thinking and feeling, the groups will not achieve the level of trust necessary for personal growth and development. Important information also may not be conveyed, which prevents the groups from helping participants gain new insights and practical tools for dealing with their work-related problems. Giving other people advice or reacting in a judgmental fashion can have similar negative effects on the individual and the group as a whole. Yet another potential pitfall is the participant who comes to dominate the group, speaking repeatedly before others have had a chance to speak at all. All of these problems have been anticipated in the protocol, and they can be avoided as long as the moderator and participants are on the lookout for such deviations and note them clearly whenever they occur.

Although the program generally was well received and largely positive in its impact, the interviews revealed that it did not have the same impact on everyone. Several of the participants thought that those who really believed in the program benefited more. One participant said, "How much you believe in it will influence how much you get out of it. If you think being a better listener is a better way to be, you'll become better at it. Some people in the group were not huge believers. So it didn't impact them as much."

Some participants also believed that a person's personality affected how he or she responded. One of the human resource directors thought that "people who were very open, who bared their souls, got more out of it." He also thought that "less flexible people had a harder time" and suggested that "the people who already have good people skills and whose jobs involve that got more out of it." A challenge for the future is finding ways to increase the readiness of participants for the program before they begin it.

Some participants raised concerns about the time investment. There were two aspects of this issue. One was the amount of time required for the monthly meetings and year-end retreats that extended over two years. The other concerned the additional amount of time required for using the new skills on the job. For instance, one of the exercises involves "dropping everything when someone comes into your office and devoting full attention to them." One of the group members tried this and reported the next month, "It really works. But it took forty-five minutes! I don't have the time for this." In this case, the group members discussed the problem and identified a need to set boundaries. No one can use all the skills all the time. It is better to think of them as tools that you use selectively.

While some participants were concerned that the program sometimes takes up too much time, one believed that it may not go on long enough. He questioned whether two years, without any subsequent follow-up, will be adequate for sustaining the changes that he and others in his group underwent. He said,

"I wish we would have had a continuing piece—maybe keep meeting every quarter or six months. If you don't exercise something, you lose a little bit of it. We tried to set up social events that would have given us continuity. But they kept falling through." One potential solution to this problem would be to use follow-up one-on-one coaching with another member of the group—in other words, peer coaching (Parker et al., 2008). In fact, the PDT protocol could serve as a basis for peer coaching. Two peer coaches could follow a version of it whenever they met for a coaching session.

Another unresolved question concerns whether the group members should come from different organizations. Although this aspect initially was a requirement, the two PDT groups for principals brought together people from the same region of a large school system. In one group, this shared experience seemed to benefit the group. However, in the other group, it seemed to contribute to interpersonal conflict and hurt feelings. The creator of the program believed that this unfortunate experience could have been avoided if the moderator had been more effective. However, the question of whether participants should come from the same organization remains an open one. As one participant noted, "The safety of the group is important. When no one in the group is from the same company, there can be more experimentation."

Another unresolved issue concerns how homogeneous the group should be in terms of age and experience. In the evaluation study, the groups were made up of senior, midlevel, and junior managers. Some participants noted that this arrangement was "great for the younger people" because they could benefit from hearing about the experiences of the older members. However, the older members did not seem to get as much out of the experience. Some participants defended the diversity in seniority. One such individual said that while it was true that people with more experience had more to contribute to business issues, everyone could contribute equally to personal issues.

A related issue concerns gender. In the evaluation study, two groups were all female by design and two others were mixed, with two females and seven males. (The other five groups were all male.) A participant in the all-female group with whom I spoke believed that it "worked out wonderfully in our case." She went on to argue for all-women groups: "Women tend to be more verbal and more emotional, and all of that blossomed in this group. We shared a lot in some ways because men weren't present. It was very open and trusting. All of us walked away as friends." A male participant in one of the mixed groups thought that the gender diversity "was fantastic." He said, "I'm glad we were in a mixed group. It gave us different experiences to draw on." A female participant said she valued "the bonding that takes place" in the groups, but she did not speak directly to how well the mixed-group format worked for her or others. The question of whether to mix men and women in PDT groups in the future thus remains an open one.

Many of these concerns relate to the question of whether the PDT program can be modified in order to adapt to different circumstances, and if so, in what ways. For instance, could the time commitment be reduced? Could it be offered as an adjunct to other leadership development programs? Although there probably are ways in which the program could be adapted in the future, any adjustments need to be evaluated carefully. For instance, forming groups within one organization has been tried, and the results seemed to be very positive in one group but a problem in another group. Based on this limited amount of experimentation, one can conclude that such an adaptation is possible, but it must be done in a way that avoids potentially negative consequences. Specifically, it needs to address confidentiality concerns and any awkwardness that could occur when people who work with one another are in the same group. If the participants are from a large organization and work in different divisions or departments, it might be possible to address these issues adequately.

Similarly, it may be possible to reduce the time commitment or change the scheduling of sessions in some way. One possibility would be to focus on just one or two of the emotional and social skills, such as listening and relationship management, and thus compress the program into one year rather than two. However, it is important to keep in mind that there needs to be several opportunities distributed over an extended period of time for the participants to be immersed in a group experience based on the protocol and to practice the skills repeatedly in their work and home environments. Without such an extended experience, it is highly unlikely that the participants' normal, habitual responses to situations will be changed. Also, the retreat seems to be crucial in helping the participants to bond in ways that lead to more significant change. Thus, the retreat would need to occur sooner, perhaps at the beginning or after the first six months. In any case, any modifications in the program need to be evaluated carefully in order to ensure that they do not weaken the program's effects.

CONCLUSION

Emotional intelligence seems to be an important missing ingredient for many senior-level leaders. A number of programs have evolved over the years for helping leaders to develop the social and emotional competencies that are so crucial for success, but many of these have limitations. For instance, when I asked one of the participants how the PDT approach compared to other executive development programs, she said that she had been "in lots of different programs over the years," but none was as effective as the PDT group. For instance, she had attended an executive management program offered by a prestigious university that included lectures, group breakouts, and discussion. She found it to be valuable but limited: "I did learn things, and I got exposed to other people. But it didn't impact skill sets, and it didn't lead to much change in outlook." She also attended many one-day seminars and called some of these "okay," but often they were disappointing because "they depend so much on who the speaker or facilitator is. Do they know their stuff? Are they charismatic?"

The PDT group is a promising new approach that addresses some of the limitations found in other types of programs. For instance, following the protocol makes the PDT group less dependent on the knowledge, skill, or charisma of a facilitator. One participant said, "Other programs like the Young President's Organization (YPO) Leadership Forum don't follow such a strict process. In PDT groups, the process comes first, which makes for a more consistently positive experience." Another participant concurred. He said that he talked to his brother-in-law who was in a YPO group, and "it was clear that his YPO group didn't work as well because they didn't have anything like the protocol to follow."

The PDT group, as well as the other models we have considered, suggests that helping leaders become more emotionally intelligent is possible. But the quest for more reliable, cost-effective approaches continues. Perhaps more organizations in the future will sponsor the kind of experimentation that is needed to advance this important area of practice.

Leadership as Relational Practice

Joyce K. Fletcher

Relational leadership is the strategic use of relational skills such as emotional and social intelligence in fulfilling one's positional role in an organization. This chapter identifies two gaps in the practice of relational leadership that executive development programs should explicitly address. It offers a practical framework for understanding the implications of these gaps and specific strategies practitioners can use to address them.

That effective leadership in today's world requires more than technical or strategic knowledge is generally agreed on (see Chapter Four in this volume, for example). Although the missing ingredient in leadership has many names and descriptions, such as *authentic leadership* (Luthans and Avolio, 2003), *quiet leadership* (Badaracco, 2002), *humble leadership* (Collins, 2001), and *connective leadership* (Lipman Blumen, 1996), all focus on a type of relational competence commonly called *emotional* or, more recently, *social intelligence* (Goleman, Boyatzis, and McKee, 2002; Goleman, 2006). This competency is considered critical because now, more than ever before, the demands of leadership require the ability to work with and through others. Indeed an argument can be made that the very concept of leadership has shifted from an individual to a relational construct. Applied approaches (for example, Kouzes and Posner, 2007; Wheatley, 2001) and scholarly approaches (for example, Graen and Uhl-Bien, 1995; Graen and Scandura, 1987; Pearce and Conger, 2003; Uhl-Bien, 2006) define leadership itself as a relationship and leadership practices as occurring in relational interactions, or what Bradbury and Lichtenstein (2000) call the "spaces between." That is, leadership is increasingly conceptualized as the practice of working in and through relationships to achieve instrumental outcomes. This conceptualization of leadership is similar to what I have called *relational practice* in that it relies on using relational skills to achieve organizational goals.

This focus on leadership as a relational construct has three elements: skills, processes, and outcomes:

- *Skills.* The leadership skills required to establish good working relationships include empathy, vulnerability, self-awareness, self-regulation, humility, resilience, and resolve (Badaracco, 2002; Collins, 2001; Cox, Pearce, and Sims, 2003; Dutton, 2003; Goleman, 1998; Goleman et al., 2002; Luthans and Avolio, 2003; Sutcliffe and Vogus, 2003; Vera and Rodriguez-Lopez, 2004).

- *Process.* Social interaction is the process through which relational leadership is enacted, exemplified by the countless microinteractions, or relational episodes, that make up what we think of as a relationship (Fletcher, 2007; Fletcher and Kaeufer, 2003; Gardner, 1990; Hosking, Dachler, and Gergen, 1995; Kahane, 2004; Mayo, Meindl, and Pastor, 2003; McNamee and Gergen, 1999). In particular, the relational interactions that typify good leadership are characterized as egalitarian, mutual, collaborative, and two-directional, with followers playing an integral, agentic role in the leadership process (Aaltio-Marjosola, 2001; Fletcher, 2007; Harrington, 2000).

- *Outcomes.* The outcomes of effective relational leadership include coordinated action, collective achievement, shared accountability, and, most important, organizational learning (Conger, 1989; Gittell, 2003; Hosking et al., 1995; Kanter, 2001; Lipnack and Stamps, 2000; Seely Brown and Duguid, 2000; Thompson, 2004; Wheatley, 2001; Yukl, 1998). Indeed, multilevel learning is the key organizational outcome of good leadership: dyadic learning when the relationship is between individuals, group learning in teams and communities of practice, and ultimately organizational learning that results in positive action (Agashae and Bratton, 2001; Heifitz and Laurie, 1999; Kim, 1993; Senge, 1990). Thus, the conventional distinction that managers "do things right" and leaders "do the right thing" (Zaleznik, 1992) is increasingly blurred as the knowledge of the "right thing" is conceptualized as something that is co-created and emergent from positive, learning relationships distributed throughout an organization (Day, Gronn, and Salas, 2004; Hill, 2004; Kayes, 2004; Kim, 1993; Vera and Crossan, 2004; Watkins and Cervero, 2000). Likewise, the leadership task is conceptualized as creating organizational conditions in which all relational interactions at work are "high-quality connections" (Dutton, 2003) that enhance organizational learning, innovation, and adaptation.

In summary, for the purpose of this chapter, there are two important points about the relationality of leadership. First, relational leadership is not only about the relational capacities of positional leaders in their individual interactions with others. It is also about the ability to create organizational conditions under which others in the organization can operate effectively in their relational interactions such that an organization has a constellation of effective working relationships throughout. Second, relational leadership is about the strategic use of relational competence in the service of the work. That is, it is not about fostering high-quality relationships for the sake of the relationships themselves, but about fostering high-quality relationships that will yield positive organizational outcomes.

HIDDEN CHALLENGES IN IMPLEMENTING RELATIONAL LEADERSHIP

Despite the increasing acceptance of the relationality of leadership, there are a number of gaps or hidden challenges in the understanding of the construct that limit the ability to fully embrace and implement leadership as a relational entity (Fletcher, 2004; Fletcher and Kaeufer, 2003). In this section I identify two of these challenges.

The first hidden challenge is that *relational leadership can be difficult to implement because it is influenced by societal-level phenomena that are rarely explicated.* New models of leadership offer a more relational paradigm of leadership practice as well as a more relational prototype (Lord and Maher, 1993) of the skills, characteristics, and attributes of an ideal leader. As some have noted (see Chapter Eight, this volume; Fletcher and Jacques, 2000), both paradigm and prototype often are abstracted or lifted from the larger organizational and, I would add, societal context and presented as context-neutral concepts. Abstracting relational principles from the larger context creates a theory-to-practice gap that can be problematic for practitioners.

The writings about relational leadership often identify the emotional skills needed to enact it, but the literature is largely silent on how individual-level social identity characteristics such as race, class, or gender might influence one's ability to enact these more relational skills and still be perceived as a strong leader. Thus, there is an opportunity to embed relational leadership within the larger organizational and societal context to better understand the external forces that influence relational leadership practice and strategize ways to address them. This is an important area to explore because of evidence that despite the rhetoric about the need for leaders who have relational skills, relational practices are often devalued or marginalized. In other words, despite the new reality, older and less relevant images of leadership are amazingly resilient, resurfacing and reinstating themselves in selection processes, success narratives, and evaluation criteria (Fletcher, 2004; Fletcher and Kaeufer, 2003; Pearce and Conger, 2003).

The second hidden challenge is that *using relational skills in the service of instrumental ends can seem counterintuitive to practicing leaders.* In management literature and elsewhere, "instrumental" versus "relational" has traditionally been thought of as a dichotomy and as variants of the basic masculine/feminine dichotomy and similar to other supposed dichotomies, such as rational/emotional, achievement/affiliation, and public/private sphere. While those who advocate using relational skills in leadership practice often highlight positive organizational outcomes (as Dutton, 2003, does), the underlying tension between relationality and instrumentality is rarely explored. The result is that many practitioners may be confused when they try to integrate the two.

In this chapter, I will use my own work in relational practice and the phenomenon I call the "disappearing dynamic" to explore these two challenges.

I will then identify the gaps in executive development these challenges reveal and suggest ways to address them. The following major sections take on three main questions:

1. What are the societal-level dynamics that can affect the practice of relational leadership and can undermine its effectiveness?

2. What are the specific ways in which relational leadership can be undermined or, in the language I have used, "disappeared"?

3. What strategies can practitioners use to address these issues?

SOCIETAL-LEVEL DYNAMICS THAT CAN AFFECT RELATIONAL LEADERSHIP

Current models of effective leadership eschew old heroic, individualistic command-and-control behavior and instead focus on the importance of teamwork, collaboration, and what Jane Dutton and others call "high-quality connections" (Dutton, 2003; Dutton and Heaphy, 2003) in the workplace. These high-quality connections require maintenance, relational competence, and what is often commonly called *emotional intelligence* (Chapter Four, this volume; Goleman, 1998) or, more recently, *social intelligence* (Goleman, 2006). Interestingly, despite the importance of these relational skills to organizational learning and effectiveness, they can be difficult to recognize as leadership skills in practice (Eagly and Carli, 2007; Fletcher and Kaeufer, 2003; Pearce and Conger, 2003) and as a result, while valued in the abstract, are often not valued in the concrete everyday interactions that exemplify them.

What accounts for this invisibility of relational leadership practices? One answer lies in what many have noted is the association of these skills with the private sphere of family life and the feminine (Calvert and Ramsey, 1992; Fletcher, 1994; Fondas, 1997; Peters, 2003). Because of this association, when individuals "do" relational practice, they run the risk of being perceived as "doing family" or "doing femininity" rather than "doing work." This aligns them with a lower power position in our historically patriarchal society and with a social role long considered inappropriate in the public sphere of paid employment in the workplace. Indeed, to the extent that we enact our social identity in all our interactions (Goffman, 1959) and "do gender" (West and Zimmerman, 1991), whenever we "do work," it is "doing masculinity" that has been most clearly aligned with the performance markers of workplace competence (Martin, 1996; Martin and Collinson, 1998).

These gender/power dynamics can complicate the practice of relational competence, exerting pressure to reconstruct stories of organizational effectiveness in order to distance oneself from relational femininity and instead align oneself with traditional images of power and leadership (Fletcher, 2004). Thus, although the rhetoric around relational skills and attributes has changed over the years and implications for organizational effectiveness and learning are clear, the underlying separation of the two spheres of life, work and family, and the underlying gender/power dynamics inherent in that separation are still in place in our society (Bailyn, 2007). This can present problems for leaders who are trying to enact current models of effective leadership and is an important dynamic for leadership development practitioners to identify when discussing the practical implications of enacting relational leadership.

Gender is not the only culprit in this story of the invisibility of relational practice. Gender dynamics, which of course affect men as well as women, often interact with other aspects of social identity, such as race, class, ethnicity, and sexual orientation, to further diminish the likelihood that relational competence will be recognized and rewarded. As Jean Baker Miller notes in her landmark book, *Toward a New Psychology of Women* (1976), in systems of unequal power (inequities based on race, class, organizational level, or sex, for example) it behooves those with less power to be ultrasensitive and attuned to the needs, desires, and implicit requests of the more powerful. In other words, in systems of unequal power, people who have less power will, by necessity, be more likely to have highly developed relational skills. This inappropriately associates the skills and behaviors of relational practice not only with femininity but also with powerlessness and vulnerability (Bartolome and Laurent, 1988; Fletcher, 2004; Kanter, 1977).

Recognizing these gender/power dynamics inherent in relational practice is important for two reasons. First, it helps us understand at a systemic level why traditional images of competence and effectiveness are so resilient and why relational competence can be risky to enact, even if it is good for the organization. The rhetoric about leadership and learning may have changed, but the association of relational practice with family, femininity, and powerlessness remains a powerful, albeit largely invisible, force, undermining the rhetoric and influencing the stories people choose to remember and tell about their own and others' behavior. Giving voice to these underlying dynamics can rescue them from invisibility and make them discussible, thereby interrupting the dynamic and creating an opportunity for change.

The second reason it is important to recognize these underlying gender/power dynamics is that it creates an opportunity to explore the concept of relational practice from a perspective Holvino (2008) calls simultaneity: the simultaneous effects and interactions of multiple dimensions of social identity on behavior and perceptions of behavior. So, for example, the concept of simultaneity would move us to ask how these dynamics would play out for people of color. How, for example, are these dynamics experienced by Asian American women who may be expected to be quiet, more passive, and less assertive than Anglo women? For African American women—and men—it would invite us to explore the intersection of race and gender in the historical context of racial oppression in this country. How, for example, are the gender/power dynamics inherent in that legacy experienced by African Americans, who may be expected to be subservient and nonassertive? Exploring questions such as these with leaders who are in our workshops and leadership development seminars has the potential to advance the discussion of relational practice in significant ways, broadening its scope to include a range of societal norms and expectations that may affect one's ability to engage in relational leadership effectively.

SPECIFIC WAYS IN WHICH RELATIONAL LEADERSHIP CAN BE UNDERMINED

Understanding the specific ways relational practices are rendered invisible is important because when we understand these dynamics and how they work, we are more likely to be able to interrupt them and make some headway in strategizing solutions. In researching the phenomenon of the invisibility of relational effectiveness, I found three distinct "disappearing acts" that can marginalize relational practice: the misunderstanding of motive, the limits of language, and the conflation of relational practice with idealized motherhood and femininity.

Misunderstanding the Motive

The first disappearing act is to misinterpret why someone would be enacting relational practice. Although it is often motivated by a desire to work more effectively, relational practice can be (mis)understood as a personal idiosyncrasy or trait. These traits sometimes have a negative connotation, such as naiveté, powerlessness, weakness, or emotional need. But they may also be more positive, as when relational practice is seen as an expression of thoughtfulness, personal style, or being nice.

Consider a team member who puts effort into keeping others informed of things that were decided in meetings they missed, passes on information others need to know so they can understand the rationale behind actions, or takes time to act as a go-between for members who are having difficulty working together. My research indicated that the motivation to engage in these time-intensive practices often comes from the belief that it is necessary for the success of the project—in other words, from the belief that the short-term investment of time and effort will pay off in long-term business results. Others, however, may be relying on relational practitioners to do this work because they believe it is work that fits their personality and style. Indeed, my research found that others attributed the motivation to engage in relational behaviors as an issue of personality and style rather than strategic intervention (Fletcher, 1999). So, for example, people who engaged in these activities were often called the glue of the team and thought of as caring or thoughtful individuals. These are fine attributes, but absent the strategic intention, they hold little value as evidence of positional leadership potential.

This disappearing act suggests that if we want to "appear" our relational practices, we have to articulate our intentions first to ourselves and then to others. It is not enough to enact relational leadership in the service of the work and then simply hope that others will understand the strategic intent of the actions. Instead, we need to make the motivation underlying our actions clear. Why are we doing what we are doing, and how is it connected to outcomes we want to achieve? Naming our intention and connecting our actions to strategic goals is an antidote to the disappearing of relational practice.

The Limits of Language

The second disappearing act has to do with language. It is often difficult to find words to describe relational work powerfully. Acknowledging and building on—rather than attacking—others' ideas is an effective way to build consensus, but it may be labeled as simply "being polite" or even "being deferential." Maintaining relationships that are critical to accomplishing the task may be dismissed as just "being nice." Someone who takes time to teach colleagues a new skill or pass on information that will help them do a better job may be described as a "nurturer" or a "caring person." Language such as this tends to feminize the behavior, associating it with family rather than work relationships and thereby weakening it. In addition, using soft, feminine language to describe relational skills can evoke more general gendered dichotomies (such as strong/weak, work/family, rational/emotional) that underlie organizational discourse, thereby reinforcing these dichotomies even when they are not explicitly mentioned (Calas and Smircich, 1991; Flax, 1990; Jacobsen and Jacques, 1997). Using such language, then, is not only limited in its ability to capture the strategic intention and effectiveness dimension of the activity, it actually serves to maintain the dichotomous thinking in which relational activity is devalued or perceived as inappropriate in organizational settings. This second disappearing act suggests that if we want to rescue relational practice from invisibility, we need to use organizationally strong language to describe it both when we practice it and when we see it practiced by others.

Confusing Relational Practice with Femininity

The third disappearing act I found in my data—how relational practice gets confused with femininity—is a phenomenon with special implications for women (Fletcher, 1999; Eagly and Carli, 2007). When men do relational practice, the first two disappearing acts might render their relational competence invisible. That is, they might be misinterpreted as weak, and they might have trouble finding language that adequately describes the power and contribution of their behavior. But for women, something additional happens. When they do relational practice, it often gets confused with their social roles in society as nurturing wives and mothers. When they engage in relational practice, women are likely to be seen as "mothering" rather than leading, as selflessly giving (expecting nothing in return) rather than modeling a new, more relational way of working. This confusion is problematic. Selfless giving is, by definition, nonmutual. And effective relational practice, whether practiced by men or women, depends on conditions of mutuality and reciprocal influence (Zaccaro, Rittman, and Marks, 2001). People who put relational leadership into practice (by, for example, seeking to develop others by coauthoring articles with junior staff or agreeing to chair an important but time-consuming community outreach initiative) have every right to expect that this stance of mutuality will be met and matched by others—that others will join them in co-creating the kind of environment where these conditions can prevail such that someone else will head up the next time-consuming initiative.

Indeed, early research on the construct of mutuality (Jordan, 1986) would suggest that the promised outcomes of newer models of leadership such as collective learning, mutual engagement, learning across difference, and mutual empowerment cannot occur under conditions of nonmutuality. On the contrary, for relational practice to be widely adopted, it must have embedded within it an invitation to reciprocate in kind. But gender expectations constrain this possibility for women. When a woman's attempt to use relational practice to work more effectively is misunderstood as "doing mothering," the expectation of reciprocity embedded in the practice is rendered invisible. Thus, women may find they are expected and even relied on to practice many of the relational aspects of leadership but to do it without a recognition that this is strategic behavior and without expecting similar behavior from others.

This third disappearing act suggests that women need to consciously and actively separate their relational practices from gendered expectations about their social roles as wives and mothers, both in their own minds and in the perceptions of others. In practical terms, this can be difficult to do. Many women find it difficult to determine whether they are responding to gendered expectations to nurture and develop others or actually engaging in intentional action to do what is best for the work. Men, who have to navigate a different set of gendered expectations, must deal with a different version of the same dilemma. For example, "doing masculinity" when mentoring can lead to a certain type of patriarchal mentoring stance that Belle Rose Ragins and Amy Verbos (2007) call "the Godfather approach," which may not be best for the protégé or for the organization's need for developing new talent.

The challenge of separating gendered expectations from doing good work is, I believe, the central challenge in enacting relational practice and brings us to the final issue I address.

ADDRESSING THE GAPS

Once leaders have an understanding of the societal-level dynamics that might be undermining their own practice of leadership and the ways in which they are perceived, the challenge is how to address this issue in practice.

One key task is to differentiate relational practice in the direct service of the work from more general relational activity that is in the service of the relationship itself, related to the work either indirectly or not at all. The two are not mutually exclusive of course, but not differentiating them can be problematic. The confusion between the two often arises because relational activity has been so long associated with the private sphere of home and family life that the rules for applying it to the workplace are unclear. Furthermore, its association with caring and thoughtfulness can be experienced as at odds with important workplace realities such as accountability and productivity.

Thus, in the name of caring, supervisors may engage in a type of pseudore-lationality, or what I have come to call *relational malpractice.* This includes things like not giving colleagues accurate feedback, suppressing rather than airing conflicts or contradictions, and retaining or protecting incompetence.

Trivial relational activities intended to show caring—things like remembering birthdays or arranging for pizza parties to celebrate organizational events—can divert the focus from more organizationally significant relational activities such as listening, mutual learning, transparency, and the accurate communication of important organizational realities. Using the word *trivial* to describe some of these "caring" activities may be unfair. Certainly celebrating together can have a beneficial effect on the overall atmosphere and in some instances might even be critical to the work. But by and large, in terms of cost to benefit, it is far more important for leaders to focus energy and time on more central relational activities that facilitate the kind of open, transparent, egalitarian connections that lead to organizational learning and collective achievement.

In working with executives on these issues, I have found that leaders have difficulty putting relational leadership into practice because stereotypical (gender-linked) notions of caring behavior (and what that looks like in practice) get confused with the goal of engaging in high-quality relational interactions in the service of the work. Over the years I have developed a rubric that I believe can help distinguish between relational practice and relational *mal*practice (see Table 5.1).

Column 1 represents a dysfunctional, nonrelational practitioner—the kind of command-and-control leader, for example, who doesn't consult with others or admit being wrong. Column 2 represents the best characteristics of a relational practitioner—a leader who thinks more fluidly about self and other, focuses on process as well as task, lets the nature of the work determine when to get input, and thinks about the needs of the work rather than career or self in determining what action to take. Column 3 represents characteristics of a dysfunctional relational leader who exhibits relational malpractice, focusing exclusively on others and their needs, afraid to move ahead with decisions, focused on meeting others'

Table 5.1
Relational Practice Versus Nonrelational Practice and Relational Malpractice

1 Nonrelational Practice	2 Relational Practice	3 Relational Malpractice
Dysfunctionally command and control	Relationally intelligent	Dysfunctionally relational
Self	Self-in-relation	Other
Task	Create conditions where task can get done (process and task)	Process
Knows everything (never gets input)	Fluid expertise (nature of task decides)	Knows nothing (always gets input)
Authoritarian	Authoritative	Authority-less
Good for my career?	Is it good for the work?	Will they like me?
Concerned with enacting masculine gender identity	Concerned with doing good work	Concerned with enacting feminine gender identity

expectations in order to be liked and accepted. Comparing where leaders are located in the columns of Table 5.1, and where the leaders perceive themselves or are perceived as being located, is a good way to understand what may be going on in terms of three dynamics underlying relational practice: a disappearing dynamic, a B-word dynamic, and a malpractice dynamic.

The Disappearing Dynamic

This dynamic occurs when one is operating in column 2 but is perceived as operating in column 3. That is, a leader is enacting relational competence but instead of being seen as doing leadership is perceived as weak, indecisive, or motivated by a desire to be liked.

If we believe this is happening, it is important to recapture the leadership and effectiveness dimensions of the behaviors that have gotten disappeared by addressing each of the three "disappearing acts" described in the previous section. Being clear about our intention and connecting it to the quality and effectiveness of the work, using strong language to describe what it is we are doing, and making sure we push back on the conflation of our behavior with femininity or powerlessness are all ways to interrupt the disappearing dynamic. Pushing back on these three disappearing acts can rescue the behavior from being devalued or unrecognized and help us remove ourselves from potentially exploitive situations.

The B-Word Dynamic

The second dynamic the rubric helps us identify refers to operating in column 2 (relational practice) but being misinterpreted as operating in column 1 (command and control). Because of gender stereotypes, this is a dynamic more likely to be experienced by women. When women are authoritative, focus on task as well as process, or make unilateral decisions when the situation calls for that, they can be perceived as bossy, bully broads, or worse (Eagly and Carli, 2007). In the 2008 presidential primary, Hillary Clinton was subject to this dynamic so often that even mainstream journalists like Nicholas Kristof in the *New York Times* commented on it (Kristof, 2008). It is one-half of the double bind in which women can find themselves. The result is that gendered expectations of women can make even simple behavior, like being brief and direct in their communication, seem inappropriately assertive.

Not all women are naturally relational, but because of gender stereotypes, most are expected to be. Female leaders who work in nonprofits note that this dynamic is especially relevant for them. People who have chosen to work in the nonprofit world because they want a different work environment may confuse relational practice with relational malpractice, holding leaders (especially female leaders) to a standard of caring, compassion, and process that can spiral into dysfunction. Efforts to stay firmly in relational practice by, for example engaging fluid expertise or making sure conflicts and contradictions are addressed and not avoided, can be challenging.

Women in workshops I've led who are faced with this challenge note that one way of addressing the dilemma is to talk about it openly—saying, for example, that after hearing all the comments and realizing that their role as director requires that they make a decision between two good alternatives, they have decided on option A for these reasons. The relationality of their leadership is expressed by their willingness to share information openly, not shying away from the role, responsibility, and accountability inherent in taking on a leadership position.

The Malpractice Dynamic

In this dynamic, we tell ourselves we are operating in column 2 but are actually operating in column 3. This is perhaps the most insidious dynamic because it gets to the heart of a widespread ambivalence about things relational.

Certainly it doesn't take long to identify extreme examples of relational malpractice. We have all been in meetings where we want to get to the bottom line and someone, maybe even the person in charge, keeps us on process, endlessly getting input and shying away from making a decision. And we have been in situations where the tough work of giving negative feedback, letting someone go, or addressing an underlying conflict has been avoided in a misguided attempt to foster harmony and a "caring" environment. In these cases, the issue is that the relational practitioner has confused relationality with nonmutual acts of deference or selflessness. This tendency is something Miller and Stiver (1997) describe as relational paradox: the tendency to move out of authenticity and mutuality in the mistaken belief that it will enhance the relationship, when in fact it does the opposite.

Not dealing with the tough issues, taking oneself out of the mix, and focusing on feelings of closeness rather than the real connection that happens when we deal with issues are all symptoms of enacting the relational paradox and ending up in column 3 when we are trying to be in column 2. Relational practice (column 2) is about effective working relationships characterized by mutuality where the goal is learning, effectiveness, and mutual growth in connection. Mutuality and authenticity mean tackling the tough issues, putting one's own needs and the needs of the work in the mix, being willing to make the difficult decisions, and knowing when to get input and when to act. However, when we are trying to change our behavior and we aren't used to the alternative, we often overcompensate.

The rubric lets us see two ways that might happen. People who want to move away from column 1 (command-and-control leadership behavior) may inadvertently move to column 3 (dysfunctionally relational) rather than column 2 (relational practice). Conversely, people wanting to move from column 3 (dysfunctionally relational) may inadvertently move to column 1 (command and control). When we think overcompensation might be at play, it is important to ask ourselves clarifying questions. What are our motives? Are we truly applying relational principles (including mutuality) to our working relationships? What would it mean to put relationality into practice in this particular case? In other words, the rubric can help us identify where we are actually operating (as opposed to where we think we might be operating), as well as explore mistakes in the perceptions of others who might misunderstand the motivation behind our behavior.

CONCLUSION

The gender dynamics underlying the practice of relational leadership are significant and affect both women and men and, more important, the practice of good leadership. It is perhaps easier to see the negative effects of the historical prescription to "enact masculinity" in the doing of leadership when a woman, like Hillary Clinton, does it. It can lead to ineffective or, worse, very costly actions (for example, in an effort to prove one is tough enough to do the job, suggesting that we "annihilate" a country with which we disagree). But the doing of gender in the doing of leadership can have much more subtle, more widespread effects. Robin Ely and Deborah Meyerson (2009), in their study of work on oil rigs, note that the conflation of "doing masculinity" and doing work has led to many ineffective, unsafe work practices, such as not admitting mistakes or not asking for help. Interestingly, they note that when leaders in an organization focus on work outcomes and clearly articulate the connection between enacting behaviors more typically thought of as feminine (admitting mistakes, asking for help) and organizational effectiveness, it is possible to disrupt the conflation of "doing gender" with "doing work." Using the three-column rubric, this would mean focusing on staying in the middle column, not because one is trying to balance competing demands but because the middle column is a way of asking ourselves about the work and making sure that the requirements of the task at hand are the guide for our behavior, rather than expectations, gendered or otherwise, about how to be perceived as a good leader.

Gender dynamics underlie the practice of leadership. Ignoring them, or keeping them hidden as most descriptions of leadership do, is not the answer. Neither is it helpful to suggest that we simply stop enacting our gender identity in the doing of work. As Goffman notes (1959), we are always socially constructing our identity in our interactions with others, and gender is an especially powerful part of that identity (Foldy, 2002). What the three-column rubric can help us with, however, is being aware of the forces operating on our leadership behavior so that we become more self-aware and can question our motives. Substituting a higher goal—doing good work—can help us decouple doing work and doing gender identity.

The How-to-Be Leader

A Conversation with Frances Hesselbein

Frances Hesselbein Girlscout leader
Kathy E. Kram

During challenging times—in fact, during all times—leaders need to know their core values, passions, and talents so that they can define a mission that serves some aspect of society and inspires others to apply their unique talents toward the same goal. Frances Hesselbein models the very character that she asserts is essential to effective leadership at this time in history. Frances is a recipient of the Presidential Medal of Freedom, the highest civilian honor in the United States, for her leadership as CEO of the Girl Scouts of the USA from 1976 to 1990, her role as the founding president of the Drucker Foundation, and her service as a pioneer for women, diversity, and inclusion. Kathy Kram spoke to her in February 2009.

LEADERSHIP AND "HOW TO BE"

Kathy Kram: Frances, what do you mean when you speak of leadership authenticity?

Hesselbein: I think it's important to begin with, "How do we describe leadership?" And I would say leadership is a matter of how to be, not how to do.

Kram: Can you tell us more about that distinction?

Hesselbein: Leaders spend most of their time learning how to do their work and helping other people learn how to do theirs, yet in the end, it is the quality and character of the leader that determine the performance and results. This has been my definition of leadership since 1981, when I was with Girl Scouts of the USA.

Kram: So the "how to be" is about character?

Hesselbein: Yes. In the end, it is the quality and character of the leader that determines the performance, the results, not the how-tos. Now that was 1981. I keep testing it today in many situations. It is even more relevant today and as powerful as it was in 1981.

Kram: You said you first discovered this definition when you were leading the Girl Scouts. Can you summarize what happened?

Hesselbein: Well, one day the President's Organization, whose members include about nine hundred company presidents, called and asked, "Would you speak on leadership to our upcoming Presidents Conference?" I was very flattered, and I said I would like to very much. And then they said, "Oh, by the way, first Peter Drucker will speak, then Warren Bennis will speak, then you will speak, and you're all speaking on the same subject, leadership."

I thought, *How am I ever going to follow those two great thought leaders?* They were friends who were also my mentors. And then I settled down and said, *Well, this happens to be the life you're leading, and if you can't define leadership on your own terms, you shouldn't be making a speech.*

Of course, I had been thinking and talking about leadership all my professional life, and I knew there had to be one sentence that would define leadership on my own terms. After a lot of introspection, also known as agony, it came through to me: leadership is a matter of how to be, not how to do.

When the three speeches were over that day, Peter Drucker came up to me and said, "Your definition of leadership was the most important thing that was said today." So that's my definition—and I keep testing it. And it becomes more relevant every day, quality and character of the leader determines the performance, the results.

Kram: Why do you say "even more so today"?

Hesselbein: Because of what is happening in our society and globally. All we have to do is look at headlines, or listen to example after example of leaders who have failed their organizations. Some of those leaders are going to jail. Some of them leave in disgrace. Across society, there is this new call for principled, ethical leaders. There are too many examples of leaders who spoke one way and behaved another.

Perhaps this discussion reflects the hunger that our society has for principled leaders. For example, Junior Achievement International, a huge youth organization, developed an award for outstanding staff members from all over the world, and every year they give a Frances Hesselbein How to Be Leadership Award. They've adopted the whole concept of "how to be." When we look at how dictionaries define *authenticity*, it is genuine, known to be true, trustworthy; they are all "how to be" qualities.

Kram: So, going back to the second part of the phrase "leadership authenticity," you equate authenticity with being genuine?

Hesselbein: Known to be true, trustworthy. These are all "how to be" qualities. Let me give you another example of how that definition evolved. When General Shinseki was chief of staff of the army [1999–2003], I was invited to review the manuscript of the new *U.S. Army Leadership Manual.* I said I would be honored. When it arrived from Fort Leavenworth, I was amazed as I opened the package and on the cover were just three words: *Be, Know, Do.* And the content of that draft for the army was so relevant, so best practice, that in reviewing the content, the only suggestion I could make was that there was one chapter that I thought they should expand by adding more on army values.

Later, on a *Harvard Business Review* roundtable, I mentioned the *Army Leadership Manual: Be, Know, Do,* and also on a television interview. Then our Leader to Leader Institute [Hesselbein is the founding president of this organization] was flooded with requests from civilians, "How can I get a copy of *Be, Know, Do?* Where can I buy it?" Fortunately for me, it was unclassified, so we could give people the information on how to order the new *Be, Know, Do: Leadership the Army Way.* And when I shared this amazing civilian response with General Shinseki, he said, "Well, why don't we adapt *Be, Know, Do* for civilians?"

It required very little adaptation, and our Leader to Leader Institute, with Jossey-Bass, our publisher, published *Be, Know, Do.* You've seen it—*Leadership the Army Way,* introduced by Frances Hesselbein and General Eric Shinseki.

And again, *Be* is the first word in the title, and the message is: quality and character of the leader. So authenticity is essential.

Kram: One of the purposes of the book in which this interview will appear is to present new ways of thinking about how to help leaders develop their character and quality. How might you go about that kind of development?

Hesselbein: Well, to begin with, there are leaders at every level of an organization. You don't have to be the CEO to be a leader. And one of the first steps is to communicate the values, the principles of the organization, and to distill the language until the message is short, powerful, and compelling. For example, I had a belief, a message with the Girl Scouts, that I keep testing for relevance:

> We manage for the mission. We manage for innovation. We manage
> for diversity. We manage for all three, or we are part of the past.
> Relevant today, relevant tomorrow.

So with our people, we talk about mission as why we do what we do. It's our purpose. It comes first. Then comes managing for innovation, and I always use Peter Drucker's definition of innovation: "change that creates a new dimension of performance." That's the second indispensable charge. The third charge is diversity. We have to manage for diversity. We have to manage for all three, or we are part of the past, spelled i-r-r-e-l-e-v-a-n-t.

Some leaders find "manage for the mission," "manage for innovation," inspiring. Then they look at diversity and don't think it's equal to *mission* and *innovation*. I've had leaders explain to me, "Oh, diversity will take care of itself," or, "Building a richly diverse, inclusive organization is a great challenge." They don't see it as the greatest opportunity for relevant, significant success, indispensable to the organization of the future. But if we don't manage for diversity, we're already part of the past, and someone else will eat our lunch.

As we preach authenticity, our values and principles as leaders, our people watch us. They look at us; they watch us very carefully. And if what we profess, what we preach is consistent with what we do, morale and productivity soar. But if we say one thing, act in the opposite way, we get negative results. Low morale, low productivity. For example, when a leader says, "Our people are our greatest asset," and then treats "our people" solely as cost, it's very disillusioning.

Kram: So that's an example of inauthentic behavior?

Hesselbein: That's right. No authenticity, then no morale, no productivity.

Hesselbein: Let me give you two examples of powerful leadership authenticity.

On November 5, 2008, The Leader to Leader Institute presented A. G. Lafley with its annual The Leader of the Future Award. His response was not about himself; it was all about his people. As he talked about Peter Drucker, he said that Peter "argued that leaders have the responsibility to ensure that jobs are fulfilling and that individuals are able to contribute as fully as they can. I agree. The most important thing I do as CEO is to develop leaders and to unleash the creativity and productivity of P&G's 138,000 knowledge workers." To which he added, "We need to be in touch with their feelings and frustrations. To be in touch is to be a listener and an observer, to be connected and collaborative, to practice and to believe passionately in diversity and inclusion. We must embrace the humanity in ourselves, in those we work and collaborate with, and in those we serve."

Right before this, *Chief Executive Magazine* had published a marvelous article on the two best companies for leaders. One was Lafley's P&G; the other was Jeff Immelt's General Electric.

If we look at Jeff Immelt's GE as one of the two best companies for leaders, it's all about education. Crotonville is famous; it's all about learning because GE is a learning institution, a learning organization—not just learning for the management team but for leaders at every level. Jeff is very famous for this. And a long time ago, I don't even remember which year, he and I were receiving an award, and we each were to speak for five minutes. What did he talk about? Not about GE and all the big corporate stuff. He talked about the importance of education for all of our children.

It was so inspiring. So here's a guy who is not just talking about the learning organization, but he lives it the way A. G. Lafley lives his authenticity.

ENCOURAGING AUTHENTICITY

Kram: What can you tell readers about how to encourage authenticity in organizations today? How can we help leaders to live authentically? There're a lot of pressures on leaders not to.

Hesselbein: Well, first you yourself live it. You can't just talk it. Every day of your life as a leader at any level, you've shared your vision of the future, the mission is why we do what we do, our reason for being, and then we've shared the values, not on a plaque somewhere; we live them. We say these are the values of the organization, and we all live them. Then, no matter what the situation, we never think, "Well, I can be slightly unethical today, but tomorrow I'll be better." It doesn't work that way. No matter now difficult the circumstances become, we stand and we act on principle.

Every day this becomes more difficult. However, I think in this period right now, I believe that we all have more hope.

Kram: So you're hopeful, even right now?

Hesselbein: Yes! Last year at this time, in speeches, I often talked about "the darkness of our times," and I no longer say that. Enormous, enormous challenges face our country. If we're talking about authenticity and serving, and in the very challenge, there are even greater opportunities.

I believe that since the beginning of our country, two institutions have sustained the democracy. One is the U.S. Army and the other is public education. We've stretched the army, and public education's house is on fire. But we cannot talk about "our children" and have millions and millions of invisible children in our country who will never have a high school diploma. For example, right now, in New York City, we have 1 million school children. Five hundred thousand will not receive a high school diploma. When I shared this in a conference with business leaders, a man came up after my speech and said, "You think one out of two is bad? I'm from Los Angeles, and we will graduate one in five."

I think a test of authentic citizenship as well as leadership is, "What are we doing to address a major threat to our sustaining the democracy?" We cannot sustain the democracy unless we educate all of our children. The education of all our American children.

Developing from Within

Kram: Are you also thinking the army has been doing a good job in terms of education and developing leadership?

Hesselbein: Yes. When Peter Drucker was asked, "Which organization in the United States does the best job of developing leaders?" it was expected that he would say GE or name some other big corporation. He shocked them when he said, "The United States Army," because the army develops its leaders from within. And that is one of the things A. G. Lafley is famous for: developing people within P&G to take leadership roles.

Kram: Can you tell us a little bit more about what goes on inside the army or P&G to develop the kind of leadership you're talking about?

Hesselbein: It's education, education, education. It means leaders at every level are responsible for the development of their own people. There are learning opportunities for everyone, and when someone comes through clearly as a leader with great potential, we develop that person. We don't say, "How can we go outside the walls of organization and buy a good vice president?" No, we're developing our leaders from within.

And so that was Peter Drucker's definition of "the best job of developing leaders"—which shocked a lot of people. But when they thought about it, they understood that you develop, you have teams at every level, you have leaders at every level. And our key responsibility is to educate, to develop our leaders.

Playing to Strengths

Kram: One assumption is that part of developing a leader's capabilities is to give them the opportunity for self-assessment and for clarifying their values. Would you include that as part of the education piece?

Hesselbein: Oh, yes. Peter Drucker said our job is to make the strengths of our people effective and their weakness irrelevant. And we really ought to tack that statement up on the wall. If we have someone who is doing very well in one area and in another area not so well, are we going to spend our time and money in developing his strengths—which is often his 90 percent? Too often, for that remaining 10 percent that he or she doesn't do well, what do we do? We focus on that 10 percent, not the 90 percent that should be our focus.

Kram: Focus on the strengths.

Hesselbein: "You make their strengths effective and their weaknesses irrelevant." I love it. When I quote Peter on that, you would be surprised to see some people looking shocked, and I know what they're thinking: "Oh, I'm doing the opposite."

Kram: By saying that we should make weaknesses irrelevant, I assume you're saying that other leaders in the organization with the counterbalancing strength can pick up that part of the work. Is that right?

Hesselbein: Yes, yes. We focus on what you do uncommonly well, and we release you to do it. We assign that other 10 percent to someone who will do well in that area. It's the team approach.

Kram: It sounds like senior leaders need to model this kind of behavior and also make sure there are consistent rewards and recognition that are consistent with those actions.

Hesselbein: That's right. And you keep testing it, and sometimes we can be surprised. We've been preaching it, and then we say, "Are we really practicing it?" And we look at some deviations, and we change; we work to meet our highest expectation of ourselves.

PRESSURES AGAINST AND FOR AUTHENTICITY

Kram: Do you think ineffective reward and recognition practices or the pressures acting on potential leaders lead toward their being inauthentic? How does that come about?

Hesselbein: I think there are pressures. Suppose I report to someone, and the message I get is, "You have to be tough, and you have to make whatever that mark is. I don't care how you do it, but you have to get there." That dooms me, the person, and the organization. We've been given a choice: either put aside our own principles, our own sense of ethics, or leave.

Kram: Yes, that's true.

Hesselbein: It takes courage, but many people walk away from those situations. There is no such thing as "slightly unethical."

Authentically Diverse

Kram: So perhaps the messages that people get from their leaders create pressure to be inauthentic.

Hesselbein: Yes. In that behavior, that language, those high expectations. But high expectations can also be supported by authenticity. For example, P&G is in 130 countries, and A. G. Lafley has 100 different countries represented in his management. If you're in the organization, you don't have to wonder how he feels about diversity and inclusion. He's behind you. You're living it.

I think the whole concept of the book in which this conversation will appear—the idea of what are the missing ingredients—is so powerful because right now I think many people are thinking in a different way. It is a new day.

Kram: Certainly President Obama models enlisting people for their strengths and what they have to offer.

Hesselbein: Yes. That's what I mean.

Kram: And it doesn't matter whether you grew up in the inner city or in a small town in the Midwest or elsewhere, his idea seems to be, "What can you bring to this effort?" That is very different from simply telling people what you want them to do.

Hesselbein: "What do you bring?"—a powerful expression of finding the best person for the job whether you're a Republican or a Democrat, whatever gender, race, ethnicity—it doesn't matter to him. He wants the best person for the job. It has been said that he faces the greatest challenge of any president since Abraham Lincoln.

And there is something about his election, when so many young people were inspired and they worked and they voted. He will be the most carefully watched leader in the country. There's something about his language, the way he speaks from the heart, from the intellect that has inspired our people.

I often think about him and about other presidents, and when people ask me which president is my favorite, which one do I admire most, they're always surprised when I say Abraham Lincoln. Because at a time when our country was torn apart, in the bloodiest war in our history, he found the language to heal and unify. And that was part of his being.

Kram: It's the idea of being inclusive, and prizing everybody no matter where they come from or what their label is.

This New Generation

Hesselbein: I spend a third of my time on college and university campuses, traveling twice a week. I have this sense of urgency. And it is from this generation of college students that I'm getting my inspiration. In my opinion, my experience, this is a very different generation from earlier cohorts.

Kram: Tell me about that. How are these students different?

Hesselbein: I talk about serving and making a difference, I talk leadership and ethics, and I say, "To serve is to live." And they look at me as if to say, "Well, of course." After events where there isn't time at the end for everyone to talk with me, I get e-mails; they want me to know the kind of volunteer work they're doing while they're in school or about last year when they went to Darfur, or where they are going.

At the end of speeches, if I've sensed this marvelous response from my student audience, I say, "Ten years from now, they may say of you, 'The future called and they responded, they kept the faith.' And twenty years from now they will say of you, 'Once again, The Greatest Generation.'" Because right now, they believe they have the opportunity to change this society with this new kind of leadership. They know democracy is everybody's business, everybody's job.

Kram: And you think that's somehow qualitatively different than the generation that I grew up in, which was the coming to adulthood during the Vietnam era?

Hesselbein: Yes, and generations after that. I think that isn't being derogatory. Here we have great leaders in every generation, who came up, but when you look at leadership right across the board and the generations on university campuses, college campuses, there is a difference right now. Once in a while I receive an e-mail that ends with a name and then, at the bottom, "To serve is to live." I find that very touching.

"BEING," "DOING," AND TRANSFORMING THE GIRL SCOUTS

Kram: If we could, I'd like to return to the period when you were transforming the Girl Scouts. What did you do to bring about change there? How would you express it in your terms of being and doing?

Hesselbein: Well, first, I didn't transform the Girl Scouts; those remarkable people did. When I came from the mountains of western Pennsylvania to New York, I had not applied for the job. I had been CEO of two Pennsylvania Girl Scout Councils in six years. Those were my first two professional jobs. I'd done a lot of volunteer work nationally and internationally, served on the National Board and on world committees, but I was invited to come to New York and talk to them about Girl Scouts of the USA, and the future, and if I were in this position what would I do.

In the sixty-seven years prior, since its founding, Girl Scouts of the USA never named anyone from within the organization as CEO. I thought they were just casting the widest net and they would choose the dean of a college—someone from the outside.

A search committee member asked me, if I were CEO, what would I do? So I described the total transformation of the largest organization for girls and women in the world and how we would build a richly diverse, inclusive organization, and we would have exemplary leadership and learning opportunities for all 650,000 men and women in the workforce. And a new program for girls heavy on math, science, technology, and highly contemporary learning opportunities for everyone. It was fun, but I never dreamed I would get a call: "We want you to come."

And so in July 1976, when I arrived in New York to head up the national organization, its 335 local councils were far apart on distant islands. How do you bring them all together in one great movement?

I asked what the demographics told us about the membership and racial/ethnic representation. The reply was, "We never ask race or ethnicity. We feel that would be discriminatory." I felt it would be discriminatory if we didn't.

So we did our research, but not from within. The National Urban League had a remarkable researcher, Dr. Robert Hill, and he had just published a book,

The Strengths of Black Families. So I went to see Vernon Jordan who was then president of the National Urban League, and said, "I need Dr. Robert Hill. We will pay his salary. We'll pay you anything, but we need him to do solid research that we can believe and respect. We want to know about those five racial/ethnic groups out there, how do they feel about us for their daughters? And I want you to look at those 650,000 adults serving two and a quarter million girls. How do they feel about building this richly diverse, inclusive organization?" Because when we got everyone on the computer, we found we were 95 percent white, and that was intolerable.

Vernon Jordan said that if we were going to do that, he would give us Bob Hill. So Bob went out and found Native American, African American, Hispanic, Asian American—didn't matter, all ethnic groups wanted us for their daughters, but they didn't know how to access the organization. Then he went inside the organization, every part of the country, it didn't matter, countrywide, and the response was that we wanted their daughters but "we were waiting for them to come in."

So we began this massive initiative. I found the most remarkable educator, consultant, Dr. John W. Work III. He went out and gave the most remarkable diversity, inclusion, training right across the organization at every level: the national board, the national staff, board members and staff leaders, our local council board and staff members, troop leaders on how to serve all of our people, all girls, all over the country. When we finished, we were able to move out with a powerful initiative to build the richly diverse organization of the future.

We had great communications people who designed huge posters for all five groupings, and each one had a real Girl Scout leader in her uniform with her Girl Scouts—five or six little girls in uniform. For Native Americans, with her girls around her, the caption was, "Your Names Are on the Rivers." We learned you don't speak directly to girls in Hispanic families. So that poster's caption was, "Girl Scouting Has Something of Value for Your Daughter." Everything based on solid research and powerful commitment.

Kram: And what was the training about?

Hesselbein: Well, the training was how to build the richly diverse inclusive organization, with rich representation at every level, respect for all people, and a highly contemporary program for girls. We quickly tripled racial/ethnic membership.

Yet five years later when I looked at those 335 local CEOs, some of them still didn't see themselves as others did. They didn't realize the impact they were having on others, even after this remarkable transformation they were part of. So I asked Dr. Regina Herzlinger, Harvard Business School professor, if she and a team of fellow professors would develop a corporate management seminar for Girl Scout executives.

She said yes, and so she, Dr. Len Schlesinger [now president of Babson College], Dr. James Austin, and three other professors developed a powerful seminar, and I said, "Oh, wonderful we'll put them through a hundred at a time." She said, "Oh, no, fifty at a time." So 335 Girl Scout Council CEOs, 100 national staff members, had the rare privilege of learning in a corporate management seminar designed just for them by a Harvard Business School professor—fifty at a time. When they finished, not only did they see themselves life-size, they were very assertive and said, "All right, what's next?"

So we asked Dr. Herzlinger to provide a week of asset management training. These were the CEOs responsible for a third of a billion dollars—it's now two-thirds of a billion dollars—cookie sales, hundreds of camps and buildings, so superior finance/asset management education was the key to the transformation. Learning never stops.

At one time, in one week, on the East Coast, there were fifty Girl Scout Council executives with the Harvard Business School team, and on the West Coast were 335 chairmen of the boards of Girl Scout Councils, and members of the National Board with Peter Drucker at Claremont in their management seminar.

Someone interviewing me on the transformation of the Girl Scouts asked, "Well, how did you know to do that, to use Harvard and Peter Drucker?" I said, "Well, it's very simple—only the best is good enough for those who serve girls."

It was a very exciting time, and people are still using the Harvard Business School case study of the transformation of the Girl Scouts of the USA, and I'm still being interviewed and asked, "How did you transform such a large organization?" I say what I said to you earlier: "No, no, those remarkable people transformed the Girl Scouts of the USA."

The Girls Scouts were founded in 1912—it's almost a hundred years old. Right now they're undergoing a remarkable second transformation. Kathy Cloninger [the current CEO of the Girls Scouts of the USA] is exactly right for her times as we thought we were for ours, and they are doing the most amazing job, a superb job of once again leading the transformation of the largest organization for girls and women in the world.

When I left, we were One Great Movement, and today that's what is happening all over again. Kathy is just the second CEO of Girl Scouts of the USA to come directly from a Girl Scout Council in almost a hundred years. Isn't that fascinating?

Kram: Yes, it is.

Hesselbein: The Girl Scouts organization/movement is thriving, and of course it's changing to meet the very special needs of girls and leaders and communities today, not those of ten or twenty years ago.

SOME POSSIBLE LESSONS

Kram: What would you say are the lessons from that experience—for organizations on Wall Street, for those in public education, and for all the various institutions that face such incredible challenges today?

What Is Our Mission?

Hesselbein: First, examine the mission. An organization that says, "Well, we don't exactly have one, but this is what we do," doesn't have a mission. But for tomorrow's world, the mission, why you do what you do, your reason for being is your most powerful message. And before you redefine your mission, you look out the window. Peter always said, "I never predict. I look out the window and see what is visible but not yet seen." What is out there not yet visible? There are emerging trends that will have a massive impact on the organization and the people you serve.

So we try to identify two or three of these massive changes that are coming our way, and we make sure that our mission statement is stated against that backdrop: this is why we do what we do—our reason for being, for the future. And Peter Drucker says it should fit on a T-shirt; so that means we distill the language until our mission does fit on our T-shirt.

Who Is Our Future Customer?

Hesselbein: Ask, "If this is our mission, then who is our customer of the future? Do we know whom we're serving today? Is it the same customer?" There are secondary supporting customers as well, but first of all, who is your primary customer? And when you determine that and all those other customers, secondary ones, you have to please, meet their needs.

What Does the Customer Value?

Hesselbein: One of the toughest challenges is listening to the customer. The toughest question is, "What does the customer value?" It's not, "We know what is good for them."

What Have We Done?

Hesselbein: Then "What have been our results so far?" When we discipline ourselves, knowing we can't do everything, we can recognize three or four strategic goals that will support and further the mission and, under the goals, objectives that will help us achieve them. And we're very careful about that language. We *further* a mission; we never *achieve* a mission. We further the mission and achieve the goals. And that may mean, for example, that your primary customer has changed.

Open to Change

Kram: New customers? Then might this process lead to an organization or a leader creating a relevant mission to today and to the future that some of the members of the organization may no longer fit?

Hesselbein: Yes. They may say, "I like the way we were. I'm going elsewhere." Thank them for their contribution, because they have made a contribution in the past. And as they leave, you'll find others arriving, saying, "I want to be a part of this exciting future."

Kram: And that's where the authenticity comes back into play, right?

Hesselbein: Yes, yes. The mission is not something you hang on the wall and print in the annual report. If I get on an elevator in your building, I should be able to say to anyone riding along with me, "What is the mission of your organization?" They ought to be able to reel it off. It belongs to all of us. The guys on the loading dock, wherever—it's theirs and they know why they do what they do.

A powerful mission statement that I've always loved comes from the International Red Cross in Geneva, which has to work in hundreds of countries and hundreds of languages, yet its mission has only five words: "To serve the most vulnerable." Nothing about, "We're going to serve everybody in the world," or "We have such a big heart." No. "To serve the most vulnerable."

At Leader to Leader, our mission is: "To strengthen the leadership of the social sector." This statement also fits on the T-shirt that Peter Drucker talked about.

Mission and Passion

Kram: I want to ask you about the connection between an individual's authenticity and this vital mission that you're describing.

Hesselbein: All right. It has to be passionate. I look at the mission, and its message has to be consistent with the purpose as I see it and believe in. If it is not as relevant as I believe it should be, if I don't think it will move us, if I cannot help redefine the mission, then I walk away. But when you read a mission and you say, "That's for me," then you want to be part of that. No lukewarm people on our team—just passionate believers.

Kram: The U.S. Army has done very well at that, hasn't it?

Hesselbein: Yes. A great example. Sometimes when I'm speaking about mission, particularly on university campuses, I talk about the U.S. Army and I hold up a little coin. I say that every soldier wears this with his dog tag: the Warrior Ethos: "I will always place the mission first. I will never accept defeat. I will never quit. I will never leave a fallen comrade."

Sometimes students will listen to me as I share the Warrior Ethos with them, and I can sense that they are translating it into their own lives. And I've watched a couple of them who had a little tear. It is amazing that the Army, which could have used the over 235 years of history of the army in a long message, chose just four lines, beginning with, as every organization should, "I will always place the mission first."

Kram: You've given us several good examples of why that's so important.

Hesselbein: But isn't that amazing? Thirteen years ago, I began to work with the U.S. Army, and I had always said that mission comes first, everything begins with mission, and here I pick up the Warrior Ethos: "I will always place the mission first." Our young, eighteen-year-old soldiers wear that, and they know and live what it means.

Duty, Honor, Country. They're living it. And it inspires us to be better people. Their leadership gives all of us a new sense of the power of leadership, of service. It's their contributions that inspire us to serve, to try to live up to their example of selfless service.

Kram: That sounds similar to the message that A. G. Lafley communicates to his organization—an expression of gratitude and humility.

Hesselbein: Yes, gratitude for their example and for what we are learning about leadership from them. And we gain a deeper appreciation of our own country because of their service and love of country. And I could say something too about the families of soldiers. They share that courage. It's a long time; fifteen months is a long time to be without your husband or wife and for little children—some of them born since the soldier left. Sometimes a second or third deployment. But it's all part of, "I will always place the mission first."

CONCLUSION

Kram: What's going through my mind right now is that when people hear you speak through this interview, they'll have an opportunity to get in touch with their own potential and how they might give their personal gifts and strengths in service to others.

Hesselbein: Yes, yes, absolutely.

Kram: The connection between the reader and what you have said in our conversation—that is, the leader learning to be, and the making of a mission that everyone in his or her organizations can connect to.

Hesselbein: That's right. And it becomes part of everything we do. Mission comes first. Everything furthers the mission. If people come with a wonderful idea that is very compelling for your school or for your organization, you look at it. And even if there's a lot of money offered, you have to have the courage to say, "Thank you. This is a wonderful opportunity, but it doesn't further our mission. May I suggest several other organizations where it would be perfect." We express our appreciation but remain faithful to the mission.

The Gap in the System

The chapters in Part Three look at applying what we already know about developing leaders to promote understanding and management of power relationships in organizations, and toward informed actions that promote inclusion in a diverse global environment.

Frankly, we ought not still be struggling in this terrain. The organizational and behavioral sciences have mapped this landscape and scouted this territory for close to fifty years. If we were to travel back in time to the 1960s, an intrepid practitioner in those fields might eagerly say to us, "How have you resolved those issues? Surely, by 2010, you have developed robust solutions. We already know what actions would resolve them. All we need is *resolve* to resolve them."

But as Warren Bennis once observed, something happened on the way to the future. The three chapters in this part of the book point us back to the right path. In Chapter Seven, Morgan McCall and George Hollenbeck put the case quite bluntly. We have over the years developed a clear understanding of how to develop leaders, but it still doesn't happen. In fact, the development of leaders is one of the key missing ingredients in the field of leadership. There is more research and practical technology that measures leadership than there is for measuring the growth of leadership. The authors provide a simple remedy: leaders must simply value leadership enough to do the hard work of developing it. It is, at the end of the day, a question of personal and organizational resolve.

Barry Oshry takes another angle in Chapter Eight, addressing common issues that we see across all levels in organizations, all the time: a lack of mutual understanding, a lack of empathy and cooperation, personal stress, blame, and an us-versus-them mentality. Oshry, who has spent his career working on these issues, has found systemic forces in organizations that make us blind to the contextual influences that mire us in these dysfunctional power dynamics. He presents a framework, the people-in-context lens, for helping us understand these organizational interactions and see the system in which we are enmeshed. He demonstrates how leaders can create more rewarding and effective relationships throughout the organization by seeing and understanding their own context and the contexts of others.

In Chapter Nine, Ilene Wasserman and Stacy Blake-Beard provide usable perspectives for building awareness around a key leadership competency: engaging diversity. With depressing regularity, the same kinds of confrontations seem to replay again and again (as this book was written, the arrest of Harvard professor Henry Louis Gates Jr., an African American, and its amplification as a black-white confrontation played nightly on American television and traveled around the world on the Internet). Wasserman and Blake-Beard point out that as our world becomes more global, more interconnected, and more complex, the need to create engagement and dialogue about diversity grows more important. Similar to Oshry's argument about power systems, the authors argue that engaging diversity requires leaders to develop a capacity for dealing with complexity. Such capacity demands self-reflection and self-awareness, the ability to observe oneself at the same time one is engaging with the other person. This is not easy, and the chapter provides frameworks and tools to help leaders learn that practice.

Important themes cut across the chapter in this part, and each puts theory into action. Recognizing one's place in a system of relations with others creates the capacity to see and to lead entire organizations, small groups, teams, and other people systems.

The Not-So-Secret Sauce of the Leadership Development Recipe

Morgan W. McCall Jr.
George P. Hollenbeck

Despite a widespread understanding of how to develop leaders, that development still does not happen at the scale and pace required to keep pace with the ever-changing and challenging context in which organizations operate. One open question related to meeting that requirement is whether there are enough leaders who value leadership development enough to develop it. Selecting leaders who value leadership development provides both the impetus for development throughout the organization and the models for development.

Why is it that so few leadership development efforts produce the leaders needed when the elements of leadership development have been well developed and researched over the past thirty years? (See McCall, 1998, for examples of development frameworks.) Even casual efforts can easily include the following:

- Links to strategy (how many and what kinds of leaders the organization will need given the strategic goals)

- Planned job experiences (everybody knows that most development takes place on the job)
- Individual and collective development efforts (executive coaching is widespread, and for a while, corporate universities and training centers sprang up like mushrooms)
- Feedback mechanisms (360-degree feedback is no longer questioned; it's a given)
- High-potential identification processes (competency models and executive reviews are everywhere)
- Succession planning (more and more a board-level issue)

And there is no shortage of benchmark companies whose leadership development practices are publicly documented and widely admired (see, for example, Byrnes, 2005; "The Top Companies for Leaders," 2007; Colvin, 2007).

With all of these pieces readily available, highly refined, and widely used, one would expect that leadership development would be a done deal. But it isn't. Leadership failure is as prevalent today as it was thirty years back, if not more so. A recent compilation of estimates of executive failures ranged from 30 to 67 percent, with an average failure rate of about 50 percent (Hogan, Hogan, and Kaiser, in press). Even if these estimates are exaggerated, many, if not most, organizations today are unhappy with their cadre of leaders and see developing better ones as one of their most important tasks (Howard, Erker, and Bruce, 2007).

As is the case with other organizational change efforts, a long list of factors both inside and external to the organization work against success in developing leaders. But with the myriad tools, techniques, and strategies available for leadership development, one might expect more progress than we see. The lack of success suggests that something is still missing—either an as-yet-to-be-discovered technique or approach, or some "secret sauce" that blends the existing ingredients so that they work better together. Although there may be new methodologies under development, including Internet-based programs and interactive simulations, we don't hold out much hope that new leadership development training, procedures, methodologies, or programs will solve the problem. Indeed, new approaches may take us into new dead ends (as competency models have done—see Hollenbeck and McCall, 2003; McCall and Hollenbeck, 2007) rather than lead us to the light.

We suggest that the solution lies not in new methods and refinements (the necessary ingredients already exist); rather, it lies in matters of selection, beginning with selecting leaders who can and will lead leadership development.

In this chapter, the first main section clarifies our underlying assumptions about leadership mastery. The second section briefly sets out the forces that work against leadership mastery. The third describes the essential role leaders must play in developing leadership mastery in others and the three key sets of leaders who play these roles: senior executives, potential leaders, and business partners.

SOME ASSUMPTIONS ABOUT LEADERSHIP MASTERY

In searching for a language to describe leadership and its development that avoids the "competency" notions prevalent in discussions today, we turned first to the literature on craftsmen (for example, Sennett, 2008) and expertise (for example, Ericsson, Charness, Feltovich, and Hoffman, 2006). The crafts provide an interesting example of the acquisition of skill and art through a progression from apprentice to journeyman to master, the highest level of that skill and art (and hence a notion of mastery in leadership). *Mastery* as we use it here does not imply an end state, as in "there is nothing left to learn." As Sennett points out, maintaining mastery—that highest level of skill—requires constant learning and effort.

The process of becoming a master leader parallels many of the research findings about other kinds of experts, from chess masters to surgeons (McCall and Hollenbeck, 2008). Among other shared qualities, acquisition of leadership expertise requires a long time, intensive effort, appropriate experience, a variety of teachers, and increasing skill across a range of cognitive and affective domains.

In the cases of both craftsman and experts, the focus is on the outcome—people capable of high performance within a domain—and on the journey through which those people achieve that level of performance. In many respects, leadership can be considered an identifiable (while extremely broad) domain, and people aspiring to mastery of that domain can be viewed as acquiring expertise through experience, practice, and performance.

The parallels between developing mastery as a leader and as a craftsman diverge when we examine the field within which each emerges. For example, the guilds that controlled craft production required that individuals demonstrate increased mastery before being allowed to move to the next higher level. The move from apprentice to journeyman required seven years of experience, culminating in a chef d'oeuvre demonstrating mastery of "elemental skills" (Sennett, 2008). To the best of our knowledge, no such demonstration of competence is required for promotion in management. Furthermore, the move from journeyman to master required another five to ten years and another demonstration of mastery, *chef d'oeuvres élevé*, which had to show "managerial competence and give evidence of trustworthiness as a future leader" (Sennett, 2008, p. 58). As desirable as it might be to require a masterwork before allowing individuals into senior leadership positions, no certificate of authenticity is required for entry to the executive suite.

This is not the place to get into a detailed discussion of the similarities and differences between the acquisition of expertise and leadership development (for that, see McCall and Hollenbeck, 2008). However, for the sake of argument we will make some assumptions about the path to mastery of leadership based loosely on some of the general principles of expertise in other areas. These include the role of experience, the need for synergy among components, the individual path across common ground, the law of serendipity, and the importance of intentionality (the link to strategic intent).

Experience Is Most Important

We first assume that experience is the most important element in leadership development (see McCall, Lombardo, and Morrison, 1988). It follows, therefore, that whoever controls the kinds of experiences (assignments, bosses, projects, and so on) that exist within the organization (availability) and who decides who will get them (access) sits in a powerful position relative to leadership development. More often than not, ultimate control, especially of key assignments, lies with line managers and executives, not with human resources (HR).

Coordination and Timing Matter

We also assume that to achieve maximum effect, the various components of development—including feedback, coaching, training, incentives, design of assignments and projects, and selection—must be coordinated, timed appropriately, and used in support of experience rather than operate independently of it or at cross-purposes. That said, these components are usually scattered across multiple functions, layers, and businesses within an organization, and even across different departments within functions like HR.

Development Is Not Mechanistic

We assume that development in general, and leadership development in particular, is neither linear nor mechanistic, even though the processes designed to produce it often are. Policies, procedures, forms, and the like may be helpful, but individuals develop in their own time, and the process, while not random, can be neither finely programmed nor predicted. As David Oldfield (1991) puts it, each of us takes a private journey to becoming what we become, even though those private journeys traverse the common ground of human experience. So it is with leadership. Each leader is forged by a unique collage of experiences and the personal lessons carved from them, yet the experiences and the lessons comprise a common landscape across which all leaders might trek. As we discuss later, you can do things to help people recognize learning opportunities when they appear and to increase the likelihood that they will take them even though there is some risk in doing so. But in the end, you can't make anyone develop, force development against an arbitrary timetable, or even force people to develop others. You can, of course, force people to go through the motions.

Serendipity Matters

We assume (and observe) that opportunities for development often are serendipitous. To the degree that development is driven by experiences such as challenging assignments and exceptional bosses, access to developmental opportunities will always be serendipitous to some extent. Not only do the experiences appear when they appear, and often unexpectedly, a given individual on that private path may not be ready or available when the opportunity appears. Even when the stars align, when an experience and the person needing it intersect in time and place, the best business decision may require giving the job to the person most qualified for the job rather than to the person who could learn the most from it.

Strategy Should Dictate What Is Wanted

Finally, we assume that the kinds and quality of leadership needed, as well as the meaning of *mastery* in a leadership context, must be part of the organization's strategy. Even so, not all organizations will (or should) make leadership development a core competency. The attention given to leadership and leadership development will vary depending on the challenges the organization faces at various points in time. When the economy is booming, all ships rise with the tide, and everyone looks like a good leader. In times of threat, effective leadership is more crucial than at any other time, but intentional leadership development often is put on hold for the duration. Furthermore, different stages in the organizational life cycle may require different kinds of master leaders—the entrepreneurial wizard needed in a start-up may not fare as well once the organization is up and running. As with other forms of expertise, leadership is in many respects situation specific, requiring unique knowledge and skills depending on time and place.

THE FORCES WORKING AGAINST LEADERSHIP MASTERY

Roughly translated, our assumptions imply that the effectiveness of leadership development is seriously compromised by anything that interferes with these:

- The availability of developmental experiences
- The coordination of developmentally relevant processes and activities with each other and with ongoing experience
- Taking into account individual differences in development (especially one-size-fits-all models)
- Taking advantage of serendipity
- Embedding leadership development directly in strategic need

As it turns out, such forces are legion, some of them the unavoidable result of conflicting business priorities or environmental circumstances. But many of them are the entirely avoidable consequence of a fundamental misunderstanding of how leadership mastery is achieved. In no particular order, here are some of the worst villains.

Fragmentation of Key Components

Key components of talent development that are critical to making the system work effectively are typically isolated from one another (and some, in this day and age, are even outsourced), often fall under the auspices of different executives, and sometimes operate at cross-purposes. For example, talent development is significantly affected by compensation (whether incentives are attached to development), succession planning (whether development is a consideration in who gets what job), performance management (the nature and frequency of performance feedback and the degree to which it is developmentally useful), organizational design (the kinds of experiences, especially assignments and projects, that are available for development), and recruitment and selection (the composition of the talent pool itself), as well as the more obvious training and development activities.

Traditionally many of these components—compensation, recruiting, performance management, training—have been driven by or housed in (at least nominally) the HR function. Some are not. But even within HR, where coordination is most likely, the components often are located in different departments with different mandates and different levels of influence. In one company we have worked with, for example, "leadership development" is housed in a different department from "leadership training" and reports through a different hierarchy to a business unit leader, while the training function reports to HR. In that same company, compensation is outsourced.

Other key components, such as incentives for self-development or for developing others, selection of individuals for key jobs, and decisions about organizational structure that directly affect the kinds of assignments available, may be scattered among various business units, report through different senior leaders, and, most likely, are driven by priorities other than development. Caught between the various business pressures, fragmentation of components, and lack of understanding among line executives about how these pieces must work together, development is often piecemeal at best.

A Surrounding Superficial or Toxic Culture

In a perfect world, leadership development is so much a part of the organizational culture that it is almost invisible. It is embedded in the DNA of the business strategy and an inherent expectation of leaders so that it just happens, without a lot of fanfare. Instead of being packaged and sent off to HR, development takes place in day-to-day placement decisions, natural coaching by managers, the ways decisions get made, and other actions. With a supportive culture, development takes place whether or not the standard HR tools are available. But sophisticated companies support a developmental philosophy with a variety of tools and processes. Many of them are the responsibility of HR, but in a healthy culture for development, they are seen as useful aids rather than as a nuisance. In effective cultures, HR (if it's even called that) has the authority to enforce standards of development, which are taken seriously by line management.

Such cultures are rare. Development is more likely to reside in an organizational culture in which commitment to it is superficial and where bits and pieces of development can be found in various places but are neither coordinated nor taken very seriously. With a training program here, a 360-degree assessment there, and the occasional job assignment for broadening a manager's skills, development is hit-or-miss. Superficial development cultures can appear to be quite elegant because the individual components in the hands of a sophisticated HR staff can be highly refined. When those pieces and parts don't come together or integrate with processes outside HR to create synergy, and when they have little meaningful connection to the business strategy, those are signs that development gets only lip service (despite sometimes extraordinary investments). Senior management may even espouse development as a crucial organizational value, but the lack of coordinated action and a low priority are the telltale signs that it isn't. Some development will occur, of course, because some people take advantage of the pieces for their own growth or because individual managers take it on themselves to develop the talent beneath them.

But the most difficult cultures for development are the highly toxic ones in which senior management doesn't even pay lip service to developing leadership talent. The philosophy, driven by a bedrock belief that leadership, if not altogether irrelevant, is something you either have or you don't, carries a sink-or-swim attitude. Challenging assignments are viewed as a test rather than an opportunity to grow and, once identified as not having "it," people are out of the running or out of the organization. Talent is bought and sold rather than developed. Ironically, even in such situations as these, some development can still occur because challenging assignments are given to people thought to have the right stuff, and almost in spite of themselves, they have to master new domains.

Misdirected Search for Return on Investment

It is with some justification that organizations are increasingly interested in what, if any, return they are getting on their investment in various HR programs. To the extent that leadership development consists of the bits and pieces managed by HR, then the costs associated with the components, if less so their impact, are readily ascertainable. Indeed a growing consulting industry has arisen that sustains itself by trying to determine the return on investment (ROI) of such things as coaching and leadership training. So if the cost of development is defined by the visible expenses of running programs, hiring coaches and consultants, paying tuitions, conducting 360-degree feedback surveys, supporting an HR staff, and other such tangible items, then fluctuations in the business cycle make those developmental activities easy targets. They are much easier to cost than to justify, and they can be seen as expensive luxuries that are used as rewards when times are plush and disappear when things get tight. This vulnerability leads to fascinating creativity when it comes to calculating the return on these investments, especially since there is little reason to expect these pieces of the puzzle to have much effect in isolation.

The real cost of development is not the highly visible budget items, but rather is embedded in giving the right people the right experiences with the right levels of support so that they become better leaders. And the real return on the investment is not short-term changes in attitudes or behavior (as might be measured by assessing training outcomes), but the increased numbers of master leaders who achieve the business strategy. This is not to say that it is any easier to measure an increase in the number of capable leaders. In fact, it is considerably more difficult to assess the quality of leadership and its relationship to organizational outcomes than it is to measure the impact of a program or process. But measuring the wrong thing more precisely does not make it useful information.

In short, errors perpetuated by misunderstanding how people acquire leadership expertise are compounded by efforts to measure ROI based on that misunderstanding. The result is not only a distraction from what should be assessed, but time, energy, and money invested in a game of smoke and mirrors to justify or not (depending on the motives of those doing the cost analysis) ongoing activities.

Opportunity Deficits

If leadership mastery is achieved through experience, then obviously decisions that affect what experiences are available and who will get them are the driving forces in development. Yet organizational architecture is rarely determined by the need for sufficient numbers and types of important developmental experiences. Clearly it is fiscally foolish to design an organization purely for developmental richness, but just as clearly the need for developmental opportunities, such as profit-and-loss responsibility or international exposure early in a career, should be factored into design decisions. Without start-ups, turnarounds, growing businesses, relevant projects, certain staff assignments, and similar important opportunities (see McCall et al., 1988, and McCall and Hollenbeck, 2002, for descriptions of developmental experiences and what can be learned from them), the opportunities for potential leaders to learn the skills they need are limited. The shortage of developmental opportunities (there have never been enough truly powerful experiences to go around) has grown even worse as competitive pressures have led to delayering, outsourcing, and lean processes. These problems are compounded by the recent emphasis on upward career movement at younger and younger ages, coupled with the breakdown of the psychological contract between employers and employees that placed a value on loyalty. Now people expect to hop across organizations—not to become better managers but to advance their upward mobility.

Because the design of an organization must first serve the strategy of the business, it is all the more crucial that developing leadership talent be integral to that strategy. Only then will design decisions take into account the importance of certain kinds of experiences for the development of talent, and the equally important task of deciding who gets those experiences. Unfortunately, many organizations see leadership development as an HR issue (see below), resulting in an organizational architecture, and selection and placement processes, that are at best orthogonal to development.

Myopic Focus on the Human Resource Function

For far too long and in far too many organizations, leadership development has been synonymous with HR programs, usually training programs, but more recently seemingly business-related interventions such as action learning (in which contrived teams are coached as they attack business problems) and on-the-job coaching. Basic tools of the trade such as coaching and mentoring programs, 360-degree feedback, needs assessment, development of competency models, and training programs are typically housed in the HR function and viewed as HR activities. Once responsibility for leadership development is delegated to HR, it is no longer necessary for it to be a serious part of the business strategy (indeed much effort by HR goes into creating a separate HR, or "talent management," strategy), or that it be an accountability of business leaders. To make matters worse, in many organizations the HR function is relatively powerless and isolated from the "real" business of the business.

Even when the HR function is given responsibility and resources, it often lacks access to the critical elements of development. Put on the spot for leadership development, HR leaders have little choice but to optimize the tools of HR.

Elsewhere we have described how competency models, as one example, allow HR to develop integrated and internally consistent programs for development disconnected from the processes by which leadership mastery is achieved. These elegant and sophisticated programs bring to mind Steinbeck's description of the equally elegant desk designed specifically for use aboard ship on his 1940 biological expedition to the Sea of Cortez:

> In a small boat, the library should be compact and available. We had constructed a strong, steel-reinforced wooden case, the front of which hinged down to form a desk. This case holds about twenty large volumes and has two filing cases, one for separates (scientific reprints) and one for letters; a small metal box holds pens, pencils, erasers, clips, steel tape, scissors, labels, pins, rubber bands, and so forth. Another compartment contains a three-by-five inch card file. There are cubby-holes for envelopes, large separates, typewriter paper, carbon, a box for India ink and glue. The construction of the front makes room for a portable typewriter, drawing board, and T-square. There is a long narrow space for rolled charts and maps. Closed, this compact and complete box is forty-four inches long by eighteen by eighteen; loaded it weighs between three and four hundred pounds. It was designed to rest on a low table or in an unused bunk. Its main value is compactness, completeness, and accessibility. We took it aboard the *Western Flyer*. There was no table for it to rest on. It did not fit in a bunk. It could not be put on deck because of moisture. It ended up lashed to the rail on top of the deckhouse, covered with several layers of tarpaulin and roped on. Because of the roll of the boat it had to be tied down at all times. It took about ten minutes to remove the tarpaulin, untie the lashing line, open the cover, squeeze down between two crates of oranges, read the title of the wanted book upside down, remove it, close and lash and cover the box again. But if there had been a table or large bunk, it would have been perfect [1951, pp. 11–12].

The reality is that even the most elaborate of HR-based talent management systems is lashed to the rail when they are disconnected from the ongoing flow of experiences and who gets them.

Disinterested or Inept Senior Leaders

If responsibility for leadership development is unfairly dumped in the lap of HR, then where does it rightfully belong? With senior management. If the people promoted into senior leadership roles don't believe in development, don't model it, don't take it into account when making decisions, don't support it, and don't understand it, it won't happen.

In other words, only through senior-level commitment and action can an organization counter the forces that work against developing talent. They must see to it that whatever is necessary is done to create synergy among elements that independently have only modest, if any, effects; create a culture supportive of development; revise cost-benefit accounting to include the results of experience-based development; design the organization to provide a rich array of developmental experiences; change assumptions about the role of HR and introduce accountability for development into line management; and select and promote managers who live and breathe the development of others, as well as their own. This is a prodigious task under the best of circumstances, suggesting that the involvement of the board may be required if senior management is to be held accountable (see Chapter Thirteen, this volume).

Actually that's not a bad to-do list for overcoming those vexing obstacles to development, but it is unfortunately a difficult list to execute. And like most other large-scale change projects, some dimensions are more important than others. The secret sauce, we suggest, is actually quite obvious: it is leadership—the very thing the process is intended to produce. We find ourselves in the proverbial catch-22: to develop leadership requires leadership. This raises the question of whether very senior leaders who are not believers can come to see the light. One has to suppose that it is possible, though our experience with senior executives suggests that it is relatively rare. By the time people reach senior rank, their views on development are often fixed by their interpretations of their own experience.

So it boils down to selection after all. If the senior leaders of the organization, the role models for developing leaders, do not believe in and demonstrate and enforce the values required to make development work, no amount of money spent on development programs, forms, consultants, or coaches will make much difference.

THE MISSING INGREDIENTS IN LEADERSHIP'S SECRET SAUCE

We are often quick to hold senior management responsible for everything from stock price to workforce diversity to product quality. To pin responsibility for leadership development on them is to acknowledge reality while at the same time throwing it into competition with everything else for a place on the priority list. That there are other priorities, sometimes more urgent ones, does not alter the fact that it is extremely hard to learn leadership in a nonsupportive environment from leaders who are not leading. If developing leadership talent is to be more than the heroic act of the occasional executive, then senior management must recognize and accept its essential role in developing leadership mastery in others. It is the senior team that must build an organizational context where selection and development of leadership talent are expected and supported and where people are held accountable for developing themselves as well as others.

Because of this responsibility at the senior levels, the selection of senior executives is one ingredient to the secret sauce of leadership development. It is senior leaders, after all, who

- Design the organization and its priorities, thereby determining what experiences are available to develop talent
- Make crucial placement decisions, thereby controlling who gets the most challenging opportunities
- By formulating strategy and values, determine the priority of development relative to other important objectives
- Select people for key jobs and entry to senior management ranks, thereby either increasing (or reducing) the number with shared commitment to development
- Decide whether to hold people accountable for development by measuring and sanctioning it
- Ensure that processes such as succession planning, compensation, performance management, and development programs support development

All of these roles are important, but senior management selection is key because there must be consistency among the senior business leaders in their belief in development or movement across boundaries for developmental reasons will be severely limited. And without shared values, it is unlikely that senior leaders will give up their most talented people easily for the sake of their development, even if exposure to other parts of the business would broaden them.

Obviously if the wrong people are at the top, there is no driving force to create the context for development. But selecting committed senior leaders, while necessary, is not sufficient. At least two other ingredients—and both of them selection decisions—must be added to the sauce. The first, an obvious one because leadership mastery is achieved only through learning from experience, is that people have to be selected for developmental experiences. The second, less obvious, is that senior leaders have neither the time nor all the necessary expertise to personally direct development of talent and so need a special brand of help—they need to select "business partners" who can help them carry out their developmental responsibilities. The right people in these two areas are the missing ingredients that make leadership development work.

Of course, no silver selection bullets exist for choosing these three types of players in the leadership mastery game (the senior leaders, the business partners, and the high potentials), any more than there are silver bullets for developing leadership mastery. As Peter Drucker observed more than twenty years ago, "There is no magic to good staffing and promotion decisions—just hard work and disciplined thought" (1985, p. 22) or as Jack Welch pointed out more recently, selecting "great people is brutally hard" (Welch and Welch, 2007, p. 102). We will argue that organizations have not done the brutally hard work and disciplined thought.

Selecting the Senior Leaders

Despite adulation of the CEO, senior leadership means more than just the top dog. Senior leadership is the cadre of executives who collectively determine the structure of the organization and, with it, a host of developmental essentials: the existence of challenging (developmental) jobs, the availability of profit and loss assignments, degree and form of globalization and the utilization of expatriate assignments, identification of cross-boundary special projects—the list is very long. That commitment to development be included among the criteria for selection or promotion into senior positions is therefore imperative.

In advocating that skills and values relevant to developing talent be among the selection criteria for senior leaders, we are not naively ignoring the importance of business results. Just as eligibility for becoming a pharaoh in ancient Egypt required first that the candidate be descended from the Sun God, performance is (or should be) a basic requirement for senior leaders. But the organization that takes leadership mastery seriously must have senior leaders with talent for both development and getting business results.

We are not proposing a behavioral competency list for selecting executives for their skill at developing leadership mastery in others. The important characteristics are valuing leadership mastery as a strategic imperative and demonstrated results in actually doing it. Assessing these does not require new or breakthrough assessment techniques. Properly applied, with Drucker's "hard work and discipline," our tried-and-true methods will do fine. Sorcher and Brant (2002), for example, describe one such method that focuses on using the information within the organization, collected and processed systematically, to make executive selection decisions. Their method is a kind of exerciseless assessment center, using executives who know the person as assessors and using their knowledge of the person in past situations to describe the person behaviorally. They take advantage of the fact that in most organizations, everybody is known by somebody, or at least partially by several somebodies who together can paint a complete picture.

Knowing where an executive stands on these characteristics should rarely be an issue—who in the organization the "development" managers are is usually well known. The trick is ensuring that the characteristics are included when selections are made and in doing the work to assess them.

Even with all of the sophisticated tools and technology available for assessment and development, it boils down to priorities. If leadership is believed to be an essential part of achieving business objectives, then it is attended to. If not, it isn't.

Selecting the Business Partners

Senior leaders do not do the work alone; they must have talented teams and staffs if they are to carry out the leadership imperative. Again, selection rears its ugly head. It was not by accident that Jack Welch devoted so much of his time to selecting the right executives and overseeing their development. But Welch did not do this alone. He was supported by an executive development staff that knew GE and understood its strategy, its development jobs, and its people.

While expertise in development resides theoretically in HR professionals, the kinds of advice and counsel needed to make leadership development work are not found in the typical knowledge base of HR. To illustrate our point, we recently happened onto a detailed HR competency model of the International Personnel Management Association, describing the roles and competencies of HR business partners and how these competencies are demonstrated. Although we are die-hard critics of competency models, that developing leadership mastery by that or any other name does not appear on HR's own list as a role, a competency, or an activity has to grab our attention.

If indeed leadership mastery is a product of experience, then the crucial expertise is in knowing the strategy of the business (which experiences are relevant); the nature of jobs, assignments, and bosses (what experiences are available and what might be learned from them); the people (who would benefit from the experiences); and the politics of the organizations (how to negotiate the shoals of moving talented people as needed to develop them). This knowledge is as likely, or more so, to be housed in seasoned executives throughout the organization than it is to be found in HR professionals, but when HR professionals have these qualities, they are what we mean by "business partners." Not only do organizations like GE, IBM, and Johnson & Johnson select and develop HR career professionals with these characteristics, but from time to time they have also drafted into development service seasoned executives with broad knowledge of the company, its goals and its people, who share the trust of others, and who no longer themselves have a stake in the politics of job assignment.

As is the case in selecting senior executives, choosing effective business partners to work with them requires hard work and discipline and a focus on the values and the kind of knowledge required. This may mean bypassing seemingly obvious candidates for those important roles in favor of those who are committed to the endeavor and have demonstrated their understanding of it. Again, the tools of Sorcher and Brandt apply, as does Mahler's accomplishment analysis, a descendant of which is used at GE (Mahler and Wrightnour, 1973). Mahler's approach goes well beyond the usual performance appraisals or manager's recommendations on a list of competencies to include the use of trained "data collectors" to collect and organize detailed information about the results obtained, work methods, leadership styles, and work characteristics of those recommended for higher-level jobs and development. Both of these approaches focus on tapping into the base of knowledge about people that exists in almost any organization but that is seldom made good use of.

Selecting People for Experiences

Given a limited number of potentially developmental experiences, identifying potential leaders who can make the most of those experiences is a critical task.

It is complicated by the fact that leadership mastery is acquired over time through multiple, diverse experiences, meaning that potential itself evolves and is a moving target. Confidence, for example, usually increases with success in tough experiences but is, at the same time, a factor in willingness to engage in those challenging experiences in the first place and in learning from them. Thus, it is both cause and consequence in increasing leadership mastery.

Given this complexity, how should we select high potentials? Collins (2001) makes the case that "good to great" companies select their people first, even before they decide on their strategies. With the right people "on the bus," many of the problems of changing direction, of motivation, of compensation take care of themselves. With the wrong people on the bus, it doesn't matter what the organization's strategy is because it can't be implemented.

But who are the right people? To some extent, every organization will answer this question differently, depending on its history, stage of development, industry, and so on. But Collins identifies a common core among effective "high potentials" that begins with what he calls character, which includes relatively enduring traits like the ability to learn and adapt, motivation and work ethic, integrity, and willingness to put the greater good above personal gain. Add to this aspect of character a demonstrated ability to achieve high performance and get results, and we have one prescription for the right people to develop (see also Hollenbeck, 2009).

Interestingly, this is consistent with the research on expertise, which suggests that those who become world-class experts in various domains not only learn more from their experiences, but have extraordinary passion for mastery and equally extraordinary discipline to achieve it (see McCall and Hollenbeck, 2008). One study of high-potential international executives (summarized in McCall, 1998) found similar qualities distinguished them from "solid performers." Indeed, those rated highest got, took, or made more opportunities to learn, and they did more things to learn from those opportunities.

The mix of tools for identifying high potentials includes assessment centers, simulations, 360-degree feedback, an assortment of measuring instruments, and group evaluation processes like the one Sorcher and Brant (2002) described, as well as performance reviews and recommendations by managers. (Recent reviews of the range and effectiveness of various methods appear in Thornton, Hollenbeck, and Johnson, in press, and in Howard, 2007.) As was the case with selecting senior leaders and their business partners, methodology and technology are not the limiting factors in selecting potential leaders. Rather, the challenge is to use these tools effectively to assess what is really important. Whether we are talking about expert performance in leadership or other domains, mastery requires commitment to growth, dedication to practice and improvement, and increasing skill in extracting meaning from relevant experience.

Who gets identified as high potential and therefore gains access to key developmental experiences ultimately determines who has the opportunities to achieve leadership mastery. With the right senior team in place, supported by the right business partners, selecting and placing high potentials are guided by the leadership needs of the organization and the best interests of the high potentials, relatively free of the ebb and flow of political and economic tides. The key word here is *relatively*. In tough times, priorities change and tough actions are necessary: lines of business made be shed, people may be laid off, cutbacks may be widespread, and resources may grow scarce. However, the very process of surviving and remaking the organization presents, in a perverse sense, significant developmental opportunities. By thinking through who could benefit from the challenges inherent in trying times, development can continue even under frightful circumstances.

CONCLUSION

When we set out in search of the missing ingredients in leadership development we did not anticipate that it would lead us into the selection arena—a bit of a paradox given the different views and assumptions of selectors and developers. We expected to slog through a quagmire of processes, philosophies, tools, techniques, research, hearsay, war stories, practices, and wisdom, perhaps unearthing some gemstones along the way. With a little luck, we thought we might even discover a breakthrough that, if not leading to fame and fortune, might at the very least move leadership development forward by a notch or two.

In retrospect we are not surprised that the grail was not there for us to find. Hands more capable than ours have dug this soil for decades, and both researchers and practitioners have contributed to a vast array of perspectives and resources that can be and are applied to the challenge of developing leadership. That the estimated failure rate among leaders remains distressingly high is not for want of potential leaders or the tools and techniques for helping them realize their potential. Rather, we concluded, the source of the problem was in a different place altogether.

Like the desk Steinbeck described, the powerful ideas and tools available for leadership development often end up lashed to the rail, covered by tarp, making little difference despite their potential. They are useful only if those facing the leadership challenges of the organization believe that leadership talent is essential to business success and that it can be developed, know that methodologies exist to aid in the identification and development of that talent, and have the knowledge and advice and support to do what needs to be done.

So inevitably we end up with selection as the obvious general type of secret ingredient in leadership development. Indeed, in the hands of the right people, even primitive tools can produce impressive results. The leadership talent pool can be significantly enhanced by selecting senior leaders who are committed to developing their own and others' mastery; selecting people to work with and support them who understand the organization's business, its people, and the experiences it has to offer—and know how to mesh them; and selecting people for those experiences who are most likely to learn from them.

To conclude that the heart of development consists of hard choices, hard work, and discipline in selecting key players is hardly electrifying enough to bring us, the authors, either fortune or fame. However, attention to these aspects of development just might move things forward a notch or two.

People in Context

Barry Oshry

In almost any organization, you will find a lack of mutual understanding, empathy, and cooperation up, down, and across structural and functional lines. Blame, and a we-versus-them position, surfaces in many interactions. You will find personal stress at all levels, and you will discover dysfunctional peer relationships at the top, in the middle, and at the bottom. This chapter presents a valuable framework—a people-in-context lens for understanding organizational interaction. Using the framework, you will see how blindness to context creates all the problems described above. More than that, the framework demonstrates to leaders how seeing and understanding their own context and the contexts of others can enable them to avoid those problems and to create satisfying and productive relationships throughout the organization that lead to alignment and better performance.

Our efforts to understand and intervene in organizational events have a persistent bias: to interpret phenomena from a personal framework. In other words, situations are to be understood in terms of the needs, motivations, temperaments, personal styles, values, and developmental stages of one or more of the individuals involved. And if the diagnostic lens is personal, then it follows that the interventions will also be personal: fix, fire, demote, replace, or suggest coaching or therapy for one or more of the parties.

I suggest an often overlooked lens that provides a deeper understanding of these phenomena and a range of more effective leadership strategies. This is a person-in-context lens in which phenomena are understood as the interactions of individuals and groups with the systemic contexts in which they and others exist. When we fail to recognize context, events are misunderstood and energies misplaced. A missing leadership competency is seeing, understanding, and mastering the systemic contexts in which we and others exist.

In this chapter, I describe the consequences of blindness to context and the productive possibilities we derive from context sight. The first main section describes four common system contexts: Top, Middle, Bottom, and Customer. The second section discusses the four contexts as they apply to individuals and the third as they apply to groups. In both sections, I describe familiar scenarios that result from context blindness and produce personal stress, strained or broken relationships, and diminished organizational effectiveness. I also lay out some principles for seeing context and describe the positive difference that seeing context can make for leaders and others in organizations.

The fourth main section of the chapter presents a case that illustrates the limitations of personal orientations while demonstrating how seeing contexts deepens our understanding of situations and reveals more comprehensive and productive leadership strategies.

Seeing, understanding, and mastering context is an essential leadership competency. There is a difference between knowing that people operate in different contexts and experiencing relationships with people from different contexts in the day-to-day turmoil of leading modern organizations. I end with a discussion of the implications for leadership development.

FOUR SYSTEM CONTEXTS

This section describes four common system contexts: Top, Middle, Bottom, and Customer (Oshry, 1994). This is not to imply that these are the only contexts in which people function, but these four are essential to our understanding of organizational interaction, and they are the four that I know very well from my work over the past forty years with both the Power Lab (Oshry, 1999) and the Organization Workshop, both described at the end of this chapter. What is important to understand is that Top, Middle, Bottom, and Customer are not just hierarchical positions; they are conditions all of us face in organizational interaction, conditions we move in and out of from event to event. So in that sense, all of us are Top/Middle/Bottom/Customers.

- *The Top context: Complexity and accountability.* We are in the Top context (Figure 8.1) whenever we have been designated responsible for a system or piece of a system—whether it is the organization as a whole, a division, unit, task force, family, project, team, or classroom. The Top context tends to be one of complexity and accountability: lots of inputs to deal with, difficult issues, issues from within and without the system, issues that aren't dealt with

Figure 8.1
A Person in the Top Context

elsewhere float up to you, and complex decisions must be made regarding the form, culture, and direction of the system. Whenever we are in that Top context, we are accountable for the system, the piece of the system, or the process for which we are Top.

- *The Bottom context: Vulnerability.* We are in the Bottom context (Figure 8.2) of vulnerability whenever we are on the receiving end of decisions that affect our lives in major or minor ways. Plants are shut down, health and retirement benefits are changed, restrictive governmental regulations are put in place, new initiatives are instituted, current initiatives are abandoned. All of this happens *to* us without our involvement.

Figure 8.2
A Person in the Bottom Context

- *The Middle context: Tearing.* We are in the Middle tearing context (Figure 8.3) whenever we are pulled between the conflicting needs, demands, and priorities of two or more individuals or groups. We are Middle between our work group and our manager, between a spouse and a child, between supplier and manufacturing, between our executive group and the board, between one executive and another.

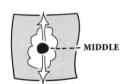

Figure 8.3
A Person in the Middle Context

- *The Customer context: Neglect.* We are in the Customer context of neglect (Figure 8.4) whenever we are looking to some individual or group for a product or service that we need in order to move on with our work, and that product or service is not coming as fast as we want, at the price we want, or to the quality we had hoped for.

**Figure 8.4
A Person in the
Customer Context**

To reiterate the basic point: regardless of what positions we and others occupy, we and they are constantly moving in and out of these contexts: sometimes as Top, sometimes as Bottom, sometimes as Middle, and sometimes as Customer.

AWARENESS OF PERSONS IN CONTEXT

We do not reflexively see context; we see people, and we tend to experience our interactions as person to person. Sometimes we are blind to the context others are living in, and sometimes we are blind to our own context. The basic point is that we are not just interacting people to people; we are people in context. Failure to recognize that can lead to serious misunderstandings, inappropriate actions, and dysfunctional consequences. In this section, I discuss the contextual principles at work on the personal level, provide some examples of what that context looks and feels like, and offer some strategies a leader can take in this situation to address the gap.

Principle 1: When We Are Blind to Others' Contexts

Principle 1: When we are blind to others' contexts, we are likely to fall into scenarios in which we misunderstand others' actions, attribute inaccurate motives to them, respond in ways that negatively affect our relationships with them, and diminish our personal and organizational effectiveness:

- *"Arrogant" Tops.* We may have a brilliant idea for organizational improvement. We send it to Top and await an acknowledgment, maybe even a promotion. To us, this is a great idea with potential for increased organization effectiveness. But to our Top, struggling to survive in this world of complexity, it may be just another complication in an already complex world. A week goes by with no response from Top. Two weeks. Nothing. Our reaction: *It's those arrogant Tops again!* We get mad, we withdraw, and we lose our enthusiasm for making any more contributions.

• *"Resistant" Bottoms.* We've just developed an exciting new initiative that could really make a difference to our workers and ultimately to the organization. For the workers, it means more involvement, more empowerment, more opportunity to make a difference. We bring it up to our workers, but there is no enthusiasm. To us, this is an exciting initiative, but to our workers living in this world of vulnerability, this is the latest installment of "them" doing it to "us" again. *What have they got up their sleeves this time? What happened to last year's exciting new initiative? Just wait it out; this too shall pass.* We conclude that our workers are just too far gone for anything to excite them.

• *"Weak" Middles.* We've just made a simple request to our Middle; it's about support we need from him on our project. That's all we're asking for. To us, it's a simple request, but to our Middle struggling to survive in a tearing world, supporting us is working against someone else who is pressing Middle to support her. So instead of a strong commitment to support, we get a weak wishy-washy *I'll see what I can do.* Where did we ever get such a weak Middle!

• *"Nasty" Customers.* We're trying to be helpful to a disgruntled customer whose product has once again been delayed. There's nothing we can do about product delivery, but we do want to soothe Customer's ruffled feathers, so we invite Customer out for coffee; we also suggest a tour of the facility and present our customer survey form. Instead of gratitude, we get an angry reaction from Customer. To us, we are making reasonable gestures; to Customer living in the world of neglect, our nice gestures are simply *more neglect! Some people are just unreachable by kindness!*

Leadership strategy 1 comes into play in all of these situations:

> *Leadership strategy 1:* Take others' contexts into account. Make it possible, even easy, for them to do what it is you and your system need them to do.

There is no arrogant Top, resistant Bottom, weak Middle, or nasty Customer. What we have are people—just like us—struggling to cope with their respective contexts of complexity and accountability, vulnerability, tearing, and neglect.

Our problem is that we have been reaching out and reacting as if these are just person-to-person interactions. In our context blindness, what we've done is increase the complexity of Top, the vulnerability of Bottom, the tearing of Middle, and the neglect of Customer, which is not what we had intended.

The challenge for us is to take context into account. This involves having an understanding of others' context, having some empathy for them, not reacting to their initial responses, staying focused on what it is we are trying to accomplish, and being strategic, that is, rather than being blind to context, taking other people's contexts into account. *Given the context they are in, how do I make it possible for them to do what I need them to do?* So, incorporated into my strategy are the following challenges: How do I reduce the complexity of Top, the vulnerability of Bottom, the tearing of Middle, and the neglect of Customer?

Principle 2: When We Are Blind to Our Own Contexts

> *Principle 2:* When we are blind to our own contexts, we are vulnerable to falling into scenarios that are dysfunctional for us personally, for our relationships, and for our systems. We respond reflexively to these contexts—not all of us, not every time, but with great regularity—without awareness or choice. It is as if these scenarios happen to us without any agency on our part.

• *Burdened Tops.* When we are Top, living in the context of complexity and accountability, we are vulnerable to reflexively sucking responsibility up to ourselves and away from others. It's not a choice we make; it simply happens. We don't see ourselves doing anything. It is just crystal clear to us that we are responsible for handling the complexity we are facing. The more regularly we do this, the more we increase our stress, the more we dilute the brainpower that can be brought to bear on situations, the more we gradually disable others so that when we need them, they aren't there for us.

• *Oppressed Bottoms.* When we are Bottom, living in the context of vulnerability, we are vulnerable to reflexively holding others responsible for our condition and the condition of the system. Again, we do this without awareness or choice. It's crystal clear to us that *they* are responsible, not us. The more regularly we do this, the more righteous we become in our victimhood and the more bitter toward others; the less energy we devote to dealing with the very problems we are facing, and the less agency we feel in our lives. The system suffers from misdirected energy that is devoted to whining, complaining, resisting, and, possibly, sabotaging—energy that could have been focused more productively on the business of the system.

• *Torn Middles.* When we are Middle, living in the tearing context, we are vulnerable to sliding in between other people's issues and conflicts and making them our own. It becomes crystal clear to us that *we* are responsible for resolving *their* issues. What makes this especially stressful is that *they* hold us responsible for resolving *their* issues. Sliding in between weakens us: we become confused, uncertain whose priorities to serve; we may not fully satisfy anyone, we get little positive feedback; and possibly we doubt our own competence. Middles cope with this tearing in different ways: some reduce the tearing by aligning themselves with Tops, others by aligning with Bottoms; in either case, they create tension with whomever they are not aligned. Other Middles cope with the tearing by bureaucratizing themselves, making it difficult for anyone to get to them. And still others burn themselves out shuttling back and forth, attempting to explain each side to the other, trying to placate all sides, struggling to please everyone. In all of these coping mechanisms is a loss of independence of thought and action. No independent Middle perspective is brought to bear, and as a consequence, the system loses whatever value such perspective could provide.

• *Screwed Customers.* When we are Customer, living in the context of neglect, we are vulnerable to staying aloof from delivery systems and holding them responsible for delivery. It becomes crystal clear to us that they, not us, are responsible for delivery. So when delivery is unsatisfactory, we feel righteously angry at the supplier and personally blameless. Since it's clear to us that we have no responsibility in the delivery process, whatever contribution we might have made to the quality of delivery is lost.

In all of these scenarios, blindness to our own context results in personal stress, fractured relationships with others, and diminished organizational effectiveness. The solution is to turn to leadership strategy 2:

> *Leadership strategy 2:* Recognize the context you are in, move past the reflexive disempowering response, and use the possibility of whatever context you are in to strengthen yourself, your relationships with others, and the system.

To master our own context, we need to understand that in system life, we are constantly moving in and out of Top, Middle, Bottom, and Customer contexts. We need to be able to recognize whatever context we are in at the moment. *Am I Top, Middle, Bottom, or Customer in this moment?* We need to be able to notice our reflex response in whatever context we are in. *Am I sucking up responsibility to myself and away from others? Am I holding THEM responsible for my condition and the condition of the system? Am I sliding in between other people's issues and conflicts and making them my own? Am I staying aloof and holding the delivery system responsible for delivery?*

Sometimes the clue to context lies in our feelings: *I'm feeling burdened or oppressed or torn or screwed. What is that feeling telling me about the context I am in, and how I am responding to it? Am I feeling burdened because I'm sucking responsibility up to myself? Am I feeling oppressed because I'm holding others responsible? Am I feeling torn because I'm sliding in between others' issues? Am I feeling screwed because I'm holding the delivery system responsible for delivery?*

Awareness allows us to avoid the negative consequences of blindness. Beyond that, it opens up more powerful and productive possibilities for responding to context, possibilities that strengthen ourselves and our systems—for example:

- In the Top context of complexity and accountability, instead of sucking responsibility up to myself and away from others, my challenge is to be a person who uses this context as an opportunity to create responsibility in others.

- In the Bottom context of things that are wrong with my condition and the condition of the system, instead of holding THEM responsible for all that is wrong, my challenge is to be a person who is responsible for my condition and the condition of the system.

- In the Middle context of tearing, instead of sliding in between and losing my independence of thought and action, my challenge is to maintain my independence of thought and action in the service of the system.

- In the Customer context of neglect, instead of standing aloof from the delivery process and holding it responsible for delivery, my challenge is to be a person who shares responsibility for delivery.

We are much more powerful and more contributing system members when, in the Top context, we are creators of responsibility in others; when, in the Bottom context, we are responsible for our condition and the condition of the system; when, in the Middle context, we maintain our independence of thought and action; and when, in the Customer context, we share responsibility for the delivery of products and services. Living from these transformative stands demands that we use more of our potential in whatever context we are in, and it enables us to focus more of our creative energies on the business of the system. These stands also raise unique challenges for us. As Tops, we need to give up some control; as Bottoms we need to give up our dependency and blame; as Middles we need to give up our need to please everyone; and as Customers we need to give up our sense of entitlement.

These are the payoffs and the prices to be paid for seeing, understanding, and mastering the systemic contexts in which we are living. In this section, we explored the leadership challenges of seeing, understanding, and mastering individuals in context. Now we turn our attention to groups in context.

GROUPS IN CONTEXT

We exist as members in organizational peer groups: in Top Executive groups, Middle Management and Staff groups, and Bottom groups. We also bring our personal bias to our group relationships, to our affinities and antipathies. When things go wrong in our groups, our tendency is to explain these difficulties in terms of personal issues: there is something wrong with you or me, or maybe we are just an unfortunate mix. And when our diagnoses are personal, so also are our usual remedies: fix, fire, rotate, separate, divorce, or recommend coaching or therapy for one or more parties.

In fact, many of the peer group breakdowns that occur are not personal at all; they become personal, but their roots lie in context blindness.

Principle 3: When We Are Blind to Our Peer Group's Context

Principle 3: When we are blind to the contexts in which our peer groups are functioning, we are vulnerable to falling into dysfunctional scenarios that cause us personal stress, weaken if not end our relationships with our peers, and detract from the contributions our peer groups could be making to the system:

• *Territorial Tops.* Members of Top peer groups may see themselves as just people with a job to do, but they are more than that; they are a group existing in a context of complexity and accountability (Figure 8.5).

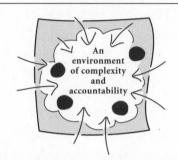

**Figure 8.5
Four Persons in a Top
Context**

Without awareness and mastery of that context, they are vulnerable to falling into dysfunctional territoriality. The process goes something like this. As members of Top teams, we reflexively adapt to the complexity and accountability of our context by differentiating, with each of us handling our own areas of responsibility. Differentiation is an essential process; without it, we would not be able to cope with the complexity and responsibility of our situation. But then a familiar process unfolds; we harden in our differentiations. Differentiations become territories. Each of us becomes increasingly knowledgeable and responsible for our area and decreasingly knowledgeable and responsible for others' areas. We develop a "mine" mentality. We become protective and defensive of our territory. And we face uncertainties about the form and future of the system: *What kind of culture do we want to create? Do we want to expand in new directions or stick to our knitting? Are we going to take financial risks or play it cautiously?*

These are complex questions with no textbook answers, yet we gradually polarize around fixed positions: the Riskers versus the Cautionaries; the Loose/Democratic System Builders versus the Bureaucratic/Authoritarian System Builders. Relationships fray. There are issues about who are the really important members of this team. Members feel they are not respected for their contributions. There are feelings about who is holding up their piece of the action. There are battles for control. Silos develop, sending mixed, confusing messages down through the system. There is redundant building up of resources in the silos; potential synergies across silos are blocked. Tensions among the Tops are high, and it all feels so personal.

• *Fractionated Middles.* Middle peer groups, whether first-line supervisors or middle managers or staff groups, may think of one another as just people and attribute their feelings about one another as simply reflections of one another's personality, temperament, motives, values, and such. But Middle peer groups exist in a tearing context, one that draws them away from one another and out toward those individuals they are to supervise, lead, manage, coach, or service (Figure 8.6).

Dispersing is an adaptive response to that tearing context; that is what Middles are hired to do. But in time, we harden in our separateness. We develop an "I" mentality in which our separateness from one another predominates; our competitiveness with one another intensifies, as does our tendency to evaluate one another on relative surface issues: emotionality, manner of speech, skin color, gender, clothes we wear, and such. This fractionation of Middles isolates them, leaving them unsupported, without a peer group, able to be surprised, and often feeling undercut by actions taken by other Middles. It leaves the system uncoordinated, and it works against potential synergies among Middles or any collective influence by Middles.

Figure 8.6
Four Persons in a Middle Context

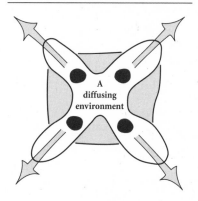

Figure 8.7
Four Persons in a Bottom Context

• *Conforming Bottoms.* Bottom peer groups exist in a context of shared vulnerability (Figure 8.7). The reflexive response is to coalesce. In coalescing, we feel (and, in fact, may be) less vulnerable. We develop a "we" mentality in which our differences are submerged and we feel connected to one another, supporting and being supported by one another. But then we harden in our we-ness—our closeness to one another and our separateness from all others, from "them." In our we-ness we become wary of all others, resistant to them, and at times antagonistic to them. In our we-ness, there is pressure from one another as well as self-inflicted pressure to maintain unity. Difference is experienced as threatening to the we, and those expressing difference are pressured to come back into line. Individual action is experienced as threatening to the we and is discouraged. The pressure toward conformity is intense. The cost to individuals is the suppression of their freedom and the opportunity to develop their individuality; the cost to the system is resistance to even the best-intentioned change initiatives and the suppression of energy that could be focused on system business.

Each of these scenarios results in stress for individual group members, causes the quality of their relationships to deteriorate, and diminishes the group's contribution to the overall system. And each of these scenarios is avoidable. Transformation becomes possible with context awareness and choice:

> *Leadership strategy 3:* Recognize the context your peer group is in; adapt to that context without allowing adaptation to harden into dysfunctionality. Develop your peer group into a Robust System, one that strengthens individual members, their relations with one another, and their contribution to the system.

Figure 8.8
A System
Differentiating

In order to develop powerful peer groups, we need to (1) understand the fundamental systemic processes underlying Robust Systems, that is, systems with outstanding capacities to survive and develop in their environments; (2) recognize how these processes are influenced by context in ways that can limit peer group effectiveness, and (3) master the processes. Any peer group—Top, Middle, or Bottom—can become a Robust System.

Figure 8.9
A System
Homogenizing

A Robust System differentiates, homogenizes, individuates, and integrates (see Figures 8.8 through 8.11). "Differentiates" refers to the fact that the system develops variety in form and function, thus enabling it to interact complexly with its environment. "Homogenizes" means developing processes for sharing information and capacity across the system. "Individuates" means encouraging individuals and groups to function separately and make independent forays into the environment, experimenting, testing, developing their potential. "Integrates" means enabling a process in which parts—individuals and

Figure 8.10
A System
Individuating

units—come together, share information, feed and support one another, and modulate one another's actions in the service of the whole.

Whether we see context or are blind to it, our groups will reflexively adapt. But some reflexive patterns of adaptation actually diminish peer group effectiveness by relying on certain processes while ignoring or suppressing others. When we see and understand context, we can strengthen our groups by bringing the ignored or suppressed processes back into the mix.

**Figure 8.11
A System
Integrating**

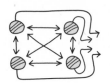

• *The formula for falling into Top Territoriality is differentiation and individuation without homogenization and integration.* For Top groups in the context of complexity and accountability, the reflexive response is to differentiate and individuate, that is, to develop a variety of forms and processes for coping with complexity *and* for the parts to function independently of one another in the pursuit of these separate strategies and approaches. Thus far, this is all to the good. It is when Top groups fail to balance differentiation and individuation with homogenization and integration that they fall into destructive territoriality. In light of this peril, how can leaders develop a robust Top peer group? The leadership challenge for Top groups is not to differentiate less but to homogenize and integrate more, to share high-quality information with one another, to spend time walking in one another's shoes, to work together on projects other than their specialized arenas, to function as mutual coaches to one another in which all Tops are committed to one another's success. Such forms of homogenizing and integrating activities serve to strengthen the group's capacity. The new formula for Top peer power becomes: *Homogenization and integration strengthen differentiation and integration.*

• *The formula for falling into Middle Alienation is individuation without integration.* For Middle groups in the tearing context, the reflexive response is to individuate: to separate and function independently as they supervise, manage, lead, coach, or otherwise service the groups they are charged with serving. This is an adaptive response to the tearing context. It is when individuation is not strengthened by integration that the fractionated pattern described previously develops. In light of this peril, how can leaders develop a robust middle peer group? The leadership challenge for Middle peers is not to individuate less but to integrate more: meet together regularly with just Middle peers, share information gleaned from across the system, use their shared intelligence to diagnose system issues, share best practices, solve problems, work collectively to create changes that individually they are unable to achieve. The new formula for Middle peer power becomes: *Integration strengthens individuation.*

• *The formula for falling into Bottom Conformity is homogenization and integration without individuation and differentiation.* For Bottom groups in the context of shared vulnerability, the reflexive response is to coalesce. Coalescence is a process in which unity is maintained by homogenizing (emphasizing commonality while suppressing differences that could divide) and integrating, that is, sharing resources and supporting one another in common cause. Coalescence is an adaptive response to shared vulnerability; it is when homogenization and integration are not balanced by individuation and differentiation that the groups fall into stifling and destructive conformity. So how to develop a robust Bottom peer group? The leadership challenge for Bottom peers is to strengthen themselves by encouraging differentiation (*Let's explore multiple approaches to coping with our vulnerability*) and individuation (*Go out there and see what unique contribution you can make*). Differentiation and individuation are not experienced as threats to unity as long as they are pursued with the goal of strengthening the we rather than weakening it. The formula of, *In unity there is strength,* is changed to, *In diversity there is strength.* In the language of group processes, the new formula for Bottom peer power becomes: *Individuation and differentiation strengthen homogenization and integration.*

Principle 4: Overcoming the Illusions of System Blindness

> *Principle 4:* Our consciousness—particularly how we experience others—is shaped by our relationship to them. Change the relationship, and we experience them quite differently.

One reaction to any of the group strategies described could be: Very interesting, but it won't work with my people. And why won't it work with your people? Well, it's because of their temperament, or needs, or motives, or level of maturity, and so forth. We find ourselves back into experiencing others through a personal rather than systemic lens. When Tops are in the "mine" mentality, Middles in the "I" mentality, and Bottoms in the "we" mentality, the feelings they have toward others feel solid, firmly grounded in the characteristics of these others. Simply a matter of who they are. And any notion that you might feel differently toward them feels far-fetched. Yet these solid, firmly grounded experiences are in fact the illusions of systemic blindness. Change the relationship, and the feelings change.

In the Power Lab experience (described at the end of the chapter), we demonstrate this illusion quite dramatically. A central feature of the program is a multiple-day intensive societal experience in which participants are randomly assigned to Top, Middle, and Bottom positions. With great regularity, Tops fall into territorial issues, Middles become alienated from one another, and Bottoms become a powerfully connected we. And all relationships seem firmly grounded in the reality of who the people are. Then there is a second experience in which all roles are shifted; the powerfully bonded Bottoms are now in different contexts: some as Tops, others as Middles, and others as Customers. And in short order, love is transformed into impatience, annoyance, competition, aggression. Previously territorial Tops and alienated Middles are now bonded Bottoms. They all experience the power of context. That can and should be a humbling experience.

There may be many roads leading to systemic understanding. As an educator, my favorite is this: I prefer to come to a system intentionally knowing nothing about it: reading no reports, interviewing no one. And then I give a talk on Top Teams and Middle Peer Relationships and Bottom Groupthink. The presentation is about context and how context shapes our experiences of ourselves and others, and the dysfunctional scenarios that can follow. The power comes when people identify themselves and their system in this pure abstraction. How does he know this about us? Clearly whatever is happening to us is not simply about us or our particular organization. Something else must be going on. And that questioning creates the opening for systemic understanding and intervention: for Tops to pay more attention to homogenizing and integrating activities, for Middles to regularly integrate with one another, and for Bottoms to strengthen themselves by building individuation and differentiation into their survival strategies. The challenge for all is to see, understand, and master systemic context.

SYSTEMS IN PRACTICE: THE CASE OF THE RIGID MANAGER

The following case illustrates the people-in-context ideas I've described in this chapter, and it also supports what could be regarded as a fifth principle toward developing system insight:

> *Principle 5:* Seeing people opens up deep but potentially limited personal interventions; seeing context opens up comprehensive systemic interventions.

A change intervention that has been successful in division A of Ace Manufacturing is being introduced into division B with the help of a team of consultants. One snag is that B's division head is less than enthusiastic about the project. *Our department managers are having enough trouble keeping up with day-to-day demands without dealing with the complexity of a whole new initiative.* Still, the initiative has been introduced, and five of the six department managers seem invested in making it work despite its apparent difficulties. Charles, the sixth manager, has been ignoring the initiative. To him, it is as if it doesn't exist. Charles is clear about his boss's priorities, and his boss's priorities are *Charles's* priorities.

The consultants have attempted to work with Charles, with little success. They interpret Charles's apparent resistance from a personal developmental framework: seeing him as being stuck at a developmental level at which he is unable to separate himself from the demands of authority. If Charles and the initiative are to be successful, Charles needs to be helped to move through that stage of development and acquire greater independence.

Meanwhile, the other department managers, each operating independently of the others, are grappling with both the requirements of the new change initiative and the continuing demands of the division head, who is increasingly unhappy with them. They have been lax on their paperwork, reports not being timely or thorough, and there have been too many complaints from people in their operations. None of this is a problem for Charles. His paperwork is fine, his reports are timely and thorough, and as far as the division head is concerned, Charles's operation is running smoothly.

Charles may in fact be stuck at this level of development, and it could be useful to help him move through that stage. But a richer understanding of this situation with more powerful intervention possibilities emerges when observed through a systems lens.

A Systemic Picture

Charles, with his apparent inability to separate himself from authority, is but one piece of a total system scenario involving the relations between and among the division head (Top) and the department managers (Middles). A deeper understanding of this situation and a more global intervention strategy emerges when we take into account the contexts in which people are functioning:

- *Top context: Complexity and accountability.* To the division head, this new initiative is being experienced as another complication in an already complex world. This feeling is reinforced by the lax reports from department managers and the complaints coming from their groups. Progress on the change initiative seems incoherent. The division head receives very different reports.

- *Middle context: Tearing.* Charles is not the only Middle torn between the requirements of the new initiative and the day-to-day demands of the job. Department managers are coping with the tearing in different ways. Charles reduces the tearing by aligning up; the division head's priorities are his priorities. The division head has no problem with Charles, but the consultants do because Charles's priorities are not their priorities. Meanwhile, the other department managers are coping with the tearing differently. Some are aligning with the consultants' priorities; the consultants are pleased with their efforts, but the division head is not. Others are attempting to please everyone with limited success.

- *Middle peer group context: Tearing.* Each department manager faces this tearing alone. There is no Middle peer group with a coherent strategy for handling their tearing and implementing (or agreeing not to implement) the change initiative.

A Systemic Intervention

The key leverage point is the Middle peer group. Currently there is no Middle group with an independent perspective on the current situation or a coherent strategy for dealing with it. Middles, being in their independent, separate "I" mentalities, do not experience the need or potential for collective power in their group. In fact, their competitiveness with and evaluations of one another, all consequences of the "I" mentality, support their *not* working collectively.

A first step in a systemic intervention is to develop system knowledge: education regarding context. Rather than approaching the situation head-on, a conceptual presentation or simulation would be aimed at illuminating context, primarily the Middle context and the challenges that context raises for individual Middles and the Middle peer group. The goal is for the abstract to illuminate the concrete current situation: why people are feeling the way they do and how the development of a powerful, independent Middle peer group can fundamentally transform the situation. Then it is up to department managers to work on developing such a group—one that meets regularly, in which members share information about what's working for them and what's not. They support one another, coach one another, and, most important, develop an agreed-on strategy for handling the change initiative.

If Middles are successful in that effort, a number of problems are resolved. The complexity of the Top (division head) is reduced; he is receiving more consistent information from his Middles, and the change initiative appears to being managed more uniformly. Individual Middles are less torn, alone, weak, unsupported; all Middles feel part of a powerful and effective peer group; the change initiative is pursued more consistently. And, one would hope, this change initiative, when implemented effectively, will have a positive effect on the lives of all system members. From this persons-in-context framework, the focus is less on "fixing" any one person than on helping all parties see, understand, and master the systemic contexts they are in.

IMPLICATIONS FOR LEADERSHIP DEVELOPMENT

Seeing context is an unnatural act. We do not see others' contexts; all we see directly are their actions or inactions. Nor do we see our own contexts; what we see and feel are specific events, actions, and conditions. So the challenge is how to educate leaders regarding context.

Conceptual Presentations

This chapter is one example of education in context. Leaders, like everyone else, welcome the opportunity to organize what appear to be random, chaotic phenomena into actionable abstractions—finding the simplicity in complexity. This framework of Top, Middle, Bottom, Customer does that. It resonates with leaders' day-to-day experiences; they can readily see themselves as moving in and out of these contexts; and those with at least minimal self-awareness can recognize the lure of the disempowering reflex responses. Along with awareness, the framework offers clear choice: alternative strategies for empowering self, others, relationships, and systems. In this sense, this is a teachable framework, whether through chapters and articles such as this, presentations, case studies, animations, theatrical dramatizations, or other media.

Executive Coaching

One-on-one coaching can be an important tool of education in context. This, of course, requires that coaches have a deep grasp of context first in their own lives and then in their ability to see it operating in others. The coach can help the leader take into account the context of others. What is their world like? What are they wrestling with? How are they likely to experience this initiative of yours? And what can you do to ease their condition in a way that makes it possible for them to do what you and the system need them to do? A coach can help leaders be aware of their own context and the choices available to them. *Are you unnecessarily sucking responsibility for this up to yourself and away from others? What are the consequences of doing or not doing that? Are you sliding in between others' issues? What are the consequences of your doing or not doing that?* The coach's job is not only to help create awareness and choice in the moment, but also to educate leaders such that context consciousness becomes a regular component of their analytical framework.

Experiential Education

Well-designed organization simulations enable leaders to experience directly the consequences of context blindness and the possibilities that come with seeing, understanding, and mastering context. There is a difference between knowing these concepts intellectually and experiencing them directly in the heat of action. In a stroke of synchronicity, as I was writing this chapter, I received an e-mail from an Organization Workshop trainer who had just completed a workshop with the executives of his organization. He wrote: "The best part of it was [that] the group has had a lot of prior exposure to [the concepts of] choice and responsibility. So this was for them a fantastic example of how the theory of choice/responsibility isn't as easy as it sounds." Experiential education can provide this kind of humbling experience that sets the stage for real knowing.

CONCLUSION

A missing leadership ingredient is the ability to see, understand, and master the systemic contexts in which we and others exist. In our person-centered orientation, we tend to be blind to context, and that blindness is costly.

When we are blind to others' contexts, we misunderstand them, have little empathy for the challenges they are facing, misinterpret their actions, react inappropriately to them, and fall out of the potential for partnership with them. When we are blind to the contexts we are in, we are vulnerable to falling into patterns that are dysfunctional for ourselves and our systems as burdened Tops, torn Middles, oppressed Bottoms, and screwed Customers. And when we are blind to our groups' contexts, we are vulnerable to falling into the dysfunctional patterns of Top territoriality, Middle alienation, and Bottom groupthink.

With system sight, all of these dysfunctions can be avoided; we are able to interact more sensitively and strategically with others who are Tops, Middles, Bottoms, and Customers; we are able to create more thoughtful, creative, and productive responses when we are Top, Middle, Bottom, and Customer; and we are able to create peer groups whose members value and support one another and who collectively make powerful contributions to their systems.

All of this can be taught—just as we know that the earth revolves around the sun even though our direct experience is the other way around. The other day, I heard my young grandson describing how the other kids in class were grousing about something their teacher had done. He said, "Don't they get it? She's just a Middle." So maybe early education would be a productive path to develop.

APPENDIX: ABOUT THE POWER LAB
AND THE ORGANIZATIONAL WORKSHOP

These immersion experiences for leaders are essential to the work of developing people-in-context ideas expressed in this chapter.

The Power Lab

The Power Lab, a total immersion experience, has been one of my main windows into systems. Devised to help leaders to deepen their knowledge, it has helped me deepen my own understanding of system phenomena.

A key feature of each Power Lab is The Society of New Hope, a three-class social system with sharp differences in wealth and power. Participants are randomly assigned to their class. The Elite (Tops) own or control all of the society's resources—among them its bank, housing, food supply, court system, newspaper, and labor opportunities. At the other end are the Immigrants (Bottoms), who enter the society with little more than the clothes on their backs. Housing, meals, and supplies are available to them only if they sign up for work (mostly low-wage physical labor) that enables them to make purchases. And between the Elite and the Immigrants are the Managers (Middles), who enjoy middle-class amenities so long as they continue to manage the institutions of the Elite to the satisfaction of the Elite. This is a total immersion experience in that there are no breaks from the experience from the moment it begins to its end. This is not a role play; there are no instructions as to how people are to handle their situations. It is more like a life-within-life: *These are the conditions into which you are born; deal with these conditions, and learn from them.*

My role in many Power Labs was to function as an anthropologist—the name assigned to staff members whose job it was to capture the society's history as it unfolded and, once the society ended, to report on that history in ways that enabled participants to see the entirety of the experience, not just the part they played. Anthropologists get the rare opportunity to see whole systems. By agreement with participants, I had access to all deliberations within and across class lines. This view from the outside allowed me to observe the regularly recurring patterns described in this chapter: the territoriality that developed at the top, the fractionation in the middle, the conforming cohesiveness at the bottom. This view from the outside also enabled me to see and describe the different contexts out of which these patterns emerged: the complexity at the top, the tearing in the middle, and the shared vulnerability at the bottom.

When each societal experience ended, participants shared in an intensive debriefing session what I could not see from my outside perspective: their experiences, thoughts, and feelings as they struggled to deal with their contexts. It was out of these conversations that I began to grasp the uniquely different forms of consciousness that developed in each context: the "mine" mentality at the top, the "I" in the middle, and the "we" at the bottom.

The Organization Workshop

The Organization Workshop experience has two functions: to educate participants about organizational life and to continue my education in systems. Unlike Power Lab, which lasts for several days, the Organization Workshop lasts only a few hours. An organization is created composed of groups of Tops, Middles, and Bottoms; outside the organization are customers and potential customers with projects for the organization to work on and funds to pay for service. Participants are randomly assigned to positions; there are no instructions on how to play one's position. The conditions are created, and participants adapt as best as they can.

While developing the Organization Workshop, I had a significant insight. For a long time, I felt responsible for helping people understand what happened over the life of the organization. (I was feeling very Top and sucking all responsibility up to myself!) I would take my yellow pad in hand and run from place to place trying to observe and make sense of events. But the action was fast-moving, and there was no way I could capture the story in this setting. Then came the insight: "TOOT" (Time Out Of Time). During TOOT, organization action stops and members in each part of the system describe what life is like for them in their context: the issues they are dealing with, the feelings they are experiencing, the nature of their peer group relationships. TOOT has a powerful simplicity. It requires only that participants listen so that they might understand the contexts in which others are living and then consider the implications that knowing has for how they feel toward each other and how they choose to interact (Oshry, 2007).

Leading Inclusively

Mind-Sets, Skills, and Actions for a Diverse, Complex World

Ilene C. Wasserman
Stacy Blake-Beard

Engaging diversity is a key leadership competency in the rapidly changing global environment. Engaging diversity requires the capacity for dealing with complexity and the capacity to be self-reflective: the ability to observe oneself (take a third-person perspective) while engaging with others (from a first-person perspective). This chapter provides frameworks and tools that will help managers imagine how to lead effectively in ways that are inclusive of others and create a greater impact.

Ambiguity, uncertainty, and interdependence characterize contemporary organizations. Leaders working in this environment sense a difference between technical problems and adaptive challenges (Heifetz, 1994; Heifetz and Linsky, 2002; Heifetz, Linsky, and Grashow, 2009). Leading inclusively clearly requires the capacity to meet continuous adaptive challenges. Technical problems call for expertise. Adaptive challenges, however, involve situations where there is no clear answer and thus require flexibility and agility. (In Chapter Ten, Santana, Las Heras, and Mao suggest that leaders use cultural intelligence as a way to adapt to these challenges and to deal with diverse perspectives.)

This chapter offers leaders an approach to strengthen their capacity to lead inclusively. Leaders begin this process by noticing how they know what they know, then expanding the possibilities for sense making, and, as a consequence, increasing their repertoire for being present in their interactions with others. To set the stage for this process, we begin with a review of the evolution of diversity and inclusion as a discourse in organizations, because how the conversation frames these issues has guided the approaches leaders have adopted. We then speak to the current discourse on diversity as encompassing a widening breadth and increasing depth of issues, in that global diversity calls for leaders to manage complex dynamics in relationship with others and among diverse teams and external stakeholders. We conclude by posing questions that leaders can ask themselves to promote their capacity to lead inclusively and develop ways of knowing, being and doing that better help them lead in this way.

THE CHANGING CONVERSATION

The terms *diversity* and *inclusion* began to permeate our language at the workplace in the latter part of the twentieth century. Each decade from about the 1960s on can be read as a turn in the social conversation and a related shift in the competencies articulated as necessary to foster inclusive cultures in organizations. These progressive turns created a path of incremental progress.

The roots of some of the conversations about diversity sprouted in the 1960s during the civil rights movement and the passing of equal employment opportunity and affirmative action legislation in the United States. Among other things, those actions sought to bring men and women of color and white women into corporations and other places where they had been traditionally underrepresented in numbers and positions of leadership. At that time, the focus of the organizational discourse was "fit in." Business-oriented programs addressed how people should dress and advised them on their speech patterns.

In the 1970s, the discourse on diversity turned toward awareness or sensitivity encounters aimed at exploring and explaining the cultural histories that marginalized groups brought to their relationships at work. Businesses often structured these development opportunities as retreats. In the 1980s, the framing of development initiatives expanded to include a wider definition of *diversity*, including ethnicity, nationality, physical ability, religion, and sexual orientation. In the 1990s, proponents of diversity argued for the importance of using the business case approach to learning (Kwak, 2003). In the twenty-first century, the discourse has broadened to include global diversity. The framing of diversity includes personal behavioral and cognitive styles, social and cultural identity, and global dimensions as they relate to the success of organizations and a connect to how leaders do their work.

Over time, the terms *diversity* and *inclusion* have come together in the general discourse. This linking demonstrates a turn in the dialogue that accommodates a view of inclusion as expanding the approach to diversity. For some speakers, using *inclusion* broadens the discourse from just race and gender to other identity groups. For others speakers, *inclusion* addressed concerns that the term *diversity* is laden with so much baggage that it invokes "diversity fatigue." The use of *inclusion* in the conversation about diversity signals a move away from the negative imagery that is often associated with *diversity*. That move acknowledges that diversity and inclusion are more than affirmative action initiatives, more than justification for the business case; they are essential to learning and development within organizations (Kochan et al., 2003; Thomas, 2004; Thomas and Ely, 1996). Based on understanding these approaches, contemporary development initiatives related to workplace diversity include how social and cultural identity affect social relations, work behaviors, and the distribution of professional opportunities in organizations. Initiatives also focus on the way in which social identity shapes perspectives, experiences, and values and how organizations can fully use these differences.

The challenges of working across dimensions of differences demand an adaptive skill set. In this chapter, we discuss the attentive mind-set required to capture opportunities from difference (know), the skills needed to translate that knowledge into practice (be), and the active integration of knowledge and practice required to shepherd organizations through times of change (do).

The motto "Be, Know, Do" was popularized in the book *Be Know Do: Leadership the Army Way* (Hesselbein, Shinseki, and Cavanagh, 2004). Many learning and development models advocate a specific ordering of these particular processes. Frances Hesselbein and her coauthors suggest that the U.S. Army leads with "be" since authenticity comes first. (See Chapter Six for an interview with Hesselbein on the subject of authenticity and other issues.) The Old Testament suggests a different approach: *na'aseh v'nishma*, or, "We will do and we will hear/understand." In the discussion that follows, we suggest that doing, being, and knowing comprise a virtuous cycle of development.

THE INCLUSIVE LEADERSHIP MIND-SET

We all develop an automatic way of engaging with others. These habituated ways of responding to others, however, can prevent us from noticing ways in which others' styles, approaches, forms of expression, and ways of knowing may be different. In some cases, we might feel uneasy or uncomfortable when we encounter such differences and not quite know why. Or we may notice and feel confused. Or we might not even notice, which has the effect of making others invisible to us. Mezirow (2003) suggests that these moments are opportunities to pause, reflect, and challenge our habits of mind and action by not only challenging what we know but how we know what we know. Focused reflection can open the door to novel ways of being, thinking, and engaging.

Given the complexity of daily organizational lives, it is likely that managers often encounter moments when they have to make a judgment call in the moment in response to competing demands. Consider the judgment call that the head nurse at a community hospital made when a man whose wife was in labor requested that no black employees assist in the delivery of his child. The nurse conceded to his request. In the complexity of that moment, her concern about the husband's temper took precedence over the hospital's stated policy: "Employees will be assigned to patient services without regard to race, creed, color, national origin or religion of either the patient or employee." In addition to going against policy, the nurse's decision did not serve the patient's health because the most capable and experienced provider for her particular situation was an African American nurse on duty at the time.

The identities, culture, experiences, and stories that emerge in such moments are complex, multifaceted, and fluid. People have multiple identities, and these identities intersect to create a complex and integrated identity (Nkomo and Cox, 1996). Frameworks that explore the interaction of multiple identities (Crenshaw, 1994; Okazawa-Rey and Kirk, 2007) can be useful for leaders in analyzing how the many dimensions of diversity play out in organizations. Armed with that understanding, leaders can begin to see how different social and cultural skills and competencies embedded in forms of knowing and enactments of power are mobilized and used in different circumstances and under different conditions (Styhre and Eriksson-Zetterquist, 2008). In the example of the head nurse, the pregnant woman, and the husband, the nurse's professional identity, rather than contexts of race, culture, gender, or other identities, would ordinarily form the overriding context for decisions. In her encounter with the husband, the nurse privileged race over professional credentials. Faced with an emotionally charged encounter, the nurse made a reactive decision based on a habit of mind (beliefs taken for granted; in this case, perhaps, the belief that avoiding a confrontation superseded the best standards of medical care) rather than reflection. Critical self-reflection in such moments opens the possibilities for transformative learning and leadership.

The head nurse's decision came to the attention of the hospital's leadership when the community protested the hospital's response, and the press reported the incident. The hospital's chief operating officer, Margaret, immediately responded to the press, saying that while the supervisors were trying to avoid a confrontation with the patient's husband, they were wrong to accommodate his demands. The hospital president called the decision to honor the request "morally reprehensible." Hospital administrators apologized to employees, formed a diversity task force, arranged for cultural sensitivity training, and revised hospital procedure to better advise in such episodes.

The hospital's leadership, with Margaret at the helm, took the community's protest as an invitation to look deeply at what the hospital's staff and leadership needed to learn to be more culturally sensitive and learn more about ways of making sense from difficult moments of difference that had been up until then, invisible. In order to expand the range of responses in future encounters, Margaret hired consultants to help the hospital look at its systems and processes, as well as facilitate a process of critical reflection on the staff's taken-for-granted mind-sets. Margaret recognized that sustained culture change required changing how people saw themselves in relationship with others.

Critical reflection with others is essential for transforming relationships, especially where there are deeply rooted stories about one another (Wasserman, 2004). This difference may stem from a different cultural narrative, different style, or significantly different life experiences. Reflecting with others not only helps us expand how we are making sense of the moment, but also helps us notice our meaning-making systems, our taken-for-granted lenses for knowing ourselves, with each other. Mezirow (2003) poses a question that speaks to why knowing by itself is not enough, asking how any of us can develop accurate and useful knowledge in a world that is changing so rapidly. As leaders navigate increasingly diverse contexts, they will need to be in touch with not only what they know but also how they represent their knowledge in the skills they bring to bear in different situations. Leaders need to have ways of knowing and methods to audit and revise their knowing when they encounter situations that require new frames. They need a set of skills to complement and enhance their knowing and to expand their capacity and flexibility for being.

INCLUSIVE SKILLS FOR LEADERS

Knowing, being, and doing are interrelated processes in a virtuous cycle. To know ourselves differently requires us to be different. We are different, in part, as a consequence of shifting how we know what we know. One such shift is toward relational leadership and away from command-and-control, charismatic, and other forms of the leader-follower dichotomy. Fletcher (see Chapter Five, this volume) describes relational leadership as a process of interacting that works in and through relationships to achieve instrumental outcomes and organizational goals. Research on leadership shows that a sense of self and authentic connection to others is a cornerstone to twenty-first century leadership (Bass, 1985; Bennis and Nanus, 1985; Burns, 1978; Kouzes and Posner, 2002). Activities of care, listening, the willingness to help, and the ability to understand provide the context for empowering the self and the other (Gilligan, 1982; Jordan, Kaplan, Miller, Stiver, and Surrey, 1991). As organizations become truly global, leaders need to learn how to strengthen their relationships with others who are different (in terms of race, gender, culture, geographical origin, first language, and other factors). The work on relational leadership offers constructive tools that can assist leaders in strengthening their repertoire of skills and their way of being (Fisher-Yoshida, Geller, and Wasserman, 2005; Fletcher, 1999).

The concept of self-in-relation is of particular relevance to being an inclusive leader. Self-in-relation theory (Miller and Stiver, 1997; Jordan et al., 1991) suggests that women thrive in situations where connections with others can be maintained and avoid situations that force them to separate themselves from significant others. Their being is in connection. The concept that our being is bound up with others transcends the research on women's relationships and is applicable across gender, ethnicity, nationality, and other dimensions of difference. Leaders are strengthened and are better able to steward their organizations if they are not only attuned to their own developmental challenges and strengths but also connected to how their experiences both affect and are affected by others.

Another way to examine this concept is by exploring the relationship between subject and object. Both bell hooks (1989) and Robert Kegan (1994, 2000) talk about a capacity for agility in moving between subject and object in relating with others. (Both theorists discuss the movement between subject and object at length in their work. We touch on only a bit of their writings here.) Kegan places the subject at the center of his framework; his theory offers a guide to the metamorphosis that occurs as the subject learns to look beyond herself to include the perspectives of others and understand her own stance in relation to others. hooks's cultural critique helps us see that leaders may emerge from groups some might consider oppressed (or low in positional power or hierarchical status) but who have valuable insights to offer through their stewardship. The distinction between hooks's and Kegan's work demonstrates what we can learn from the different position or standpoint of traditionally dominant and marginalized cultural groups.

From Kegan's perspective (1994, 2000), transformative learning happens not when someone changes behavior, emotional responses, and cognitive awareness, but when that person also changes the way that he or she knows the world and others (for a more in-depth discussion of Kegan's theory, see Chapter Three, this volume). Although we have been talking about the capacity to reflect on one's self in relationships, Kegan (2000) suggests that transformation requires leaders to have the capacity to step back, reflect on events that have transpired, and then make decisions about those events. Kegan frames this transformation or learning as the increasing capacity to distinguish subject (that which we take for granted as our way of being) from object (that which is separate and distinct and therefore more easily observable).

The part of Kegan's theory on which we are focused involves the flexibility and agility to move meaning making from subject to object. Kegan notes, "We *have* object; we *are* subject" (1994, p. 32). He suggests that the capacity for engaging the complexity that inclusive leadership demands is related to the ability to differentiate subject and object—to hold out our taken-for-granted ways of thinking and relating for our own observation.

As a feminist theorist, hooks urges leaders to move from object to subject. She talks about the capacity for movement between subject and object being tied to transformation. Her work focuses our attention on the phenomenon of how members of marginalized groups silence or tone down their voices and on the criticality of being self-authoring.

In the feminist literature, this movement from object to subject is interrelated with coming to voice from a place of silence. Those who have lived more on the margins might be more challenged by the act of giving voice. As hooks notes, "Speaking becomes both a way to engage in active self-transformation and a rite of passage where one moves from being object to being subject.... It is only as subjects that we can speak. As objects, we remain voiceless—our beings defined and interpreted by others" (1989, p. 12). Through hooks's work, we can see the importance of how a leader embodies the notion of voice. The lesson for being a relational leader is to invite voice in the silence. Lorde (1984) notes, "In the transformation of silence into language and action, it is vitally necessary for each one of us to establish or examine her function in that transformation and to recognize her role as vital within that transformation" (p. 43).

Leaders coming to voice is about more than the physical sound of speaking. Voice is about taking a stance, knowing oneself, and listening with respect to others' realities. It is the capacity of not discounting and dismissing alternative experiences. To solicit voice is to seek out perspectives that are different from your own.

As leaders move from subject to object, they understand that others may be on parallel journeys of object to subject. They should understand that sometimes they may be or may represent forces that silence or shut down alternative realities and that they and their organizations lose when such censoring happens. hooks sees the shift from object to subject as a platform from which leaders can use voice in a liberatory manner—not just in the service of their freedom but also as a way to provide an opening and a space for other voices that have traditionally been muted, drowned out, or silenced. hooks (1989) challenges leaders to take up a different stance of voice: "The struggle to end domination, the individual struggle to resist colonization, to move from object to subject, is expressed in the effort to establish the liberatory voice—their way of speaking that is no longer determined by one's status as object—as oppressed being. That way of speaking is characterized by opposition, by resistance. It demands that paradigms shift—that we learn to talk—to listen—to hear in a new way" (p. 15).

Leaders need to have the flexibility and agility to move between subject and object in order to deal effectively with issues of diversity and to lead inclusively. Both hooks and Kegan focus on enhancing flexibility in mindfully moving between subject and object as we relate to one other. Leaders situated in different positions of dominance (and subordinance) may approach self-in-relation differently. While we speak of Kegan being particularly attuned to the context when the subject is at the center and hooks speaking to context where the subject is on the fringes, both acknowledge that leadership is nuanced. The same leader can embody both—by being at the center and on the edge.

If we return to Margaret and the hospital, we might see her at times in a dominant position. Certainly her role as an executive-level officer in her organization provides a level of power and centrality in relation to others. Yet there may also be times when, as a woman, she finds herself on the edges of the power discourse. The concept of intersectionality, the idea that we comprise several important identity dimensions that are uniquely valuable and overlapping, illuminates the process of self-in-relation to others.

One of the most powerful ways that leaders can seek out alternative perspectives and increase their agility in moving between subject and object is by building diverse developmental networks. Higgins and Kram (2001) endorse the importance of creating a developmental network, which they define as "the set of people a protégé names as taking an active interest in and action to advance the protégé's career by providing developmental assistance" (p. 268). This group can be an invaluable source of support, providing feedback that enables leaders to hear different voices and consider alternative perspectives.

Blake-Beard focuses on the importance of one type of developmental relationship: mentoring. Mentoring partnerships have been identified as a powerful tool to enable the careers of those advancing through the ranks in organizations (Blake-Beard, in press; Blake-Beard, Murrell, and Thomas, 2007). Mentors support their protégés by providing career support, including exposure and visibility, sponsorship, coaching, protection, and challenging assignments. Mentors also provide psychosocial or emotional support to their protégés, including acceptance and confirmation, counseling, friendship, and role modeling (Kram, 1983). The focus in mentoring is often on what mentors (often in some type of leadership role) provide to potential leaders. But leaders acting as mentors also stand to gain. Mentoring relationships provide a mechanism for leaders to gain access to alternative perspectives and experiences. In light of shifting demographics, including an increasingly diverse workforce, globalization, and technological advances, the use of mentoring as a tool for leaders managing in times of change will become even more critical.

The importance of being able to facilitate the process of knowing in new ways is critical for leaders for several reasons. Leaders need increasing capacity to access not just their thoughts and reactions but to have the capacity to reflect on self-in-action (Schön, 1991). The capacity to reflect on self-in-action or in relationship develops a leader's relational agility. Our interdependence means that leaders need to shift their focus from themselves as creating and transmitting leadership to being a leader who invites, considers, and incorporates other perspectives and new ways of making meaning in relation to those perspectives. The capacity to move between subject and object facilitates the leader's ability to leverage differences (and the rich opportunities and challenges that diversity brings). Traversing levels from individual to systems, taking up voice, reflection on experience, and welcoming others through a network of diverse developmental relationships are all aspects of this skill of moving between subject and object. These are the essential ingredients for leading well in today's complex organizational reality.

LEADERSHIP TOOLS TO FOSTER INCLUSION

Being a relational leader who is mindful of inclusion requires agility in coordinating meaning and action with others. "Creating and maintaining an inclusive culture is a complex and ongoing process that requires continuous self-examination and thoughtful reflection by leaders and all members of the organization" (Wasserman, Gallegos, and Ferdman, 2008, p. 181). Specifically, leaders foster inclusion in four ways:

- Explicitly defining the boundaries and rules for acceptable behavior
- Creating the conditions for conversations to explore differences
- Modeling and communicating an understanding of and valuing of diversity
- Being authentic and using personal experiences strategically (Wasserman et al., 2008)

Each of these requires agility and flexibility in engaging others, particularly when people are making sense of situations in very different ways. To build agility and flexibility, we need tools and frameworks to support us. The coordinated management of meaning (CMM) is a practical theory that provides models and tools that guide us in coordinating and management meaning together (Pearce, 2004). Here, we introduce the basic models and tools of CMM as a guide for leaders in defining boundaries for acceptable behaviors, creating conditions to explore differences, modeling the valuing of diversity, and being authentic.

CMM guides us in looking at what we do in the ongoing turns and processes of our conversations, social encounters, and other communication events, and, consequentially, the ongoing process of meaning making. At the heart of the communication approach is the premise that we make sense in the process of communicating. Taking a communication approach means that we shift attention from the content (what you said and what I said, and what each of us intended), to the impact or the consequential meaning that is made in the patterns of our coordinating actions and managing meaning. These patterns include making "us–them" alliances, nurturance and support, and possibly even curiosity about historically rooted, deeply held differences. In our everyday interactions, some moments are more critical than others, and some choices of how we engage and what choices we make are more consequential than others. Those consequences come to light when we notice that while we intended to create a bond, another's response makes an offense. CMM guides us in seeing our role in creating the consequences of our communication, elevating our responsibility in relationships while mitigating blame.

The capacity for self-reflection, or looking at what we do and make in relationships with others, is a critical part of relational responsibility (McNamee and Gergen, 1999). Marsick (1990) suggests that we need to attend to the structures or mind-sets that serve as our guiding principles in order to develop deeper and broader understandings of ourselves, others, and the contexts we create. Martin Buber describes the possibilities we can create in relationships as a dialogic moment: "when one acknowledges and engages another with a willingness to put one's own story at risk, to suspend one's certainty, and to foster new meaning in the context of relationship" (quoted in Cissna and Anderson, 1998, p. 186).

Although there are many facets to CMM, our analysis of the tool in this chapter focuses on three models: the Serpentine Model, the Daisy Model, and the Hierarchy Model.

The Serpentine Model (Figure 9.1) looks at how we make sense within the boundaries of an episode. We can punctuate or frame an episode and look at how the next moment or how expanding the bracketing of an episode reshapes what

Figure 9.1
Serpentine Model

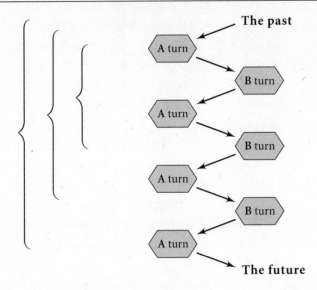

precedes it or comes after. The model is called the Serpentine Model because its description of turns takes on a serpent shape.

When the meaning we make with another person is coherent and coordinated, we feel in sync. When we are not making sense together, this model helps us look at how we might be bringing different pasts and futures to the moment. Consider the episode bounded by the situation of the head nurse and the husband in our hospital story. It is quite likely that the nurse did not know what story the husband was bringing to this episode and being influenced by. It is also likely that the husband did not know hospital protocol. Margaret held a broader view of the episode, contextualizing it in a commitment to high-quality medical care while protecting the respect of her staff. Her subsequent actions demonstrated her commitment to act toward a future when her staff would make different choices in a moment of pressure.

Our stories are based on influences we bring from our past experiences and the stories we inherit. CMM's Daisy Model depicts the particular voices or influences we bring forth to interpret or make sense of the episode. We each choose, with more or less self-awareness, what frames of reference we foreground in a particular episode. In the hospital case, the husband may have had a bad experience with someone of African American descent and felt that that his demands protected his wife in a time of vulnerability. Furthermore, he may have assumed that he had to make demands to get a response (see Figure 9.2). The nurse who made the judgment call was responding to the husband's emotional expression, foregrounding that over hospital policy. In making that decision and going against protocol, the nurse held a commitment to respond to the patient's needs (see Figure 9.3).

Figure 9.2
Daisy Model: Patient's Husband

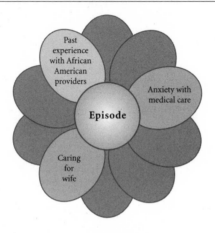

Figure 9.3
Daisy Model: Head Nurse

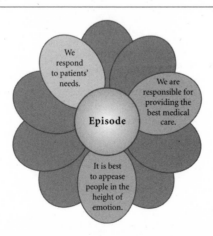

The meaning we make of any encounter is dependent on the context in which it occurs, and our encounters are always in multiple contexts. CMM's Hierarchy of Meaning model directs our attention to the levels of context we bring to the episode and the order in which we organize those contexts. Meaning can shift depending on what we rank as central, first, and foremost, and whether we are arranging different contexts in different levels of hierarchy than the other person whom we encounter.

Figure 9.4
Hierarchy of Meaning Model: Husband's Mental Model of the Situation

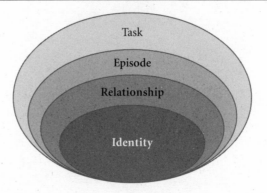

Figure 9.5
Hierarchy of Meaning Model: Nurse's Mental Model of the Situation

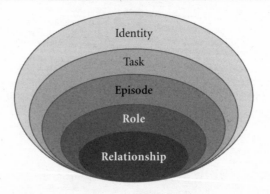

The husband (Figure 9.4) in the hospital story was making cultural identity (identity) more central to his choice of the nurse he wanted to provide medical care for his wife (relationship). The husband emphasized his prejudice toward African Americans. The nurse (Figure 9.5) who responded to the husband's request emphasized easing the husband's temper and avoiding a confrontation (relationship), and put less emphasis on choosing the best provider for his wife's care (role, episode, task). The hospital administration elevated the context of the hospital's policy protecting the treatment of and respect for its employees as well as quality of care.

Our narratives are always emerging in the moments of engagement with each other. Leaders must invite the conversations that foster the coordination and management of meaning, particularly in complex relationships. In so doing, they define the boundaries and rules for acceptable behavior that foster a culture of inclusion. Leaders must also create the conditions for conversations to explore differences, modeling an understanding of and relative comfort with diversity and being authentic.

Engaging diversity, particularly in our global environment, requires agility and flexibility in engaging others. We cannot take for granted that how we know is the same for others. Leaders create relational eloquence when they stay engaged and reflect together on moments where confusion, insults, or just plain discomfort arises, creating more robust narratives for what is possible (Wasserman, 2005). The tools of the CMM model help us move from acting our stories in opposition to one another to looking at our stories and articulating what meaning we are each making with them. We can then create a new, shared narrative for what meaning we want to make to foster an inclusive culture.

CONCLUSION

This chapter has emphasized the need for leaders to know, be, and do differently—to know how they know as well as what they know, to be aware of themselves and others as being both object and subject, and to work together to formulate a new, shared narrative. How do leaders acquire and hone these necessary dimensions? Throughout our discussion, we have suggested questions for leaders to ask themselves to promote their capacity to lead inclusively. In summary, leaders can ask themselves the following series of questions, based on the guideposts of knowing, being, and doing:

- How do you know? With whom do you surround yourself? Are your networks composed of individuals and groups representing people from perspectives and cultures that are different from your own? If not, what opportunities might you pursue to diversify your developmental networks and expand your taken-for-granted ways of knowing?

- What would others say about your being? How do you engage those around you? How might you explore opportunities to engage difference—to welcome the difficult conversations that, when authentically taken up, have the potential to enhance our work together? How do you invite feedback or critiques of your leadership? Do you welcome alternative views or seek out people who might experience themselves on the margins? How do you strengthen opportunities for leaders to engage a liberatory voice—one that acknowledges their own and others' realities?

- How do you enact inclusive leadership? How might you use the CMM tools to expand how you are making judgments and decisions? How might you notice the opportunities to shift from an image of being infallible (is next to impossible in a changing world) to modeling the acknowledgment of mistakes as opportunities for learning, developing, and expanding your approach?

The traditional skills that leaders have always needed are still necessary. But leaders also need to expand the stewardship of their organizations through different, inclusive approaches to knowing, being, and doing. The demands and challenges of the twenty-first-century organization require nothing less.

PART FOUR The Gap at the Institutional Level

Part Four turns toward the external environment for a perspective that may be missing most often in writings on leadership. Perhaps this view is missing because we often tend to think of leadership as focusing on the relationship between the leader and those who report to him or her. But the process of managing up or out is generally even more important than managing down. We have recruited authors with extensive personal experience, not just academic training, to help us navigate this territory.

This level of analysis is often called the *institutional level* because the players are generally representative of powerful institutional forces: government, labor, social movements, nongovernmental organizations, generational cohorts, consumer groups, religious groups, educational organizations, political action groups, and the like. These kinds of groups exert tremendous impact on organizations and the people who lead them.

The following chapters discuss four major external influences on the leader and the organization. First, we consider the world. As business has become more global, it has become increasingly important for leaders to be able to comprehend the complex cultural forces that are in play as national boundaries become more permeable. In particular, this puts a demand on leaders for greater cultural intelligence and its concomitant behavioral adaptability. Laura Santana, Mireia Las Heras, and Jina Mao introduce us to the concept of cultural intelligence and discuss ways that leaders can develop it. Like many other leadership qualities, this one is learned best through experience.

Trina Soske and Jay Conger make a persuasive case for a significant shift in current approaches to executive development. Specifically, they argue for a move away from the traditional focus of individual leader development and a move toward developing an organization's collective leadership capability. Such a shift requires changing the overall frame of executive development, the definition of leadership, and how development initiatives are designed, governed, measured, and implemented. (For an expanded treatment of this shift, its implications, and its practices, see Van Velsor, McCauley, and Ruderman, 2010.)

Another set of changes confronting leaders today in the external environment is the evolving requirements of customers and consumers, the new social environment with its myriad stakeholders, the physical environment and challenges of sustainability, and an ever-changing legal and ethical context. Guided by the wisdom and extensive practical experience of Peter Cairo and David Dotlich, we examine the ways that leaders seek to manage these forces over which they appear to have little control. The work here goes beyond the familiar issues of social responsibility and ethics. It involves being a social change agent, a political scientist, an inspirational figure, and even a bit of a fortune teller.

Finally, we consider the leader's "boss": the board of directors. What exactly is the appropriate role of the board, the point at which it is exerting oversight and fiduciary responsibility and not straying into areas that are management's prerogatives? Guided by Peter Browning, a seasoned CEO and turnaround artist, we hear about the different facets of the board's responsibility for selecting the right individual for a leadership position, the right person for a particular time and place. Once that person is in place, how can the board contribute to the development of the organization's internal talent without interfering? How does a board determine if it is time for a change? Because of the sensitive nature of the board's work, we rarely get to observe many of the backstage processes of the board, so this is a rare opportunity for readers to step behind the scenes.

In the final chapter, the editors synthesize the different perspectives that this book offers to its readers, and they look forward to the consequences of filling the gaps that open in the development trajectories of senior leaders. The practice of leadership takes on added complexity not only because the external environment demands it, but because the potential for any individual or group to rise to an ideal depends on internal, and perhaps eternal, challenges. The perspectives gathered in this book make some headway toward exploring the terrain surrounding those challenges. They emphasize the need to let go of old assumptions and to collaborate in building new understanding for leadership and learning.

Developing Leaders with Cultural Intelligence

Exploring the Cultural Dimension of Leadership

Laura Curnutt Santana
Mireia las Heras
Jina Mao

These times require leadership strategies for dealing with diversity and complexity in the context of cultural difference. Leaders who seek to be effective in working in this context understand that they need to learn how to best engage and capitalize on the diversity of perspectives that arise in teams and other groups in which various cultural viewpoints find their voice. Leaders need to be aware that cultural dimensions affect leaders and their performance; that awareness allows them to address missed opportunities in which people fail to develop critical relationships because of their culturally limited perspectives. This chapter offers two strategies, cultural training and border crossing, that promote cultural competence and intelligence and help managers fill this gap in their leadership capacity.

An international business owner creating a manufacturing division within the United States hired primarily immigrants from developing countries. All had experience working within the industry, and some had a university education. In an intentional strategy to develop his leadership pipeline, the owner empowered his experienced workforce to harness their ideas and create self-directed work teams. He encouraged them to take on leadership roles within their areas and establish efficient procedures.

His communication was met with varied reactions: blank stares, looks of fear, or heads nodding in agreement but apparently without understanding what was being asked. After some time without results, it was clear that the employees were not volunteering information and did not seem to assume responsibility or authority. Without structure, direction, or instruction, they had no idea how to function even though each was highly skilled at his or her craft. Without intervention from a higher level, teamwork did not happen. The company was eventually successful at creating an effective work environment, but only after cultural paradigms were identified and the parties engaged in dialogue about how to work together. The dialogue surfaced cultural assumptions that are often invisible. The owner leader had initially missed an important cultural aspect of working across difference—a cultural intelligence.

ADDING THE CULTURAL INGREDIENT

Our viewpoint in this chapter complements the thinking reflected in this book's other chapters and offers an additional layer to each discussion—a cultural dimension. Our contribution is informed by decades of working with leaders and leader development initiatives across many countries and languages. We have each crossed borders, working and living as expatriates. Collectively we have lived in China, Spain, France, Mexico, and the United States, and we have worked in Europe, Asia, the Middle East, South America, and North America. As reflective practitioners crossing cultures, we often find that being effective requires standing outside our own paradigms and beliefs in order to entertain different perspectives and value diverse viewpoints. Many leaders with whom we have worked felt they were increasingly effective by doing the same. Our chapter offers suggestions to individuals, providers of leadership development initiatives, and systems and organizations whose intentional organizational strategies for the leadership pipeline may be informed by the cultural ingredient.

The shifting trends of workplace demographics indicate that working across values, worldviews, and cultures is increasingly critical for those who assume the role of leader in times of more inclusive and relational leadership. Our discussion begins by noting those trends and positioning cultural intelligence as a framework to examine development for leaders who do not want to miss this cultural ingredient. We then present an array of ideas that individuals and organizations may use strategically for development and leadership effectiveness. We separate these ideas into two main categories: cultural awareness training and border crossing.

We believe that leadership has individual and collective aspects; here, we mostly address the individual, with a full understanding that these ideas can also be applied to collectives (see, for example, Chapter Eleven).

SHIFTING TRENDS: WHAT LEADERS COULD BE MISSING

Over the past two decades, workplace demographics and the values people place on their work have changed remarkably throughout the world. The workplace has become more diversified, with an increase of highly educated women, minorities, and immigrants who bring their own sets of values (Ruderman and Ohlott, 2004; Mainiero and Sullivan, 2006). The newer generation of the labor force also brings its unique values to work. Younger workers give as much importance to work as to family (Moen and Roehling, 2005), and they pay more attention to global issues such as environmental concerns and social justice.

Whether leading within one's own culture or across geographies, effective leadership requires the ability to deal with the diversity of perspectives that people bring to their work and their world (McCauley, Drath, Palus, O'Connor, and Baker, 2006). Leaders need to interact in an increasingly complex work environment where decision making is often distributed in virtual work teams in a highly heterogeneous environment. These shifts call for more collaborative relationships (Criswell and Martin, 2007). U.S.-centric paradigms about leadership, which emphasize heroism by one individual, need to be complemented with paradigms of leadership as an inclusive, collective, relational, and social practice (see Chapter Five). All of these changes require leaders to develop more complex

Table 10.1
Factors That Increase the Need for Leaders to Work Effectively with Culturally Diverse Groups

Increasing number of highly educated women in the workforce	Women tend to make up 50 percent of college graduates and bring different values than men do to the workforce (Ruderman and Ohlott, 2004; Mainiero and Sullivan, 2006).
Generation Y entering the workforce with values that are substantially different from those of previous generations	Generation Y brings new relational skills, more altruistic values, and increasing technology savvy to the workplace, and leadership needs to capitalize on their contributions (Alexandre-Bailly and Delay, 2006).
A diversified consumer base	Requires a matching workforce that understands diverse needs, values, and preferences (Thomas, 2004).
A diversified workforce resulting from immigration	Necessitates integrating people from diverse cultural backgrounds to guarantee the best talent working together (Bordas, 2007).
Business globalization	Implies working across boundaries even when people do not travel and working for clients in other regions (Hewlett and Luce, 2006).

understanding of human dynamics such as motivation, needs, and relationships under differing cultural norms and assumptions.

Leaders today face complex challenges for which no preexisting solutions or expertise exist (see Table 10.1 for a summary). Heifetz (1994) suggests that "we should be calling for leadership that will challenge us to face problems for which there are no simple, painless solutions—problems that require us to learn new ways" (p. 2). To do so, leaders need to understand what people from different constituencies bring to the workplace. They need to create spaces in which people feel valued and motivated to contribute.

Are future leaders ready to address the diversity they will face in their career progression? Whether coping with diversity of styles within one's social identity group or within an expatriate assignment, who will be effective and successful as a leader? What will the owner of a small business need to be effective at in order to understand the attitudes and values of his employees with diverse backgrounds? Will John, the U.S. home-schooled technology-savvy youth, find that his Facebook and Second Life experience has prepared him to interact face-to-face with people in the office? Can Hans, a Dutch compliance officer, be effective as he leads the company's team in Brazil? Will Mai-Tuan, a Chinese woman working for the multinational company, be able to get six people from different nationalities to work efficiently together on her geographically dispersed team? How can developmental assignments for a French man—working for an American firm in West Africa—help him understand the needs of the team that drives business results and then communicate that back to the home office?

We know that leadership deals with diversity in the workplace, the task of leadership is more complex than before, and leadership is increasingly relational and inclusive. To deal with diverse perspectives, leaders must have more than just information. They must develop cultural intelligence: an overall perspective and repertoire that results in the ability to function effectively across cultures, whether they are national, ethnic, or organizational (Van Dyne, Ang, and Livermore, in press). Development is critical (also see Chapters Three and Five).

Leadership is a source of competitive advantage (Day, 2000). In what ways can we accelerate the development of individuals and collectives for leadership that transcends and capitalizes on difference? To answer this question, we introduce the concept of cultural intelligence into our discussion of the challenges that today's leaders face, in addition to ways in which leaders can overcome these challenges. We start by explaining what we mean by *culture* and what culture means to leadership.

WHAT IS CULTURE, AND WHY DOES IT MATTER TO LEADERSHIP?

People develop, grow, and live within societies that develop different assumptions, beliefs, and rituals over the years as a result of diverse religious beliefs, legal and economic systems, and social structure, among other factors. Those may be within the boundaries of nations, companies, and occupational or professional groups. Culture can be thought of in terms of immediate surroundings (family, company, or organization) or increasing scope (region, nation, or world). One of the most prominent researchers on culture, Shalom Schwartz (2006), defines culture as a "rich complex of meanings, beliefs, practices, symbols, norms and values prevalent among people in a society" (p. 3). Cultural values emphasize, shape, and justify "individual and group beliefs, actions, and goals" (p. 3), whether those belong to an organization's culture or a country's culture. According to Schein

(1985), culture exists simultaneously on three levels: on the surface, there are artifacts; underneath artifacts lie values; and at the core are basic assumptions. Assumptions represent taken-for-granted beliefs about reality and human nature. Values are social principles, philosophies, goals, and standards considered to have intrinsic worth. Artifacts are the visible, tangible, and audible results of activity grounded in values and assumptions. In Schein's words, culture is "the pattern of basic assumptions that a given group has invented, discovered, or developed in learning to cope with its problems of external adaptation and internal integration, and that have worked well enough to be considered valid, and, therefore, to be taught to new members as the correct way to perceive, think, and feel in relation to these problems" (p. 9).

Three Dimensions of Culture

According to Schwartz (2004), there are six cultural-level values that can be presented as three bipolar dimensions: autonomy versus embeddedness, hierarchy versus egalitarianism, and mastery versus harmony.

Autonomy Versus Embeddedness   Autonomy emphasizes freedom to pursue one's own ideas, independence, and affectively positive experience, while the other end of the continuum, embeddedness, describes a value set centered on framing life in a collective context in which people identify with the group and a shared way of life. This value type emphasizes the status quo and opposes action that would disrupt the traditional order (Schwartz, 2004). Here is where it has become interesting for leading across differences: generally the United States is considered a culture in which people strive for autonomy, in contrast to Asian Confucian countries that are very high in embeddedness.

When people from two sides of the same continuum work together, unique challenges can arise. For example, Alvaro, a Mexican executive, had to coach his colleague Dave, from the United States, who was an expatriate in Mexico City, about how to reward his sales team. Alvaro had to explain that contrary to what Dave thought, salespeople would be very happy being awarded with the company's traditional "130 trip." The 130 trip was an award given to the members of a team that as a whole had performed above 130 percent of the annual goals. The team members were invited, together with their partners, to spend a three-day weekend in Cancun, a Mexican beach resort. Several teams would participate in the same weekend, and the pictures would later appear on the organization's intranet site. Dave had thought that each person would prefer to spend the money as he or she wished, and he was skeptical of the idea that people would like to be rewarded for team achievements rather than for personal ones. Only after he experienced one of the 130 trips himself did he realize what it meant for each person of the team: a recognition before their spouses, a time for sharing with other high-performance team members, and external recognition in front of other company sales teams.

Hierarchy Versus Egalitarianism   Hierarchy corresponds to ascribed roles and obligations and is the opposite of egalitarianism, which views people as being on equal footing and cooperation, based on a voluntary ground. For example, U.S. managers often find that a participatory management style does not work well in China. Chinese workers are much less willing to challenge authority or speak their mind than American workers are. This reflects the respect people pay to established structure and roles within a culture that values hierarchy.

Mastery Versus Harmony   The cultural values of mastery are characterized by assertive attempts to change the environment when such action is seen as contributing to positive individual or group outcomes. In contrast, cultures that stress harmony emphasize that it is more important to fit into the world as it is rather than try to change it (Briscoe et al., 2007). The unwillingness of Chinese workers to speak their mind in formal meetings also reflects the desire for agreement and collaboration, and they will do everything possible to avoid conspicuous conflict.

As an example, consider how Betty, an Australian manager recently deployed in China, had trouble understanding what her colleague Wai-teen was telling her after a meeting. Betty assumed that the lack of interventions during the meeting to approve the following year budget meant that people were in agreement with her. She assumed such silence meant that they had understood that the new budget made more sense within the current economic situation and with new products out in the market. However, Wai-teen was confident that most of the people who attended the meeting were very angry, since Betty had changed the budget substantially and some of them would probably have trouble achieving their goals after the changes. Betty wondered why they did not express their anger or ask questions. A couple of days later, Betty got the first sign that Wai-teen was right. One of her managers resigned, saying that for family reasons, he had accepted an offer from another company. Wai-teen explained to Betty that Chinese people often showed respect to superiors by not challenging them, not asking questions, and not complaining overtly. Those manifestations, which in some countries could be understood as a sign of agreement, may not be understood in the same way in other countries. The Chinese employees' education had emphasized the importance of respect to those in a higher position, especially in school, in the family, and at work.

The Dimensions and Cultural Regions

Using the three bipolar dimensions, Schwartz (2006) compartmentalizes similar country cultures into seven similar cultural regions: Confucian Asia, Eastern Europe, English speaking, Latin America, Southeast Asia, Sub-Saharan Africa/Middle East, and Western Europe. Israel represents a unique combination that is not replicated in other regions. Table 10.2 summarizes Schwartz's findings on regional variation in cultural values. We present the summary as a guideline for understanding and engaging in meaningful dialogue, not as a portrayal that reduces human beings to one variable of culture.

Table 10.2
Dominant Cultural Dimensions in Seven World Regions

	Autonomy	Embedded-ness	Mastery	Harmony	Egalitarian-ism	Hierarchy
English speaking	High	Low	High	Low	Low	Average
Western Europe	High	Low	Low	High	High	Low
Eastern Europe	Varies	Average	Varies	Varies	Varies	Average
Confucian Asia	Varies	High	High	Low	Low	High
South Asia	Low	High	Varies	Varies	Low	High
Africa/ Middle East	Varies	High	Varies	Varies	Low	Varies
Latin America	Average	Average	Average	Average	Average	Average

Sources: Prepared by Briscoe et al. (2007), and based on Schwartz (2004, 2006). Used with permission.

People from different backgrounds bring different values to work. The challenge for leaders lies in the fact that culture is rooted in basic assumptions, which leaders may not recognize because assumptions are taken for granted. Leaders need to be adept at reading cues, understanding behaviors, and drawing inferences. Assumptions are ingrained in decision making and communication processes, and they affect outcomes that leaders depend on. Understanding those assumptions is particularly crucial when leaders collaborate with people who potentially hold assumptions different from their own. The effectiveness of leaders who deal with diverse groups—for instance, when they oversee operations in different countries or lead geographically dispersed teams—depends on their capacity for understanding their own presumptions as well as those of others and on the fact that presumptions may differ. When cultural assumptions are not shared or well understood, they might create misunderstandings that reduce the effectiveness of leaders.

Assumptions exist within communication exchanges. Different assumptions about interpretations and meanings can lead to misunderstandings where even more basic words have drastically different meanings. "Tomorrow," for instance, may translate into "twenty-four hours" in many U.S. contexts; in Spain, it can mean, "I cannot do it now; I'll try to get it to you in a couple of days." In Mexico it could mean "not today, and not clear when." The word *deadline* means an agreed-on due date in the United States but within an estimated time frame in Latin America. *Impossible* may mean "we need to negotiate how we're going to do this" in Greece. These reflect the differences in how people from diverse cultural backgrounds regard and use time. Consider other subtleties of communication that convey a variety of messages and how they can affect the work of leading others.

Communication styles may convey an unanticipated message within different cultural contexts. Jeff, a leader who transferred to Latin America, was surprised when he realized that for no apparent reason, his new work group was responding coldly to him. Upon closer observation of his group and their behavior, Jeff questioned his assumptions about his own typical greeting style—a general head nod to all. As a way of experimenting, Jeff began to greet each person every day one by one, with a handshake and a "good morning." Soon he witnessed a substantial shift in the behavior from his coworkers, who began to respond more positively toward him.

Another example can be found in Erika's story. She is an Argentinean manager working in China. After being in China for a few weeks and shopping by herself several times, she realized that in the open market, shoppers need to bargain for everything and that the process is, in her words, like a show, in which both roles embody a part. It took her a while to realize that bargaining, according to her, is part of Chinese mentality. As she puts it, "To bargain is a part of all processes." It is necessary to learn how to conform in order to be effective in day-to-day managing and leading.

Without reducing people to cultural stereotypes, leaders need to understand cultural subtleties to lead effectively across differences. How do organizations prepare people to lead teams composed of people with diverse ethnic, national, and social backgrounds? How do they train people to lead dispersed teams with members in different cultural regions of the world without falling into cultural reductionism (Essed, 2001)? One answer lies in approaching local cultures with respect and listening to the voice of the other. Instead of labeling the other as simply different, and perhaps inferior, strive to hear the voice that understands the context of that particular society. Instead of assuming that all Americans are cold, or all Latinos are warm, or all French are romantic, engage in discourse that helps to address cultural viewpoints and allow for difference. It is important to transcend values-based stereotyping (Earley and Peterson, 2004) or identity-based conflict that is linked to a person's belonging in a certain race, gender, ethnicity, or country (for a larger discussion on identity-based conflict, see Hannum, McFeeters, and Booysen, in press). An openness to wider perspectives implies development (see, for example, Chapter Three, this volume), and practicing in the context of difference can help leaders develop cultural intelligence.

CULTURAL INTELLIGENCE

Cultural intelligence refers to the ability to interpret and respond to unfamiliar cultural signals in an appropriate manner (Earley, Ang, and Tan, 2006). Individuals differ significantly in their capacity to deal with cross-culture issues, regardless of whether it is crossing national boundaries or organizational group boundaries. The next sections focus on how to understand and develop leaders capable of working effectively across cultures and diverse environments.

An individual's effectiveness in working with people from different national cultural backgrounds at home or abroad depends on his or her ability to apply knowledge and skills to produce culturally intelligent behavior (Earley et al., 2006). Beyond rational or emotional intelligence (see Chapters Four and Five) the concept of cultural intelligence invites cultural backgrounds and their impacts to be part of the discussion. There may be cues that even a person with high emotional intelligence in his or her native culture may not be able to read or manage in other cultural settings (Earley and Peterson, 2004).

In any given social interaction, the ability to adapt may contain elements of emotional intelligence as well as cultural intelligence. For example, after an intense week of working together in a leadership development program, the facilitator said a heartfelt good-bye to a participant from another country in a different language. The participant was offended and refused to speak, turning and leaving without the chance to make sense of the situation. The facilitator realized something was wrong and extended an e-mail apology; the reply was short: "unfortunate incident and let's not speak of it again. I am offended you used that language." Emotional intelligence helped the facilitator understand her words had been offensive; cultural intelligence helped her realize why her words offended the participant. Having greater emotional intelligence and cultural intelligence on both sides will help to dissipate confusion and build understanding across cultures. Greater emotional intelligence helps reach across cultural misunderstandings. Greater cultural intelligence helps to resolve those misunderstandings. In this sense, emotional intelligence and cultural intelligence are complementary in cross-cultural settings.

Cultural intelligence has four dimensions: metacognition, motivation (and emotion), cognition, and behavior (Earley et al., 2006; Earley and Mosakowski, 2004). The dimensions are facets of a person's ability to adapt to a new culture. People having high cultural intelligence are capable of mastering and acquiring new knowledge and skills while working through setbacks and obstacles. While some elements of cultural intelligence might be innate, most of the relevant behavioral skills can also be acquired and developed. Intercultural training and border crossing may be useful for developing leaders who can quickly and accurately acquire and master knowledge and skills when leading in a culturally diverse environment.

Metacognition

This first dimension of cultural intelligence, metacognition, refers to "thinking about thinking" (Earley and Peterson, 2004). It refers not only to what an individual knows about the beliefs, customs, and taboos of foreign cultures but also to his or her learning strategies. Those who have been expatriated understand that it is impossible to know everything about a culture in which they are living and working. Rather, people must develop a capacity to apply their learning strategies to novel situations. The ability to strategize about the way they learn is critical to their success in adapting to new environments. For instance, expatriates are better off when they develop rich developmental networks: a group of individuals with whom a protégé has a developmental relationship. The developmental relationship becomes a source of learning, social support, and other career-enhancing resources (Higgins and Kram, 2001). Thus, strategizing about one's developmental network, and making sure that it includes diverse people who are a rich source of learning about the country culture and practices, as well as the company expectations, is a way of ensuring learning and adaptation.

Motivation

The second dimension of cultural intelligence, the emotional or motivational dimension, refers to the individual's desire to adapt. As Earley and Mosakowski (2004) point out, adapting to a new culture means overcoming obstacles and setbacks. Being motivated and confident about one's own ability to work through these obstacles and setbacks goes a long way in fostering individual adaptation. Self-efficacy, in which the individual believes in his or her capacity to take action and have an impact, enables him or her to act intelligently in culturally novel settings. A person with low self-efficacy is likely to disengage after experiencing early failures. Knowing how to help leaders overcome anxiety and stress stemming from early failures is often the first critical step in moving forward.

Cognition

The third dimension of cultural intelligence, knowledge, provides a cognitive understanding of basic cultural clues (Van Dyne et al., in press). Understanding the norms and values of a culture's system—such as time, relationships, child rearing, or other ways of organizing the culture—contextualizes cultural cues. This information is important but not always sufficient. Combining the cognitive understanding with the fourth dimension, the behavioral, enables the capacity for engaging in a culture with appropriate actions.

Behavior

This fourth dimension refers to one's capacity for translating cognitive and emotional understanding into appropriate actions and behaviors. Successful adaptation to a culturally diverse environment requires the development of a behavioral repertoire that is appropriate for the new environment. This physical dimension of cultural intelligence also includes more subtle behavioral dynamics such as the capacity to recognize and respond appropriately to body language and gestures (Earley and Mosakowski, 2004). A person's ability to act in accordance with the habits and mannerisms of a new culture, and to acquire new habits and mannerisms when they are missing, can have a dramatic impact on that leader's effectiveness in communicating with others. Some business environments promote greeting with handshakes, bows, or kisses. Leaders who recognize and respond with appropriate behavior may be more effective because colleagues feel more comfortable and better understood in their context.

DEVELOPING LEADERS WITH HIGH CULTURAL INTELLIGENCE

The need for global leaders who can effectively manage across cultures, coupled with the shortage of people capable of doing this, presents a challenge for many companies undertaking globalization strategies. As a result, developing leaders with a high level of cultural intelligence is becoming a priority (Alon and Higgins, 2005). Although there is a growing literature about leadership across social identity groups (Ruderman, Glover, Chrobot-Mason, and Ernst, 2010), this section draws on ideas and strategies from leadership development and expatriate training to explain how organizations can use culture training as a tool to develop global leaders.

Intercultural Training

The cognitive and behavioral dimensions of cultural intelligence require that leaders have a repertoire of knowledge that is appropriate for diverse cultural environments. As reflected in Table 10.2, people in Asian cultures tend to be strong in hierarchical values, which means they tend to confer power and respect to those in leadership positions. Not surprisingly, the participatory management style that works well in the United States, a country average in hierarchy values, may not be as effective in Asia, where followers tend to expect more direction and presence from their leaders. Leaders who are not familiar with Asian cultures may misinterpret these cues as evidence of a lack of motivation, when the underlying reasons for the behavior may have more to do with cultural assumptions about the nature of effective leadership. Another example is the importance of *guanxi* (relationships) in doing business in China (Deresky, 2008). A leader who knows the importance of relationship-building rituals in China will be more comfortable participating in these rituals and be more likely to be deemed effective. The differences in assumptions about time and space mentioned earlier illustrate how an understanding of cultural differences and the appropriate cultural behavior can go a long way in contributing to a leader's effectiveness at picking up and interpreting cues during interactions.

Companies can provide training sessions, language training, books, and personal coaches to help leaders acquire the necessary knowledge to be able to behave in a culturally appropriate manner. These programs are often reserved for people working on international assignments, but the need may be extended to others as well. With an increasingly diverse workforce in the United States, as well as in other countries with high levels of immigration, all leaders could benefit from these training techniques.

While it is easier to help leaders gain knowledge about a particular culture, it is much more difficult to develop leaders who can adapt across different cultures. This is what researchers call metacognition—a person's ability to switch between his or her own frame of reference and that of another culture's frame of reference, to think about his or her own thinking. Molinsky (2007) uses the term *cross-cultural code switching* to refer to the act of purposefully modifying one's behavior in an interaction in a foreign setting in order to accommodate different cultural norms for appropriate behavior. Since people develop a dominant frame of reference in their own culture and most of the time use that reference at an unconscious level, working in a cross-cultural setting requires individuals to become aware of their own values and assumptions and become capable of functioning with or understanding different ones.

The Cultural Assimilator   One popular technique that helps leaders with their metacognition is the cultural assimilator—a cross-cultural training program that presents participants with a collection of cross-cultural "critical incidents" that occur between a sojourner, for example, an American in a specific foreign country, and a host national, a person from the specific foreign culture (Sanchez-Burks, Lee, Nisbett, and Ybarra, 2007). Each vignette is followed by a relevant question and several alternative interpretations of the host national's behavior. Trainees choose one interpretation and then receive feedback. Critical incidents have been developed to highlight unique cultural concepts as well as key dimensions as cultures vary. In short, the purpose of the cultural assimilator program is to train participants to make responses and interpretations similar to those of people from the host culture.

Research has found that although these training sessions provide a basis for cultural understanding, they do not do enough to broaden a person's mind-set. In addition to intercultural content, experience-based programs are used to develop leaders. Some consider these programs more effective than classroom training programs (Palus and Drath, 1995).

Experience-Based Programs   An experience-based program is one in which participants from the same or different countries have exposure to different yet equally interesting or valuable perspectives represented by differing worldviews. This type of program can be used to gain cultural awareness. As a collective, the participants share stories, best practices, and challenges. Many report afterward that the interaction with cohort members was a developmental stretch and a valuable learning that being open to other viewpoints can be an effective strategy.

Developmental Stretch   While both learning and development are important, distinguishing the two is helpful: learning allows new information to be taken in, while development invites new ways of sense making, sometimes requiring reaccommodation of an existing worldview (Palus and Drath, 1995). After parties learn about differences, the developmental stretch may be in cultivating new behavior that demonstrates acknowledgment of difference or perhaps finds value in a different perspective. Whether a program designed for a public audience or an initiative customized for one organization, including diversity of backgrounds, worldviews, or personality styles can be a valuable tool for appreciating difference and examining alternative worldviews.

Consciousness-Raising Programs   Consciousness-raising programs are also effective to train people in several cultural dimensions (Mirvis, 2008). Unlike training programs, which focus on content for transmitting knowledge to the students (learning), consciousness-raising programs are experience-based programs aiming to help people cultivate self-awareness, deepen an understanding of others, deal with diverse peoples and interests, and, broadly, relate to society and the natural world. Their underlying premise is that experiences that stimulate introspection and include time and space for inner work (development), whether in the forms of reflection, meditation, prayer, or journaling, deepen one's sense of self. Mirvis details a consciousness-raising program:

> Thirty Ford Motor Company functional and business unit heads, participants in a global leadership program, talk with board members, managers, and staff at Homes for Black Children, an adoption service in inner-city Detroit. They share life stories, current challenges, and future aspirations with their nonprofit counterparts in leader-to-leader dialogues. The two sides identify similarities and differences in their upbringing, values, and philosophies of leadership and talk shop about issues faced in running a business and an orphanage, respectively. The day ends with the participants singing songs with the children and pledging to build ongoing relationships [p. 173].

The purpose of programs like this one is to expose people to a variety of people and their cultures, particularly people unlike themselves and cultures different from their own, with the aim of shedding new light on unfamiliar assumptions (Mirvis, 2008). This can be done by volunteering for a nongovernmental organization or serving on the board of an organization. The key is to bring the dominant frame of reference to the conscious level and get leaders to understand that in a different cultural environment, their deeply rooted assumptions may no longer be true. Development would include being open to others' assumptions.

Among the many types of consciousness-raising programs are adventure education and service training (Mirvis, 2008). Adventure education (for instance, mountain climbing, river rafting, Outward Bound types of experiences, or urban anthropology) can be a mentally and physically engaging experience. Service experiences allow the business leaders involved to listen and respond to different points of view, exercise soft influence (higher-order) skills, and cultivate the common touch. This is an effective exercise, especially if leaders are to make meaningful connections with the people they encounter (Mirvis, 2008).

Feedback-Intensive Programs   Feedback-intensive programs, using a blend of methodologies, assessment-for-development tools (such as 360-degree feedback), experiential interactions, and peer and staff coaching (King and Santana, 2010), can be developmental and instrumental in examining the "growth and elaboration of a person's ways of understanding the self and the world" (McCauley et al.,

2006). These programs represent a best practice in the Center for Creative Leadership's work to help leaders learn and develop.

Assessing Cultural Adaptability The same culture training techniques used to train expatriates can be used to help leaders develop a capacity to adapt to diverse cultural values. Leaders are particularly exposed to a wider range of cultures. Recognizing the importance of having leaders with high cultural intelligence, companies can facilitate programs and experiences that raise their leaders' cultural intelligence and facilitate their cultural adaptation. Exhibit 10.1 provides an example of a quick self-assessment on cultural adaptability.

The GLOBE study (House, Hanges, Javidan, Dorfman, and Gupta, 2004) identifies universally positive attributes across sixty-one countries that contribute to leaders being seen as outstanding (such as being trustworthy, just, communicative, decisive, dependable encouraging, and honest); there are also universal characteristics that inhibit a person from being seen as an outstanding leader (loner, asocial, irritable, egocentric, noncooperative). Some characteristics are culturally contingent—"when in Rome, do as the Romans do"—and will be seen as positive or negative depending on the culture (ambitious, cautious, class conscious, risk taker, orderly). Although this study brings an inclusive international representation of positive leadership attributes, the information is not always enough. Sometimes a leader needs to learn by doing, which is the behavioral facet of cultural intelligence, and become aware of the learning that accompanies living across difference, such as border crossing.

Border Crossing

While the management literature invites managers to join a borderless world in which corporate operations could be seamless, real operations that work across geographical, time, and linguistic zones, including diverse cultural and socioeconomic areas, are far from smooth (Dalton, Ernst, Deal, and Leslie, 2002). Some writers predict that cultural differences will simply dissolve (Sinclair and Wilson, 2002). However, there is no evidence that this is happening, so leaders will benefit from addressing, understanding, and appreciating those differences. The new task of leadership is border crossing—the experience of being an outsider and making sense of that (Sinclair and Wilson, 2002). Doing business across borders, even when one does not move from one's own country, is increasingly common, making geography "increasingly irrelevant" (p. 9).

Exhibit 10.1
Cultural Adaptability Assessment

This short activity deals with attitudes and behaviors that are important for working with people from other countries. Rate your present level of skill on a scale of 0 to 5 as described below, and write the corresponding number in the blank to the left of each statement. This worksheet is for your use only, so be as candid as possible.

5 = one of my greatest strengths

4 = something I am good at

3 = something I can do but I need to improve a little

2 = something I can do but I need to improve a lot

1 = something I am not able to do

0 = don't know

_____ I can operate effectively in a foreign language, even if through translation.

_____ I am sensitive to differences between cultures.

_____ I work hard to understand the perspectives of people from other cultures when we are working together.

_____ I like to experience different cultures.

_____ I am quick to change my behavior to match a new environment (for example, when assigned to a foreign country).

_____ I enjoy the challenge of working in countries other than my own.

_____ I understand how culture influences the way people express disagreement.

_____ I can use cultural differences as a source of strength for the organization.

_____ I am aware of my own deeply held beliefs when dealing with others.

_____ I know when to hold fast to personal values and when to consider others' values.

_____ I effectively surface my own and others' deeply held assumptions, values, or beliefs before making important decisions.

_____ I can manage culture shock.

_____ I can adapt my management style to meet cultural expectations.

(continued)

Exhibit 10.1
(continued)

Total score _____

Score	Percentile	Assessment
32–42	Bottom 25 percent	Novice. I have limited experience working across cultures and am not particularly aware of the ways this influences my interactions.
43–52	Middle 50 percent	Intermediate. With conscious effort, I can anticipate cultural differences, see others' perspectives, and change the way I interact with them.
53–64	Highest 25 percent	Expert. I am able to easily work across cultures, perhaps in multiple languages. I am knowledgeable about many cultures and can adopt an appropriate style for most interactions.

Source: Deal and Prince (2003). Used with permission.

Border-crossing represents an unconventional path in leadership thinking and development. Both the academic literature on crossing borders (Sinclair and Wilson, 2002; Bordas, 2007; Earley and Peterson, 2004) and our anecdotal evidence from two decades of working across boundaries indicate that regular border crossing can contribute to effective leadership across cultural difference, as well as to human development (Hoppe, 2001b). Our experience suggests that leaders who have moved multiple times in childhood or their school years, accepted expatriate assignments, and worked across cultures gain skills and are more adaptable and confident to lead effectively across cultures. Learning by doing can be a powerful developmental experience. By living abroad, they often gain cultural intelligence and develop a perspective that comes from standing outside their own worldview to examine the value of a differing paradigm.

Individuals who had earlier life experience crossing borders and learned the value of difference and accommodation often have successful expatriate assignments (Wilson and Dalton, 1996). They may have lived in ethnically diverse areas, had parents from a different country, or been relocated from one part of the country to another. Joanne Ciulla, of the University of Maryland's Jepson School of Leadership, acknowledges that "world leaders are rising to this challenge: 45% of heads of state had been educated in another country—and this experience, she notes, allowed them to build bridges and to expand their ability to work with people from many cultures" (Bordas, 2007, p. 4).

Cultural intelligence development can be a part of leadership development strategy. Gillette International and Coca-Cola, for example, transfer professional and managerial staff to other countries to gain broader experience and develop skills working across cultures (Day, 2000). According to reports by many expatriates, over half of the leadership capacities to lead across cultures have come from understanding and doing the work of leading across cultures (Santana, 2008). Managers who are crossing borders report that learning different operational procedures, observing people's interactions in the workplace, listening to their meeting style, and including their viewpoints in decision making help effectiveness in a new setting. With strategies that use classroom preparation, addressed in intercultural training section, reading and discussing theories help some learn cognitively about crossing cultures. Submerging themselves within another culture, getting to know the people as human beings, showing respect and interest, and working toward solutions together allow some to live a developmental experience that can expand worldviews, values, attitudes, and beliefs. Both can be important strategies for developing cultural intelligence in leaders.

To live and work with people who hold assumptions different from one's own can be a powerful motor that increases self-awareness, but it does not always do so. We have observed expatriates who focused mostly on differences, refused to learn from a new culture, and interacted only with people from the home culture. Refusing to learn language skills, these people often criticized the new culture and counted the days until they would return home. But for many others, Hoppe (2001b) contends, leading those unlike ourselves "will call us to come to grips with our own personal and cultural assumptions, values, and beliefs in order to facilitate mutually rewarding intercultural interactions" (p. 2). Holding two opposing thoughts simultaneously and making sense of them can enrich one's perspective and contribute to integrative thinking about an experience. As Martin (2007) puts it, the complexity that we face when working and living with others who have different values "leads us to require new tools, we add depth and clarity to our stance ... a broader perspective [to] problems with a more diverse set of tools" (p. 102). This is what some academics call adult development (see Chapter Three), which refers to the ability to hold one's own cultural viewpoints as objects to be examined rather than to be subject to them.

People are able to cross borders effectively to the extent to which they can observe themselves, their beliefs, and their assumptions while recognizing value in differing views. Thus, personal development is critical for those who lead in "today's interdependent, multi-cultural, boundary-transcending world" (Hoppe, 2001a, p. 1) and can also determine to a large extent how open one can be to a different point of view (Kegan, 1982). However, adult development does not automatically happen. It requires elements of both being challenged and getting support (Kegan 1994). A person who chooses to surround himself or herself with like people, even in a border-crossing experience, limits the exposure to the challenge that interaction with difference implies. This might hinder his or her capacity to develop personally and develop cultural intelligence.

Life or developmental experiences can help individuals learn the complexity of thought and openness that permit objectifying one's position in order to be open to the value of that different position brings. Hoppe (2001b) affirms that "to lead in a multicultural environment we need a framework of cognitive complexity and openness to others" (p. 7). According to experienced border-crossing leaders, life experiences have positioned them for the complexity of cross-cultural success. This success is important not only for individuals but for teams as well. Teams that "build momentum from their commonalities" (Earley and Peterson, 2004, p. 112) and initially resist focusing on differences can develop cultural intelligence in collectives. Groups that initially focus only on differences will have more difficulty building cultural intelligence in their group.

CONCLUSION

Leaders face the challenge of taking action and getting things done (see Chapter Two) as they lead across differing value systems, varied worldviews, complex social identities, and diverse organizational or professional cultures. Given the shifting demographics of the workforce, the increasingly global focus of some organizations, the fading of previously existing borders and divides, individuals and teams that fail to develop the capacity to lead across boundaries, borders, cultures, and paradigms may arrive at key positions missing an important ingredient: cultural intelligence—the ability to effectively stand outside of one's own beliefs and examine them. This is of foremost importance as leadership becomes increasingly collective (Criswell and Martin, 2007). We have presented ideas for developing this intelligence, focusing on two strategies: intercultural training and border crossing.

From our own border-crossing experiences, as well as those of the leaders in our leadership development programs, we assert that those who assume the roles of leadership will find a critically important edge for leading effectively as they are aware of their own cultural assumptions and can be open to experience value in others' beliefs and assumptions. Differences are often invisible. Making visible the invisible experience of difference with intentional awareness is a powerful human capacity. This personal and organizational capacity for cultural awareness is something each individual can nurture, leadership development practitioners can include in designs of development experiences, and organizations can intentionally adopt to strategically develop the leadership pipeline. By learning from our experience with the cultural ingredient, we can adopt effective and culturally informed behaviors and also develop wider worldviews, positioning individuals and collectives to cross borders effectively.

The Shifting Paradigm of Executive Leadership Development

Moving the Focus to the Impact of the Collective

Trina L. Soske
Jay A. Conger

Today's approaches to executive development fall seriously short and signify a need for rethinking and change. Specifically, we must shift our emphasis from individual leader development to collective leadership capability. This requires a change in the overall frame for executive development, a new definition of leadership, and a change in the mechanics of how programs are designed, governed, measured, and implemented. IBM is used as a field example to illustrate this new approach.

The number of leadership development initiatives has exploded over the past twenty years. Leadership has become a hot business topic, with thousands of books and articles on the subject having been printed in that time frame. Until recently, business school executive education programs and consultancies that provide these services have enjoyed double-digit growth rates year over year. Keeping pace, most corporate learning and development functions have expanded to include senior positions and supporting staff focused exclusively on executive and leadership development.

With all of this activity and expense, it seems appropriate to ask:

- Has the investment in these efforts paid off, however the return is measured?
- Is the caliber of business leadership stronger today than it was twenty years ago?
- What are we doing well, and where are we dropping the ball?

More fundamentally:

- Are we truly competent as a development industry?
- Do we understand the real impact of our interventions, and do we apply them to the appropriate situations?

And not least:

- If any one of us was a CEO evaluating the various levers to improve organizational performance, would we select leadership development versus the alternatives?

Complete answers could fill several books. In this chapter, however, we can make several assertions about the state of practice in executive development today. Furthermore, we argue a case for change and describe what one part of that change might look like. We also provide a case example of one company's attempts to move in this direction. In so doing, we hope to provoke a fresh evaluation of the goals and methods of leadership education for executives. We hope to reframe how we think about the what, why, and how of developing executives to become effective leaders.

CURRENT PRACTICE IN LEADERSHIP DEVELOPMENT FOR EXECUTIVES

Although the practice of executive development varies, most programs today have some standard components (Conger and Benjamin, 1999). At the risk of oversimplification, the learning experience is structured around a two- to five-day format that includes:

- Senior leader speakers and sponsors, especially at kickoff and closing
- Classroom-based pedagogy focused on an array of content domains (leadership, strategy, organizational change, finance) that may include both plenary and small group breakout sessions
- Personal coaching on assessment feedback around specific leadership behaviors
- The creation of an individual development plan
- Any variety of guru or topic-expert speakers, experiential activities (outdoor team building or metaphoric learning or community service), benchmarking field trips, business simulations, and action learning projects

Some companies have recognized the limits of this multiday episode approach to learning and have instead opted for a twelve- to eighteen-month experience with bookend events and activities to sustain continued learning and provide reinforcement. But even these organizations are still prisoners of a learning paradigm built around highly contained and strictly bounded educational events.

In theory, the process of designing the learning experience starts with a needs analysis to identify the mind-sets and skills that the executives need to develop. More often than not, the analysis includes benchmarking how the executives score on a leadership competency model. From there, the executive development staff defines learning objectives, develops the program architecture, and makes specific design decisions regarding content, learning methods, and outcomes. The outcome objectives for these programs range from strengthening individual leadership skills, to accelerating adaptation to a new business model, to a more singular focus on facilitating growth, innovation, cross-company collaboration, or developing a global mind-set.

Most internal executive development groups supplement their internal staff with outside contract resources to design, develop, and deliver the programs. These outside firms bring their own standardized frameworks, models, and pedagogies. Most of their leadership competency models are sourced from research based on large samples of managers representing many different industries. As a result, the competency models behind many executive programs are generic. In other words, the promise of truly customized programs is largely illusory. Similar programs are being delivered within and across industries. Well-customized materials, frameworks, and models are rare.

Most programs are deemed a success if the participants enjoyed them and rate them highly on end-of-program evaluations. Some organizations go further and follow up with 360-degree feedback evaluations to see whether individuals have made any progress on their development plans or in the areas they identified for improvement during the program. In cases that use action learning projects, organizations may or may not measure the business results subsequently produced by projects.

And finally, the genesis for many of these programs arises from chasing a seal of approval associated with having them in place (the assumption is that if an organization has an executive development program, then its leadership development process is in order) and "keeping up with the Joneses" (ensuring that your company is doing the latest and greatest and keeping up with industry peers). More seriously, some programs are a response to succession planning and talent issues of concern to the senior leadership team and board of directors.

WHY TODAY'S APPROACHES FALL SERIOUSLY SHORT

If our description is, in the main, a valid profile of the majority of executive education programs, we can identify a number of critical shortcomings and specious assumptions embedded in the ways that we're approaching development. We begin by looking at certain realities about leadership development itself and how those realities challenge our past assumptions and approaches. All these realities, which we examine next, mean that we must shift our emphasis in executive education toward collective development and content focused on useful application.

Leadership Is Not an Individual Act

For the most part, the exercise of leadership in organizations is not an individual act. Despite the continued popularity of the "great person" theory of leadership and our romantic attachment to the idea of a rugged individual who is going to ride in and save the day, leadership is a team sport. Why? One reason is that the complexity, interconnectedness, and transparency of today's organizations mean that no individual can get much accomplished alone. The nature of most challenges and opportunities is systemic. Leadership in an organization is more distributed, and hence change requires a more collective sense and a coordinated set of actions.

A second reason is that most leadership is exercised within a team or broader organizational context—whether a project team, intact leadership team, or cross-functional team. But if it's all about leading together—and that's the way work gets done and change happens—then why does so much of the field still focus on developing people as individual leaders? We suspect that the answer lies in the fact that the field is a prisoner of a long history of models and pedagogies built around an emphasis on the individual leader.

In turn, individual leader development has led to a focus on leadership behaviors and attributes rather than leadership issues facing the enterprise. For this reason, most programs are designed around behavioral competency models. A lot of time and money are spent thinking about leadership behaviors, while real leadership issues facing the organization are left unattended—for example, critical shifts in the enterprise strategy, problems in the product innovation process, or new competitive threats.

Preoccupation with Programs

As leadership and executive development programs have arisen and matured, they have become self-contained and functionally specific human resource (HR) ends in and of themselves. As a result, in too many cases, learning and development staff create award-winning programs for companies that afterward continue to suffer a host of business leadership problems. Investment banks just two years ago had some of the so-called best leadership programs in the industry. It is difficult to witness what has happened to an entire industry and not wonder about the real leadership failings that these programs never addressed. One is reminded of Florida Public Power and Light, which received one of the first Malcolm Baldrige Awards for Quality and a year later filed for bankruptcy.

The risk of a programmatic approach to leadership is that it becomes separate from the business instead of being an in situ practice. Programs are something that the HR folks worry about, line management attends them, and then everyone gets back to real work after they end. Leadership development that becomes distinct from what leaders do every day poses substantial risks to the quality of leadership practice within the organization. It is unlikely that enduring developmental change will take place.

Learning Professionals Versus Line Leaders

Separating leadership development from actual situational leadership problems segregates the activities behind leader development as the domain of HR, learning professionals, academics, and consultants instead of extending the design and content of such activities to line leaders themselves. One could ask, "How can people who are not leading line organizations teach anything to others about leadership?" If leadership is treated as an academic topic, focused on theories and research, then the faculty-driven programs might be acceptable, albeit limited. But the live exercise of leadership is not an academic activity. It is about real people trying to get real things done in a highly particular context, multiple times throughout the day. Leadership shows up—or not—in a series of real-life moments. Therefore, we think it suspect that so many leaders are being taught by individuals who have no experience with the leadership tensions, paradoxes, and crucibles that the participants handle every day. This is one of the primary reasons that executive education programs have increasingly involved senior line leaders among the faculty.

Individual Leader Focus Inconsistent with Desired Change

Individual leader development is not synonymous with the purported changes in behavior that designers and sponsors often say they want to see. Very often executive development programs are commissioned to address organizational goals of culture, mind-set, or other types of overarching organizational change as their proclaimed aim. Yet much of the content is focused on generic behavioral competencies and abstract concepts and frameworks. It is as if the top two or three hundred executives spending two to five days listening to content experts exploring ideas will somehow fundamentally alter the organization's performance. Absent a larger architecture for the organizational transformation that is desired, the executive development program's potential contribution to it is largely wasted. Top executives, like anyone else in the organization, will do what's rewarded. Unless some of the critical systems, processes, and structures necessary to support and reinforce the new behaviors are in place, the purported changes aren't likely to happen. In the end, changes in performance assessment dimensions, rewards, and promotions are likely to be far more powerful drivers of behavioral change than a training program.

A Measurement Conundrum

Measuring the contribution of individual leader development remains elusive. While organizations often measure a change in the multirater behavioral profile of a participant, it is next to impossible to translate the cumulative changes in individual assessment data to business impact. Hence, most professionals take it on faith that leadership development is a good investment. Although this assumption certainly has some face validity, real questions remain as to whether these investments clear the organization's hurdle for rates of return and how the returns compare with alternative efforts and expenses.

This measurement conundrum has also led to a potentially dangerous separation between leadership development and leadership outcomes. In almost any other arena, it is difficult to imagine talking about good leadership without the mention of equally good results. Can any of us think of a great coach, great politician, or great business leader without a winning season, policy coup, or outstanding growth or profits? While results may be necessary but insufficient, the corollary is that they are the sine qua non.

Mismatches with Adult Learning

Educational approaches are often at odds with what we know about adult learning. For example, we know that adult learners require high levels of perceived relevance in order to be open to new ideas. Yet programs often draw few compelling links between program content and the participants' on-the-job performance. We know that learning while doing is a highly effective method for facilitating individual and organizational learning. Yet actual application experiences may be few and far between. Instead case discussions and competency feedback sessions comprise the bulk of the educational experience. We also know that learning will not result in behavior change unless it is reinforced over time. In spite of this, 75 percent of most budgets are spent on the learning episode (a singular moment involving a relatively short span of time), with little time, attention, or resources spent supporting, reinforcing, and otherwise putting the learning into action, or embedding the concepts in the way things get done around the organization.

Our Continuing Ignorance

In truth, we don't know that much about how to affect deep transformation through executive development interventions at the level of the individual or the collective. While HR and leadership development–oriented professionals are personally drawn to the notion of creating that profound moment of learning—the moment when a program participant experiences an aha! and with determination begins to transform himself or herself—the reality is that the field does not yet have a way to assess learner readiness (a key determinant of what sticks to the learner). In addition, we cannot know for sure what educational inputs (content, process, or experience) will produce a particular desired outcome in an individual or a collective. In other words, our interventions are a hit-or-miss in terms of outcomes. Even academic research on executive learning (a small body of work) offers limited insights.

Variation in Readiness

This reality is confounded by the wide variation in the degrees of readiness to learn among any pool of executives. It would be one thing if all individuals in the executive pool were in similar developmental places, but that is never the case. What is relevant to one executive learner may be entirely irrelevant to another. Developmental receptivity therefore varies widely across an executive audience. Yet design choices about the content and educational processes are either reduced to that of the lowest common denominator (not very inspiring) or produce a smorgasbord approach that aims to provide a little bit of everything, in the hope that everyone walks away with something. What we do know about individual development is that it is just that: an individual process, with potentially as many segments of learners as there are individuals in the room.

THE NEW FRAME: COLLECTIVE DEVELOPMENT AND ENTERPRISE APPLICATIONS

The shortcomings we have identified tell us we need to rethink and change the current practice of executive development. And considering the radically difficult economic climate and the tough trade-offs that senior teams urgently need to make about how to spend limited resources to improve organizational performance, we need to change quickly.

A Shift to Collective Aims

Many of the weaknesses of current practices would be ameliorated if executive development efforts shifted emphasis from individual leader development to collective leadership capability. We are not suggesting that we simply discard individual leader development; organizations can do both individual and collective work as separate activities, and the collective development will continue to depend in part on successful individual leader development. But we are urging that collective leadership become the primary, foreground development goal versus a secondary, background concern.

As its frame for leadership initiatives, we propose that executive development adopt the construct of shared leadership that has emerged in the academic literature. Under this construct, leadership is defined as "a dynamic, interactive influence process among individuals in work groups in which the objective is to lead one another to the achievement of group goals" (Pearce and Conger, 2003, p. 1). This definition more realistically recognizes that leadership is greater than one individual and moves the field away from a traditional focus on a superior's downward influence on subordinates.

A Shift Toward Application

The second critical shift—to application-oriented content geared to enterprise challenges—has been gaining momentum since the growing popularity of action learning programs in the 1980s, especially those popularized by General Electric. Enterprise leaders today face marketplaces characterized by constant change and great complexity. As such, learning how to lead the direction, intensity, and speed of strategic and organizational change is today's key driver of corporate success. Leadership development interventions should support these drivers. Such interventions are likely to have the greatest payoff and are likely to be the easiest to sell to the organization. This emphasis on enterprise applications will demand that educational initiatives become far more customized and tightly integrated to the organization's strategic agenda. Their aim will be to build leadership capabilities while simultaneously facilitating progress toward critical strategic objectives.

Benefits of the New Frame

Multiple benefits accrue from this reframing of executive development toward collective development and enterprise applications. First, this new frame would provide greater alignment between goals and methods, in addition to a more visible connection to business results and outcomes. Second, it would leverage the potential energy of the senior managers who are spending concentrated time together. One could argue that the opportunity to influence the hearts and minds of this group is hugely underestimated and underleveraged as a lever for performance and change. For example, executive development could be used to establish clarity about the direction, provide a platform for coordinated and aligned action, and articulate the values in action that would guide the exercise of their leadership and judgment as a collective. Third, the new frame would provide a more relevant learning environment, and one in keeping with what we know about how adults learn. Fourth, the new frame would place leadership issues squarely where they belong: in the hands of enterprise leaders. Fifth, it would address one of the vexing executive development issues today: How do organizations get their top leaders to think and behave like enterprise-wide leaders and address in unison enterprise challenges?

The reality is that many senior leadership teams are not teams at all because they have no real shared agenda or set of initiatives that they are responsible for driving collectively. Their conversations are simply reports to one another on how their function or geography is doing. Individual executives are mostly held responsible for their own personal results. Imagine this phenomenon replicated through an entire executive corps. And then contrast this with the very real succession needs of most organizations for a ready-to-go group of enterprise leaders. A huge benefit of more collectively focused development interventions is that they support this enterprise leader perspective, sense of responsibility, and shared leadership identity.

AN ENTERPRISE STRATEGIC CHANGE AGENDA

To shift how we practice executive development requires a change in the overall frame for executive development and in how programs are designed, governed, measured, and implemented. We will start with the overall new frame in which two guiding questions shape initiatives: What must the organization do in order to win in its marketplace? How can the executive group be best used as a lever to achieve these ends?

The starting point is thus an enterprise-level strategic change agenda, or some proxy thereof. From here, there is the open-ended inquiry into how to best engage and deploy the senior-most resources to drive change. The potential answers to this latter question may include an executive summit or off-site meeting, a strategic set of conversations or town hall meetings, a process to give life to corporate values, a reinvigorated business planning process of a new way of thinking about the business, a set of processes to generate strategic alignment and fine tune execution, or an executive development program or process.

This lens is strategic, first defining the business outcomes that are to be achieved, then evaluating the efficacy of various possible means to those ends. We define the problem or opportunity before selecting a solution. Once the desired change is articulated, the purpose of any interventions can be clearly defined and the interventions themselves refined accordingly.

From the perspective of organizational transformation, change interventions involving the executive cohort can significantly accelerate the transition to a desired future state. And those interventions need to be augmented by parallel streams of work to support the overall change effort.

This new frame contrasts markedly with the current executive development frame. Now, most organizations determine that they want or need an executive development program and then go about trying to figure out what the program content and pedagogical approach should be. Often this need is simply described as "greater leadership capacity." This approach presupposes a solution and then backs into the potential needs it could fill.

Differences are stark between the old (individual) and new (enterprise or collective) organizational frames:

- The new one is enterprise-wide and strategic. The old is functionally specific (HR) and more tactical and behavioral.

- The new one is more integrative and systemic. The old one is more siloed and disconnected.

- The new one regards executive development as a vehicle to achieving a higher-order organizational goal. The old one regards development as an end in and of itself.

- The new frame acknowledges the primary responsibility of the executive corps to improve performance and promote change. The old frame tends to back into what leaders must do differently as individuals to make the change happen and then tries to answer the question of "what change?"

- The new frame asks, "Where does the organization need to go, how is it going to get there, and what do we need to do—as a group of leaders—to make this change happen?" The old frame asks, "How do our executives' 360-degree assessment data look compared to the competencies in our leadership model? What strengths can we build on, and what weaknesses do we need to shore up?"

Bluntly put, the new frame directs efforts in service of a mission-critical goal, while the old one often amounts to programs in search of a purpose. Finally, the new enterprise frame ensures crystal-clear alignment between the goals and methods, making us consider that perhaps the most appropriate way to mobilize executives in support of the future state is not an educational program at all.

More systematically, what follow are brief discussions of nine critical ways or dimensions by which the new enterprise frame improves on the old individualistic frame. We summarize those dimensions in Table 11.1.

Unit of Analysis

Through the enterprise frame, organizations view the top executives as an entire cohort, along with its potential to drive change, as the relevant unit of analysis. Their collective role in driving change is at the forefront, both instrumental to and synonymous with the achievement of a mission-critical goal or strategic agenda. The topic of leadership, then, is neither an abstraction nor purely behavioral. It is real and context dependent. The exercise is about results and action. Developmental interventions are therefore used to foster an enterprise-level leadership identity, way of thinking, and sense of accountability. In contrast, the unit of analysis for many current development initiatives is the individual executive.

Overarching Purpose

First and foremost, the purpose of a collectively focused leadership activity is to address strategic change and collective leadership issues. Interestingly, these goals may or may not suggest a programmatic or educational approach as executive development has been hereto defined. In contrast, the central purpose of an individual development frame is to strengthen the personal leadership capabilities of individual executives.

Needs Analysis

With the enterprise approach, the diagnosis that precedes prescription has more to do with a deep understanding of the strategic issues facing the firm and

Table 11.1
Dimensions of Individual Versus Collective Executive Development Approaches

Dimension	Individual-Focused Leader Development	Collective-Focused Leadership Development
Unit of analysis	Individual leaders as agents of change	Executive cohort as the agent of change
Overarching purpose	Develop leadership qualities, attributes, and competencies	Address strategic change and build collective leadership identity
Needs analysis	Competency models, 360-degree assessment data	Critical business issues, change agendas
Desired outcomes	Individual development as a leader	Collective capability to drive business results
Program interventions	Time away from business on education	Time spent on the business, learning in situ
Timing and resourcing	Short, bounded confines of program; HR funded	Longer, blurred boundaries; business unit funded
Faculty	External leadership, expert content, and subject matter expert speakers	Senior leaders, peer learning
Supportive HR capabilities	Program design and development	Organizational development or organizational effectiveness process consulting skills
Governance	Led by HR or leadership development, with group executive input and approval	Group executive led, with HR or leadership development as partner

the leadership challenges associated with achieving them. This contrasts quite significantly with many of today's programs that focus on the development of individual leadership qualities, attributes, behaviors, and characteristics. In these cases, the needs analysis is often a comparison of 360-degree feedback data relative to a competency model.

Desired Outcomes

The desired outcome of collective capability-focused leadership efforts is executive-led organizational transformation versus the individual development of the leaders. Although this does not preclude individual leadership competencies being picked up along the way, the focus is on supporting top leaders in their efforts to drive change.

Goals typically include strategic alignment, execution, change, development of a common culture or modus operandi, accelerated work on a strategic agenda, and senior executive role modeling. In contrast, individual development programs have the more typical goals of preempting leadership derailments, managing career transitions, and supporting personal change.

The key metrics for collective-focused efforts are the measurement of cost savings, revenue growth, or other direct business results from key initiatives, in addition to a more qualitative acceleration or completion of a strategic agenda. It is also common to take notice of an executive's contribution to the effort, the team, and their individual performance or growth. In the last regard, the data tend to be observational—a function of the process consultant, coach, senior-level champion, or sponsor's live interactions with the individuals throughout the process. Although these qualitative data about how they showed up in the process are less precise than changes in 360-degree feedback, many organizations believe that these data are a better indication of real leadership capability and potential. This emphasis on business results and fishbowl observations in the line of real work compares to more traditional metrics such as a change in 360-degree assessment data, participant survey data, and derailment and retention data.

Program Interventions

Since the interventions are built around a specific business issue, the connection to business results is direct. Executive time is spent on the business instead of away from the business. The executives work on real projects critical to the organization's performance rather than projects made up as a vehicle for learning. This contrasts markedly with the carefully crafted portfolio of action learning projects that organizations typically assemble to provide a platform for cross-functional work and individual learning. Normative criteria regarding scope, timing, requisite resources, geography, and others are used to define action learning projects so that they conform to the strict boundaries of the development program, especially time.

Timing and Resourcing

Organizational and strategic change takes time and, in most cases, money. It certainly does not take place within the strictly bounded confines of a two- to five-day program, absent any new data, analysis, or thought. Transformative efforts involving the top executives can often take months, if not years, to fully complete—and even longer to completely tally the results. In addition, the analytical efforts can require external consulting resources, extensive internally conducted analysis, travel dollars to support customer and market research, and so forth.

Faculty

In collective leadership interventions, the senior leaders generally assume a strong "leader as teacher" role. This line-led learning is complemented by peer exchange learning and supplemented by relevant outside expertise. This model, borrowing from Noel Tichy's notion of the teachable moment and the various leadership practices that support Senge's learning organization, contrasts sharply with the external faculty and subject matter experts that pepper the typical two- to four-day program. This is not to say that these collective initiatives do not use external speakers and new ideas. Rather, they do not confuse exposure to new ideas with radically changed Monday morning performance.

Supportive HR Capabilities

Whereas the typical executive development program requires expertise in leader development, individual assessments, program design and development, and adult learning, the more collective capability efforts demand a broader and more organizational lens. This view means that practitioners must understand how strategic agendas are enacted in complex organizations, how to stage organizational learning that supports key organizational transformations, and the nexus of strategy, leadership, and learning—in addition to the previously mentioned areas of expertise. It also requires more of a line than staff perspective and a corresponding focus on business results instead of ideas.

Collective interventions tend to require a lot of courage and real-time consultative and facilitative capability. Since the processes are more openly designed, and much of the work takes place live, the interactions are not as carefully controlled, and many unexpected things can happen in the learning container and leadership laboratory created.

Governance

In all cases we have seen, the CEO is the sponsor of the initiative, exercising significant influence on the scope and nature of the activities. Not only is his or her role crucial to the launching and chartering of these efforts, but the CEO's continued availability and willingness to act as a thought partner throughout the process is key to success. Direct reports to the CEO often act as champions, but they can also be assigned project lead responsibility. This type of involvement contrasts sharply with the keynote or closing speeches that most CEOs or senior leaders provide to traditional programs, or their occasional involvement as the "leaders as teachers" portion of the program.

In terms of overall governance, decision rights belong to the CEO and his or her team, with support from the HR or LD (leadership development) functions. Again, this contrasts starkly with some of the more programmatic development efforts, where HR or LD owns the program and many of the decision rights, with input and approval by the CEO and top executives.

In this collective model, top leaders assume active responsibility for the development of leadership in their organization. In the traditional model, top leaders have a more passive role, mostly facilitated by others (HR).

A CASE EXAMPLE: NEW EXECUTIVE LEADERSHIP DEVELOPMENT AT IBM

In this section, we take a deep look into IBM's ongoing efforts to mobilize and deploy its top three hundred senior executives to achieve its strategic change agenda. This case illustrates richly the implications and questions regarding the collective leadership development paradigm we have been describing. In particular, we look at how IBM approaches the specific set of leadership development dimensions we have outlined.

Purpose: Creating the Integrated IBM

In fall 2005, Sam Palmisano, chairman and CEO of IBM, determined that he needed to galvanize his senior leaders around the theme of an integrated IBM. The company had unmatched breadth in its product and service offerings among its industry peers. But Palmisano felt there needed to be far greater coordination among the company's operating groups—computer hardware, software, and services—to truly leverage this breadth of offerings to customers.

To begin the enterprise integration process, in January 2006, Palmisano formed a new leadership body of approximately three hundred executives from across the organization. This group was named the Integration & Values Team (I&VT). Their explicit mission was to lead enterprise integration as well as to model a new set of leadership values that had recently been promoted. The new values emerged from a process launched in 2004 called a "values jam"—a threaded conversation across its fifty thousand employees. From this conversation, three core leadership values were confirmed: dedication to every client's success; innovation that matters—for the company and the world; and trust and responsibility in all relationships. Having completed the process of identifying the new values, it was time to breathe life into them by having the senior-most leaders model the values.

Membership on the I&VT team was a result of a highly deliberate and collective conversation about those executives who were most capable at moving the organization forward on its integration goals. Eventually three selection criteria emerged and formed the basis for membership decisions: their formal role in the organization, their three-year performance history, and their leadership in the areas of growth and integration and the IBM leadership values.

A Shift in the Leadership Paradigm

Prior to this initiative, IBM had focused largely on developing leaders as individuals. As a result, it tended to be assessment center or career transition oriented in its program approaches. The company's programs were also more focused on introducing executives to new ideas than they were toward achieving business results. So, for example, action-based learning was absent from the company's portfolio of development programs.

But the company's concept of leadership was shifting away from an individual frame of reference to a collective one. Much of this shift was due to the thinking of Mike Markovits, vice president of business and technical leadership. Mike had been a career HR professional at GE, working across various businesses and alternating among HR generalist, leadership development, and change management responsibilities. He had also led leadership education at Crotonville. His mandate at IBM was to think fresh, build on the already rich heritage, and take it to the next level. Mike explains, "I didn't come in to create this leadership initiative. It was something we figured out. Given how interconnected global companies like IBM are, we believed that no individual can do anything by themselves. It's all about leading together, and leading together—or collective leadership—is about two things: thinking together and acting together. So if this is how stuff gets done in organizations, then why would we continue to develop people as individual leaders? It was clear that we needed to develop them with the collective capability in mind, getting them to think together, work together, and lead together for collective and enterprise results. Personally I think this shift is just beginning to happen in the leadership development industry."

Top Executives as a Key Change Lever

Since the goal of this effort was a transformation in the enterprise, and leadership is the most critical and yet most often neglected lever of large scale change, a road map was needed for clarifying the roles that leaders in the organization would play in making change happen. A one-page change engagement process was created that identified the primary roles. Sam, the CEO, was responsible for architecting and setting the agenda for change. His sixteen senior vice presidents (SVPs) were responsible for identifying significant enterprise integration imperatives. The role of the I&VT collective (the 300 or so members) was to lead the enterprise imperatives at the executive level, while IBM managers (30,000 or so) would lead the change at the level of day-to-day operations and enlist the other more than 300,000 IBM employees to identify what is needed to move the enterprise. It was a theory of progressive engagement, with a steady build of ownership.

Deploying Senior Executives to Drive Integration and Values

Sam Palmisano's enterprise change agenda contained approximately fifteen critical initiatives. These were items that kept the chairman "up at night" and were considered mission critical. They became the backbone for the leadership development initiative at the executive level. The idea was for the top three hundred to spend time working on these most critical challenges to deliver on the promise of "one IBM." The enterprise nature of the projects would force participants to broaden their perspectives. Palmisano said, "I'm really trying to get more people at IBM to think like me. They need to let go of their identity as a HR person, a SW [software] person, etc. and begin to think of the whole—the one IBM."

Once the three hundred members of the I&VT had been selected, IBM launched and chartered its first action learning group of twenty-five to thirty executives to address one of the mission-critical initiatives: Client Value. Additional action learning teams would later be launched to address initiatives such as Enable Cross-Enterprise Integration, Win SMB, and Enable the Globally Integrated Enterprise. Since these initiatives were part of an overall change agenda, the timing and scope of each launch was dictated by a critical path and a set of project prerequisites and dependencies.

I&VT Initiatives: A Process Overview   The action learning experience was built around a four-phase I&VT process: launch, discovery, recommendations, and implementation. In the launch phase, participants received their mandate directly from Palmisano. They were given a draft charter that they discussed and debated during the first two days. They could go back to their executive champion and seek to modify their charter if they wished. If the changes were significant, Palmisano had to sign off on the new changes. The teams then produced their work plans for attacking the problem. These had to be approved by the champions. Then the groups began building their team and setting their development agenda. In the discovery phase, participants interviewed the various stakeholders. They traveled outside IBM and examined best practices and market data. During the recommendation phase, the teams consolidated their learnings and developed a recommended course of action. This phase culminated in a presentation and dialogue with the chairman and team. These first three phases typically lasted between four and six months. The final phase, implementation, involves ensuring key stakeholder ownership and support, transitioning responsibility to line owners, and maintaining ongoing accountability for implementation of the various recommendations. This responsibility could last for years.

Throughout the first three phases, members also participated in team and individual assessments and coaching. For example, in preparation for the launch, participants take online assessments including a 360-degree feedback survey. They receive one-on-one feedback during the first week of the process and then contract with their consultant to help them on two or three leadership competencies of their choice. There are checkpoints and feedback opportunities along the way. At the end of the four months, they have one follow-up meeting with a consultant. In some cases, the consultants and the initiative members have maintained their coaching relationship.

Even when members of the I&VT are not actively assigned to an initiative (there are only twenty-five to thirty members of an active team at a given time), they are expected to provide counsel and support to their peers on the current action learning team. Observational data on these assists are tracked, noted, and included, albeit on a more anecdotal basis, in the individual performance evaluation process.

I&VT Member Self-Assessment   At the end of each year, the HR SVP sends a self-assessment consisting of five questions to every I&VT team member (see Exhibit 11.1). This self-assessment is an input as to who continues to be on the team and who is removed. A member who is removed may be invited back in the future, but it is generally not perceived as a positive outcome.

Other Assessments   The consultants who offer process consulting to the teams also provide observational data on team members regarding their individual participation and performance within the learning teams. Mike explains: "The team process is an incredible window to watch people in action. There is

Exhibit 11.1
I&VT Member Self-Assessment

- Describe one to two substantive actions that you've personally driven to more effectively integrate IBM this year.
- Describe one to two actions that you have taken to increase diversity for IBM and/or your organization, e.g., executive diversity—US Minorities and Women WW, Diversity Network Groups, Mentor Relationships, etc.
- Describe one to two key successes you have had this year with your partnership accounts, e.g. revenue growth, key meetings, critical situations resolved, etc.
- Describe one to two actions that you have taken to build a performance oriented culture, e.g. climate/culture improvements, MIS, IDPs, etc.
- Describe one to two incidents where you have modeled the behavior of leading by the Values.

Source: IBM. Used with permission.

no hierarchy, as it's a group of peers. So they have to establish their own leadership structure to support the work. It is interesting to see who wants to play leadership roles, who are asked by peers to play leadership roles. The most interesting variation is in the domain of thought leadership—who really has a compelling idea and is able to carry the day with their influence. Collaborative influence became something we watched carefully. While people do not get graded, we have a clear idea of who are the high, medium, and low contributors. That information is funneled through the succession planning process to Palmisano."

Reinforcing and Rewarding the Expectations In order to support and reinforce the I&VT initiative, IBM has put in place a chairman's I&VT bonus (a noteworthy amount) for which the team members are eligible. Criteria for receiving the reward include demonstrated evidence of breaking barriers and teaming across IBM, modeling the leadership behaviors for integration and the IBM values, and contribution beyond the scope of the I&VT member's official job role. In addition, participants know that their behavior and performance on the team is being observed, and these assessments will be fed into the performance management and succession planning systems. Finally, I&VT initiatives are well communicated throughout the organization. In his company Webcasts, Palmisano discusses the role of the I&VT as a key lever for change. I&VT initiative members are asked to present at company leadership development programs and discuss what they have learned as leaders by going through the process.

Desired Outcomes

The I&VT initiatives are chartered to accomplish specific business results, with a pragmatic emphasis on outcomes. Two measures are used to determine success. The first is the business project results: increased revenues, cost savings, process improvements, and so forth, depending on the nature of the project. These are identified in the initial team launch and the chartering process, and the outcomes are approved by the project champions and Palmisano prior to the official launch of a team project. The second measure of success is the development of a cadre of leaders with an enterprise perspective, leading enterprise changes consistent with IBM values. This outcome is measured though behavioral assessments, observational data (the sources are Palmisano, his senior team, and Mike's team), and participant self-assessments.

Because the projects are the real work of promoting change at IBM, it was recognized that tangible outcomes may take a year or more to fully tally in terms of the business results. In fact, project recommendations from the third quarter of 2006 are still being implemented to this day, given the far-reaching nature of the changes proposed. Hence, although IBM can see benefits, it cannot begin to quantify the results over the short term. Mike explains: "This is something that was unanticipated. At General Electric, we would have a three-week action learning experience, and everything was wrapped up with a presentation to the chairman. Then the recommendations were passed along to line management. In contrast, our teams at IBM are theoretically never terminated. Many of their recommendations involve changing the culture, and that doesn't happen overnight. The first team we launched still meets occasionally to take stock of the status of the implementation of their recommendations and to act as a guide to line managers involved in the actual implementation. They make certain that the original intent of their efforts is not lost."

The Program Approach

For this new generation of executive development initiatives to have an impact, their designs and content must be highly customized. Mike describes how critical this element of customization is to a successful outcome:

> I had been at General Electric for twenty years, and I'd been warned that you have to understand your context. In other words, you can't simply take best practices from GE, plop them into another context, and expect them to work. Having worked extensively with action learning courses at GE, I thought their designs were very effective. But IBM's culture and business are different. First, many of our senior leaders are responsible for closing our biggest business deals, unlike GE. So there's no way we can take even one of these three hundred IBM executives and lock them in a room for three weeks. Without them out with clients, the business would be brought to its knees. So while GE routinely takes executives off-line for three-week projects, we ended up designing involvement in the I&VT as something executives did in parallel with their real jobs.
>
> Second, while GE is very good about top-down execution, IBM is a less directive and more participative and collaborative culture.

This means that a lot can happen in between a chairman's approval of an initiative and final implementation of it. Understanding this, we determined that the team's work could not conclude at the point of making recommendations. The teams would have to stay involved throughout the implementation phase to ensure that recommendations materialized into concrete actions.

Third, Palmisano wanted to cultivate a much more sophisticated understanding of the external marketplace. So we wanted a process that didn't rely on the information in people's heads. The business required robust insight into customers' changing needs and the opportunities for IBM to address them in a more coordinated way. Therefore, we designed a process that allowed time to collect new and fresh market perspectives, thoroughly analyze the data prior to recommendations, and think deeply about implementation and change issues.

This eye toward deeply understanding the organization, its history, and what this meant for designing an effective intervention also led Mike and his team to design a somewhat surprising kickoff course module on the topic of "hope." Although this was not a traditional offering in content design menus, it seemed essential to address at the beginning of this process. Mike expounds on this design choice:

The topic of organizational change can be a loaded one for people. Some executives had witnessed or been a part of unsuccessful change efforts in the past, and this accumulated experience can really close the window of what someone believes is possible. When you are asking for ideas and recommendations, you can end up with an underlying level of pessimism and cynicism that is a profound barrier to change. So we addressed this head on with the topic of hope, and the notion that it is an attitude that can be chosen. We discussed how discouragements and defeats can either immobilize us or make us more resilient. We encouraged people to reconnect with personal stories of something they had wanted when they were young and how they went about getting it. The goal was to instill a sense of personal power to make change while also managing their internal motivations and expectations.

As readers will discern from Mike's last comment, he was able to leverage individual leader learning as a vehicle for collective learning, blending the older model of individual development with the newer frame.

Another content issue the design team addressed was strategic risk taking. The near-death experience that IBM went through in the mid-1990s was a scarring experience—a significant emotional event that had a continuing impact on the behavior of IBMers. When the design team looked at the set of leadership competencies, this dimension was the weakest. It was critical to address risk aversion head-on because of the need to source breakthrough ideas, not incremental plans, for the enterprise initiatives. So in the beginning, Palmisano chartered the teams with the clear expectation that they were to generate bold ideas. Throughout the action learning process, the SVPs assumed responsibility to ensure that aspirational ideas were generated.

Organizational Development Skills   All organizational development and organizational effectiveness resources of IBM already reported to Mike. In fact, this had been one of the reasons the role was so attractive. Prior to launch, however, Mike realized that he needed to redeploy organizational development and organizational effectiveness resources from business-unit based projects to work on these new enterprise initiatives in order to support the process. He also needed to build the consulting muscles of his team. So one of the initial steps was to increase their capability in the area of process facilitation so they could fully support the teams.

Each of the action learning teams had three to four consultants to support the discovery and learning process, as well as the leadership development components. The consultants were not content experts chartered with providing answers or advice to the team; rather, they provided coaching and process facilitation experience. They provided consulting on-the-fly, offering real-time interventions with the teams at the individual, team, and executive levels.

Timing and Resources   IBM is still implementing recommendations from its action learning team chartered in the third quarter of 2006. The plans have been so far-reaching that it will take years to quantify the results. According to Mike, this is something that was unanticipated, and the design team has adjusted its expectations about timing based on learning along the way. Mike describes the change in thinking:

> At first, we really wanted to get as many people through the process as possible. But, that was thinking more like a traditional training program. Once we realized these projects were about culture change and performance improvement, with some leadership development sprinkled in, it slowed the pace. There is only so much change the organization can stomach at a time. Hence, the sequential fashion that we're using to roll these initiatives out.

Careful pacing is a critical dimension of these programs.

The process has fostered new data collection, analysis, reflection, and fine tuning, and the analytical rigor of the team recommendations has been strong, especially around critical stakeholders. Mike noted: "In general, most of our teams have spent a lot of time with clients, and this source has had the most significant influence on the recommendations. They have additionally spent time with employees. As recommendations became more formulated, they also spoke to key stakeholders, both internal and external."

In addition, the market research function and other parts of IBM have all been available to the teams for whatever support they needed. The market intelligence group has tended to get tapped for every initiative. The teams could commission new analysis. In addition, IBM has its own consulting function, Global Business Services. Some of the teams commissioned new studies from this group or went outside to hire external consultants, speak with experts at universities, and so on.

How were these market research efforts funded? As Mike puts it, "HR did not fund these initiatives. The business funded them. In addition to all of the previously mentioned IBM resources being available, these executives are big people, with big jobs and big budgets. In the event they needed travel and out-of-pocket expenses to fund their data analysis and market research, they came up with the money out of their own budgets and made it happen without any additional funds." This point drives home the critical importance that support from the senior-most executives takes multiple forms and is essential for these initiatives to move beyond simple action learning projects.

Governance   Palmisano sponsored the entire I&VT effort. He chartered each team, made himself available to the teams throughout the process of analysis and recommendations, and then acted as a coach to the teams prior to the presentation of their recommendations. At each team's initial kickoff meeting, he shared a lot of his views about its particular issue or challenge. In between, some teams availed themselves of Palmisano's input, while others chose not to engage him prior to the prerecommendation meeting. At the prerecommendation meeting, Sam provided coaching, particularly about the challenges the teams would encounter when they presented their recommendations.

According to Mike, Palmisano often coached by asking questions. In doing so, he was modeling a specific leadership behavior for his executive team. Mike illustrates Palmisano's approach:

> A typical set of coaching questions and discussion with Sam might be as follows: "SVP so-and-so is going to struggle with this idea. He might view it as inconsistent with his view on the market. How do you think you could get him on board?" Then the team would have a group discussion with Sam and determine how to better prepare for the presentation. Typical coaching themes included how to gain organizational acceptance for an idea, appreciating the roadblocks and barriers associated with some of the recommendations. He would help the teams think about the organization's realistic appetite for change and the appropriate phasing (how much/how fast), and so forth. Sam didn't see his role as one of providing answers; rather, he facilitated the team's own thinking and acted as a role model. He was very mindful of how to encourage enterprise-wide thinking and to use these forums as a vehicle to affect the key mind-set shifts required in the business.

Each of Palmisano's direct reports, the SVPs, was assigned as a team champion. Each initiative had two SVPs assigned to it. Sam selected the SVP champions, with guidance from Mike's team. Mike's team, which was working with the initiative teams on an ongoing basis, would coach the SVPs on how to engage the teams at the start, notify them of the areas they needed to press the team on, and otherwise help the SVPs to promote a healthy dialogue and team progress. In particular, the SVPs' biggest challenge was to balance the tension between feasibility and aspirations without dampening the team's hopes and enthusiasm.

Useful Lessons from IBM

The transformation process is still ongoing at IBM. Mike and his team, in addition to everyone else who touches the I&VT process, continue to learn, and the design is revised accordingly. Many of the lessons learned from the IBM experience are generalizable to the new generation of executive leadership development approaches. As you consider moving your own initiatives toward a more collective and enterprise focus, some of the important lessons to remember include the following:

- *CEO sponsorship is essential.* Palmisano's deep commitment to and engagement with the process has been crucial.

- *When transformational change is the goal, with leadership development as an integrated outcome, organizations may have to slow the pace of their effort.* It's not about efficiently "sheep-dipping" the executives through a program. It's about discerning the scope and rate of change that the organization can successfully digest. Pacing is critical, according to Mike: "The thinking . . . is that IBM is still digesting the five initiatives already begun. We know the next initiative needs to be smaller and more focused. We've realized it's a great tension point in the design of these efforts."

- *You have to be very strategic in the use of outside subject matter experts.* If the teams perceive that the faculty is taking time away from the business or that they have to put project progress on pause, then they will resist the outside resources. It is critical to construct the right conditions for these individuals to provide value. IBM learned that these external resources need to be tightly integrated into the initiative design and delivery. Their content must be seen as integral to the projects.

- *The HR, LD, and OD support required for executive-led change efforts and in situ learning looks very different from those required to support a more typical three-day program.* Specifically, a deep understanding of how to facilitate large-scale change and strong process facilitation and coaching skills are critical success factors for these initiatives. Organizations that lack these internal skills may need to rely on external suppliers for their deeper experience base and credibility with senior-level leaders.

- *There is a need for a common nomenclature and set of models regarding change.* In the case of IBM, the organization already had a change model—a clear sense of process and language to rely on. In addition, Mike and his team socialized a model of organizational change that senior leadership used widely. Without this accepted standard, a critical capability gap would have to have been filled.

- *The launch of the initiative teams must be supported by a degree of readiness on the part of the larger organization.* Mike recalls, "When we launched our first one, my team was in good shape, but the rest of the organization didn't really understand, appreciate, or know how to support the initiative process. It had never been done before. So senior leaders, members of the initiative teams, and their team members didn't know what to expect. We also hadn't thought about how to alert the organization about what this new responsibility would involve. By the second time, we brought in past participants within the first week to help the new participants know what to expect."

- *Degrees of individual, team, and organizational change will vary over the process.* In the beginning (the first half of a project initiative), the mix of emphasis on change by level was probably 40 percent individual, 40 percent team, and 20 percent organizational learning. Then the mix switched quickly to 20 percent individual, 20 percent team, and mostly (60 percent) organizational change. There was a scaffolding quality to the change process.

- *A key challenge is to allow and reinforce learning at multiple points throughout the experience.* Particularly important is the creation of learning opportunities after a team project officially ends. For example, Mike and his team established retrospectives: structured opportunities where the teams come together and look at what's happened or not happened since the project recommendations. Teams are asked to reflect on what they've learned about leading change on a collective and individual level. These are held at least annually, and sometimes more frequently. They can be as long as a day or as short as a thirty-minute conference call. They can be in person and are often scheduled adjacent to other key gatherings of executives.

Beyond these specific requirements, this new generation of executive development initiatives will require general shifts in the mind-sets and actions of senior leadership teams, their organizations, and program designers and providers. The initiatives will require more CEOs and senior leadership teams to assume greater responsibility for the development and mobilization of their executive talent pool. All too often when senior leadership contemplates issues of engagement, commitment, alignment, and leading change, they delegate them (dare we suggest, internally source them) to HR.

A second general shift is that this new generation of initiatives requires a greater appetite for the messy work of making change happen in organizations. These interventions blur lines between formal education and learning while doing, between time spent on the business and time spent doing the business, between lines of business and functions, and between a formally bounded effort and the longer time frame required to drive change.

A third shift is requiring a greater supply of compelling models, methods, and approaches. IBM and others that use some variant of executive-led change efforts all provide fascinating examples of moving in this direction. That said, the field needs to begin to research and classify these interventions and create a clearinghouse to highlight the variety of performance improvement and change leadership initiatives involving the executive ranks.

A fourth shift is to cultivate a nonprogrammatic perspective and orientation toward executive development, supported by a different tool kit and tradecraft than most executive development or leadership professionals possess. A more enterprise-wide and consultative view from the start would be required to ensure that diagnosis precedes prescription and approach. If leadership is to be tapped as a critical lever of large-scale change, then those designing and supporting the process must be experienced at orchestrating change. While an understanding of where and when to support the effort through education and skill transfer is essential, it is a small piece of the overall architecture.

Questions You Can Ask

Examples like IBM will surely whet some people's appetite for a wholesale shift in the way we think about developing the collective leadership capabilities of top executives and the potential opportunity lost by not doing so. Short of an entire redesign, however, there are some questions readers can respond to as they reposition their initiatives toward an enterprise and collective executive development model:

- What are your most pressing enterprise issues in the near future? Which of these could provide platforms for the leadership development of your executive talent as a collective? For example, are there specific enterprise issues that require collaboration across the executive team?

- Can you craft some of these challenges into concrete project learning formats that will become longer-term learning vehicles?

- Are your senior-most leaders committed to addressing these using a developmental format? Do they have a sense in concrete terms of the collective leadership demands required to succeed? Do senior leaders need to change the way they get work done—the ways they think together, work together, and make decisions together?

- Are the senior-most leaders willing to be champions of the process and provide resources such as time and money? Are they able to model the mind-sets and behaviors you are promoting through the initiative?

- Does your leadership development team possess the facilitation and change leadership backgrounds necessary to manage complex action learning projects focused on change?

- Are your senior-most leaders aware of the systemic demands of change and their own role in making that change happen, and do they have the appetite for the endeavor now? Are they willing to address the organizational systems, structures, and processes to enable enduring change?

- Can you realign your leadership development metrics around business results related to the project outcomes?

- Can you identify the individual, team, and organizational capabilities that need to be developed while driving project-based results and accelerating the strategic agenda?

- Can you pace the work in a way that does not rush the process and ensures deep and continuous learning?

CONCLUSION

The leadership development field perpetuates a long-standing romance with the great man/great woman theory of leadership. Whether it is politics on CNN, sports on ESPN, or business on CNBC, we spend inordinate amounts of time talking about the leadership of individuals, extolling the virtues of a person but mostly lamenting the lack of such persons. At the same time, most people and pundits in the United States, if not the entire world, openly decry what they perceive as an absence of leadership. Objectively one might ask whether we can continue to rely on our individualistic notion of leadership. Given our lack of conscious competence about how to develop such heroic figures, are there likely to be enough of these "great men" and "great women" to tackle the multitude of challenges facing all of the large global organizations? Will these great leaders be able to transcend the intrinsic intransigence of the rest of the organization as they attempt to drive change, or will their good intentions more likely be swamped if they don't have legions of help? We firmly believe that our existing leadership paradigm gets in the way of creating a more effective container for the development of the very leadership we so desire.

The challenges of the world today require more and better leadership. From our perspective, the leadership odds and the business outcomes look a lot brighter if we shift focus from the individual leader to the collective leadership capability of organizations. That is where we will have the greater payoffs in the field of leadership development.

On the Other Side of the Divide

How Leaders Must Lead in the Post-Boom Era

Peter C. Cairo
David L. Dotlich

A historical emphasis on selecting and promoting leaders based on educational credentials, intellect, and business acumen has resulted in companies around the world relying on a cadre of leaders who are technically competent but perhaps ethically unconscious or emotionally stunted. Today's challenges and those in the future require leaders who have strong character, who possess an awareness of and ability to lead in an increasingly uncertain context, who encourage an environment where creativity drives innovation and problem solving, and who demonstrate a deeply held commitment to leadership and the responsibilities of their positions. We challenge our colleagues in the field of leadership development to join us in looking in the mirror to ask what role we have played in contributing to today's leadership crisis and what role we can now play in producing the leadership we require.

About four years ago, we conducted a senior executive program for a major U.S. bank. The program was designed to develop the top two hundred executives into enterprise leaders who would have a clear point of view, make good decisions, and develop the business. This well-known company was enjoying unprecedented success, especially in providing financing and mortgages for the accelerating housing market. The leaders in this program were confident and impressed by their own ability to achieve outstanding performance. At the same time, the company recognized the importance of discussing corporate values.

We invited an external speaker to address the group—a former CEO of a global firm that had failed spectacularly due to questionable ethics on the part of some of its senior leaders. He warned these leaders about the dangers of hubris and reminded them that success frequently contains the seeds of future failure. He challenged them to truly lead, to think for themselves rather than simply enact whatever their institution asked of them. Recalling his early training in a Jesuit university, he challenged the senior leaders of this successful bank to look deeply inside themselves and ask some tough questions: Who are you? Whose are you? and Where are you going? He asked them to think about whom they were leading, why they were leading, and what their real purpose was as leaders of a great company. The evening session was contemplative, even solemn, and throughout the room, heads nodded. It was clear these questions provoked serious reflection for the entire group, and everyone turned in for the evening describing the impact the speaker had made on them.

But by the next morning, his message had evaporated. In the light of day, these hard-charging bankers were back to discussing what they believed were the real requirements of leadership: derivatives, mortgage-backed securities, and profit margins. Although we could not realize it at the time, the underpinnings of the 2008 financial services industry crisis were materializing beneath us. These leaders were not honing their leadership ability. Rather, they were lining up with the current expectations of their culture, their CEO, and their industry. Figuratively, they were heading off a cliff, and we were helping them. The aha! moment of the day before had been forgotten as the group pursued its real leadership agenda: making more money faster. And it worked: the firm's performance over the next couple of years was so outstanding that we wrote a case study about how the program contributed to its success.

The leadership challenges raised by our external speaker that evening were ignored by these Wall Street titans, as they were by many other financial firms at the time. We have often reflected on that moment in these trying times for our client. If we had pushed the dialogue begun by that speaker, could some of the problems have been avoided? Would the leaders in that room have been challenged to become better leaders instead of just better moneymakers? Were there ways that we could have made those lessons, so profound at the time, stick?

We share this story to highlight the challenges facing leaders and leadership development professionals. Our view is that the events leading up to the financial crisis and the ensuing recession challenge the assumptions of our historical view of leadership and leadership development. Traditional approaches to typical problems will no longer work in the unfolding era. The tried-and-true approaches for developing leaders may be most in need of rethinking. How will we produce leaders who can lead according to their values and beliefs without sacrificing organization performance? How will we produce leaders who can think and act systemically? How do you embed leadership behaviors in an organization that is relentlessly focused on short-term results? Our view is that these issues can no longer be ignored, and our inability to achieve the right balance among competing values in the past has resulted in leaders who have ignored the long term and the enduring in pursuit of immediate wealth and short-term profits.

Many of the problems that arose in the fall of 2008 were disguised by the economic boom over the past two decades. In this chapter, we examine the leadership issues that contributed to those problems, including challenges that were with us before the current crisis, such as globalization, technology, the rising importance of social responsibility, consumer and customer power, generational changes, and a more demanding regulatory environment. The second part of the chapter offers ideas for responding to what we conclude is a great crisis of leadership facing companies (and society) today. We argue that our historical emphasis on selecting and promoting leaders based on educational credentials, intellect, and business acumen has resulted in a cadre of leaders who are technically competent but perhaps ethically unconscious or emotionally stunted.

We think the world now faces a shortage of leaders who can deal with the complexity of the challenges before us, and that what's required now are leaders who have strong character, possess an awareness of and ability to lead within an increasingly uncertain environmental context, encourage an environment where creativity drives innovation and problem solving, and demonstrate a deeply held commitment to leadership and the responsibilities of their positions.

This chapter also invites our colleagues in the field of leadership development to join us in looking in the mirror to ask what role we have played in contributing to the leadership crisis and what role we can now play in producing the leadership the world requires. Finally, we share six specific actions that leaders can take to survive in today's environment and succeed in the future and implications for those of us in the field of leadership development.

HOW DID WE GET HERE? A BRIEF HISTORY OF THE BOOM

The past two decades have been an era of extraordinary optimism, euphoria, and denial. Consumers, business leaders, and governments enjoyed a consistently positive view of the global economy and confidence in solving even the most vexing problems. Recounting recent history and looking at the future of finance, author Edward Carr (2009) writes: "For a quarter of a century finance basked in a golden age. Financial globalization spread capital more widely, markets evolved, businesses were able to finance new ventures and ordinary people had unprecedented access to borrowing and foreign exchange. Modern finance improved countless lives" (p. 1).

Few complained as the era made a lot of people very rich. Even those who did not acquire staggering amounts of wealth were able to finance lifestyles that gave them the illusion of prosperity. Entrepreneurs opened businesses, renters purchased homes for the first time, and homeowners used the rapidly rising equity in their homes as banks for financing cars, vacations, home improvement projects, education for their children, and memberships to exclusive clubs that they had previously only dreamed of.

This era of easy money and excessive lending came to a screeching halt in the middle of 2008 with the rapid plunge of global stock markets and the sudden credit freeze in the financial system. What people had suspected for some time was soon confirmed: the United States officially entered a recession in December 2007. During the last half of 2008 and early 2009, the reckoning continued, and many began to suggest that the U.S. economy had been growing not through increases in productivity or output, but through complex financial instruments that propelled consumption but also accumulated debt. The economy continued its rapid decline as the subprime mortgage crisis triggered the collapse of venerable financial institutions, unemployment rates rose to levels not seen since the early 1980s, and even healthy companies had their stock value battered by forces that were outside their control. There grew among business leaders, government officials, and consumers a pervasive sense that the global economy had crossed a dividing line into a new era and that all the old assumptions about growth, economic well-being, and even the American dream were suddenly open to question and were perhaps becoming irrelevant.

The future fallout of this era is still largely unknown, but it's safe to say that along with the titanic challenges organizations are facing comes recognition of a future that will require new ways of leading. The complexity of the challenges in front of us, from the environment to health care to geopolitical conflicts, has combined with a global recession and credit crisis to force leaders and leadership development professionals to look hard into the proverbial mirror. For two or three decades, it has been relatively easy to be a leader, and even poor ones have looked effective. Now the question on many minds is whether current leaders in key roles can establish stability and prosperity, or whether we require different leaders with new mind-sets and ideas. Whether we are facing fundamental shifts in the environment or a swing in a predictable business cycle, the future will require leadership characteristics that have been underemphasized or ignored for some time.

THE DIVIDING LINE: 2008

Psychology has a rich tradition of examining the relationship between individuals and their environments. As far back as the 1950s, researchers in vocational psychology studied the fit between personal characteristics and occupational demands to determine the impact on career success and satisfaction (Swanson, 1996).

The field of organizational development and behavior has long held the view that forces in the external environment have a dramatic effect on organizational performance. Open systems models have demonstrated that the ability to understand and respond to what's happening outside the boundaries of an organization—economic trends, competitive shifts, social changes, political events—is a prerequisite to developing an organization that can succeed.

In essence, these models imply that organizations will be more or less successful based on the degree to which they fit with the demands of the environment in which they operate (Burke and Litwin, 1992).

Studies of leadership have concluded that the circumstances in which leaders find themselves dictate how to respond and that not every leader is equipped to handle every type of leadership challenge. The skills required to start up an organization are different from those required to turn one around and are in turn different from those required to accelerate growth (Adizes, 1988). The point is that understanding the environment in which a leader operates is important to understanding the skills and characteristics required to be successful. At no other time has this challenge been greater than today.

The events of 2008 and 2009 highlight how quickly things change. Events of the recent past have caused all of us to realize in tangible ways that the pace of change is accelerating and that the problems confronting organizations and leaders are interrelated. The costs of health care, for example, have an impact on competitiveness because costs must be embedded in the price of products and services. Global commerce, travel, and interdependent markets produce potential pandemics of unfathomable dimensions. The complexity and pace of change affect all organizations and challenge entrenched behaviors, assumptions, and practices of leaders everywhere. Leaders who are able to handle complexity can flourish, while those who persist in seeing the world more traditionally in terms of what's good versus bad or right versus wrong are disadvantaged. We have arrived at a point in which the forces accelerating change cannot be turned back. Several factors must now be accepted and embraced as keys to the future.

The Illusion of Growth

The bursting of the economic bubble painfully demonstrated that much of the economic growth over the past two decades simply wasn't real. The success of many companies was fueled by easy credit, lax regulation, overly complex financial tools, and greed. While U.S. corporate earnings consistently averaged 8 percent of GDP over the last decade of the boom, among nonfinancial companies, the average was closer to 5.3 percent of GDP—an average consistent since the mid-1980s (Mandel, 2008). The truth is that the large profit boom of the past decade was mainly contained in the financial services sector. In addition, while the U.S. Bureau of Labor and Statistics reported that productivity grew at 2.6 percent annually over the last decade of the boom, even that statistic may be illusory: "If the economy was artificially boosted by excess borrowing, that would show up as higher output and, presumably, higher productivity. The implication is that once borrowing recedes to the historical average, actual underlying productivity growth might be lower than we thought" (Mandel, 2008, p. 2).

Even the flurry of mergers and acquisitions that occurred during the past two decades played a role in contributing to the illusion of growth. While the reduction in operating expenses that comes from two companies merging and consolidating resources might show an improved return on investment and a better balance sheet, many mergers failed to increase top-line revenue significantly. Bottom-line improvements do not necessarily indicate the creation of new products and services that add real value for customers.

The merger of DaimlerBenz and Chrysler is a prime example of an attempt at growth that failed in part because the real value wasn't there. When DaimlerBenz purchased Chrysler in 1998 for $37 billion, it grew overnight into one of the world's largest automakers. But despite Daimler's best efforts, the merger failed on a number of fronts, and by the time Daimler sold Chrysler in 2007, both companies were struggling. One business article summed up the merger in 2005, before the sale of Chrysler: "Beset with humbling quality problems, a money-losing small car business, and high production costs, Mercedes had gone from being the global benchmark for quality and one of the most profitable automakers in the world to a money-losing shambles. For the first half of 2005, the premium carmaker lost $1.1 billion" (Edmondson, Welch, Thornton, and Palmer, 2005).

With Chrysler sold to a private equity group in 2007, Daimler became free to focus once again on its luxury car and truck businesses. But Chrysler continued to struggle and eventually filed for bankruptcy, and Daimler is still caught in an incomplete separation from the American car company. Between continuing to carry a 20 percent stake in Chrysler and an overall steep decline in the auto industry since the global recession began, the company reported a net loss of 1.53 billion euros ($1.93 billion) in the last quarter of 2008 (Bemis, 2009).

Many leaders encouraged the bubble by promoting growth that didn't really create value for anyone. The other side of the divide will present a new growth challenge for leaders: the challenge of producing real value, real products, or real services that save people money, improve their lives, or help them be more productive.

"Blame the Leader"

The current crisis has brought a rash of public criticisms of leaders, and not just in the financial services industry. Questions about executive compensation, wasted taxpayer money, inequitable distribution of wealth, rewarding failure, and the continuing criticism of leaders who just "don't get it" fill the media. One public opinion poll from February 2009 showed that only 22 percent of American adults view the CEOs of the country's largest corporations favorably—a rating even lower than that of Congress at 26 percent! Stockbrokers and financial analysts, by comparison, were viewed favorably by 37 percent of American adults (Rasmussen Reports, 2009).

When consumers struggle and businesses underperform, executive behaviors come under greater scrutiny than during good times. In uncertain economic times, we look at leadership practices much more carefully and hold leaders to higher standards. Furthermore, as anxiety rises, we look to our leaders to instill confidence and model the behaviors they expect of us. But too often cold logic, misguided objectivity, and excessive reliance on analytics trump judgment. When we see leaders behaving with poor judgment in difficult times, we ask ourselves, *What were they thinking?* and wonder, *Where are the leaders who questioned the wisdom of these decisions?* The inevitable question that follows is, *Can any leader be trusted?*

The difficult truth is that a lot of poor leaders who otherwise might have been weeded out thrived in the economic boom. The boom obscured a lot of flaws, and a lot of leaders were rewarded for being in the right place at the right time. As the saying goes, "a rising tide lifts all boats." At the same time, although media and public attention is now focused on the egregious mistakes some high-profile leaders have made, it's important to recognize that the focus on these poor leaders obscures the vast majority of others who are performing well and making wise, well-considered decisions. It would be a mistake to tar all leaders with the same brush. Many outstanding leaders during this time of crisis have been shown to have done the right thing and prevented their organizations from being swept up in the herd mentality that has brought many to their knees. Now these responsible leaders are the ones charged by default to rebuild trust with a skeptical public—no easy task, as PepsiCo CEO Indra Nooyi wrote in *Fortune Magazine*: "To the consumer, the idea of value is about a lot more than price. It is about a sustainable relationship, the knowledge that this is a transaction that can be trusted . . . . A company is not just an engine for shareholder value (2009, p. 67).

Executive Compensation

The gap between executive pay and average worker pay continues to widen. According to a study by the Institute for Policy Studies and United for a Fair Economy, the average worker in the United States earned $29,544 in 2006. The average Fortune 500 company CEO earned $10.8 million in total compensation, or more than 364 times as much as the average worker (Anderson, Cavanagh, Collins, Pizzigati, and Lapham, 2007). In light of the economic hardships that many middle- and lower-class Americans are experiencing, this issue has attracted intense scrutiny and shined a light on questions of equity and fairness. The light is particularly bright when the perception is that the compensation is without merit or that executives are not seen as having earned these large sums.

In the oil industry, for example, leaders took advantage of enormous increases in the price of oil that led to revenue growth, increased profitability, and huge paychecks. An analysis in *BusinessWeek* from the middle of 2008 reported on oil industry CEO compensation; the magazine asked executive compensation research firm Equilar to analyze oil industry CEO compensation from 2006 to 2007. For that time period, the compensation of CEOs of the twelve largest U.S. oil outfits rose 5.8 percent, from a median of $14.6 million to a median of $15.4 million. During the same time period, compensation for CEOs of S&P 500 firms rose only 1.3 percent, from a median of $8.7 million to a median of $8.8 million. Furthermore, bonuses for these oil industry executives increased 71 percent, while bonuses for executives at S&P 500 firms decreased 4.9 percent (Herbst, 2008). It's unlikely that these wide disparities in compensation were a function of more effective leadership.

As average workers in the United States look at rising unemployment and falling 401(k) balances and home values, they are understandably concerned and frightened about the future. At the same time, executives are focusing in an unseemly way on their pay. When executives complain, even whine, about their pay being capped or their bonuses being cut or about being unmotivated due to a reduction in pay, it's hard for the majority of the public to be sympathetic. Many executives get swept up in this mentality without looking at the implications of the pay gap between them and their employees or even asking themselves whether the gap is justified. The spotlight on executive pay and the perception that many leaders have too often been overpaid for underperformance will continue to bring sharp scrutiny on the other side of the divide until there is a more rational sense of equity and fairness in compensation.

The Inevitable Impact of Human Nature

Financial crises have occurred over and over again throughout our history. From Tulipomania in the seventeenth-century Netherlands to the most recent housing bubble, the boom-and-bust economic cycle has always been with us. Many noted economists, including John Kenneth Galbraith in his *A Short History of Financial Euphoria* (1994), have documented these bubbles and warned against them. Yet every couple of decades, a new boom takes hold, and a new bubble grows, only to be burst suddenly and dramatically as investors, consumers, and leaders lose money and jobs in the aftermath. Why do we never learn? What prevents us from drawing on previous experiences to avert these crises?

A number of factors have played into the amnesia that led to the current bubble and may simply be explained by reflecting on human nature. We tend to ignore many of the lessons of history and forget about the transgressions of earlier eras. While we like to think of ourselves and our leaders as learners, the fact is that most of us have short memories and rarely take the time to reflect on our experiences before moving on to the next challenge.

In addition, many fundamental human biases exacerbate the problems associated with these periodic boom-and-bust cycles. Based on research in social psychology and the emerging science of behavioral economics, Brafman and Brafman (2008) described some of the human perils when it comes to making decisions. They point out the deep-seated biases that affect how all leaders make decisions. For example, we know that leaders tend to be more optimistic about outcomes they believe they can control and to which they are highly committed—regardless of what the facts might indicate. This can lead to excessive confidence in a deal the leader believes in and an underestimation of the risks. We also know that leaders often exhibit a sunk-cost bias by throwing good money after bad to justify what has already been invested. Other biases having to do with the inability to reevaluate an initial evaluation of a situation, the tendency to go to great lengths to avoid perceived losses, or the difficulty of resisting the pressure to conform to group dynamics have all, in one way or another, played a role in the current crisis (Krohe, 2007).

It is not hard to imagine that these natural tendencies, when combined with hubris and the inability to manage personal appetites, would lead to some of the excesses and poor decisions we have seen in recent times. CEOs are not immune to the effects of human nature. We know that personality factors can undermine even the brightest leader's efforts to succeed (Dotlich and Cairo,

2003). Arrogance, volatility, habitual distrust, and eagerness to please are just some of the characteristics that can cause leadership derailment. When leading is relatively simple, it's easier to keep these derailers in check. But when pressures in the environment reach a breaking point, a leader can lapse into self-destructive behavior without knowing it. Under pressure, some confident leaders exhibit hubris, or leaders who normally show healthy skepticism will lapse into cynicism that demotivates their people. The inability to anticipate and manage these vulnerabilities can lead to dramatic failures.

THE NEW ENVIRONMENT

To complicate matters further, several trends emerged in the five or ten years before the bust, already presenting challenges to leaders across industries and markets. When the economy was booming, these challenges were met, overcome, or ignored with the confidence that comes from a vibrant economy and the belief that whatever happens, we'll all be okay.

Now, on this side of 2008, with a new view of reality, leaders have to reexamine many of these same challenges and address them in light of the behaviors that helped contribute to the current crisis. This will require a keen understanding of the environmental forces that were present even before the economic meltdown and a greater appreciation of a world where consumers grow cautious and perhaps cynical, governments pursue greater regulatory oversight, and ecological concerns threaten the planet. Following are six environmental forces that have accelerated in the past decade or so that have changed the leadership landscape and suggest to many that business itself will need to be conducted in a new way.

Globalization

First, the pace and scale of globalization presents huge challenges and opportunities for leaders today. Friedman's popular book, *The World Is Flat* (2005), brought many of these challenges to light in describing global connectedness. Certainly the interdependence of the global financial system has been made much more transparent by the economic crisis. Credit, rapid trades of currencies, and global investments have revealed that no company and no country is autonomous, and emerging markets may no longer be satisfied with consuming the products of developed markets without competing there as well. Leaders must now understand that interdependency connotes complexity and new responsibilities.

The structural, cultural, and strategic issues of globalization put pressure on leaders as they face expansion into new markets outside their own countries. Some of the challenges are structural. Do they organize by markets, for instance, or by region, or by product franchise? Most global organizations have evolved to some form of matrix in order to be responsive to local needs while also trying to ensure efficiency and flexibility to changing demands. This poses specific challenges when it comes to alignment, allocation of resources, assessing performance, and decision making. Other challenges associated with globalization are cultural. How do leaders acquire the cross-cultural sensitivity to understand their customers and employees when they are located thousands of miles from their headquarters? How do they understand and take advantage of diversity?

Some companies are making globalization work, even in the middle of a recession. An important key they have discovered is mixing global and local. McDonald's, for instance, developed common standards and consistent practices, but left menus, pricing, promotions, and publicity in the hands of local franchises. Likewise, the U.K.-based Vodafone has sixty thousand employees in twenty-five countries, and although it maintains some consistent standards and practices, it also allows individual offices to take on some local character. CEO Arun Sarin says, "In Germany, we feel German. In Italy, we feel Italian. In Spain, we feel Spanish. In India, we feel Indian. Here, we feel British. But there are [still] common values and common skills we look for" (Dotlich, Cairo, and Rhinesmith, 2009, p. 77). Successful leaders will learn how to balance global and local in the increasingly complex global marketplace.

Technology

A second force, the explosion and convergence of technology over the past decade, means that businesses, markets, and organizations move at faster rates than ever before. Some leaders have found ways to exploit technology to their advantage. For example, CEO blogs are on the rise. Jonathan Schwartz of Sun, who predicted the executive blogging trend, uses his blog to increase Sun's brand equity (Schwartz, 2005). Other CEOs such as Craig Newmark of Craigslist, Mark Cuban of the Dallas Mavericks, and Alan Meckler of WebMediaBrands blog regularly. Schwartz predicted in 2005:

> The rise of social media continues to break down barriers between executives and their employees, customers, and peers. In addition to

blogs, many companies and leaders are beginning to use Facebook, Twitter, and YouTube to communicate through a variety of methods and means and encourage feedback from employees, customers, and consumers. Some executives have seen real value arise from using these social media to communicate. Blendtec's CEO Tom Dickson stars in a video campaign titled "Will It Blend?" The videos feature Dickson attempting to blend various objects in his company's appliances. After the videos were posted on YouTube, sales of the company's blenders quintupled [Fraser and Dutta, 2009, p. 20].

These new forms of connection yield a dark side as well. Misinformation spreads equally fast, and interest groups freely challenge leadership behavior online and in global forums. Leaders are being held to higher standards, and missteps are quickly tracked, reported, and transferred around the world. Leaders must grasp that they now exist in a social community that requires a sense of responsibility and commitment to the larger good, as well as to individual goals and objectives. They must coexist in a world of conflicting objectives and constituencies that are both vocal and forceful.

Social Responsibility

The challenge of social responsibility is the third force that has gained power in recent years. Companies and leaders are being pressured from their consumers and the public at large to create sustainable organizations. The ecological consequences of the past thirty years of growth are coming home to roost, and it may not be long before we have to face another crisis—one that is far more significant than an economic recession and cannot be addressed by government stimulus plans and easing credit. Imagine that sea levels rise ten or fifteen feet and put coastal cities under water, or that expanding deserts take over vast areas of vital farmland, or that population growth outstrips the ability of the land to support it. These scenarios are discomforting but real, and they have to be confronted. They represent dramatic outcomes of an unsustainable way of life that can't simply be legislated away. Corporate leaders and companies can no longer turn a blind eye to ecological issues. They must begin to imagine that the next disaster could be irreversible and act as if their very lives depend on swift, intelligent action.

Nike provides a useful example of responses to the sustainability movement. In 2008, the company began featuring its Considered Design products in all six of its key categories. Considered Design is Nike's sustainable product line; the line aims to minimize environmental impact in all stages of production by reducing waste in the design and development process, using environmentally preferred materials, and eliminating toxic materials. The company was a pioneer in the sustainability movement; it introduced a Reuse-A-Shoe recycling program in 1993 and has since used recycled shoes as surfaces on basketball courts, running tracks, and playgrounds (Nike, 2009). Now Nike is extending the Considered Design to include other factors such as labor and determining how best to communicate the results of its own Considered ratings with consumers.

One question for all companies today is whether sustainability and the pressure for social responsibility will survive the current economic meltdown. Some believe that these issues will take a back seat as long as organizations and companies are consumed by threats to their own survival. Others suggest that the issues of organizational responsibility are too vital to long-term survival to be put aside during the crisis. Our view is that these issues cannot be approached as a dichotomous choice. The sustainability and ultimately the survival of the planet cannot be separated from the survival of any company or industry. Leaders will need to think in more complex ways about the definition of success and figure out ways to maintain the momentum they've created so that they will be able to accelerate these efforts when the economy ultimately rebounds. The risks of failing to do so are too great to do otherwise.

Shift of Power

The fourth force is a shift in power from businesses and organizations to their customers and consumers (Stringer and Cates, 2009). Customers and consumers now have access to more information than they have ever had before. This has given them the opportunity to bargain for everything from lower prices to improved customer service and to require increased levels of customization. The shift in power means that leaders will have to listen to consumers and customers more closely than before. Only organizations that are tightly connected to their customers will succeed. No longer will consumers just speak with dollars; they will speak in blogs, social networks (Facebook, Twitter, and YouTube, for example), and other public forums where the world can learn about their experiences with products and services.

Companies that engage their customers and consumers through online communities are reaping the rewards that highly targeted marketing can bring without the high costs of traditional focus groups. Kraft Foods, for example, wanted to develop and market a line of diet foods based on the popular South Beach Diet. After giving three hundred women in their online community the opportunity to provide input, the company used its insights to bring a line of forty-eight new South Beach Diet products to market. In the first six months these products were on the market, the line reached $100 million in sales and garnered high praise from consumers (Communispace Corporation, 2007).

Generational Changes

Significant generational changes are occurring. Much has been written about the differences between the values and attitudes of baby boomers, Gen Xers, and millennials. With boomers set to retire over the next ten years or so, Generation X taking on leadership roles, and millennials continuing to enter the workforce and establish careers, leaders at all levels will have to connect with people—both employees and consumers—whose values, expectations, and lifestyles are different from their own. Howe and Strauss (2007) described some of the cross-generational tensions in a *Harvard Business Review* article: "To younger generations in the workplace, old Boomers will appear highly eccentric.... However much the rising generations may respect Boomers for their vision and values, they may also dismiss them as insufficiently plugged in" (p. 48). Generation Xers, for their part, will enter leadership roles with a different outlook and a greater pragmatism from their boomer predecessors. "As business leaders, Gen Xers will be more effective at pushing efficiency and innovation than any other generation in memory," say Howe and Strauss. They also note that "even as mature workers, Gen Xers will want to be free agents" and that they will "seek new ways of removing professional middlemen (lawyers, accountants, brokers, advisors) from business transactions" (p. 49).

Regulation

Finally, leaders will have to face the pressure of new regulatory issues as governments look at how to prevent some of the abuses that have taken place in recent years. Ben Bernanke, speaking to the Council on Foreign Relations, indicated that an overhaul of U.S. financial regulations would be required in the aftermath of the current crisis (McMahon, 2009). The emerging regulatory guidelines could inhibit the activity of free market economics. While leaders understand the desire of government and the public to bring hedge funds and other such businesses under the authority of the Securities and Exchange Commission, for example, these same leaders know that even the best-intentioned regulations can have an unintended ripple effect throughout the economy and hamper businesses that have conducted themselves in an ethical manner. Too much regulation could prove costly and hamper growth. Nevertheless, the backlash in response to the excesses of the past couple of decades will inevitably lead to much greater oversight of free market practices.

HOW LEADERS MUST RESPOND

We are in an uncharted and complex environment on this side of the divide. It requires leaders and leadership development professionals to confront the reality that much of what we have done to produce effective leaders may be inadequate for the challenges in front of us. We need to wrestle with what will be expected of leaders and how to identify and replicate the attributes, behaviors, characteristics, practices, and qualities required for success. This is a time of transition, and it offers an opportunity to challenge our assumptions and professional practices. Although the full implications of the current crisis are unknown, we believe that the four assumptions for leaders that follow will be critical to their success in the future:

• *Character still matters.* It's a timeless message, but leaders today need to be reminded of what is enduring and what really matters. Character is too often overlooked, perhaps because we don't appreciate its importance until we see the consequences of its absence. Character is rarely examined as long as a company grows and meets or exceeds performance expectations. There have been times historically, but not recently, when character was central to assessing leadership effectiveness. We believe that leaders of strong character who can take a stand based on clear values and ethics, make difficult trade-offs, do the right thing, form a clear point of view, and act on principles as much as their intellect and acumen will be the ones who survive and prosper. More important, we must recognize that leaders with character frequently challenge the status quo, make others uncomfortable, and resist efforts to make them fit in or toe the party line. These consequences of character must be embraced as a way to foster healthy debate that leads to the right course of action.

- *Context is more important now than ever before.* Leaders must be acutely aware of what's happening outside their organizations and the system in which their organizations live and thrive. This is not a new idea; some argue that context has always been more important than content. However, the context of the current environment is unlike any we've ever seen in terms of complexity and uncertainty. Leaders who can understand the interdependencies of the external forces around their organization and encourage adaptive, nimble responses will have an advantage over those whose internal focus prevents them from seeing what's going on around them. Leaders will need to embrace curiosity, participate in dialogue that leads to insight, give nondefensive responses to ideas that challenge their assumptions, and recognize that they are dealing with a whole new set of rules. In short, they will have to be relentless learners.

- *Creativity that drives innovation can save us.* Given that the new world we live in requires new approaches, leaders will need to relentlessly pursue new, innovative, and unique ideas everywhere. Solutions to seemingly intractable problems and challenges will occur only if leaders emphasize that creativity and new thinking are welcome and create through their behavior the type of climate in which innovation and breakthrough ideas can flourish. Many organizations and leaders focus on incremental innovations to current products and solutions. We now require transformational approaches and ideas.

- *Commitment makes a difference.* In the past, when all boats were rising as the tide came in, it was easier to be a leader. It was possible to succeed without committing to a specific point of view, a group of followers, or a long-term mission. Now, on this side of the divide, a leader who is wholly committed to a vision, an organization, and a group of followers will have an advantage over one who isn't. These committed leaders will need a passion for leading. In an environment where it might not be as easy or even as desirable to be a leader whose actions undergo constant scrutiny, those who aren't sure of themselves or their commitment will have little chance of success. Those who can face tough issues such as globalization, sustainability, social responsibility, diversity, and growth driven by real value will have the best chance at long-term success.

Reflecting on the current leadership landscape and our own experience in the field over the past thirty years, we believe there are five actions that leaders must take to survive the present and flourish in the future.

Embrace Global Interdependence

If nothing else, the current economic crisis has shown how interdependent and interconnected the world is. China fuels the U.S. recovery efforts by purchasing billions of dollars worth of treasury notes at the same time that the slumping U.S. economy reduces demand for Chinese exports that slows that country's growth. Plunging demand for oil as a result of the worldwide economic decline threatens the economic foundation of Russia and other oil producers.

Employing a global mind-set not only requires recognition of the world's interdependency, but a genuine appreciation for diversity—though not diversity as it has been traditionally defined in the United States. Leaders will have to show empathy, understanding, and the ability to respond to new customers, employees, and other stakeholders. They will have to ask themselves tough questions:

- Does our management team or board reflect the diversity of our customers and employees?

- Are we providing the types of global experiences required to develop the right skills and mind-sets for our people?

- Do I seek out diverse points of view when it comes to making the critical decisions that affect our organization?

- Should I ask some of our most senior people to work with orphans or in a medical clinic for a few days to increase their understanding of and sensitivity to the world around us?

Approach Issues Systemically

This means leaders will have to be able to manage trade-offs and paradoxes like never before (Dotlich et al., 2009). They will need to acknowledge that there are not always right or wrong answers. In the new environment, answers to the most vexing questions don't come easily, and even the best analytics may not always be enough to provide clear-cut options.

The fundamental challenge of leadership today is not how to solve problems so that they will go away, but how to manage ongoing dilemmas or paradoxes that have no long-term solution: achieving short-term goals without sacrificing investment in the future; ensuring that cost efficiencies do not inhibit innovation; focusing relentlessly on performance while still creating an environment in which people feel valued; or leading a global organization from the center without losing touch with local markets. Managing these types of inherently ambiguous issues will require stamina, resilience, and the ability to live without real closure.

Reestablish and Reinforce Trust

The current environment has undermined the credibility of leaders from all sectors. Although it is unfortunate that many, if not most, leaders have drawn unfair scrutiny because of the bad examples of others, every leader is saddled with the obligation to reestablish trust and credibility. The obligation to meet commitments, act in a way that is consistent with words, create real value, and inspire confidence and trust in others has rarely been so important. This is hard work in a complex environment, but without trust, nothing else the leader does will make a difference.

Form Partnerships and Alliances Outside Traditional Organizational Boundaries

Fewer and fewer organizations will be able to succeed in this increasingly interdependent world if they try to go it alone. Interdependence involves relinquishing full control, which can be difficult. However, giving up some control is vital in forging partnerships that result in mutually successful enterprises.

Apple recognized the value of nontraditional alliances in 2006 when it partnered with the band U2 for the release of its U2 Special Edition iPod. Pharmaceutical companies partner with independent research organizations to drive innovation and build their pipeline of new products. Consumer products companies seek the insights of professional groups to test the efficacy of their new products. Educational institutions in the United States partner with European schools to augment their curricula and expand the experience of their faculty and students. The ability to establish collaborative relationships will be critical to real growth and sustained success in the future.

Relentlessly Engage Employees

We know that the state of engagement worldwide is not positive. Most employees do not report being fully engaged. BlessingWhite (2008) reported that only 29 percent of employees in North America are "fully engaged" and 19 percent are actually "disengaged." In South Korea, only about 8 percent of workers report being "fully engaged," and in Hong Kong, only 5 percent of workers report being "fully engaged." Only about 3 percent of Japanese workers report being "fully engaged." And as an organizational practice, we understand that "employee engagement" has nearly become a cliché. It covers a range of practices, many of which have nothing to do with the actions required to achieve authentic engagement.

At the same time, we know that employee engagement is the lifeblood of innovation, talent retention and development, long-term growth, and ultimately organizational success. Engagement is more than satisfaction. It involves leaders who develop an open, honest, authentic dialogue with employees. Engaged employees feel fully involved in their work, are enthusiastic about their jobs, and are committed to their organization's success. They trust their leaders because the leaders treat them as the adults they are and allow transparency about everything within the organization. Leaders must treat engagement not as a soft issue or an afterthought but as an organization imperative.

Avoid the Trap of Letting Intellect and Acumen Trump Character and Integrity

How many times have we heard someone refer to a leader as "brilliant," "a rocket scientist," "gifted," or "a genius"? Without underestimating the intellect required to tackle some of the complex problems leaders face, part of the current mess we're in has to do with relying on those whose intellectual ability was not tempered with sound judgment and strong character. Too often leaders were intent on being the "smartest person in the room" and failed to understand (or care) about the consequences of their actions or the impact on others affected by their decisions.

IMPLICATIONS FOR LEADERSHIP DEVELOPMENT PROFESSIONALS

Our colleague Linda Clark-Santos (in press) has written a provocative piece that challenged all leadership development professionals, of whom she is one, to reflect on our culpability for the current crisis. After all, were we not drinking from the same well as the leaders and organizations that are now under such punishing scrutiny? She poses some important questions: How could this leadership crisis have happened? How could the smart and capable people we supported lead us into the abyss? How could we have missed what was really going on? How did we fail to recognize how fragile some presumably powerful organizations really were? These are not easy questions, and we don't pretend to know all the answers.

However, we do think that recent events have implications for those of us who have devoted our careers to developing leaders:

- Throw out past leadership models for development.
- Refocus on enduring leadership qualities.
- Not everyone needs to be a leader.
- High potentials are not a special class.
- Make people accountable before moving them on.
- Do not ignore the B players.
- Help people leverage their current capabilities.
- Let leaders teach leaders.

• *Start by throwing out all of the leadership models we've used to guide our development efforts.* These models have done a disservice to leadership by taking leaders and development professionals alike to a dead end. Selecting leaders against a competency model hasn't been productive; instead, it's produced, or tried to produce, a cadre of leaders who all look and say exactly the same things. If you placed the leadership models of ten organizations side by side, there would be few differences, even if they came from radically different industries. Furthermore, the breadth of most models suggests attempts to create the perfect leader. Could Winston Churchill, Mahatma Gandhi, Martin Luther King Jr., or Nelson Mandela be appointed to a first-line supervisor job in most companies today, given the range of requirements of supposedly effective leadership? Rather than develop a new list of seventy-five behaviors in a ten-part competency model, let's look at the handful of capabilities that really matter in the effort to develop true leaders.

• *Return to a focus on developing hard-to-develop, enduring leadership qualities.* This will be challenging since there continues to be a reasonable debate about what qualities are inherent in leaders and which can be developed. Many leadership "programs" are insufficient to develop true leadership, especially in a three- or four-day off-site meeting. What may be required are relationships that are developmental over time. Leadership coaching is still in its infancy as a methodology, but truly effective coaches may be required to probe, prod, and nurture a leadership sense of self that occurs over time and across situations. We have argued in earlier books that the coaches are not therapists, but the dividing line in developing truly capable leaders is now less clear. Effective coaches will need to explore new ways to help leaders integrate rather than resist complexity, and this work may be accomplished in an ongoing, deep relationship:

• *Acknowledge that not everyone needs to, or should be, a leader.* It's time for development professionals to help leaders and those who follow them to revisit the definition of a successful career. It is possible for people to be upwardly mobile and have high-quality careers without being forced to focus on a leadership position that they may not even want, much less be able to do well. We have seen many people take on positions they didn't want or be moved up when they weren't ready. All too often these people fail when a little more time or a simple refocusing of career goals would have helped avoid the problems they encountered. It's time to encourage the conversation about the value people offer and the many ways that we can define success that are not necessarily linked to the number of people for whom you are formally responsible.

• *Recognize that high potentials are not a special class.* Leadership capability varies over a lifetime, with potential appearing at different times for different people. Many companies decide once who is high potential and mindlessly promote and rotate these individuals in an effort to maximize return. The result is a group who are often protected and promoted rather than challenged and hungry.

• *Make people accountable for results before moving them on to another development experience.* One side effect of the boom economy has been the rapid movement of people from position to position before the full impact of their leadership is determined. While this has been a chronic problem in many organizations for a long time, the recent growth cycle has exacerbated this tendency. Furthermore, sometimes it was possible to show growth without being really responsible for it because the overall economy was doing so well. People need to be in positions long enough to demonstrate real skills and a real ability to achieve the results expected of them.

Professionals should also expand efforts to put leaders in situations that test their character and require cultural sensitivity, openness to learning, resilience, and the ability to operate in complex and ambiguous situations. And rather than focusing on whether people have had certain experiences (overseas position, staff job, operations experience) in order to qualify for leadership positions, we need a renewed focus on the quality of experience in terms of what learning actually took place.

• *In our never-ending quest to find high-potential A players, do not ignore the B players.* This encompasses two issues. First, with our strong emphasis on academic pedigree and length and type of experience, we have probably neglected some very talented people who have the natural qualities that make good leaders. We may need to look differently at the way in which these distinctions are made. Second, we may want to renew our effort at creating innovative development opportunities for B players. In a time of resource constraints, it's easy to devote most resources to those judged to be the highest potential. However, this carries with it the risk of ignoring those whose efforts are equally critical to the success of their organizations and assumes more precision in differentiating A players from B players than experience suggests is reasonable.

• *Help people find the best ways to leverage their current capabilities by putting them in positions consistent with their strengths.* Development professionals and senior leaders are often focused on closing gaps. This suggestion does not ignore the very real importance of development, but rather acknowledges that an important part of any development professional's role is to ensure that leaders are in positions that play to their strengths.

• *Let leaders teach.* It's time to let the leaders teach leaders. This concept has also been around for a while, but in reality it too often means scripted events that avoid really tough issues. And too often dialogue is about organizational or business issues and not about the tough challenges of leadership. Bill Weldon, CEO of Johnson and Johnson, is an exception. He has been very successful in leading two-day, unstructured forums on leadership. The leaders and high-potential employees in these sessions talk with candor and openness about the future of leadership, the company, qualities that are needed going forward, and anything else of importance to them. These discussions get to the heart of what leadership requires and how tough it really is to be a leader.

CONCLUSION

We have a sense that a line has been crossed as a result of the current economic turmoil. The boom that characterized the previous twenty-five years brought with it staggering wealth, innovation, and political changes that no one would have predicted fifty or sixty years ago. But at the same time, there have been significant consequences for our society and institutions, and they have equally significant implications for leadership. The current environment, rife with uncertainty and anxiety, is also a time of great opportunity. Alternative energy, a shrinking globe, technology innovations that hold hope for millions who suffer from disease and poverty: potential abounds everywhere. Leaders who are willing to challenge assumptions, learn from experience, and draw energy from the changes that are occurring will find reason to be hopeful about the world on this side of the divide.

Leadership in the Corner Office

The Board's Greatest Responsibility and Challenge

Peter C. Browning

The most important responsibility of the board of directors of a publicly traded company is to ensure that the right CEO is leading the corporation. To meet its primary responsibility, the board must grapple with three questions: Does the organization have the right CEO? Does the organization have a robust process for developing incumbents? And if it's necessary to go outside, how can the board ensure that it picks the right candidate? There are proven practices to help the board answer these questions and meet its most important obligation.

After World War II, the U.S. economy experienced a period of unfettered growth and development. Most people enjoyed lifelong careers with the same company. Succession to the CEO position took many years and generally was given to the most senior executive who maintained that term of office until retirement. As the U.S. economy entered the 1970s, global competition arrived and the circumstances in organizations changed. White-collar ranks and the executive suite became as susceptible to reductions in force as workers on the plant floor. Lifelong employment was no longer assured, CEO longevity became less certain, and the long-serving, most senior person was no longer the given choice. The question became, Who is best equipped to lead the organization at this time under these circumstances?

The turnover rate of CEOs is not just a U.S. issue. In fact, Europe, with its strict governance standards, is an even more difficult environment for CEOs, as the ten-year average rate of CEO successions shows:

- United States, 27 percent
- Europe, 37 percent
- Japan, 12 percent ("Succession Planning," 2008)

These trends show what's at stake as organizations work to secure the right leader to install in the top position. In response to that interest, discussions of leadership abound. It is hard to find a business book, magazine, or newspaper today that doesn't touch on or address some aspect of leadership: how we define it, how we identify it, how we teach it, whether it is nature or nurture—all parsing the secrets of leadership that can aid and abet the process of developing the most effective leaders. One thing we have learned since Plutarch's *Parallel Lives* reported on the strengths and flaws of Greece's and Rome's leaders almost two thousand years ago is that the right person in the right place at the right time makes all the difference. Some individuals have a way of overcoming obstacles and difficulties that plagued their predecessors and can reach goals that previous leaders were unable to accomplish.

Another lesson we have learned is that leadership comes in all shapes, sizes, personalities, gender, and colors of skin. As Peter Drucker (2004) wrote, "An effective executive does need to be a leader in the sense that is now most commonly used. Harry Truman did not have an ounce of charisma. Some of the best business and non-profit CEO's I've worked with over a 65-year consulting career were not stereotypical leaders. They were all over the map in terms of their personalities, attributes, values, strengths, and weaknesses. They range from extroverted to nearly reclusive, from easy going to controlling, from generous to parsimonious" (p. 59).

Despite these years of observation, erudition, ink, and evolving views on what constitutes leadership, we may know it when we see it, but we unfortunately see it only with the benefit of hindsight. Training programs, job rotation, industrial psychologists, and all the other means at our disposal are not litmus tests for prospective CEOs that provide certainty when it comes to putting the right leader in the right spot. Only time spent in office will tell if the right choice sits in that chair. You are never likely to hear board members use the words Matthew J. Paese (2008) suggests: "I am still waiting for the true realist to emerge from the board room and announce, 'We are making this CEO succession decision recognizing that it probably won't work out and that next year at this time we will be looking for a replacement.' Of course, it is absurd to imagine any board openly condemning an incoming CEO but if board members were appointed purely to make accurate predictions, that's precisely what many of them would be compelled to do. The data supports it: Over the last decade CEO turnover has increased by over 50% and performance related departures by over 300%" (p. 19).

THE HIGH COST OF FAILED CEO LEADERSHIP

The price for failed leadership at the CEO level, whether the candidate is internally developed or hired from the outside, is almost incalculable (see, for example, Stoddard and Wychoff, 2008).

What can happen when choices go wrong? The saga of Bob Nardelli's tenure as CEO of Home Depot remains fresh. Although Nardelli had an outstanding record of accomplishment and success at GE, becoming one of three finalists to succeed Jack Welch, in less than five years, in a number of well-documented ways, Home Depot's market capitalization fell and its debt rose. The organization became a poster child for bad governance and failed leadership.

The story is instructive for all of us. After a storybook run of success, the two founders of Home Depot, Bernie Marcus and Arthur Blank, who were considering retirement, realized they had not developed an internal successor. Once Bob Nardelli became available, the board acted quickly (in retrospect, too quickly) to bring in this proven leader from the company many experts viewed as a paragon for developing leadership talent. As it turned out, Nardelli was the wrong person in the wrong job at the wrong time.

Organizations can quantify the cost of failure in terms of loss of shareholder value, but the cost associated with employee turnover, low morale, loss in productivity, and the time it takes to turn around the business—call them opportunity costs—are equally extraordinary. These penalties clearly reinforce the importance of making the right choice. What lessons, insights, and knowledge can boards of directors draw from to deal with this risk?

In 1990, John Kotter extolled a view of leadership that described powerful personas providing extraordinary vision, coalescing and exciting the people in their charge to create profound change. Clearly Kotter was influenced by dramatic changes in the U.S. economy during the 1980s. In that period, annual reports carried vision and value statements, and the general and trade press printed hundreds of stories that focused on the charismatic CEOs who led these changes. The elevation of leaders who possessed "the missing ingredient" carried into the 1990s, when the bubble burst, and suddenly many of those bigger-than-life personalities revealed feet of clay. Organizations like Enron, WorldCom, and Tyco, and the people in them and the people who did business with them, suffered incredible damage. Regardless of the size of the institution, it is not difficult for the wrong person in the CEO's chair, over a short period of time, to destroy significant shareholder value and to wreak havoc on hundreds, even thousands of lives.

Since then the focus of the conversation has shifted to examining the understated natural "leader of men." Jim Collins captured that stereotype in 2001: "Compared to high profile leaders with big personalities who make headlines and become celebrities, the good to great leaders seem to have come from Mars. Self-effacing, quiet, reserved, even shy, these leaders all produce a blend of personal humility and professional will. They are more like Lincoln or Socrates than Patton or Caesar" (pp. 12–13).

What kind of leader is right for the organization? What is the right model of leadership practice? Should a board use a one-size-fits-all perspective, or should it follow the latest business fashion? The truth is, for any senior leader, most often he or she never performs quite as well, or as badly, as the numbers indicate. When things are going well for the company and the industry, it produces a halo effect on a leader: he or she can do no wrong. Extraordinary leaders may possess capabilities that create extraordinary results, and perhaps such leaders can replicate those results in almost any organization. Or maybe such leaders are the consequence of the board's putting the right person in the right place at the right time.

THE CHALLENGE TO THE BOARD

After forty years of experience in the business world, starting as a sales trainee and rising through responsibilities as division president of two different businesses and finally to CEO of two different publicly traded companies, and having served on boards of directors for eleven different publicly traded companies, I have developed a keen interest in the questions and issues of leadership at the CEO level. So I am familiar with the challenge of CEO turnover. In fact, since January 2000, I have served on the board of directors of six companies that have made a change of CEO at least once.

Wachovia Corporation is an example. In this instance, the board asked the CEO to step down and brought in his replacement from the outside. In the case of EnPro Industries, when the incumbent CEO retired, the board search for a successor also brought in someone from outside the company. In the remaining four examples, Acuity Brands, Lowes Companies, Nucor Corporation, and Phoenix Companies, the CEO's successor came from within—in some cases as the clear candidate and in other cases after discussion and review of several prospective internal candidates.

After the sad sagas of Enron, Tyco, WorldCom, and other organizations, the responsibility of the boards of directors of publicly traded companies is increasingly scrutinized. You can find almost as many articles on the subject of board governance as on leadership. Some of these growing expectations are well founded, but others reflect a lack of understanding about what a board can or cannot do. As Jack and Suzy Welch (2009) note, "The real fallacy of corporate governance in this crisis is not what boards did or didn't do but what was expected of them. The [board's] job is to hire and fire the CEO based on his performance, values, the quality of a team and the coherence of his business model" (p. 102).

Without question, among the board's many obligations, its most important is selecting the CEO, followed by supporting a process to ensure the selected leader is effective. Despite the ultimate responsibility for the enterprise, the board does not run the organization: the CEO and the executive leadership team run the company, and the stakes in terms of performance are the highest.

THREE QUESTIONS A BOARD MUST ANSWER

How does a board fulfill its most important obligation and responsibility to ensure it has the best person possible leading the organization? It might be helpful to look at this problem from three perspectives:

1. Does the organization have the right CEO?

2. When a change of succession is at hand, how does the board select the best candidate?

3. If it is necessary to search outside the organization, how does the board find the optimal candidate?

Before addressing these issues, I want to consider several points. First, my operating definition of *leadership* is the capacity to elicit the willing collaboration of others toward a worthwhile goal over an extended period of time with sustainable outcomes. Although the wrong person in the wrong place at the wrong time can destroy significant shareholder value alone, regardless of the size of the organization, the right person in the right place at the right time cannot right the ship alone. Senior executives require the help of others, and securing that help takes leadership. It is, to put it simply, "the quality that persuades others to follow" ("Tough at the Top," 2003). No less than William Shakespeare tapped that essential capacity to lead, when in *Henry IV Part I,* Glendower boasts, "I can call spirits from the vasty deep," to which Hotspur replies, "Why so can I, or so any man, but will they come when you do call for them?"

Second, the operating assumption for approaching these three questions is that there is no single missing ingredient or set of ingredients that every successful leader must possess. CEOs fail or succeed for different reasons: the wrong choice for the organization (as with Nardelli at Home Depot), circumstances in an organization or in the environment outside the organization change, what previously worked for a leader works no longer, staying too long in the job. The board must continually assess the situation. The evidence for deciding one way or another may not be clear or definitive (it seldom is), and in most cases the board waits too long to effect change.

The Right CEO

Despite the challenges and difficulties described, boards do reach effective and appropriate decisions regarding the CEO. They must do several things on an ongoing basis. First, the board must establish a process for interacting with the CEO. This includes board meetings where the CEO is seen with the senior team answering questions and leading the discussion. Such meetings for reviewing and discussing strategies with the CEO and the executive team can take several forms: annual or biannual events, for example, spread out over a couple of days, outside the boardroom.

Another important component is a regularly scheduled session between the board and the CEO alone, with an open dialogue on any or all issues. These issues might include long-term and short-term successors, problems with direct reports, and strategic issues. There is no better way for a board to begin understanding how the organization's top leader thinks than through such conversation. In addition, the entire board should engage in a robust annual assessment of the CEO. Observations and recommendations that emerge from that assessment should be communicated to the CEO by at least two board members, including the lead director or a proxy.

An executive session of the board, where it meets only with the independent directors, should occur at every board meeting. This is another opportunity for the board to review and discuss performance. During these discussions, the role of lead director is critical to ensure constructive discussions that address the individual or collective concerns of the board so that members can build confidence that the organization has the right leadership or, if faced with a problem, decide how best to address it.

An example of the dilemma presented to boards when considering whether the organization has the right person in the job can be found in the story of GE's board of directors and its choice of Jeffrey Immelt as a successor to Jack Welch (Table 13.1 summarizes the story's facts). As reported in *Business Week,* "Along with the burden of replacing the most celebrated CEO of his generation, Immelt inherited an inflated stock price—the so-called Welch premium fostering unrealistic expectations. Yet he has still managed to produce 14% growth in annual earnings and 13% annual revenue gains" (McGregor, Jespersen, and Zegel, 2008, p. 36). The article goes on to highlight the leadership eras of five GE CEOs over fifty years and to provide a measurement of GE's stock price performance during each of their tenures.

What should the board of GE do in Immelt's case? Does GE have the right leader? Does Immelt possess the right mix of ingredients, or is it time for change? Boards of directors face similar dilemmas every day. A CEO is never quite as

Table 13.1
GE Leaders, 1958–Present

CEO	Tenure	Stock Price Return
Ralph Cordiner	1958–1963	45.1%
Fred Borch	1963–1972	7.5
Reg Jones	1972–1981	−28.8
Jack Welch	1981–2001	140.2
Jeffrey Immelt	2001–present	−30.2

Source: McGregor, Jespersen, and Zegel (2008).

good as the numbers and never really never quite as bad. Reg Jones, during his tenure as the leader of GE, was considered the consummate CEO, developing a rigorous strategic planning process adopted by most corporations and beginning the globalization of GE's business. The company doubled sales and earnings yet suffered negative stock returns.

During Jones's tenure, the Dow Jones fell below 1000 and never returned to that level. As Jones prepared to retire, he pushed the selection of a controversial maverick GE manager, Jack Welch, arguably the most celebrated CEO of his era and the archetype of the strong, bold, bigger-than-life corporate leader. During Welch's tenure, GE's market cap grew from $14 billion to $410 billion, and GE Capital expanded from contributing modestly to the organization's income to contributing close to 50 percent of earnings. During this period, the Dow grew from below 1000 to 11,000. Immelt guided GE to 14 percent average growth in earnings between 2005 and 2009, but also saw GE's stock price decline more than 30 percent (McGregor et al., 2008). With the financial services industry in turmoil, what should the GE board have done? What conclusions can we draw in considering a board's ongoing task of determining whether it has the right person—a leader with all the ingredients for meeting the challenges at hand? From this perspective, it is fair to argue that had Jack Welch remained at the helm of GE, the financial outcome and circumstances would be no different.

Developing and Selecting from the Inside

From the board's point of view, the development of one or several successors from inside the institution to succeed a current CEO is the clear preference between selecting an insider or an outsider (Gribben, 2008). Although there never has been and never will be a perfect process for developing internal talent, the opportunity for the board to watch, observe, judge, measure, and assess individuals over a long period of time offers a significantly lower risk than bringing a leader in from the outside, no matter what that leader's track record shows. Critics of CEO compensation often point to the failed internal development of a successor as leading to inflated compensation because it costs more to hire from the outside.

For example, Equalar (a company that tracks executive pay) found that during the period 2007 to early 2008, the median compensation of external hires was 65 percent higher than the median compensation for internally promoted CEOs. Among bigger organizations, the discrepancy was more pronounced: outside hires were compensated at a rate 75 percent higher than internal hires (Tuna, 2008).

Given that an inside candidate is a known quantity, that hiring an outsider is considerably more costly, and that a board of directors' most important responsibility is to ensure that the organization it governs has the right CEO, how should the board approach the succession issue?

First, it is important to distinguish between succession of a successful CEO and replacing a failed one. With rare exceptions, the successor for the successful CEO leading a consistently high-performing institution should come from within the organization. Understanding the culture, values, successful operations model, and key people are critical to the continuous success of a high-performing enterprise and a newly selected CEO. According to John Gabarro (1987), the challenges and successes that internal candidates face are decidedly different from those faced by external candidates. For one, the challenges are greater and the failures more likely for an external candidate. The lack of experience with the organization and the effect of that inexperience on carrying out the CEO assignment, in addition to undeveloped relationships with important players in the organization, contribute to those bigger challenges and higher failure rates. Risk rises when boards recruit from outside the organization. There is no substitute for allowing an individual with increasing responsibilities to lead through the crucible of good times and bad and to demonstrate the development of all the ingredients that are right for the organization at that time. Different circumstances or environmental changes can require different skills.

When a business is not doing well or its CEO has failed as part of a challenged culture, environment, or team, then often the board's best option lies outside the organization. To use a sports analogy, it may be time for a coaching change. The board should be aware, however, that there may be a talented leader in the organization who knows the business, values, and people but was held back by the incumbent CEO. New CEOs of troubled companies need to hit the ground running, and some advantages accrue to promoting from within a dysfunctional organization if the right person is available.

The question remains, How does the board help select the best candidate? In times past, the incumbent CEO would recommend his successor to the board, and there would be easy and ready concurrence. Times have changed. For a number of reasons, not the least of which are the New York Stock Exchange listing requirements, with the rising tide of performance expectations, and requests of boards to be directly involved, circumstances have dramatically altered. So if expectations of board engagement and responsibility for CEO succession have changed, how should the selection process work?

The answer is that the selection process requires a robust organization with a fully developed and active performance management system. There is no one form, no singular approach to developing leaders other than one led by the CEO and the CEO's direct reports, supported by a strong human resource department. Such a system should operate proactively to identify and develop talent across the organization. The top leaders in the organization put this process on display not by what they do but by what they say. Whom they hire, fire, pay, and promote—these decisions say everything about the true values of the institution and its commitment to developing leaders. An organization that aligns these elements with careful and thoughtful sorting of those who can and do deliver results the right way from those who are not and cannot deliver possesses a truly robust system. The outcome of that system should significantly improve the odds for selecting the best possible candidate for continuing the success of the institution.

Companies develop the best leader by creating an environment that permits developmental learning over time. The quality of development does not depend so much on whether that learning to lead comes from a business school or an executive training. Most learning comes from on-the-job experience. As Noel Tichy puts it, "Leadership is a clinical art and people need experience. You don't train a physician by getting a researcher to perform open heart surgery" (quoted in "Tough at the Top," 2003, p. 11). Still, no matter how robust an organization's development process is and no matter how confident the board is that it has selected the perfect person, the truth of how an individual will perform when standing alone in the CEO office will not be visible until that person has been in the job for a period of time and the board can assess if the potential and capabilities it saw during the selection process are evident in its choice.

Managing succession is hard work, requiring the board and CEO to be actively engaged in an ongoing dialogue and discussion through an agreed-on process. Every time the board meets alone with the CEO, which should take place at every board meeting, the board should be comfortable that they are in agreement with the CEO on who should succeed the CEO in case of a disaster. The board and the CEO should also revisit, as needed, appropriate prospective successor candidates to build a consensus on backup succession and prospective succession.

Looking Outside for a New CEO

How does the board fulfill its most important obligation and responsibility in ensuring the best person possible is leading the organization if, after careful deliberation, a suitable candidate cannot be found within the company? Under these circumstances, the tried-and-true method is to select an executive search firm. Boards can work specifically with an individual in that firm that the chairman of the governance committee or chairman of the search committee determines can best understand the needs of the organization. It is essential to work with someone who can provide effective give-and-take communication. The role of the lead director and nonexecutive chairman, in the event they are not the designated head of the search committee, is to work openly and together with the full board to ensure that all board members have an opportunity to participate constructively and thoughtfully in the selection of the next CEO.

The challenge to finding the right leader outside the organization rests in how the board moves beyond very strong and powerful résumés of prospective candidates (because they will all look good) to determine to the best of its ability that the candidate has the right skills and chemistry necessary to take on the job at hand.

Two examples from my own experience might prove useful here. In the case of Wachovia, after the decision was made to ask the incumbent CEO to step down, the board decided that the best course was to look inside and outside the company to ensure the appropriate and necessary experience was found to lead the organization through its financial crisis. Ultimately, after considerable board discussion and deliberation, it was decided that the best candidate under the circumstances would be found outside the company.

Another example is EnPro Industries, a company created through the spin-off of a series of disparate businesses, including asbestos claims and insurance from its parent Goodrich in 2002. Over a six-year period, the CEO who had been executive vice president over these businesses at Goodrich did an effective job of creating a new culture, effecting necessary change so that the new company was able to grow profitably. As he approached retirement age, it was determined after careful review and consideration by the board that finding his successor from within the company would be unlikely. A search was initiated, led by the nonexecutive chairman and the chairman of the compensation committee, who worked with the board, and a successor was selected in spring 2008.

A different kind of story about outside selection emerges from how the board of Hewlett-Packard (HP) struggled with Carly Fiorina's fate. The board brought Fiorina in from the outside with much fanfare (she had led AT&T's successful 1996 spin-off of Lucent Technologies), and for some time the business press reported positively about her tenure, even lionizing the way she led HP. But dissension emerged on the board when she proposed acquiring Compaq Computers. A very public dispute with certain members of the board leaked to the press, showcasing the board members' differences and the governance transgressions on the part of some members. These events culminated in Fiorina's termination, although in hindsight, it appears that the Compaq acquisition was the right strategic move.

Even when a board believes it has the right leader in the right position at the right time, the board's choice may be susceptible to forces beyond its control. Consider the case of General Motors. After announcing record losses for the second quarter of 2008, George Fisher, lead director for General Motors, said, "We are absolutely convinced we have the right team under Rick Wagoner's leadership to get us through these difficult times and on to a bright future" (Vlasic, 2008). In April 2009, under pressure from the U.S. government, Wagoner was asked to step down.

These examples illustrate the dimensions of the challenge that faces a board of directors when it must determine if it has the right CEO in place or should select a successor. That challenge has never been more daunting. As Luke Johnson (2008), one of the leading partners in Risk Capital Partners, a private equity firm, recently said, "This is the eternal question in business: When a company succeeds or fails, is management or the business itself responsible? There is a touching faith among many that certain gifted individuals are superstars who single-handed make everything wonderful. I am much more impressed by companies where the founder steps back but the operation continues to thrive."

Here is an another example from the field. In 1981, I was given my first responsibility as general manager of a division of the Continental Can Company. The business had lost money for four consecutive years and was doing so poorly an effort to sell it was unsuccessful. The only option left was to close it down or perform a high-risk radical surgery. The company closed plants, reduced the division's sales organization from over one hundred people to ten, and made other severe cuts. Survival was the only objective.

That was the scene I stepped into. Immediately a number of simultaneous actions took place. The first was deliberate overcommunication. We held meetings every six months with each shift in the two remaining plants (one union and the other nonunion) and in the home office. We used question boxes to elicit concerns that arose while the division addressed the strategic effect of those meetings. Second, because its workforce had been reduced so dramatically, the division was allowed to select the fittest and, as needed, the best additions that it could find. Third, the division placed a strong focus on product quality, innovation, and improvement, and it combined that focus with an intense effort to build relationships with all key customers. All of these actions were combined by open, aggressive leadership on the part of the five key members of the management team.

During this period, the business environment was undergoing its own transformation. The paper disposables industry was in turmoil. Our competitors, Dixie Cup, Lily Tulip, and Sweetheart, had their own problems. But our new team was in the right place at the right time with the right strategy. Not only were we able to turn the business around; it grew by taking significant market share from our competitors and eventually by looking for acquisitions. At first, no one believed it could survive, let alone prosper. The CEO sent auditors, the head of corporate human resources, and made personal visits to find out if the change was real.

The next thing I knew, I was being asked to give speeches on the turnaround, to answer questions about what I did—not what *we* did. People looked for some secret ingredient or unique approach that they could emulate, but there really was none. The point is that too often we look for simple solutions or formulas when in fact the answer is much more complex. Successful outcomes quite often are due to a much larger series of inputs than a single individual. When a board is considering candidates for the CEO position, the challenge is to sort through circumstances and outcomes so in order to truly measure the impact and capability of the person it is considering for a leadership position.

OTHER CHALLENGES TO BOARDS SEEKING TO FILL THE GAPS IN LEADERSHIP

Another difficult challenge a board can face is determining when an extraordinary leader, loved and admired by all, has stayed too long. The board's group dynamics, which can shift over time as members join or leave, also poses a challenge. Changing circumstances in the external environment can also create difficulties for boards trying to choose the right leader.

One of the examples of the "good to great leaders" that Collins (2001) cites in his book is Ken Iverson of Nucor. For over forty years, Ken led the creation of a unique and powerful culture that combined risk taking and innovative manufacturing processes to help Nucor change the very landscape of the domestic steel business. Although Ken stepped down as CEO in the mid-1990s, he remained a very influential chairman. Ultimately the board, consisting of only one independent member, voted him out of office and off the board, causing Collins to write a postscript on Nucor and Ken, speculating that maybe he wasn't the "level 5 leader" Collins writes about because of that failed transition.

However, what happened at Nucor might be attributable to more than a lack of level 5 leadership, as Collins calls it. In Nucor's case, although Ken and the board had participated in the selection of his successor, Ken remained powerful, influential, and involved in the day-to-day activities of the company as the executive chairman in his early seventies. It took courage, determination, tears, and considerable debate to reach the point where the board could vote to remove him from his responsibilities.

Following his departure, a transition of leadership involved the incumbent CEO and the promotion of a director to executive chairman. During several years of transition, the renewed board, now with a majority of independent directors, was able to establish a process for selecting the next generation of leadership. Today Nucor is bigger and stronger than ever, maintaining the extraordinary culture Ken created. The next generation of leadership has taken the company to new heights. Over the past nine years, Nucor and its CEO, Dan DiMicco, have been cited again and again as leaders in the steel industry, and the company's stock price rose substantially.

Another challenge to consider is the simple fact that no two boards are the same; each board has its own unique dynamics, and so there is no universal best way for any board to put a leader into place. Differences are attributable to many factors, including the culture of the company, the personality and character of the CEO, and the character and personality of the board members. When things are going well, the question of board dynamics and process is not nearly as important as when a critical strategic issue emerges, questions regarding selection arise, or the board is faced with managing a succession. The key role of the lead director or nonexecutive chairman in working with fellow independent board members to ensure constructive ongoing dialogue during the best and worst of times cannot be overemphasized. It is critical that board members' voices are voiced and opinions aired so that constructive discussion can take place.

Group dynamics always pose a challenge to consensus within a group around its most difficult decisions. That challenge can sometimes take the form of groupthink, where the pressure for unanimity offsets the motivation to pursue difficult alternative action. Another way of describing the challenge was articulated by Jerry Harvey (1988): "The inability to manage agreement is a major source of organization dysfunction" (p. 18). Jason Swzeig (2009) put his finger on it when he wrote that well-performing groups are better than their individual members, but badly performing groups are worse than their individual members. "Committees and other groups tend to either follow the leader in a rush of conformity or to polarize into warring camps" (p. B1).

Somehow, over time, board members must develop the capacity to learn how to work together in a way that permits them to overcome these dysfunctions so that they are capable of effectively addressing the critical issues that come before them. Part of the answer, when it comes to selecting an organization's leader, is to have an appropriate mix of perspectives and points of view and individuals who can be effective in raising uncomfortable questions and in disagreeing with the group in a way that fosters constructive debate.

As a consequence, the right lead director, nonexecutive chair, or presiding director (call it what you want) is paramount. A board cannot function well if the board's lead director thinks he or she has more answers than the CEO or aspires to leadership of the business. What is needed is someone who is deft at allowing all views to emerge while moving critical discussions toward a satisfactory conclusion so that the board feels that it has had sufficient opportunity to reflect together toward the best outcome.

While internal group dynamics create internal challenges for a board, keep in mind that external circumstances can also change, creating different kinds of challenges. A rising tide lifting all boats can provide the illusion of significant success and outstanding leadership, but that tide can suddenly go out and leave the organization grounded when economic and industry environmental factors turn sour. And not only the circumstance, but the leader the board selects can also change over time. Skills once thought of as unique and extraordinary seem to no longer exist or are unhelpful in current circumstances.

For better or worse, unless the outcomes are egregiously bad, it takes time to truly determine whether it is the leader, the environment, or circumstances that bring on a lack of performance or even failure. For all of Bob Nardelli's publicized mistakes, he inherited a very difficult circumstance: the transition in leadership from the Home Depot founders was not handled well, a PE ratio in the thirties at the time of Nardelli's succession could not be sustained (the law of large numbers), and the company was much too decentralized to sustain itself given its size and a new, focused competitor with a better model. There are reasons that it took the Home Depot board almost five years to sort through the question of whether it had the right leader. The length of time it took to decide to have Nardelli step down also reflects how difficult the process and decision making can be.

CONCLUSION

What are we to conclude? Are there missing ingredients for extraordinary leadership that boards can look for and measure when placing leaders in the CEO's chair? Absolutely. But those gaps present themselves in different ways and at different times, depending on circumstances. Clearly the wrong person in the wrong place at the wrong time can have a dramatically deleterious effect on an organization's morale and effectiveness, putting the very security of the enterprise at risk, regardless of its size. Conversely, the right person in the right place at the right time—the person with the capacity to select the right team and to bring people together around purpose and strategy—can outperform any peer. Regardless of the strength of experience, résumé, credentials and reference, and regardless of whether a leader is selected from inside or outside an organization, a board will not know if it has chosen the right mix of leadership skills until time has passed in office.

Despite these uncertainties, difficulties, and challenges, the practices that I have described in this chapter can reduce risk and increase certainty on the board that it has the best possible person running the business or that it has selected the right leader to succeed a CEO who is leaving the post. Finding and selecting the right person to lead has been and always will be hard work, requiring the members of the board to work together constructively and thoughtfully. After all, the study of leadership has been with us since the writings of the first historian Herodotus in the fifth century B.C.E. Even across the chasm of twenty-three hundred years, the strengths and flaws of leaders remain a source of powerful gaps that can undermine extraordinary leadership. Like Diogenes' unending quest for the "honest man," to borrow from another ancient author, putting the right person, at the right time, into the right place remains a challenge of utmost concern for boards and the organizations they serve.

Looking Forward

Creating Conditions
for Extraordinary Leadership

Kathy E. Kram
Douglas T. (Tim) Hall
Kerry A. Bunker

This book project has brought us wisdom and hope about our collective future regarding the possibilities for extraordinary leadership. We realize that the world we now live in is more complex than ever before, and it is ever changing. As a consequence, our approaches to leadership development must offer certain opportunities for leaders to learn, reflect, experiment, and dare to be vulnerable. Only with such opportunities will individuals, groups, and organizations generate the capacities to effectively respond and adapt to changing conditions as they unfold.

"Leaderly learning," as Peter Vaill calls it (Chapter Two), is now a necessity. Those who are leading others (and themselves) must regularly reflect on their experiences and learn from them. Furthermore, leaders must reflect more deeply (on their assumptions about how the world works and their role in it) and more rapidly (in time to handle novel and challenging situations) than ever before.

We recognize that this is the primary challenge that we all face—those of us who help leaders meet today's complex challenges and those who lead. Together we must create conditions where such transformative learning can happen even amid permanent turbulence and situations that defy our comprehension.

This book has brought multiple perspectives to this challenge. When we began discussing the idea of a book on this topic, it was unclear what these unique lenses might collectively illuminate and how we might move forward with new wisdom and practical tools. Now we can conclude with excitement and with greater clarity about our vision for the future and how we can move toward it. We hope that readers will embrace at least some of the new perspectives that the chapter authors have articulated and join us in creating new opportunities for individuals and organizations so that they can flourish. The contributors to this book emphasize the need to let go of old assumptions and old practices that no longer serve us, embrace the realities of what is, and collaborate in order to create new assumptions and approaches for leadership and learning.

DEVELOPING LEADERS NOW

The political, social, and economic changes that can touch every sector of our economy became dramatically clear in the fall of 2008. The stability and predictability of earlier decades no longer defines our environment. Organizations must adapt to a very different marketplace in order to survive and thrive, and individuals are having to change jobs—and careers—more often than they ever envisioned. As several of our authors explain, current leadership development practices are insufficient to adequately prepare current and future leaders for the challenges they face.

Peter Cairo and David Dotlich (Chapter Twelve) call for a focus on collective leadership development. In order for individuals and organizations to become sufficiently adaptable and adept at facing persistent and rapid changes in economic conditions, technology, and workforce demographics, approaches to leadership development must necessarily involve, simultaneously, work with individuals, groups, and the organization as a whole. Similarly, in Chapter Eleven, Trina Soske and Jay Conger illustrate with a compelling IBM case study that leadership development can bring about the kind of transformative learning that is needed only through intensive work tailored to the readiness of various groups and individual actors within the system. Morgan McCall and George Hollenbeck

(Chapter Seven) point out that many of our approaches to individual leader development and organization development are still relevant, but in order to address current and future challenges effectively, leaders must give development a high priority—as they do with strategy, performance, and customer service.

These dramatic changes in the external environment have significant implications for current and aspiring leaders. Several chapter authors note that the traditional knowledge, skills, and attitudes that account for executive success are no longer sufficient, and many are outdated, no longer relevant, and even, in some cases, impediments to the communication and innovation essential in today's volatile markets. In her interviews of successful top-level leaders, Naomi Marrow (Chapter One) found a consistent pattern of authenticity, a steady moral compass, and a capacity to build a wide range of connections with individuals inside and outside the organization. These practices were far more essential than the expertise and technical competence once considered essential to leadership success.

Many of our other contributors also noted that authenticity, knowing one's core values, and developing a meaningful and shared vision that clearly addresses a problem larger than the organization's survival itself are now essential to effective leadership. In reflecting on her own leadership journey, her work with the U.S. Army and with the Leader to Leader Institute, and her observations of several contemporary leaders, Frances Hesselbein (Chapter Six) emphasizes the importance of self-knowledge, core values, and a compelling personal and organization mission—the "how to be" leader.

Consistent with this focus on authenticity, transparency, and core values, several authors elaborated on the personal work that brings these attributes alive and transforms the ways that leaders go about their work. Cary Cherniss (Chapter Four) highlighted how critical emotional competence is to the work of leadership in the current context. He illustrated a new peer-group-based technology for enabling individuals to acquire these competencies. Deborah Helsing and Lisa Lahey (Chapter Three) note that a leader's developmental position can limit capacity to achieve personal change goals and stymie effective leadership actions. They offer a method of intensive coaching that addresses such immunity to change and enables individual leaders to move to a more satisfying and effective developmental position. Joyce Fletcher (Chapter Five) points out the social and cultural barriers to relational leadership, in which leaders form empowering connections with others that foster mutual learning and creative work outcomes.

Recognizing the need for greater cognitive complexity and adaptability in our leaders, Barry Oshry demonstrates how critical it is for leaders to understand the forces acting on them as well as the strategies available to them to cope effectively (Chapter Eight). Armed with a people-in-context lens, leaders can more readily create alignment throughout their organizations and avoid the dysfunctional positions that undermine collective leadership.

Similarly, Laura Santana, Mireia las Heras, and Jina Mao (Chapter Ten) point out how critical it is for leaders to develop cross-cultural competence so that they can effectively connect with people of diverse backgrounds and leverage the wide range of differences that comprise the contemporary workforce. Along the same lines, Ilene Wasserman and Stacy Blake-Beard (Chapter Nine) assert that as a result of the dramatic changes we are witnessing, leading inclusively is absolutely essential. They illustrate how embracing relationships with those who bring different perspectives and experiences to the workplace makes it possible to effectively address adaptive (as opposed to technical) leadership challenges. A leader's ability to question personal assumptions and taken-for-granted practices will enable him or her to build diverse developmental networks and diverse teams that lead to both personal learning and innovation at work.

None of these ideas and approaches is entirely new to the discourse on leadership and leadership development. Yet too few leadership development efforts have successfully fostered their adoption and practice. Peter Browning, retired CEO and business educator, describes how boards of directors have a critical role in making sure that CEOs embody the new requirements of individual and collective leadership (Chapter Thirteen), so that they can model effective leadership and reward transformative learning and collaborative leadership among constituents.

We are advocating new definitions of success and competence and new approaches to leadership development that offer promise for addressing complex problems and an increased pace of change. These changes in approach to leadership development and to leadership itself are extremely difficult to bring about; they require letting go of old paradigms and embracing new ones—work that comes with a sense of loss, grief, and fear.

The chapter authors acknowledge those difficulties. Creating the necessary conditions for leaders to let go of old assumptions and approaches to their work, to move toward authenticity, transparency, emotional competence, and maturity, and to develop the courage to be vulnerable is a very tall order. Together, over months of conversation, we came to an important realization: personal learning and the acquisition of new leadership approaches require deep learning of the kind that is difficult to achieve in the context of a high-stress, rapidly changing context.

CREATING CONDITIONS FOR DEEP LEARNING

Early on in our work together, as we discussed senior leaders who had succeeded and those who had derailed, we saw commonalities across the two groups. As other scholars and practitioners have noted, authenticity, a strong sense of core values, transparency, emotional competence, the willingness and ability to continuously learn and adapt, and the drive to create a meaningful, shared vision to have an impact on some aspect of society for the better, were essential characteristics of extraordinary leaders (Day, Zaccaro, and Halpin, 2004; Day, Harrison, and Halpin, 2009). Less clearly known are the strategies for helping aspiring and experienced leaders to develop these critical attributes. Ultimately, however, we discovered several core elements that comprise the leadership development practices that lead to transformative learning.

Beyond the Classroom

The idea that leadership development efforts must extend beyond the formal classroom is not new (McCauley and Van Velsor, 2004). It has been demonstrated that 360-degree feedback, combined with conceptual and experiential learning in a classroom setting, can be very helpful in enhancing leaders' self-awareness and the motivation to continue learning. Due to an increasingly complex and fast-paced environment at work, the trend has been toward shorter programs that do not take managers away from their jobs for too long. As a consequence, the potential for deep learning is curtailed.

Recognizing the limitations of such learning modules, CCL and other leadership development providers have added coaching within the classroom event and as a follow-up to the event. Coaching can reinforce key lessons and provide opportunities for learners to continue to reflect on experiences and apply insights gained at the off-site experience. Furthermore, leadership development practitioners have consistently noted that the right job assignments, combined with ongoing coaching, enhance learning (Kets de Vries and Korotov, 2007).

Relational Learning as a Core Process

One important common element that emerged from our conversations is the idea of relational learning as a core technology for personal learning and development

(Hall, 1996). By this, we mean that learning about self and challenging basic beliefs about self, work, and leadership occur in dialogue with trusted others. This includes coparticipants in an educational program, executive coaches, peer coaches, bosses, subordinates, mentors, and peers back on the job. Indeed, a rich developmental network is critical to continuous learning at work (Kram and Higgins, 2008).

In the past decade, an entire program of research on positive relationships at work has emerged (Cameron, Dutton, and Quinn, 2003; Dutton and Ragins, 2006). Scholars and practitioners are discovering the facets of high-quality connections that lead to mutual learning, increased zest, skill development, innovation, increased self-esteem, and self-confidence (Miller, 2004; Dutton and Heaphy, 2003). These connections offer opportunities for leaders to deepen self-understanding and try out ways of being that lead to authenticity, transparency, and the capacity to inspire others to make a collective, positive difference at work.

These high-quality connections (Dutton and Heaphy, 2003) are not easily established, however, particularly in high-stress environments. Several of the chapter authors have proposed new methodologies as solutions to this dilemma. We hope that development practitioners will adopt those or similar methods. It is our belief that leaders need to develop along these lines. There is no shortage of turbulence, no slacking in the need to get things done, and no substitute for a vision that adapts to changing circumstances but remains true to core values. Leaders at all levels can model effective and productive responses to their organizational environment and encourage others to do the same. The job of leadership development experts is to create space for people to learn and practice these leadership skills and approaches together, even during times of constant urgency. Traditional methods of leadership development have much to offer, but they are no longer sufficient for creating relationships that will sustain the necessary learning back on the job.

Opportunities to Be Vulnerable

Another common theme among the chapter authors is the call for leadership development practitioners, and leaders themselves, to create conditions that enable individuals to be vulnerable. Only with sufficient space and safety can individuals receive useful feedback, reconsider basic assumptions, and experiment with the discomfort sparked by new assumptions and behaviors (Bunker and Wakefield, 2005). The space of vulnerability is where the opportunity to acquire new beliefs and responses is possible and where the encouragement and support of trusted others are essential.

We now know that high-quality relationships with bosses, mentors, peers, and coaches are important vehicles for creating these conditions. At the same time, individuals need a baseline of emotional competence in order to seize the opportunities inherent in relational learning. So anyone charged with developing others needs to find ways to create that platform of emotional competence so that relational learning can begin. This is the trajectory senior leaders must model as a step toward creating a developmental culture in their organizations where individuals are encouraged and recognized for investing in personal learning (Hall, 1996, 2002).

Fortunately, there is a spirit of experimentation among the more forward-looking members of the development community. Some CEOs and other senior leaders are committed to learning how to be vulnerable and how to model this for their constituencies. Executive coaches and leadership development practitioners are partnering with these leaders and learning with them about how to enable others to move through a difficult and often painful learning process. The urgency of contemporary global challenges drives some leaders to mark development as a luxury. But leaders who have experienced a transformation in their approach to leadership and leadership development regard the experience and the promise of extraordinary leadership as essential because of contemporary global challenges.

Balancing Reflective Work with Action

Since leadership education began, there has always been a concern for creating a space for reflection-on-action (Schön, 1987). Traditionally the classroom was viewed as that space. When research revealed that learning becomes more relevant and sustainable when it occurs on the job while working on real problems, development professionals created action learning technologies that enable individuals to develop leadership skills while addressing vital business issues (Raelin, 2000).

The chapter authors have all in one way or another embraced the quandary of designing the appropriate venue and balance of reflective work and action. At this point, if they come to this discussion after spending some time with the book, readers will have engaged with a rich array of approaches that invite systematic reflection and with structured designs that encourage this critical activity while also accomplishing what needs to get done at work. Collectively, we are suggesting that leaders regularly ask these questions of themselves and others to ensure that old assumptions (now outdated) do not guide current behavior. In addition, we are suggesting that this reflective work can and should occur in the classroom, in work teams, and, most important, in relationships with mentors, coaches, bosses, peers, subordinates, and relationships outside the work context. Whether a leader is asking how occupying a specific position in the organization shapes a particular experience and his response to it, or asking how a particular relationship is problematic due to cultural differences that she has not yet understood and explored, posing and answering some of the questions surfaced by our chapter authors will guide leaders to new answers, innovative solutions, and positive work outcomes.

The trend toward reducing classroom time for leadership education is understandable in today's environment. This does not mean, however, that reflective work designed to foster personal learning has to be reduced as well. Quite the contrary. Armed with thought-provoking questions and high-quality relationships that enable vulnerability, self-disclosure, and honest feedback, it is possible for leadership learning to occur while work of strategic importance gets done well. And as with more traditional approaches to leadership development, we will need to assess their impact and hone their effectiveness over time.

CONCLUSION

We are most grateful to the thought leaders who joined us in this book project and helped us to create new approaches to developing leaders and leadership capability in organizations. It is clear that our multiple lenses and varied experiences were essential in uncovering the missing ingredients in leadership development practices. Our hope is that this book will inspire collaborations among individuals who aspire to lead, those already in leadership roles, and the many practitioners whose work it is to enable individuals, teams, and organizations to continuously learn how to develop leadership capacity while meeting persistent challenges posed by the current global context.

This is no small challenge. Each of us involved in developing leaders and the leadership of organizations must be willing to take the same stances toward learning and action that we are asking of them. We also must be vulnerable, authentic, creative, reflective, and risk taking as we seek more effective ways to address the entirely new challenges of today's context. We also need to model what we expect of leaders as they strive to develop the new capabilities described in this book, and we need to provide the relational support that makes it possible for others to strive toward the necessary reflection, self-understanding, and challenge of trying out new and difficult actions. If managers and executives are to develop their critical leader capabilities on a timely basis, they will need to think systemically, establish and live by a set of core ethical values, and consistently challenge old assumptions about gender, power, and other forms of diversity that have historically limited the potential of individuals and organizations in significant yet hidden ways. Combined, these challenges are a tall order that none of us can fill alone. We must establish and nurture growth-enhancing relationships with our colleagues, clients, coaches, teachers, and researchers and together learn what is essential to learn.

There is no choice now but to adapt, advance, and thrive. Let us move forward now.

REFERENCES

INTRODUCTION

Booz Allen Hamilton. (2007). CEO turnover remains high at world's largest companies. Retrieved May 22, 2007, from http://www.boozallen.com/news/36608085.

Bunker, K. A., Kram, K. E., & Ting, S. (2002). The young and the clueless. *Harvard Business Review*, *80*(12), 80–87.

Bunker, K. A., & Wakefield, M. (2005). *Leading with authenticity in times of transition*. Greensboro, NC: Center for Creative Leadership.

Bunker, K. A., & Webb, A. D. (1993). *Against the grain: How we learn from experience*. Unpublished manuscript, Center for Creative Leadership.

Cascio, W. F. (2003, November-December). Responsible restructuring: Seeing employees as assets, not costs. *Ivey Business Journal*, 1–5.

Grint, K. (1994). Reengineering the labyrinth: The Ariadne option. *Focus on Change Management*, *1*(1), 21–23.

Henry, D., & Jespersen, F. F. (2002, Oct. 14). Mergers: Why most big deals don't pay off. *BusinessWeek*, 60–70.

Lucier, C., & Wheeler, S. (2007). *The era of the inclusive CEO*. Strategy and Business Webinar. Retrieved August 16, 2007, from http://www.strategy-business.com/webinars/webinar/webinar-inc_ceo?pg=0.

Marks, M. L., & Mirvis, P. H. (1998). *Joining forces*. San Francisco: Jossey-Bass.

Spencer, S. (2007). *Navigating the barriers to CEO succession*. Retrieved July 2007 from http://www.spencerstuart.com/research/succession/1162.

Super-star CEOs are out; inclusive in. (2007). *Economic Times*. Retrieved June 19, 2007, from http://economictimes.indiatimes.com/Jobs/Super-star-CEOs-are-out-inclusive-in/articleshow/2186370.cms.

Weisman, R. (2008). Being a CEO has its perks, but tenure isn't one of them. *Boston Globe*. Retrieved May 14, 2008, from http://www.livemint.com/ 2008/05/14000154/Being-a-CEO-has-its-perks-but.html.

PART ONE

Hogan, R., & Warrenfeltz, R. (2003). Educating the modern manager. *Academy of management learning and education, 2*(1), 74–84.

CHAPTER ONE

Bennis, W. (2003). *On becoming a leader* (Rev. ed.). New York: Basic Books.

Bennis, W. G., & Thomas, R. J. (2002). *Geeks and geezers: How eras, values, and defining moments shape leaders.* Boston: Harvard Business School Press.

Bunker, K. A., Kram, K. E., & Ting, S. (2002). The young and the clueless. *Harvard Business Review, 80*(12), 80–87.

Dolnick, S. (2009). Third Satyam exec detained after fraud scandal. *Huffington Post*. Retrieved July 16, 2009, from http://www.huffingtonpost.com/huff-wires/20090110/as-india-satyamscandal/diff_D95KE1IG0_D95KEI5O0.html.

Friedman, T. L. (2008). *Hot, flat, and crowded: Why we need a green revolution and how it can renew America.* New York: Farrar, Straus and Giroux.

Goleman, D. (2000). *Working with emotional intelligence.* New York: Bantam Books.

Johansen, B. (2007). *Get there early: Sensing the future to compete in the present.* San Francisco: Berrett-Koehler.

McCall, M. W., Jr. (1998). *High flyers: Developing the next generation of leaders.* Boston: Harvard Business School Press.

McCall, M. W., Jr., Lombardo, M. M., & Morrison, A. M. (1988). *The lessons of experience: How successful executives develop on the job.* New York: Free Press.

Sorcher, M. (1985). *Predicting executive success: What it takes to make it into senior management.* Hoboken, NJ: Wiley.

Welch, J., & Welch, S. (2007, January 29). Hiring wrong—and right. *Business Week*, 102 .

CHAPTER TWO

Ackoff, R. L. (1974). *Redesigning the future*. Hoboken, NJ: Wiley.

Barnard, C. (1938). *The functions of the executive*. Cambridge, MA: Harvard University Press.

Bennis, W., & Slater, P. (1998). *The temporary society*. San Francisco: Jossey-Bass.

Charan, R., & Colvin, G. (1999, June 21). Why CEOs fail. *Fortune*, 68–78.

Frankl, V. E. (2006). *Man's search for meaning*. Boston: Beacon Press.

Koontz, H., & O'Donnell, C. (1968). *Principles of management: An analysis of managerial functions* (4th ed.). New York: McGraw-Hill.

McGregor, D. (1960). *The human side of enterprise*. New York: McGraw-Hill.

Pattakos, A. (2004). *Prisoners of our thoughts*. San Francisco: Berrett-Koehler.

Vaill, P. B. (1978). Toward a behavioral description of high-performing systems. In M. W. McCall & M. M. Lombardo (Eds.), *Leadership: Where else can we go?* (pp. 103–125). Durham, NC: Duke University Press.

Vaill, P. B. (1996). *Learning as a way of being*. San Francisco: Jossey-Bass.

Vaill, P. B. (1998). *Spirited leading and learning: Process wisdom for a new age*. San Francisco: Jossey-Bass.

CHAPTER THREE

Basseches, M. (1984). *Dialectical thinking and adult development*. Norwood, NJ: Ablex.

Belenky, M., Clinchy, B., Goldberger, N., & Tarule, J. (1986). *Women's ways of knowing: The development of self, mind, and voice*. New York: Basic Books.

Cranton, P. (1994). *Understanding and promoting transformative learning: A guide for educators of adults*. San Francisco: Jossey-Bass.

Daloz, L. A. (1986). *Effective teaching and mentoring: Realizing the transformational power of adult learning experiences*. San Francisco: Jossey-Bass.

Drath, W. H. (1990). Managerial strengths and weaknesses as functions of the development of personal meaning. *Journal of Applied Behavioral Science, 26*(4), 483–499.

Eigel, K. (1998). *Leader effectiveness: A constructive-developmental view and investigation.* Unpublished doctoral dissertation, University of Georgia.

Harris, L. S. (2005). *An examination of executive leadership effectiveness using constructive-developmental theory.* Unpublished master's thesis, University of Georgia.

Joiner, B., & Josephs, S. (2007). *Leadership agility: Five levels of mastery for anticipating and initiating change.* San Francisco: Jossey-Bass.

Kegan, R. (1982). *The evolving self: Problem and process in human development.* Cambridge, MA: Harvard University Press.

Kegan, R. (1994). *In over our heads: The mental demands of modern life.* Cambridge, MA: Harvard University Press.

Kegan, R. (2000). What "form" transforms? A constructive-developmental approach to transformative learning. In J. Mezirow (Ed.), *Learning as transformation* (pp. 35–69). San Francisco: Jossey-Bass.

Kegan, R. (2001). Competencies as working epistemologies: Ways we want adults to know. In D. S. Rychen & L. H. Salganik (Eds.), *Defining and selecting key competencies* (pp. 192–204). Kirkland, WA: Hogrefe & Huber.

Kegan, R., & Lahey, L. L. (2001). *How the way we talk can change the way we work: Seven languages for transformation.* San Francisco: Jossey-Bass.

Kegan, R., & Lahey, L. L. (2009). *Immunity to change: How to overcome it and unlock the potential in yourself and your organization.* Boston: Harvard Business School Press.

Kohlberg, L. (1984). *Stage and sequence the cognitive developmental approach to socialization: The psychology of moral development.* San Francisco: HarperSanFrancisco.

McCauley, C. D., Drath, W. H., Palus, C. J., O'Connor, P.M.G., & Baker, B. A. (2006). The use of constructive-developmental theory to advance the understanding of leadership. *Leadership Quarterly, 17,* 634–653.

Mezirow, J. (1991). *Transformative dimensions of adult learning.* San Francisco: Jossey-Bass.

Piaget, J. (1952). *The origins of intelligence in children.* New York: International Universities Press.

Senge, P. (1990). *The fifth discipline.* New York: Doubleday.

Strang, S. E. (2006). *Big five personality and leadership development levels as predictors of leader performance.* Unpublished master's thesis, University of Georgia.

Torbert, B., & Associates. (2004). *Action inquiry: The secret of timely and transforming leadership.* San Francisco: Berrett-Koehler.

Wagner, T., Kegan, R., Lahey, L., Lemons, R. W., Garnier, J., Helsing, D., et al. (2006). *Change leadership: A practical guide to transforming our schools.* San Francisco: Jossey-Bass.

Weathersby, R. (1976). *A synthesis of research and theory on adult development: its implications for adult learning and postsecondary education.* Unpublished qualifying paper, Harvard Graduate School of Education.

CHAPTER FOUR

Bar-On, R., Handley, R., & Fund, S. (2005). The impact of emotional intelligence on performance. In V. Druskat, F. Sala, & G. Mount (Eds.), *Linking emotional intelligence and performance at work: Current research evidence* (pp. 3–20). Mahwah, NJ: Erlbaum.

Belbin, R. M. (1996). *Team roles at work.* Burlington, MA: Butterworth-Heinemann.

Boyatzis, R. E. (2006). Core competencies in coaching others to overcome dysfunctional behavior. In V. Druskat, F. Sala, & G. Mount (Eds.), *Linking emotional intelligence and performance at work* (pp. 81–96). Mahwah, NJ: Erlbaum.

Boyatzis, R. E., & Saatcioglu, A. (2008). A twenty-year view of trying to develop emotional, social and cognitive intelligence competencies in graduate management education. *Journal of Management Development, 27,* 92–108.

Cavallo, K., & Brienza, D. (2002). *Emotional competence and leadership excellence at Johnson & Johnson: The Emotional Intelligence and Leadership Study.* Consortium for Research on Emotional Intelligence in Organizations, Rutgers University. Retrieved October 20, 2009, from http://www.eiconsortium.org/pdf/jj_ei_study.pdf.

Cherniss, C., & Adler, M. (2000). *Promoting emotional intelligence in organizations.* Alexandria, VA: ASTD.

Goleman, D. (1998, November-December). What makes a leader? *Harvard Business Review, 76*, 92–102.

Goleman, D., Boyatzis, R., & McKee, A. (2002). *Primal leadership: Realizing the power of emotional intelligence.* Boston: Harvard Business School Press.

Hopkins, M. M., & Bilmoria, D. (2008). Social and emotional competencies predicting success for male and female executives. *Journal of Management Development, 27*(1), 13–35.

Judge, T. A., Colbert, A. E., & Ilies, R. (2004). Intelligence and leadership: A quantitative review and test of theoretical propositions. *Journal of Applied Psychology, 89*(3), 542–552.

Kerr, R., Garvin, J., & Heaton, N. (2006). Emotional intelligence and leadership effectiveness. *Leadership and Organization Development Journal, 27*, 265–279.

Lehrer, J. (2008). Colombian defense chief describes risks, planning for hostage rescue. *Online Newshour.* Retrieved July 3, 2008, from http://www.pbs .org/newshour/bb/latin_america/july-dec08/colombiarescue_07–03.html.

Liautaud, J. P. (2006). *Application, protocol and theory of PdEI.* Chicago: Liautaud Graduate School of Business, University of Illinois at Chicago.

Lombardo, M. M., Ruderman, M. N., & McCauley, C. (1988). Explanations of success and derailment in upper-level management positions. *Journal of Business and Psychology, 2*, 199–216.

Mayer, J. D. (2006). A new field guide to emotional intelligence. In J. Ciarrochi, J. P. Forgas, & J. D. Mayer (Eds.), *Emotional intelligence in everyday life: A scientific inquiry* (2nd ed., pp. 3–26). Philadelphia: Psychology Press.

McClelland, D. C. (1998). Identifying competencies with behavioral-event interviews. *Psychological Science, 9*(5), 331–339.

Palmer, P. J. (2004). *A hidden wholeness: The journey toward an undivided life.* San Francisco: Jossey-Bass.

Parker, P., Hall, D. T., & Kram, K. E. (2008). Peer coaching: A relational process for accelerating career learning. *Academy of Management Learning and Education, 7*, 487–503.

Rosete, D. (2007). *Does emotional intelligence play an important role in leadership effectiveness?* Unpublished doctoral dissertation, University of Wollongong, Wollongong, New South Wales, Australia.

Seligman, M.E.P. (1993). *What you can change and what you can't: The complete guide to successful self-improvement*. New York: Knopf.

Seligman, M.E.P. (2002). *Authentic happiness: Using the new positive psychology to realize your potential for lasting fulfillment*. New York: Free Press.

Yalom, I. V. (2005). *The theory and practice of group psychotherapy* (5th ed.). New York: Basic Books.

CHAPTER FIVE

Aaltio-Marjosola, I. (2001, June). *Charismatic leadership, manipulation and the complexity of organizational life*. Paper presented at the MIT Sloan School of Management Organizational Studies Seminar Series, Cambridge, MA.

Agashae, Z., & Bratton, J. (2001). Leader-follower dynamics: Developing a learning environment. *Journal of Workplace Learning, 13*(3/4), 89–103.

Badaracco, J. (2002). *Leading quietly*. Boston: Harvard Business School Press.

Bailyn, L. (2007). *Breaking the mold: Women, men, and time in the new corporate world* (2nd ed.). New York: Free Press

Bartolome, F., & Laurent, A. (1988). Managers: Torn between two roles. *Personnel Journal, 67*(10), 72–83.

Bradbury, H., & Lichtenstein, B. (2000). Relationality in organizational research: Exploring the space between. *Organization Science, 11*(5), 551–566.

Calas, M., & Smircich, L. (1991). Voicing seduction to silence leadership. *Organization Studies, 12*, 567–602.

Calvert, L., & Ramsey, V. J. (1992). Bringing women's voice to research on women in management: A feminist perspective. *Journal of Management Inquiry, 1*(1), 79–88.

Collins, J. (2001). *Good to great*. New York: HarperBusiness.

Conger, J. (1989). Leadership: The art of empowering others. *Academy of Management Executive, 3*, 17–24.

Cox, J., Pearce, C. & Sims, H. P. (2003). Toward a broader leadership development agenda: Extending the traditional transactional-transformation duality by developing directive, empowering and shared leadership skills. In S. Murphy & R. Riggio (Eds.), *The future of leadership development*. Mahwah, NJ: Erlbaum.

Day, D., Gronn, P., & Salas, E. (2004). Leadership capacity in teams. *Leadership Quarterly, 15*(6), 857–868.

Dutton, J. (2003). *Energize your workplace: How to create and sustain high-quality connections at work.* San Francisco: Jossey-Bass.

Dutton, J. E., & Heaphy, E. D. (2003). The power of high-quality connections. In K. S. Cameron, J. E. Dutton, & R. E. Quinn (Eds.), *Positive organizational scholarship: Foundations of a new discipline* (pp. 263–278). San Francisco: Berrett-Koehler.

Eagly, A. H., & Carli, L. L. (2007). *Through the labyrinth: The truth about how women become leaders.* Boston: Harvard Business School Press.

Ely, R., & Meyerson, D. (2009). *Undoing gender in a traditionally male workplace.* Manuscript submitted for publication.

Flax, J. (1990). *Thinking fragments.* Berkeley: University of California Press.

Fletcher, J. K. (1994). Castrating the female advantage. *Journal of Management Inquiry, 3*(1), 74–82.

Fletcher, J. K. (1999). *Disappearing acts: Gender, power and relational practice at work.* Cambridge, MA: MIT Press.

Fletcher, J. K. (2004). The paradox of post heroic leadership: An essay on gender, power and transformational change. *Leadership Quarterly, 15*, 647–661.

Fletcher, J. K. (2007). Leadership, power and positive relationships. In J. Dutton & B. Ragins (Eds.), *Exploring positive relationships at work* (pp. 347–372). Mahwah, NJ: Erlbaum.

Fletcher, J. K., & Jacques, R. (2000). *Relational practice: An emerging stream of theorizing and its significance for organizational studies.* Working paper, Center for Gender in Organizations, Simmons School of Management, Boston. Retrieved October 21, 2009, from www.simmons.edu/som/cgo.

Fletcher, J. K., & Kaeufer, K. (2003). Shared leadership: Paradox and possibility. In C. Pearce & J. Conger (Eds.), *Shared leadership: Reframing the hows and whys of leadership* (pp. 21–47). Thousand Oaks, CA: Sage.

Foldy, E. (2002). *Be all that you can be.* Unpublished doctoral dissertation, Boston College.

Fondas, N. (1997). Feminization unveiled: Management qualities in contemporary writings. *Academy of Management Review, 22*, 257–282.

Gardner, H. (1990). *On leadership*. New York: Free Press.

Gittell, J. (2003). A theory of relational coordination. In K. Cameron, J. Dutton, & R. Quinn (Eds.), *Positive organizational scholarship* (pp. 279–295). San Francisco: Berrett-Koehler.

Goffman, E. (1959). *The presentation of self in everyday life*. New York: Doubleday.

Goleman, D. (1998). *Working with emotional intelligence*. New York: Bantam Books

Goleman, D. (2006). *Social intelligence*. New York: Bantam Books.

Goleman, D., Boyatzis R., & McKee, A. (2002). *Primal leadership*. Boston: Harvard Business School Press.

Graen, G. B., & Scandura, T. A. (1987). Toward a psychology of dyadic organizing. In L. L. Cummings & B. M. Staw (Eds.), *Research in organizational behavior* (pp. 175–208). Greenwich, CT: JAI Press.

Graen, G., & Uhl-Bien, M. (1995). Relationship-based approach to leadership: Development of leader-member exchange (LMX) theory of leadership over 25 years: Applying a multi-level multi-domain perspective. *Leadership Quarterly*, 6(2), 219–247.

Harrington, M. (2000). *Care and equality*. New York: Routledge.

Heifitz, R., & Laurie, D. (1999). Mobilizing adaptive work: Beyond visionary leadership. In J. Conger, G. Spreitzer, & E. Lawler (Eds.), *The leader's change handbook*. San Francisco: Jossey-Bass.

Hill, L. (2004). New manager development for the 21st century. *Academy of Management Executive*, 18(3), 121.

Holvino, E. (2008). Intersections: The simultaneity of race, gender and class in organization studies. *Gender, Work and Organization*, 15, 968–993.

Hosking, D., Dachler, H. P., & Gergen, K. J. (Eds.). (1995). *Management and organization: Relational alternative to individualism*. Aldershot, UK: Ashgate Publishing.

Jacobsen, S., & Jacques, R. (1997). Destabilizing the field. *Journal of Management Inquiry*, 6(1), 42–59.

Jordan, J. V. (1986). *The meaning of mutuality* (No. 23). Retrieved from http://www.wcwonline.org.

Kahane, A. (2004). *Solving tough problems.* San Francisco: Berrett-Koehler.

Kanter, R. M. (1977). *Men and women of the corporation.* New York: Basic Books.

Kanter, R. M. (2001). *E-volve!* Boston: Harvard Business School Press.

Kayes, D. C. (2004). The 1996 Mount Everest climbing disaster: The breakdown of learning in teams. *Human Relations, 57*(10), 1263–1285.

Kim, D. H. (1993). The link between individual and organizational learning. *Sloan Management Review, 34,* 37–50.

Kouzes, J., & Posner, B. (2007). *The leadership challenge* (4th ed.). San Francisco: Jossey-Bass.

Kristof, N. D. (2008, June 12). The sex speech. *New York Times.*

Lipman Blumen, J. (1996). *The connective edge.* San Francisco: Jossey-Bass.

Lipnack, J., & Stamps, J. (2000). *Virtual teams.* Hoboken, NJ: Wiley.

Lord, R. G., & Maher, K. J. (1993). *Leadership and information processing: Linking perceptions and performance.* Boston: Routledge.

Luthans, F., & Avolio, B. (2003). Authentic leadership development. In K. Cameron, J. Dutton, & R. Quinn (Eds.), *Positive organizational scholarship* (pp. 241–258). San Francisco: Berrett-Koehler.

Martin, P. Y. (1996). Gendering and evaluating dynamics: Men, masculinities and managements. In D. Collinson & J. Hearn (Eds.), *Men as managers, managers as men* (pp. 186–209). Thousand Oaks, CA: Sage.

Martin, P. Y., & Collinson, D. L. (1998). Gender and sexuality in organizations. In M. M. Ferree, J. Lorder, & B. Hess (Eds.), *Revisioning gender.* Thousand Oaks, CA: Sage.

Mayo, M., Meindl, J., & Pastor, J. (2003). Shared leadership in work teams: A social network approach. In C. Pearce & J. Conger (Eds.), *Shared leadership: Reframing the hows and whys of leadership* (pp. 21–47). Thousand Oaks, CA: Sage.

McNamee, S., & Gergen, K. J. (1999). *Relational responsibility: Resources for sustainable dialogue.* Thousand Oaks, CA: Sage.

Miller, J. B. (1976). *Toward a new psychology of women.* Boston: Beacon Press.

Miller, J. B., & Stiver, I. (1997). *The healing connection.* Boston: Beacon Press.

Pearce, C., & Conger, J. (2003). A landscape of opportunities: Future research on shared leadership. In C. Pearce & J. Conger (Eds.), *Shared leadership: Reframing the hows and whys of leadership* (pp. 285–304). Thousand Oaks, CA: Sage.

Peters, T. (2003). *Re-imagine!* New York: DK Publishing.

Ragins, B. R., & Verbos, A. K. (2007). Positive relationships in action: Relational mentoring and mentoring schemas at work. In J. Dutton & B. Ragins (Eds.), *Exploring positive relationships at work* (pp. 91–116). Mahwah, NJ: Erlbaum.

Seely Brown, J., & Duguid, P. (2000). *The social life of information*. Boston: Harvard Business School Press.

Senge, P. (1990). The leader's new work: Building learning organizations. *Sloan Management Review, 32*(1), 7–23.

Sutcliffe, K., & Vogus, T. (2003). Organizing for resilience. In K. Cameron, J. Dutton, & R. Quinn (Eds.), *Positive organizational scholarship* (pp. 94–110). San Francisco: Berrett-Koehler.

Thompson, L. (2004). *Making the team* (2nd ed.). Upper Saddle River, NJ: Prentice Hall.

Uhl-Bien, M. (2006). Relationship leadership theory: Exploring the social processes of leadership and organizing. *Leadership Quarterly, 17*(6), 654–676.

Vera, D., & Crossan, M. (2004). Strategic leadership and organizational learning. *Academy of Management Review, 29*(2), 222–240.

Vera, D., & Rodriguez-Lopez, A. (2004). Strategic virtues: Humility as a source of competitive advantage. *Organizational Dynamics, 33*(4), 393–408.

Watkins, K. E., & Cervero, R. M. (2000)., Organizations as contexts for learning: A case study in certified accountancy. *Journal of Workplace Learning, 12*(5, 6), 187–194.

West, C., & Zimmerman, D. (1991). Doing gender. In J. Lorber & S. Farrell (Eds.), *The social construction of gender* (pp. 13–37). Thousand Oaks, CA: Sage.

Wheatley, M. (2001). *Leadership and the new science: Discovering order in a chaotic world*. Thousand Oaks, CA: Sage.

Yukl, G. P. (1998). *Leadership in organizations* (4th ed.). Upper Saddle River, NJ: Prentice Hall.

Zaccaro, S., Rittman, A. L., & Marks, M. A. (2001). Team leadership. *Leadership Quarterly, 12*(4), 451–484.

Zaleznik, A. (1992). Managers and leaders: Are they different? *Harvard Business Review, 70*(2), 126–136.

CHAPTER SIX

Hesselbein, F., Shinseki, E. K., & Cavanagh, R. E. (2004). *Be know do: Leadership the army way, adapted from the official army leadership manual.* San Francisco: Jossey-Bass.

Hill, R. B. (2003). *The strengths of black families* (2nd ed.). Lanham, MD: University Press of America.

CHAPTER SEVEN

Byrnes, N. (2005, October 10). Star search. *BusinessWeek*, 68–78.

Collins, J. (2001). *Good to great*. New York: HarperBusiness.

Colvin, G. (2007, October 1). Leader machines. *Fortune*, 98–106.

Drucker, P. F. (1985, July-August). Getting things done: How to make people decisions. *Harvard Business Review*, 22–26.

Ericsson, K., Charness, N., Feltovich, P., & Hoffman, R. (Eds). (2006). *The Cambridge handbook of expertise and expert performance.* Cambridge: Cambridge University Press.

Hollenbeck, G. (2009). Executive selection: What's right and what's wrong. *Industrial and Organizational Psychology: Perspectives on Science and Practice, 2*, 130–143.

Hollenbeck, G. P., & McCall, M. W., Jr. (2003). Competence, not competencies: Making global executive development work. In W. Mobley & P. Dorfman (Eds.), *Advances in global leadership*. Greenwich, CT: JAI/Elsevier, 2003.

Hogan, J., Hogan, R., & Kaiser, R. B. (in press). Management derailment: Personality assessment and mitigation. In S. Zedeck (Ed.), *American*

Psychological Association handbook of industrial and organizational psychology. Washington, DC: American Psychological Association.

Howard, A. (2007). Best practices in leader selection. In J. Conger & R. Riggio (Eds.), *The practice of leadership: Developing the next generation of leaders.* San Francisco: Jossey-Bass.

Howard, A., Erker, S., & Bruce, N. (2007). *Selection forecast 2006/2007.* Pittsburgh, PA: Development Dimensions International.

Mahler, W., & Wrightnour, W. (1973). *Executive continuity: How to build and retain and effective management team.* Homewood, IL: Dow Jones-Irwin, 1973.

McCall, M. (1998). *High flyers.* Boston: Harvard Business School Press.

McCall, M. W., Jr., & Hollenbeck, G. P. (2002). *Developing global executives.* Boston: Harvard Business School Press.

McCall, M. W., Jr., & Hollenbeck, G. P. (2007). Getting leader development right: Competence not competencies. In J. Conger and R. Riggio (Eds.), *The practice of leadership.* San Francisco: Jossey-Bass.

McCall, M. W., Jr., & Hollenbeck, G. P. (2008). Developing the expert leader. *People and Strategy, 31,* 20–28.

McCall, M., Lombardo, M., & Morrison, A. (1988). *The lessons of experience.* Lanham, MD: Lexington Books.

Oldfield, D. (1991). *Private paths, common ground.* Washington, DC: Foundation for Contemporary Mental Health.

Sennett, R. (2008). *The craftsman.* New Haven, CT: Yale University Press.

Sorcher, M., & Brant, J. (2002, February). Are you picking the right leaders? *Harvard Business Review,* 78–85.

Steinbeck, J. (1951). *The log from the Sea of Cortez.* New York: Viking.

Thornton, G. C., III, Hollenbeck, G. P., & Johnson, S. K. (in press). Selecting leaders: Executives and high potentials. In J. Farr & N. Tippins (Eds.), *Handbook of employee selection.* Philadelphia: Psychology Press.

The top companies for leaders. (2007, October 1). *Fortune,* 109–116.

Welch, J., & Welch, S. (2007, January 29). Hiring wrong—and right. *Business Week,* 102.

CHAPTER EIGHT

Oshry, B. (1994). *In the middle*. Boston: Power + Systems.

Oshry, B. (1999). *Leading systems: Lessons from the Power Lab*. San Francisco: Berrett-Koehler.

Oshry, B. (2007). *Seeing systems: Unlocking the mysteries of organizational life*. San Francisco: Berrett-Koehler.

CHAPTER NINE

Bass, B. N. (1985). *Leadership and performance beyond expectations*. New York: Free Press.

Bennis, W., & Nanus, B. (1985). *Leaders: The strategies for taking charge*. New York: HarperCollins.

Blake-Beard, S. D. (in press). Mentoring as a bridge to understanding cultural difference. *Adult Learning*.

Blake-Beard, S. D., Murrell, A. J., & Thomas, D. A. (2007). Unfinished business: The impact of race on understanding mentoring relationships. In B. R. Ragins & K. E. Kram (Eds.), *The handbook of mentoring*. Thousand Oaks, CA: Sage.

Burns, J. M. (1978). *Leadership*. New York: HarperCollins.

Cissna, K. N., & Anderson, R. (1998). Theorizing about dialogic moments: The Buber-Rogers position and postmodern themes. *Communication Theory*, *8*(1), 63–104.

Crenshaw, K. W. (1994). Mapping the margins: Intersectionality, identity politics, and violence against women of color. In F. M. Albertson Fineman & R. Mykitiuk (Eds.), *The public nature of private violence* (pp. 93–118). New York: Routledge.

Fisher-Yoshida, B., Geller, K., & Wasserman, I. (2005, February). *Transformative learning in human resource development: Successes in scholarly practitioner applications: Conflict Management, Discursive Processes in Diversity and Leadership Development*. Paper presented at the Academy for Human Resource Development Proceedings, Estes Park, CO. Retrieved October 20, 2009, from http://www.eric.ed.gov/ERICDocs/data/ericdocs2sql/content_storage_01/0000019b/80/1b/db/df.pdf.

Fletcher, J. K. (1999). *Disappearing acts: Gender, power, and relational practice at work*. Cambridge, MA: MIT Press.

Gilligan, C. (1982). *In a different voice: Psychological theory and women's development*. Cambridge, MA: Harvard University Press.

Heifetz, R. (1994). *Leadership without easy answers*. Cambridge, MA: Harvard University Press.

Heifetz, R., & Linsky, M. (2002). *Leadership on the line: Staying alive through the dangers of leading*. Boston: Harvard Business School Press.

Heifetz, R. A., Linsky, M., & Grashow, A. (2009). *The practice of adaptive leadership: Tools and tactics for changing your organization and the world*. Boston: Harvard Business School Press.

Hesselbein, F., Shinseki, E. S., & Cavanagh, R. E. (2004). *Be know do: Leadership the army way, adapted from the official army leadership manual*. San Francisco: Jossey-Bass.

Higgins, M. C., & Kram, K. E. (2001). Reconceptualizing mentoring at work: A developmental network perspective. *Academy of Management Review, 26*(2), 264–288.

hooks, b. (1989). *Talking back: Thinking feminist, thinking black*. Boston: South End Press.

Jordan, J. V., Kaplan, A. G., Miller, J. B., Stiver, I. P., & Surrey, J. L. (1991). *Women's growth in connection: Writings from the Stone Center*. New York: Guilford Press.

Kegan, R. (1994). *In over our heads: The mental demands of modern life*. Cambridge, MA: Harvard University Press.

Kegan, R. (2000). What "form" transforms? A constructive-developmental approach to transformative learning. In J. Mezirow (Ed.), *Learning as transformation* (pp. 35–69). San Francisco: Jossey-Bass.

Kochan, T., Bezrukova, K., Ely, R., Jackson, S., Joshi, A., Jehn, K., et al. (2003). The effects of diversity on business performance: Report of the diversity research network. *Human Resource Management, 42*(1), 3–21.

Kouzes, J. M., & Posner, B. Z. (2002). *The leadership challenge* (3rd ed.). San Francisco: Jossey-Bass.

Kram, K. E. (1983). Phases of the mentor relationship. *Academy of Management Journal, 26*, 608–625.

Kwak, M. (2003, Spring). The paradoxical effects of diversity. *MIT Sloan Management Review*, 7–8.

Lorde, A. (1984). *Sister outsider: Essays and speeches.* Trumansburg, NY: Crossing Press.

Marsick, V. J. (1990). Action learning and reflection in the workplace. In J. Mezirow (Ed.), *Fostering critical reflection in adulthood: A guide for transformative and emancipatory learning.* San Francisco: Jossey-Bass.

McNamee, S., & Gergen, K. J. (1999). *Relational responsibility: Resources for sustainable dialogue.* Thousand Oaks, CA: Sage.

Mezirow, J. (2003). Transformative learning as discourse. *Journal of Transformative Learning, 1*(1), 58–63.

Miller, J. B., & Stiver, I. P. (1997). *The healing connection: How women form relationships in therapy and in life.* Boston: Beacon Press.

Nkomo, S. M., & Cox, T., Jr. (1996). Diverse identities in organizations. In S. R. Clegg, C. Hardy & W. R. Nord (Eds.), *Handbook of organization studies* (pp. 338–356). Thousand Oaks, CA: Sage.

Okazawa-Rey, M., & Kirk, G. (2007). *Women's lives: Multicultural perspectives* (4th ed.). New York: McGraw-Hill.

Pearce, W. B. (2004). The coordinated management of meaning (CMM). In B. G. (Ed.), *Theorizing about communication and culture.* Thousand Oaks, CA: Sage.

Schön, D. A. (1991). *The reflective turn: Case studies in and on educational practice.* New York: Teachers College Press.

Styhre, A., & Eriksson-Zetterquist, U. (2008). Thinking the multiple in gender and diversity studies: Examining the concept of intersectionality. *Gender in Management: An International Journal, 23*(8), 567–582.

Thomas, D. A. (2004). Diversity as strategy. *Harvard Business Review, 82*(9), 98–108.

Thomas, D. A., & Ely, R. J. (1996). Making differences matter: A new paradigm for managing diversity. *Harvard Business Review, 74*(5), 79–90.

Wasserman, I. (2004). *Discursive processes that foster dialogic moments: Transformation in the engagement of social identity group differences in dialogue.* Unpublished doctoral dissertation, Fielding Graduate Institute, Santa Barbara, CA.

Wasserman, I. (2005, August). Appreciative inquiry and diversity: The path to relational eloquence. *AI Practitioner*, 36–43.

Wasserman, I. C., Gallegos, P. V., & Ferdman, B. M. (2008). Dancing with resistance: Leadership challenges in fostering a culture of inclusion. In K. M. Thomas (Ed.), *Diversity resistance in organizations: Manifestations and solutions.* Mahwah, NJ: Erlbaum.

PART FOUR

Van Velsor, E., McCauley, C. D., & Ruderman, M. N. (2010). *Center for Creative Leadership Handbook of Leadership Development* (3rd ed.). San Francisco: Jossey-Bass.

CHAPTER TEN

Alexandre-Bailly, F., & Delay, B. (2006). *Above the clouds.* Sheffield, EFQM: Greenleaf Publishing.

Alon, I., & Higgins, J. (2005). Global leadership success through emotional cultural intelligence. *Business Horizons, 48,* 501–512.

Bordas, J. (2007). *Salsa, soul, and spirit: Leadership for a multicultural age: New approaches to leadership from Latino, black, and American Indian communities.* San Francisco: Berrett-Koehler.

Briscoe, J., Chudzikowski, K., Mayrhofer, W., Unite, J., Las Heras, M., Didi, M., et al. (2007, July 5). *Career success across cultures: Dancing to the beat of their own drummers.* Paper presented at the annual conference of the European Group for Organization Studies, Vienna, Austria.

Chen, Z., M. Wakabayashi, & Takeuchi, N. (2004). A comparative study of organizational context factors for managerial career progress: Focusing on Chinese state-owned, Sino-foreign joint venture and Japanese corporations. *International Journal of Human Resource Management, 15*(4/5), 750–774.

Criswell, C., & Martin, A. (2007). "Ten trends: A study of senior executives' views on the future." White paper, Center for Creative Leadership, Greensboro, NC.

Dalton, M., Ernst, C., Deal, J., & Leslie, J. (2002). *Success for the new global manager: How to work across distances, countries, and culture*. San Francisco: Jossey-Bass.

Day, D. V. (2000). Leadership development: A review in context. *Leadership Quarterly, 11*(4), 581–613.

Deal, J., & Prince, D. (2003). *Developing cultural adaptability: How to work across differences*. Greensboro, NC: Center for Creative Leadership.

Deal, T. E., & Kennedy, A. A. (1982). *Corporate cultures: The rites and rituals of organizational life*. Reading, MA: Addison-Wesley.

Deresky, H. (2008). *International management: Managing across borders and cultures* (6th ed.). Upper Saddle River, NJ: Pearson Education.

Earley, P. C., Ang, S., & Tan, J. (2006). *CQ: Developing cultural intelligence at work*. Palo Alto, CA: Stanford University Press.

Earley, P. C., & Mosakowski, E. (2004). Cultural intelligence. *Harvard Business Review, 82*(10), 139–146.

Earley, P. C., & Peterson, R. S. (2004). The elusive cultural chameleon: Cultural intelligence as a new approach to intercultural training for the global manager. *Academy of Management Learning and Education, 3*(1), 100–115.

Essed, P. (2001). Multi-identifications and transformations: Reaching beyond racial and ethnic reductionisms. *Social Identities, 7*(4), 493–509.

Hannum, K. M., McFeeters, B. B., & Booysen, A. E. (Eds). (in press). *Understanding and leading across differences: Cases and perspectives*. San Francisco: Jossey-Bass/Pfeiffer.

Heifetz, R. (1994). *Leadership without easy answers*. Cambridge, MA: Harvard University Press.

Hewlett, S. A., & Luce, C. B. (2006). Extreme jobs: The dangerous allure of the 70-hour workweek. *Harvard Business Review, 84*(12), 49–59.

Higgins, M. C., & Kram, K. E. (2001). Reconceptualizing mentoring at work: A developmental network perspective. *Academy of Management Review, 26*(2), 264–288.

Hoppe, M. (2001a). *Working with others (significantly) unlike yourself: An adult development perspective.* Presentation to the International Association for Cross-Cultural Psychology, King Alfred's College, Winchester, U.K.

Hoppe, M. (2001b). *Leading in an international environment: An adult development perspective. Concepts, challenges, and realities of leadership: An international perspective.* Selected proceedings from the Salzburg Seminar on International Leadership. Retrieved April 15, 2008, from www.academy .umd.edu/scholarship/casl/salzburg/chapter1.htm.

House, R. J., Hanges, P. J., Javidan, M., Dorfman, P. W., & Gupta, V. (Eds.). (2004). *Culture, leadership, and organizations: The GLOBE study of 62 Societies.* Thousand Oaks, CA: Sage.

Kegan, R. (1982). *The evolving self: Problem and process in human development.* Cambridge, MA: Harvard University Press.

Kegan, R. (1994). *In over our heads: The mental demands of modern life.* Cambridge, MA: Harvard University Press.

King, S., & Santana, L. (2010). Feedback-intensive programs. In E. Van Velsor, C. D. McCauley, & M. Ruderman (Eds.), *The Center for Creative Leadership handbook of leadership development* (3rd ed.). San Francisco: Jossey-Bass.

Mainiero, L. A., & Sullivan, S. E. (2006). *The opt-out revolt.* Mountain View, CA: Davis-Black Publishing.

Martin, R. (2007). *The opposable mind: How successful leaders win through integrative thinking.* Boston: Harvard Business School Press.

McCauley, C., Drath, W., Palus, C., O'Connor, P., & Baker, B. (2006). The use of constructive-developmental theory to advance the understanding of leadership. *Leadership Quarterly, 17,* 634–653.

Mirvis, P. (2008). Executive development through consciousness-raising experiences. *Academy of Management Learning and Education, 7*(2), 173–188.

Moen, P., & Roehling, P. (2005). *The career mystique: Cracks in the American dream.* Lanham, MD: Rowman & Littlefield.

Molinsky, A. (2007). Cross-cultural code-switching: The psychological challenges of adapting behavior in foreign cultural interactions. *Academy of Management Review, 32*(2), 622–640.

Palus, C., & Drath, W. (1995). *Evolving leaders: A model for promoting leadership development in programs*. Greensboro, NC: CCL Press.

Ruderman, M. N., Glover, S., Chrobot-Mason, D., & Ernst, C. (2010). Leadership across practices in social identity groups. In K. M. Hannum, B. B. McFeeters, & A. E. Booysen (Eds.), *Understanding and leading across differences: Cases and perspectives*. San Francisco: Jossey-Bass/Pfeiffer.

Ruderman, M. N., & Ohlott, P. J. (2004, Winter). What women leaders want. *Leader to Leader, 31*, 41–47.

Sanchez-Burks, J., Lee, F., Nisbett, R., & Ybarra, O. (2007). Cultural training based on a theory of relational ideology. *Basic and Applied Social Psychology, 29*(3), 257–268.

Santana, L. (2008). *Border crossing as a leadership development strategy*. White paper, Antioch University.

Schein, E. H. (1985). Organizational culture and leadership: Defining organizational culture. In J. M. Shafritz & J. S. Ott (Eds.), *Classics of organization theory*. Belmont, CA: Wadsworth.

Schwartz, S. H. (2004). Mapping and interpreting cultural differences around the world. In H. Vinken, J. Soeters, & P. Ester (Eds.), *Comparing cultures: Dimensions of culture in a comparative perspective* (pp. 43–73). Boston: Brill.

Schwartz, S. H. (2006). *A theory of cultural value orientations: Explication and applications*. Unpublished manuscript, Hebrew University of Jerusalem.

Sinclair, A., & Wilson, V. (2002). *New faces of leadership*. Victoria, Australia: Melbourne University Press.

Thomas, D. A. (2004, September). Diversity as strategy. *Harvard Business Review*, 98–108.

Van Dyne, L. Ang, S., & Livermore, D. (in press). Cultural intelligence: A pathway for leading in a rapidly globalizing world. In K. M. Hannum, B. B. McFeeters, & A. E. Booysen (Eds.), *Understanding and leading across differences: Cases and perspectives*. San Francisco: Jossey-Bass/Pfeiffer.

Wilson, M., & Dalton, M. (1996). *Selecting and developing global managers: Possibilities and pitfalls*. Unpublished manuscript, Center for Creative Leadership, Greensboro, NC.

CHAPTER ELEVEN

Conger, J. A., & Benjamin, B. (1999). *Building leaders: How successful companies develop the next generation.* San Francisco: Jossey-Bass.

Pearce, C. L., & Conger, J. A. (2003). *Shared leadership.* Thousand Oaks, CA: Sage.

CHAPTER TWELVE

Adizes, I. (1988). *Corporate lifecycles: How and why corporations grow and die and what to do about it.* Upper Saddle River, NJ: Prentice Hall.

Anderson, S., Cavanagh, J., Collins, C., Pizzigati, S., & Lapham, M. (2007). *Executive excess 2007: The staggering cost of U.S. business leadership.* Washington, DC: Institute for Policy Studies and United for a Fair Economy.

Bemis, T. (2009, February 17). Daimler's tales of caution: Commentary: Still paying for the Chrysler "deal." *MarketWatch.* Retrieved October 20, 2009, from http://www.marketwatch.com/story/daimlers-still-paying-its-chrysler-deal.

BlessingWhite. (2008, April). *The state of employee engagement 2008: North American overview.* Princeton, NJ: Author.

Brafman, O., & Brafman, R. (2008). *Sway: The irresistible pull of irrational behavior.* New York: Doubleday.

Burke, W. W., & Litwin, G. H. (1992). A causal model of organizational performance and change. *Journal of Management, 18*(3), 532–545.

Carr, E. (2009, January 22). Greed—and fear: A special report on the future of finance. *Economist.* Retrieved October 20, 2009, from http://www.economist.com/specialreports/displaystory.cfm?story_id=12957709.

Clark-Santos, L. (in press). Of dragons, caves, and rock stars: The new reality of leadership development. In D. L. Dotlich, P. C. Cairo, S. H. Rhinesmith, & R. Meeks (Eds.), *The 2010 Pfeiffer annual: Leadership development.* San Francisco: Jossey-Bass.

Communispace Corporation. (2007). *ClientStory: Kraft.* Retrieved October 20, 2009, from http://communispace.com/assets/pdf/C_Cli_casestudy_kraft_final.pdf .

Dotlich, D. L., & Cairo, P. C. (2003). *Why CEOs fail: The 11 behaviors that can derail your climb to the top—and how to manage them.* San Francisco: Jossey-Bass.

Dotlich, D. L., Cairo, P. C., & Rhinesmith, S. H. (2009). *Leading in a crisis: Navigating through complexity, diversity, and uncertainty to save your business.* San Francisco: Jossey-Bass.

Edmondson, G., Welch, D., Thornton, E., & Palmer, A. T. (2005, August 15). Dark days at Daimler. *BusinessWeek.* Retrieved October 20, 2009, from http://www.businessweek.com/magazine/content/05_33/b3947001_mz001.htm.

Fraser, M., & Dutta, S. (2009, March 11). Yes, CEOs should Facebook and Twitter. *Forbes.com.* Retrieved October 20, 2009, from http://www.forbes.com/2009/03/11/social-networking-executives-leadership-managing-facebook.htm.

Friedman, T. L. (2005). *The world is flat: A brief history of the twenty-first century.* New York: Farrar, Straus and Giroux.

Galbraith, J. K. (1994). *A short history of financial euphoria.* New York: Penguin Group.

Herbst, M. (2008, June 17). Oil CEOs: High prices, fat paychecks. *BusinessWeek.* Retrieved October 20, 2009, from http://www.businessweek.com/investor/content/jun2008/pi20080616_449469.htm.

Howe, N., & Strauss, W. (2007). The next 20 years: How customer and workforce attitudes will evolve. *Harvard Business Review, 85*(7/8), 41–52.

Krohe, J., Jr. (2007, November-December). Money changes everything. *Conference Board Review*, 48–52.

Mandel, M. (2008, January 23). How real was the prosperity? *BusinessWeek.* Retrieved October 21, 2009, from http://www.businessweek.com/magazine/content/08_05/b4069000016691.htm.

McMahon, R. (2009, March 10). *Bernanke: Regulatory overhaul needed to prevent future global financial shocks.* Retrieved October 21, 2009, from http://www.cfr.org/publication/18734 .

Nike. (2009). *Considered design and the environment.* Retrieved October 21, 2009, from http://www.nikebiz.com/responsibility/considered_design/index.html.

Nooyi, I. (2009, April 22). Business has a job to do: Rebuild trust. *Fortune Magazine*. Retrieved October 20, 2009, from http://money.cnn.com/2009/ 04/19/news/companies/nooyi.fortune/index.htm.

Rasmussen Reports. (2009, February 18). *CEOs hit rock bottom, less popular than Congress*. Retrieved October 20, 2009, from http://www.rasmussenreports .com/public_content/business/general_business/ceos_hit_rock_bottom_ less_popular_than_congress.

Schwartz, J. (2005, November). If you want to lead, blog. *Harvard Business Review*. Retrieved October 20, 2009, from http://hbr.harvardbusiness.org/ 2005/11/if-you-want-to-lead-blog/ar/1.

Stringer, R., & Cates, T. M. (2009). Leading for loyalty. In D. L. Dotlich, P. C. Cairo, S. H. Rhinesmith, & R. Meeks (Eds.), *The 2009 Pfeiffer annual: Leadership development* (pp. 225–245). San Francisco: Jossey-Bass.

Swanson, J. L. (1996). The theory is the practice: Trait-and-factor/person-environment fit counseling. In M. L. Savickas & W. B. Walsh (Eds.), *Handbook of career counseling theory and practice*. Palo Alto, CA: Davis-Black.

CHAPTER THIRTEEN

Collins, J. (2001). *Good to great*. New York: HarperCollins.

Drucker, P. F. (2004). What makes an effective executive. *Harvard Business Review, 82*(6), 58–63.

Gabarro, J. (1987). *The dynamics of taking charge*. Boston: Harvard Business School Press.

Gribben, K. (2008, September 2). Large companies overwhelmingly choose inside CEOs. *Agenda, A Financial Times Service*. Retrieved May 19, 2009, from http://www.agendaweek.com/articles/20080902/large_companies_ overwhelmingly_choose_inside_ceos.

Harvey, J. B. (1988). The Abilene paradox: The management agreement. *Organizational Dynamics, 17*(1), 17–43.

Johnson, L. (2008, August 13). Dangerous myths of the business superstar. *Financial Times*. Retrieved May 19, 2009, from http://www.ft.com/cms/ s/0/b718f978-6899-11dd-a4e5-0000779fd18c.html?nclick_check=1.

Kotter, J. P. (1990). *Force for change: How leadership differs from management*. New York: Free Press.

McGregor, J., Jespersen, F. F., & Zegel, S. (2008, July 28). GE: The heat on Immelt. *Business Week*, 34–37.

Paese, M. J. (2008, November-December). Your next CEO. *Conference Board Review*, 45(6), 18–23.

Stoddard, N., & Wychoff, C. (2008). The cost of CEO failure: Getting it wrong costs the economy as much as $13.8 billion. *Chief Executive*, 237, 66–70.

Succession planning: A snapshot of recent CEO turnover. (2008, September 18). *Agenda: A Financial Times Service*.

Swzeig, J. (2009, April 25). How group decisions end up wrong-footed. *Wall Street Journal*, p. B1.

Tough at the top. (2003, October 25). *Economist*, 3–7. Retrieved May 19, 2009, from Business Source Corporate database.

Tuna, C. (2008, July 28). Hiring a CEO from the outside is more expensive. *Wall Street Journal*. Retrieved May 12, 2009, from http://online.wsj.com/article/SB121719208233988107.html.

Vlasic, B. (2008, August 6). G.M.'s directors stand behind Wagoner. *New York Times*. Retrieved May 12, 2009, from http://www.nytimes.com/2008/08/07/business/07auto.html?scp=2&sq=wagoner&st=nyt.

Welch, J., & Welch, S. (2009, January 26). The WelchWay: Of boards and blame. *Business Week*, 102.

CHAPTER FOURTEEN

Bunker, K., & Wakefield, M. (2005). *Leading with authenticity in times of transition*. Greensboro, NC: Center for Creative Leadership.

Cameron, K. S., Dutton, J. E., & Quinn, R. E. (Eds.). (2003). *Positive organizational scholarship: Foundations of a new discipline*. San Francisco: Berrett-Koehler.

Day, D. V., Harrison, M. M., & Halpin, S. M. (2009). *An integrative approach to leader development: Connecting adult development, identity, and expertise*. New York: Taylor & Francis.

Day, D. V., Zaccaro, S. J., & Halpin, S. M. (2004). *Leader development for transforming organizations: Growing leaders for tomorrow*. Mahwah, NJ: Erlbaum.

Dutton, J. E., & Heaphy, E. D. (2003). The power of high-quality connections. In K. S. Cameron, J. E. Dutton, & R. E. Quinn (Eds.), *Positive organizational scholarship: Foundations of a new discipline* (pp. 263–278). San Francisco: Berrett-Koehler.

Dutton, J. E., & Ragins, B. R. (Eds.). (2006). *Exploring positive relationships at work: Building a theoretical and research foundation.* Mahwah, NJ: Erlbaum.

Hall, D. T. (Ed.). (1996). *The career is dead—long live the career: A relational approach to careers.* San Francisco: Jossey-Bass.

Hall, D. T. (2002). *Careers in and out of organizations.* Thousand Oaks, CA: Sage.

Kets de Vries, M.F.R., & Korotov, K. (2007). Creating transformational executive education programs. *Academy of Management Learning and Education, 6*(3), 375–387.

Kram, K. E., & Higgins, M. A. (2008, September 22). A new approach to mentoring. *Wall St. Journal,* p. R10. Retrieved October 22, 2009, from http://online.wsj.com/article/SB122160063875344843.html.

McCauley, C. D., & Van Velsor, E. (Eds.). (2004). *The Center for Creative Leadership handbook of leadership development* (2nd ed.). San Francisco: Jossey-Bass.

Miller, J. B. (2004) Preface. In J. Jordan, L. Hartling, & M. Walker (Eds.), *The complexity of connection* (pp. i–iv). New York: Guilford Press.

Raelin, J. (2000). *Work-based learning: The new frontier of management development.* Upper Saddle River, NJ: Prentice Hall.

Schön, D. A. (1987). *Educating the reflective practitioner: Toward a new design for teaching and learning in the professions.* San Francisco: Jossey-Bass.

NAME INDEX

A

Aaltio-Marjosola, I., 122
Ackoff, R. L., 59
Adizes, I., 276
Adler, M., 105, 106
Agashae, Z., 123
Alexandre-Bailly, F., 220
Alon, I., 229
Anderson, R., 207
Anderson, S., 279
Ang, S., 221, 226
Avolio, B., 121, 122

B

Badaracco, J., 121, 122
Bailyn, L., 126
Baker, B., 78, 219
Barnard, C., 60
Bar-On, R., 99, 104
Bartolome, F., 126
Bass, B. N., 202
Basseches, M., 72
Belbin, R. M., 98
Belenky, M., 72
Bemis, T., 277
Benjamin, B., 240
Bennis, W., 31, 35, 58, 202
Bilmoria, D., 103

Blake-Beard, S., 197, 205
BlessingWhite, 289
Booysen, A. E., 226
Booz Allen Hamilton, 2
Bordas, J., 220, 235, 236
Boyatzis, R., 99, 105, 106, 121
Bradbury, H., 122
Brafman, O., 280
Brafman, R., 280
Brant, J., 169, 171
Bratton, J., 123
Brienza, D., 103
Briscoe, J., 223
Browning, P. C., 295
Bruce, N., 156
Bunker, K. A., 1, 4, 5, 34, 43, 313, 318
Burke, W. W., 276
Burns, J. M., 202
Byrnes, N., 156

C

Cairo, P. C., 271, 280, 282
Calas, M., 129
Calvert, L., 125
Cameron, K. S., 318
Carli, L. L., 125, 129, 133
Carr, E., 274
Cascio, W. F., 5

Glover, S., 229
Goffman, E., 125, 135
Goldberger, N., 72
Goleman, D., 33, 99, 101, 107, 121, 122, 125
Graen, G., 122
Graen, G. B., 122
Grashow, A., 197
Gribben, K., 302
Grint, K., 2
Gronn, P., 123
Gupta, V., 233

H

Hall, D. T., 1, 114, 313, 318, 319
Halpin, S. M., 317
Handley, R., 99
Hanges, P. J., 233
Hannum, K. M., 226
Harrington, M., 122
Harris, L. S., 80
Harrison, M. M., 317
Harvey, J. B., 309
Heaphy, E. D., 125, 318
Heaton, N., 104
Heifetz, R., 197, 220
Heifitz, R., 123
Helsing, D., 69
Henry, D., 2
Herbst, M., 279
Hesselbein, F., 137, 199
Hewlett, S. A., 220
Higgins, M. A., 318
Higgins, M. C., 205, 228, 229
Hill, L., 123
Hoffman, R., 157
Hogan, J., 156
Hogan, R., 11, 156
Hollenbeck, G. P., 155, 157, 158, 163, 171
Holvino, E., 127
Hhooks, b., 203, 204

Hopkins, M. M., 103
Hoppe, M., 235, 236, 237
Hosking, D., 122, 123
House, R. J., 233
Howard, A., 156, 171
Howe, N., 285

I

Ilies, R., 98

J

Jacobsen, S., 129
Jacques, R., 124, 129
Javidan, M., 233
Jespersen, F. F., 2, 301
Johansen, B., 17
Johnson, L., 306
Johnson, S. K., 171
Joiner, B., 94
Jordan, J. V., 130, 202
Josephs, S., 94
Judge, T. A., 98

K

Kaeufer, K., 122, 123, 124, 125
Kahane, A., 122
Kaiser, R. B., 156
Kanter, R. M., 123, 126
Kaplan, A. G., 202
Kayes, D. C., 123
Kegan, R., 71, 72, 73, 74, 77, 78, 79, 81, 85, 86, 203, 237
Kerr, R., 104
Kets de Vries, M.F.R., 317
Kim, D. H., 123
King, S., 232
Kirk, G., 200
Kochan, T., 199
Kohlberg, L., 72
Koontz, H., 65
Korotov, K., 317

CEO, 305–307; selecting right person as CEO, 300–302; selecting wrong person as CEO, 297–298
Border crossing, 233, 235–237, 238
Brown, David, 48
Browning, Peter, 44
Buber, Martin, 207

C

Caring. *See* Relational leadership
Case studies, 66, 148
CEOs: board of directors' responsibility for selection of, 299; developed and promoted from inside company, 302–305; hired from outside company, 305–307; interviews with six successful, 15–41; selecting right people as, 296–297, 300–302, 310–311; staying on too long, 308; turnover of, 2, 296, 297
Change: in context for leadership after financial crisis of 2008, 275–281; continual, as environment for managerial leaders, 53, 56–59; decision making when implementing, 23–25; desired, vs. focus on individual leader development, 244–245; emotional intelligence needed for, 100–101. *See also* Immunities-to-change process
Character: importance of, for leadership in future, 286; as part of authentic leadership, 138; of people selected for development experiences, 171
Chrysler, 277
Ciulla, Joanne, 235–236
Clinton, Hillary, 133, 135
Cloninger, Kathy, 148–149
Coaching: executive, to educate leaders about context, 193; to implement immunities-to-change process, 91–92; to improve relational skills, 34, 38; to

increase emotional intelligence, 105, 106; leadership, in future, 291–292; leadership style moderated through, 26–27; peer, 114, 118
Coca-Cola, 237
Cognition, as dimension of cultural intelligence, 228
Collaboration: CEO's success attributed to, 28–29; as factor in leadership success, 33; in nontraditional alliances in future, 289. *See also* Relational leadership; Working with others
Collective-focused leadership development, 246–254; IBM's shift to, 254–267; vs. individual-focused leadership development, 248–254; proposed shift to, 246–248, 267–268
Commitment, 287
Communication: of complexity, 32–33; cultural assumptions in, 225; of learning, 50–51; of mission/vision, 52–56; quality of, and change efforts, 25; skills in, 32
Compensation: of externally hired vs. internally promoted executives, 303; for workers vs. executives, 279
Competencies: associated with emotional intelligence, 99–100, 102–104; of human resources, 169–170; leadership models based on, 241, 291; needed for Kegan's Self-Authoring stage, 78–79
Confidence, as factor in leadership success, 33
Consciousness-raising programs, 231–232
Constructive-developmental theory: constructive aspect of, 71–72; developmental aspect of, 72; on gap between mental complexity and psychological demands, 72; leadership as demanding Self-Authoring stage of, 78–80, 93–94; on moving from Socializing to

Self-Authoring stage, 77–78; stages of development in, 75–76

Context: importance of, for leadership in future, 287; for leadership after financial crisis of 2008, 275–281; trends affecting, for leadership in future, 281–286. *See also* Contexts, system

Contexts, system, 175–196; commonly overlooked, 175–176; four common, 176–178; implications of, for leadership development, 192–193; intervention based on, 190–192; Organization Workshop experience of, 195–196; of other people, 178–180; our own, 180–183; overcoming illusions due to blindness to, 188–189; of peer group, 183–188; Power Lab experience of, 189, 194–195

Continental Can Company, 307

Coordinated management of meaning (CMM) theory, 206–212; Daisy Model of, 208–209; Hierarchy of Meaning Model of, 210; Serpentine Model of, 207–208

Creativity, 287

Crises: decision making during, 23–25; importance of leadership presence in, 18–20. *See also* Financial crisis of 2008

Cuban, Mark, 282

Cultural adaptability, assessment of, 233, 234–235

Cultural assimilator, 230–231

Cultural intelligence: applying, in social interactions, 226–227; defined, 221, 226; dimensions of, 227–229; methods for developing, 229–237; need for, 218–219, 237–238

Cultures: defined, 221–222; dimensions of, 222–226; diverse, ability to deal with, 219–221; organizational, as

obstacle to leadership development, 161–162

Customers: and leadership authenticity, 149–150; shift of power to, 284–285

D

DaimlerBenz, 277

Decision making: identity dimensions influencing, 200–201, 205, 208–211; and Kegan's developmental perspectives, 74–76; during restructuring, 23–25

Deferring, as factor in leadership success, 33

Democracy: importance of education for, 142; institutions sustaining, 142

Developmental stretch, 231

DiMicco, Dan, 308

Diversity: cultural, ability to deal with, 219–221; evolution of conversation about, 198–200; necessity of appreciating, 288; and transformation of Girl Scouts, 146–149. *See also* Inclusion

Doing: vs. being, 137–139, 199–200; leaders as immersed in, 44, 45, 56. *See also* Action

Drive: to learn, 46–47; of managerial leaders, 53, 56

Drucker, Peter: on focusing on strengths, 143; on Hesselbein's definition of leadership, 138; innovation as defined by, 140; on mission, 149, 150; on need for CEOs to develop leaders, 140–141; and transformation of Girl Scouts, 148; on U.S. Army as developing leaders, 142

E

Education: experiential, 193; importance of, for democracy, 142; leadership development as, 142–143. *See also* Learning

L

Lafley, A. G., 140–141, 142

Language, and relational leadership, 128–129

Layoffs, 30

Leaders: behaviors of, contributing to financial crisis of 2008, 272–273; biographies of, 66, 67; blamed for financial crisis of 2008, 278; common skills of, 31–33; staying on too long, 308. *See also* Managerial leaders; Top executives

Leadership: academicization of, 44; caution on equating success with, 292; coaching to moderate style of, 26–27; definitions of, 138–139, 247, 300. *See also* Relational leadership

Leadership capability: collective, 247, 267–268, 269; lifetime variation in, 292; need for, revealed by financial crisis of 2008, 16–17

Leadership development: challenge of, for future, 1–2; deficit of opportunities for, 163–164; as education, 142–143; new view of, for future, 4–6. *See also* Collective-focused leadership development; Individual-focused leader development

Leadership development programs: common components of, 155–156, 240–242; creating conditions for learning in, 317–320; ideas on improving, in future, 314–317; implications of financial crisis of 2008 for, 290–293; importance of selection process to, 167–172, 173; increase in number of, 239–240; questions for assessing, 240; reasons for ineffectiveness of, 242–246

Leadership failure, 2, 17–18, 64–65, 156, 297–298

Leadership gaps: hypothesis underlying, 2; within individuals, 7–8, 11–13; at institutional level, 9, 213–215; need to embrace learning to overcome, 3–4; at organizational level, 8, 153–154; in relationships between leaders, 8, 95–96

Leadership mastery: assumptions about, 157–160; obstacles to, 160–166; senior executives' role in developing, in others, 167–172

Leadership models: competency-based, 241, 291; great man/great woman, 268–269, 301–302; need for revised, 291

Leadership presence, 18–20, 32

Leadership the Army Way (Hesselbein and Shinseki), 139

Learning: adult, 245; content of, by managerial leaders, 52, 53, 65; creating conditions for, 317–320; by managerial leaders, 45–51; need for continual, 51–52, 313–314; to overcome leadership gaps, 3–4. *See also* Education

Learning premise, 51

Liautaud, Jim, 107

Lincoln, Abraham, 145

Listening: improving skill in, through immunities-to-change process, 70, 71, 73, 74, 76, 77, 81–82, 83, 87–89; process-designed training rule on, 107–108

Lowes Companies, 299

M

Managerial leaders: content of learning by, 52, 53, 65; continual change as environment for, 56–59; described, 44–45; drive of, 56; learning by, 45–51; need for continual learning by, 51–52; purposing by, 52–56; and relationships, 61–65; system of problems confronted by, 59–61; training, 66–67

Marcus, Bernie, 297

Markovits, Mike, 255–256, 258–259, 260–261, 262–263, 264, 265–266

Mastery, as cultural value, 223–224. *See also* Leadership mastery

Mayer-Salovey-Caruso Emotional Intelligence Test (MSCEIT), 104

McDonald's, 282

Measurement: of emotional intelligence, 103–104; of individual leader development, 245; of outcomes in IBM's collective-focused leadership development program, 259; of ROI in leadership development, 162–163

Meckler, Alan, 282

Mentoring: and gender, 130; to improve inclusive skills, 205–206; to improve relational skills, 34, 38

Metacognition: cultural assimilator technique to increase, 230–231; as dimension of cultural intelligence, 227–228, 230

Mission: communicating, 52–54; link between leadership authenticity and, 149–152; purposing, 52–56; vision vs., 54–55

Motivation: as dimension of cultural intelligence, 228; misunderstanding, and relational leadership, 127–128

N

Nardelli, Bob, 297–298, 310

Network building: developmental, 205; as factor in leadership success, 32

Newmark, Craig, 282

Nike, 283–284

Nucor Corporation, 299, 308

O

Obama, Barack, 144–145

Olsen, Lynn, 45

Organization Workshop, 194–195

P

Palmisano, Sam, 254, 256, 259, 261, 264

People, importance to managerial leaders, 61–65

Perdue, Frank, 47–48, 54

Peters, Tom, 47

Phenomenological studies, 66–67

Phoenix Companies, 299

Power: and relational leadership, 125–127, 135; shifting to customers, 284–285

Power Lab, 189, 194–195

Problem solving: interrelatedness of predicaments and, 59–61; involving others in, 21–22; vs. managing ongoing dilemmas, 288; of technical problems vs. adaptive challenges, 197–198; vs. working with others, 29–30

Process-designed training (PDT), 106–120; compared to other programs, 120; ground rules of, 107–108; overview of, 106–110; problems and unresolved issues with, 116–119; reasons for effectiveness of, 114–116; results achieved by participation in, 109–114

Procter & Gamble (P&G), 141, 142

Purposing, 52, 53, 55–56

R

Race, and relational leadership, 127. *See also* Diversity

Raju, Ramalinga, 17–18

ABOUT THE CENTER FOR CREATIVE LEADERSHIP

The Center for Creative Leadership (CCL) is a top-ranked, global provider of executive education that unlocks individual and organizational potential through its exclusive focus on leadership education and research. Founded in 1970 as a nonprofit, educational institution, CCL helps clients worldwide cultivate creative leadership—the capacity to achieve more than imagined by thinking and acting beyond boundaries—through an array of programs, products, and other services.

Ranked in the top ten in the *Financial Times* annual executive education survey, CCL is headquartered in Greensboro, North Carolina, with campuses in Colorado Springs, Colorado; San Diego, California; Brussels, Belgium; and Singapore. Supported by more than four hundred faculty members and staff, it works annually with more than twenty thousand leaders and two thousand organizations. In addition, twelve Network Associates around the world offer selected CCL programs and assessments.

CCL draws strength from its nonprofit status and educational mission, which provide unusual flexibility in a world where quarterly profits often drive thinking and direction. It has the freedom to be objective, wary of short-term trends, and motivated foremost by its mission—hence our substantial and sustained investment in leadership research. Although CCL's work is always grounded in a strong foundation of research, it focuses on achieving a beneficial

365

impact in the real world. Its efforts are geared to be practical and action oriented, helping leaders and their organizations more effectively achieve their goals and vision. The desire to transform learning and ideas into action provides the impetus for CCL's programs, assessments, publications, and services.

Capabilities

CCL's activities encompass leadership education, knowledge generation and dissemination, and building a community centered on leadership. CCL is broadly recognized for excellence in executive education, leadership development, and innovation by sources such as *BusinessWeek, Financial Times, The New York Times,* and *The Wall Street Journal.*

Open-Enrollment Programs

Fourteen open-enrollment courses are designed for leaders at all levels, as well as people responsible for leadership development and training at their organizations. This portfolio offers distinct choices for participants seeking a particular learning environment or type of experience. Some programs are structured specifically around small group activities, discussion, and personal reflection, while others offer hands-on opportunities through business simulations, artistic exploration, team-building exercises, and new-skills practice. Many of these programs offer private one-on-one sessions with a feedback coach.

For a complete listing of programs, visit http://www.ccl.org/programs.

Customized Programs

CCL develops tailored educational solutions for more than one hundred client organizations around the world each year. Through this applied practice, CCL structures and delivers programs focused on specific leadership development needs within the context of defined organizational challenges, including innovation, the merging of cultures, and the development of a broader pool of leaders. The objective is to help organizations develop, within their own cultures, the leadership capacity they need to address challenges as they emerge.

Program details are available online at http://www.ccl.org/custom.

Coaching

CCL's suite of coaching services is designed to help leaders maintain a sustained focus and generate increased momentum toward achieving their goals. These coaching alternatives vary in depth and duration and serve a variety of needs, from helping an executive sort through career and life issues to working with an organization to integrate coaching into its internal development process. Our coaching offerings, which can supplement program attendance or be customized for specific individual or team needs, are based on our model of assessment, challenge, and support (ACS).

Learn more about CCL's coaching services at http://www.ccl.org/coaching.

Assessment and Development Resources

CCL pioneered 360-degree feedback and believes that assessment provides a solid foundation for learning, growth, and transformation and that development truly happens when an individual recognizes the need to change. CCL offers a broad selection of assessment tools, online resources, and simulations that can help individuals, teams, and organizations increase their self-awareness, facilitate their own learning, enable their development, and enhance their effectiveness.

CCL's assessments are profiled at http://www.ccl.org/assessments.

Publications

The theoretical foundation for many of our programs, as well as the results of CCL's extensive and often groundbreaking research, can be found in the scores of publications issued by CCL Press and through the center's alliance with Jossey-Bass, a Wiley imprint. Among these are landmark works, such as *Breaking the Glass Ceiling* and *The Lessons of Experience,* as well as quick-read guidebooks focused on core aspects of leadership. CCL publications provide insights and practical advice to help individuals become more effective leaders, develop leadership training within organizations, address issues of change and diversity, and build the systems and strategies that advance leadership collectively at the institutional level.

A complete listing of CCL publications is available at http://www.ccl.org/publications.

Leadership Community

To ensure that the Center's work remains focused, relevant, and important to the individuals and organizations it serves, CCL maintains a host of networks, councils, and learning and virtual communities that bring together alumni, donors, faculty, practicing leaders, and thought leaders from around the globe.

CCL also forges relationships and alliances with individuals, organizations, and associations that share its values and mission. The energy, insights, and support from these relationships help shape and sustain CCL's educational and research practices and provide its clients with an added measure of motivation and inspiration as they continue their lifelong commitment to leadership and learning.

To learn more, visit http://www.ccl.org/community.

Research

CCL's portfolio of programs, products, and services is built on a solid foundation of behavioral science research. The role of research at CCL is to advance the understanding of leadership and to transform learning into practical tools for participants and clients. CCL's research is the hub of a cycle that transforms knowledge into applications and applications into knowledge, thereby illuminating the way organizations think about and enact leadership and leader development.

Find out more about current research initiatives at http://www.ccl.org/research.

For additional information about CCL, visit http://www.ccl.org or call Client Services at (336) 545–2810.